A CULTURE OF FACT

Also by Barbara J. Shapiro

John Wilkins, 1614–1672: An Intellectual Biography (1968)

Probability and Certainty in Seventeenth-Century England:
A Study of the Relationships between Natural Science, Religion,
History, Law, and Literature (1983)

"Beyond Reasonable Doubt" and "Probable Cause":
Historical Perspectives on the Anglo-American Law of Evidence (1991)

A Culture of Fact

ENGLAND, 1550–1720

BARBARA J. SHAPIRO

CORNELL UNIVERSITY PRESS   ITHACA AND LONDON

First published 2000 by Cornell University Press
First printing, Cornell Paperbacks, 2003

Printed in the United States of America

Library of Congress Cataloging-in-Publication Data

Shapiro, Barbara J.
    A culture of fact : England, 1550–1720 / Barbara J. Shapiro.
        x, 284 p. ; 23 cm.
Includes bibliographical references (p. 219–271) and index.
    ISBN 0-8014-3686-9 (cloth : acid-free paper)
    ISBN 0-8014-8849-4 (pbk. : acid-free paper)
    1. England—Intellectual life—17th century.   2. Great
Britain—History—Tudors, 1485–1603—Historiography.   3. Great
Britain—History—Stuarts, 1603–1714—Historiography.   4. Curiosities
and wonders—England—Historiography.   5. Physical
sciences—England—Historiography.   6. England—Intellectual life—16th
century.   7. England—Intellectual life—18th century.   8. Law and
fact—England—History.   9. Knowledge, Theory of.   10. Facts
(Philosophy)   I. Title.
    DA380 .S52 2000
    942.05—dc21   99-035076

Cloth printing   10   9   8   7   6   5   4   3   2   1

Paperback printing   10   9   8   7   6   5   4   3   2   1

For Eve, Leigh, Kristen, and Matthew Ridgers

Contents

Acknowledgments

Like most scholarly efforts, this one is heavily indebted to many institutions and individuals. I have been assisted by research grants from the Huntington Library, the University of California, Berkeley Committee on Research, and a University of California, Berkeley Professorship in the Graduate School. My very able graduate student assistants were Michael Witmore, Kirsten Anderson, and Jennifer Culbert. *Albion* has permitted me to use portions of my presidential address to the North American Conference of British Studies, "The Concept 'Fact': Legal Origins and Cultural Diffusion," XXVI (1994), 227–252. Portions of Chapters 1 and 7 appear as an essay "Legal Fact-Finding and Restoration Religious Discourse," in *Law, Crime, and English Society, 1680–1840*, edited by Norma Landau (Cambridge, forthcoming). Commentators on papers given at the History of Science Association, the American Historical Association, and conferences at the University of California, Irvine, and the Huntington Library have helped sharpen my views and enlarge my perspective. Librarians and staff of Huntington Library, the Williams Andrews Clark Memorial Library, Boalt Hall Library, and the Bancroft Library have been uniformly helpful. The Baker service of the University of California, Berkeley Library has been essential to the completion of this book.

I have benefited from discussion and commentary from Michael Mascuch, Linda Peck, Barbara Donagan, Paul Sniderman, Alice Stroup, Lorraine Daston, Victoria Kahn, Michael Witmore, Harold Cook, Blair Worden, Larry Klein, and Donald Kelley. Paul Seaver, Steven Shapin, and Margaret Osler have been especially supportive. Although I have more often than not deviated from their conclusions, this study has been especially stimulated by the work of Margaret Osler, Lorraine Daston, Steven Shapin, Simon Schaffer, and Peter Dear. I would also like to thank Roger M. Haydon and Candace Akins of Cornell University Press, and Kim Vivier, for their thoughtful assistance.

Martin Shapiro has read the manuscript more times than he wished, in its many and varied manifestations. His own obligations were all too often put aside to deal with the dilemmas and difficulties of this book. As with all my earlier books and articles, this project could not, and would not, have been completed without his assistance and persistence.

BARBARA J. SHAPIRO

A CULTURE OF FACT

Introduction

The concept "fact" has been a part of European culture and especially English culture for a very long time. Indeed, it has become so much a part of the general furniture of the mind that it has, until quite recently, largely been taken for granted. Every schoolchild has heard of "historical facts" and "scientific facts." "Fact" has played and continues to play a significant role in the natural sciences, the social sciences, historiography, and the news media as well as ordinary speech. It is commonplace to employ distinctions between fact and theory, fact and opinion, fact and fiction, and fact and value.

Historical interest in "fact," perhaps not coincidentally, has developed just at the moment when the concept itself has become increasingly problematic. Philosophers, historians, scientists, and literary critics have questioned and to some extent undermined the conventional wisdom. We hear that "facts" are constructed, that is, "made" by individuals and groups at particular moments in time and place and that what counts as "fact" for one generation may not for another, that one's person's fact is another's fiction, or that there are no differences between factual and fictional narratives. There has been far less recognition that the concept "fact" itself has undergone considerable modification over time and has served a variety of disciplinary enterprises and functions.

My purpose here is to explore part of that evolution by examining the role of "fact" in English intellectual and cultural development during the early modern period, the period in which it was adopted by a variety of disciplines and was beginning to take on something of its modern meaning. This book continues my explorations of early modern English intellectual life in *Probability and Certainty in Seventeenth-Century England*. It shares that book's concern for the relationships among disciplines and the degree of certainty or probability that could be attributed to "matters of fact." It extends the story of the English legal tradition's contribution to epistemological development and evidentiary traditions. More generally, it examines key conceptual and epistemological concerns that crossed disciplinary boundaries.[1]

My investigations intersect with the innovative work of Steven Shapin and Simon Schaffer on the construction of early modern English empirical natural philosophy, Lorraine Daston's on the history of objectivity and marvels, and Peter Dear's on "experience" and "experiment." These historians of science leave no doubt that "fact" was an important conceptual category for early modern, English natural philosophy. I argue that "fact" does not begin with natural phenomena and was, if anything, a rather late arrival in natural philosophy, having become a well-established concept elsewhere before it was adopted by the community of naturalists.

I begin with law. Although "questions of fact," "questions of law," "mixed questions of fact and law" are standard tools of day-to-day legal analysis, neither legal historians nor legal philosophers have been much drawn to the evolution of the concept "fact" in law. Chapter 1 deals with the nature of "fact" in the European and particularly the English legal context and the characteristic features of fact determination in early modern English common law. Most studies of the epistemological and evidentiary aspects of English law have focused on either the medieval era or the eighteenth century and beyond. Although once almost entirely "internalist" and focused on the evolution of legal doctrine, much legal history has now adopted a "law and society" approach roughly analogous to what historians of science label "externalist." This approach focuses on the function that law plays in society and for the groups or interests it serves. Law and legal doctrine are thus seen as responsive to or reflective of social conditions and socioeconomic interests.[2] My focus on the conceptual framework of legal fact finding may be viewed as more "doctrinal" or "internalist" than "social" but less concerned with disciplinary autonomy than with the development of "fact" in a variety of interdependent institutional contexts.

Beyond such sociolegal writings, legal doctrinal work tends to focus on political issues. With a few notable exceptions early modern legal historians have not attempted to integrate legal concepts and traditions into the general fabric of intellectual and cultural history. We know a good deal about concepts of sovereignty, legitimacy, the state, and property but little about the truth-finding assumptions and procedures of early modern courts or the relationship between legal and other methods of establishing "truth" or "belief."

Chapter 1 argues that the concept "fact" that emerged in the legal arena helped to shape and sharpen the epistemological assumptions and methods of a wide range of intellectual enterprises and played a key role in the development of English empiricism. In particular I explore the distinctions between "matters of fact" and "matters of law" and discuss early modern legal approaches to ascertaining facts. In this connection I draw attention to the institutional differences between canon and civil law fact finding on the one hand and common law practices on the other, suggesting that the lay participation of common law jurors in fact finding played a significant role in the broad cultural diffusion of the concept of fact.

Subsequent chapters explore how the legally derived concept "fact" and legal methods of establishing "matters of fact" were adopted by other disciplines and intellectual projects and became part and parcel of the generally held habits of thought characteristic of late-seventeenth- and early-eighteenth-century culture.

Chapter 2 focuses on "fact" in history and historiography. Despite the impressive scholarly work on the subject of early modern historiography, there has been little investigation of the role of "fact." This chapter charts the ways in which classical and humanist conceptions of history were modified by contact with legal methods of fact determination, the development of a more document-oriented history, and the study of historical antiquities. I emphasize the evolving distinction between fact and fiction and the norms of truthfulness and impartiality that historians absorbed from both classical historiography and the legal tradition. If early modern historiography remained inextricably tied to rhetoric, it was a rhetoric that came to emphasize "fact," truth, and impartiality, to be suspicious of artfulness, partiality, and ornamented style, and to prefer firsthand witnesses over citations to authority.

Chapters 3 and 4 deal with genres rather than disciplines, genres that describe both human and natural "facts." Chapter 3 investigates travel reporting and chorography, which described places visited, "things" or conditions observed, or events experienced or witnessed. These narratives were linked to history writing and non-narrative descriptions of foreign places, peoples, and objects. They are also related to the support by the English scientific community, and especially the Royal Society, of studies that dealt with natural events and conditions and human customs and practices, that is, with human and natural "facts."

Chapter 4 focuses on the reporting of "news" and "marvels." I attempt to show how the genres associated with "news" adopted "matter of fact" as their reason for being and employed the conventions of legal and historical fact finding with their emphasis on credible witnesses and particular events. Then as now, news focused on unusual events. If it shared the historiographer's interest in political, diplomatic, and military "facts," early modern news also reported less politically relevant events such as murders, shipwrecks, and robberies. "Marvels" were news. Two-headed calves, earthquakes, floods, and unusual cloud formations became newsworthy "facts." The "news" genres, like the chorographic and travel genres, played a role in transforming "fact" from a category limited to human actions and deeds into one that comprehended both human and natural phenomena. In the process these "discourses of fact" adopted from law and history their norms of impartiality and fidelity and their emphasis on firsthand credible witnessing. These two chapters suggest the broadening conceptual and cultural domains of "fact."

The next two chapters focus directly on the development of the "scientific" or "natural" fact. Chapter 5 traces the development of "fact" as a constituent part of the new natural history. This chapter argues that in the early seventeenth century the concept "matters of fact" and the procedures for proving them were well established in law and history before they were adopted in natural philosophy. The lawyer, historian, and natural philosopher Francis Bacon played an important role in their transfer to the natural philosophical and experimental community of the following generation. Legal notions were adopted and adapted by the English scientific community and particularly in the Royal Society's emphasis on "fact" in natural history. I take up the Baconian emphasis on experiment, the connection between "fact" and the new-style natural history, the nature of scientific witnessing, and the role of observational aids such as the telescope and microscope. The conditions of scientific investigation, experiment, and decision making in some ways resembled and in others differed from those of the law court. This chapter explores how the institutions, processes, and participants in fact finding and fact making in various disciplines altered the nature of the fact-finding process to meet their own particular needs. Witnessing and credibility are given extended treatment. Some attention is paid to "fact" in the work of Continental naturalists and experimenters in order to better assess the degree to which the centrality of "matter of fact" in seventeenth-century natural investigation should be treated primarily or initially as an English development.

Chapter 6 is devoted to three specific aspects of the development of fact in natural philosophy. The first is the role of gentlemanly and aristocratic values of trust and mutual respect in establishing a scientific culture of fact hypothesized by Steven Shapin and Simon Schaffer. While I view the evidence from the naturalist community itself as showing more concern for observational opportunity and expertise than gentility, my major point is a different one. The mode of establishing scientific matters of fact practiced by the virtuosi is not a peculiar feature of the "gentlemen" of the Royal Society but instead is part of a culture of fact developed earlier and simultaneously in other disciplines as well, especially law. Lawyers and virtuosi shared an emphasis on truth, an insistence on fact over fiction and imagination, a preference for firsthand and credible witnessing, and a rhetoric of impartiality. The courtroom and the rooms of the Royal Society shared a great deal, and whatever the courtroom was, it was certainly not a place of shared, gentlemanly trust.

The second part of this chapter explores the relationship between "fact" and causal explanations involving "principles," "hypotheses," "conjecture," "theory," and the "laws of nature." It compares these efforts in natural philosophy with the historians' and newsmen's use of "conjecture," "reflection," and "inference."

Finally, this chapter examines the mode of discourse practiced in English natural history and natural philosophy. The rhetoric and stylistic norms advertised by the Royal Society and its members were actually common to all the discourses of fact. In the context of other changes in rhetoric and developments in religious epistemology, it becomes clear that the development of the polite, "gentle," noncontentious modes of discourse of the virtuosi was at least in part promoted by the epistemological implications of the concepts of fact they employed rather than by their social position or aspiration.

Chapter 7 attempts to show how the concept "fact" and essentially legalistic approaches to proofs for "matters of fact" were adopted by a variety of post-Restoration religious controversialists. In this context, "fact" is used to support "belief" in principles of natural theology and key portions of the Bible, to argue against Roman Catholic claims, to prove the existence of spirit, and to underpin ecclesiastical history. I argue that the successful deployment of the proofs of matter of fact in the sphere of religion played an important role in making "fact" a central cultural category. As Protestant Christianity came to rely on arguments from matter of fact to establish and support belief in the central tenets of Scripture, "fact" came to have a more and more central role in English thinking and culture.

The final substantive chapter deals with the elaboration and diffusion of "fact" in English culture. It begins with Locke's role in elevating fact into a generally applicable philosophical category no longer tied to particular disciplines. By the early eighteenth century we can begin to speak of England as participating in a general "culture of fact." We look beyond 1700, if only briefly, to suggest something of the continuing evolution and importance of "fact," which became deeply embedded in eighteenth-century British philosophy, itself much taken with the continuing legal writing on fact. This chapter also reviews the relationship between "fact" and "fiction," suggesting how changes in this relationship made it possible for the conventions of reporting "matters of fact" to shape the fictional genres of the late seventeenth and early eighteenth centuries. "Fact" became incorporated in a new kind of fiction, the "fictional facts" of the early novel.

The conclusion provides a summary and suggests how this study fits into existing traditions of intellectual and cultural history.

It is necessary to say a few words about chronology, terminology, and categories. The chronological span suggested by the title needs some comment since my treatment of the various disciplines is not identical. The law and history chapters focus on the sixteenth and early seventeenth centuries because developments dealing with "human" facts precede and help shape those that deal with "natural" facts. The chapters dealing with mixed modes of human and natural facts and those dealing with natural facts emphasize the second half of the seventeenth century. The adoption of arguments from "fact" by religious polemicists being on the whole a rather late development, the religious chapter is largely concerned with the late seventeenth century. The penultimate chapter on cultural elaboration, which refers to a number of disciplines and genres, carries the discussion into the eighteenth century and is meant to point the way to further research. Although a main theme of this book is the interrelatedness of the various discourses of fact, I have organized chapters roughly along modern lines of law, history, science, and religion, an organizational format that makes it possible to chart cultural connections *and* disciplinary development.

Some new work by historians of science views natural philosophy as a category that encompassed much of both "science" and "religion" and also excluded parts of each. I draw attention to these revisionary efforts but retain the more traditional categories, in part because a firmly agreed recategorization scheme has not yet emerged and in part because however much natural philosophy may have concerned itself with Divine creation, there were still broad streams of religious and naturalist endeavors and writings that were and were perceived at the time to be relatively distinct.

Current and early modern terminologies do not always convey the same meaning, and the early modern usages were themselves somewhat confusing. I occasionally use the terms "science," "scientist," and "scientific fact," but these terms are anachronistic. I sometimes use "naturalist," a term that includes both natural historians and natural philosophers. Certainly "science" and "scientists" would not have made sense to early modern practitioners of "natural history" and "natural philosophy." Natural history involved the description of particular empirical phenomena and covered a much broader range of inquiries than is implied by our modern "natural history." Natural philosophy treated of causes and principles that often included some we think of as theological. The same persons were frequently engaged in both natural history and natural philosophy and often were referred to as "experimental philosophers," "new philosophers," or "virtuosi." "Scientist" now carries the suggestion of a professionalism that did not exist then. I sometimes use the term "virtuosi," though it may connote either amateurism or virtuosity. The word "science" itself was employed then in several different ways, ranging from any body of knowledge or skills to what today we would call a discipline, and implied a level of certainty that few natural philosophers would claim. In the seventeenth century natural philosophy included the nature of the deity and his Creation, and there were "civil," "natural," "ecclesiastical," and "divine" histories.

Although at times I point to related Continental developments and in some instances to the need for a comparative perspective, this study is focused on early modern English developments and English cultural venues. Although limited in time and space and in what aspects it considers of the various disciplines it explores, this book traces how the concept "fact" became a central feature of several intellectual enterprises and of the general English intellectual landscape. I describe a widening circle of influence from law that with time extended to historiography, news, marvels, the study of natural phenomena, religion, and the pseudohistory and pseudobiography we call the novel. As it is adopted by different intellectual enterprises with different problems to solve, "fact" may come to have different functions and different roles in the different disciplines. As it moves from one discipline to another, "fact" is transformed in many ways—but a common core of meaning persists that becomes central to English culture.

CHAPTER ONE

"Fact" and the Law

The concept of "fact" took shape, I have suggested, in the legal arena and was then carried into other intellectual endeavors until it became part and parcel of the generally held habits of thought of late-seventeenth- and early-eighteenth-century English culture. So now we must turn to that legal arena.

Although my focus is primarily on England and English culture, examination of the English legal tradition of fact finding cannot be limited to the common law. Despite its frequent claims to uniqueness, the common law drew on the Romano-canon legal tradition. The English were constantly exposed to that tradition and its variants in Chancery, Admiralty, and the ecclesiastical and prerogative courts. Civil law learning informs many of the authoritative sources of the common law, most notably Bracton. The Romano-canon tradition, formalized earlier than English common law, had developed a complex evidentiary system during the Middle Ages. The ordeals and other irrational proofs were replaced by rational inquiry and the critical sifting and evaluation of the available evidence by professional judges. Witnesses played a central role in the rationalization of evidence, perhaps the single most important change in later medieval law.[1] The system quickly developed into one of written depositions in answer to written interrogatories prepared by legal professionals. Complex rules established the credibility of witnesses and excluded incompetent, biased, or interested testimony. In serious criminal offenses for which the evidence of two good witnesses or the confession necessary for "full proof" was lacking, the testimony of less credible witnesses, a single witness, or other *indicia* or signs were sufficient to order judicial torture of the defendant to elicit the confession that would constitute full proof. Drawn from the ancient rhetorical tradition, these *indicia* included the age, sex, education, social status, and reputation of the individual in question. Similar criteria were invoked in assessing witness credibility and circumstantial evidence.[2]

The Romano-canon system distinguished between fact and law, a distinction embodied in the civil law proverb "You give me the facts, I give you the law" and in the numerous procedural manuals that developed from the twelfth century onward.[3] "Fact" or "factum" in law implied human actions or events in which human beings participated that might be known even if not directly observed at the time of adjudication. Typically, they were actions, such as a murder or a robbery, that had been committed some time in the past. The "facts," which were to be established by both written documents and witness testimony, provided the basis for belief and judgment. The distinction between matters of fact and matters of law was found in the law of all jurisdictions that derived all or part of their law from the civil law that had developed in Italy and elsewhere during the medieval era.[4]

Some, but not all, of this legal technology was also to be found in the English common law. Three somewhat related features of the common law system are particularly relevant to our inquiry. The first is the legal usage of "fact" and the distinction between "matters of fact" and "matters of law." The second is the development of lay jurors as fact evaluators, particularly of witness testimony. The third is the value the legal system placed on impartial public proceedings and unbiased judgment.[5]

"Matter of Fact" and "Matter of Law"

Unlike the Romano-canon law, the common law separated the determinations of "matters of fact" from "matters of law" institutionally, placing the former in the hands of lay jurors and the latter in the hands of professional judges. One of the most important results for our purposes is that experience with "facts" and fact determination became familiar to that quite substantial group of ordinary individuals eligible to serve on juries.[6] English self-congratulation on the jury of "twelve good men and true" helped enhance the sense of jury fitness to undertake its fact-finding task. The quite widespread experience and familiarity with legal institutions and the language of fact and methods of fact determination thus brought facts easily to the attention of the English so that they became part of the "furniture of the mind." I suggest that it was precisely this familiarity and this confidence in juries that made "fact" so easily transportable to a variety of nonlegal contexts.

The term "fact" as used in English law had two related meanings. The first, and more general, referred to any human act or deed of legal significance that had, or would, take place. In the second, "fact" referred to the act constituting the crime of which the defendant stood accused. The act, the fact, thus required proof. A judge demanded that "Evidence be given of the truth of the Fact, that Gentleman did murder himself is this."[7] The "fact" in question might be an act that occurred on a particular occasion, for example, "the evening of the fact," or a series of acts such as adultery or treason that might take place over some time. A prisoner who pled not guilty "denieth the fact." The accused had been "taken in the Fact" of arson. We also find references to the "Heinousness of the Fact" and to "malefactors" and the still common legal usage "before the fact" and "after the fact."[8] William Lambarde's popular *Eirenarcha* employed similar categories, categories also to be found both in Cicero's *De inventione* and the *Rhetorica ad herennium*. Lambarde's "precedent" category, analogous to "before the fact," included the "will to do the fact" as well as the "power to commit the act." In dealing with the "present" category, justices of the peace were to consider whether the accused had been present at the fact and conditions in the absence of which "the fact could not follow." "Subsequent" acts are "after the fact."[9] The language of fact as act or deed, particularly of a criminal nature, became familiar English usage.

Although the origin of the distinction between matter of fact and matter of law in English law remains unclear, it was well known in the sixteenth century.[10] The Latin maxim *ad quaestionem facti non respondent judices, ad quaestionem juris non respondent juratores* was much quoted by Coke, who attributed it, perhaps incorrectly, to Bracton.[11] The first example of the distinction between matters of fact and matters of law in English I have encountered is Sir Thomas More's *Debellacyon of Salem and Bizance* (1533). Here the terms are employed in ways suggesting common use and widespread understanding rather than innovation. More, whose work was written for a fairly broad audience, was attacking Christopher St. Germain's *Salem and Bizance*, which examined procedural and evidentiary differences between English ecclesiastical courts in cases of heresy and the common law courts in cases of felony. The distinction between fact and law is employed by both More and St. Germain as they discuss the nature of witnesses, assessments of their credibility, and the perjury of witnesses in heresy trials. Both also clearly distinguish jurors from witnesses and insist that in common law trials jurors are "judges of the fact." In this instance, as in so many others, the distinction between fact and law is employed in the context of distinguishing the work of the judge from that of the jury.[12]

From the sixteenth century, if not earlier, jurors were seen as "judges of the fact." Statements to that effect appeared with some regularity in judicial charges to the jury and in judicial summing-up of evidence. Jurors and others who attended or heard about criminal trials would have been familiar with the idea that juries were assigned the task of determining whether the "fact" alleged in the case was to be considered proved. "Fact" in this context implied a human deed or action which had occurred in the past and which had to be substantiated or proved to the satisfaction of the jurors, who were "judges of the fact." The "fact" or "matter of fact" was not considered "true" or suitable to be believed until satisfactory evidence had been presented. A "matter of fact" was an *issue* placed before a jury as to whether a particular person had performed a particular act or set of acts. "Fact" in the legal context therefore did not mean an established truth but an alleged act whose occurrence was in contention.

Although there are relatively few records of early-seventeenth-century trials, the charge of the attorney general in the notorious case of the earl of Somerset, accused of poisoning Sir Thomas Overbury, uses the language of fact in the typical legal sense. Here the fact in question is murder, and the fact is distinguished from the evidence that would establish the fact. The prosecution, which first made "a Narrative or Declaration of the Fact itself," then promised to "Break and distribute the Proofs," consisting of "witnesses," "examinations," and various writings.[13]

The best-known jurist of the late Elizabethan and early Stuart era, Sir Edward Coke, insisted that judges in the common law courts were not to answer questions of fact, nor were juries to answer questions of law, but that in Chancery judges would decide fact questions on the basis of the depositions of witnesses. Witness testimony in common law trials was "but evidence to a jury," and juries were sworn "to inquire of the matter of fact." Giles Duncombe characterized the jury as "sworn Judges in matter of fact, evidenced by witnesses and debated before them." He insisted that the public nature of English trials meant that "the Fact is settled, with greater certainty of truth" in English courts than elsewhere. It was common knowledge that the office of the jury was to find the truth of the facts; that of the judge, to declare "veritatem juris."[14] In practice the convention of facts for the jury and law for the judge was not always rigorously followed. Occasionally, there were claims that jurors were properly judges of law as well as of fact.[15]

Juries

Jurors were not initially fact evaluators but rather "knowers" of the facts, selected locally because they were expected to bring some prior knowledge of the facts and/or the litigants to the trial. Witness testimony to establish facts began in the fourteenth or fifteenth century but seems to have become a regular and accepted part of common law proceedings only in the course of the sixteenth century. Thomas More and Christopher St. Germain treated the proposition that jurors were not witnesses but judges of fact as if it were common knowledge.[16] Soon legislation attempted to ensure that suspects and witnesses would appear in court. Subpoena procedures developed, and perjury made a statutory crime. The justices of the peace were active in the pretrial examination of witnesses in the mid-sixteenth century. As witnesses became more common, the courts more clearly distinguished not only between jurors and witnesses but between witnesses and accusers. A kind of cross-examination of witnesses by counsel during trial became possible.[17] In the early seventeenth century Sir Edward Coke insisted juries were to be led to their verdicts by the witness testimony they heard in court, and Sir Francis Bacon, then Lord Chancellor, indicated that the law of England "leaveth the discerning and credit of testimony wholly to the juries' consciences and understanding."[18] Jurors in both civil and criminal cases were required to determine the truth or falsity of the evidence presented to the court. Although jurors legally retained the right to personally know the facts at issue, they were, for all practical purposes, limited to evaluating the documentary and parole evidence presented to them.[19]

Matters of fact in most situations were to be proved either by the testimony of witnesses or by "authentic" documents. Legal and other dictionaries thus distinguished between "matters of deed" and "matters of record." In civil cases there was a strong belief that written records were superior to witness testimony because they were not subject to the fallibility of human memory.[20] In criminal cases the testimony of witnesses was central.

Assumptions and Epistemological Issues

Although law as a discipline is typically approached as a matter of normative rather than empirical inquiry, in everyday legal practice questions of empirical epistemology necessarily arise. Once witness testimony became central to English legal proceedings, how the jurors are to discern the truth of the facts alleged in court became an important practical question. Early modern common law courts, however, are rather difficult to analyze sharply in epistemological terms because they are a combination of institutional elements and procedures. Some, like the jury, had been created in the distant past. Others, like the witness, were a more recent innovation. Because the common law trial combined lay and professional elements, it incorporated both lay and professional epistemological assumptions and patterns of thought. In the process of attempting to cope with current social and political contexts and with changing patterns of belief about how judgments should be made, the common law courts developed an evolving set of rules about evidence. For instance, early modern courts retained the older device of oaths, grounded in earlier epistemological beliefs but also reinforced by Reformation concerns with conscience. The relationship between the old oaths and the developing rational criteria for assessing witnesses was unclear. This tension was important because at that time only some parties and some witnesses could testify under oath.

A number of assumptions underlay the modes of inquiry of early modern courts. The first was that it was possible to gain adequate if not perfect knowledge of events that could not be seen, heard, or repeated in court. Neither judges, jurors, nor lawyers would actually "see" the killing or the land transaction at issue. The law dealt with "transient things" of no "constant being." Firsthand sensory experience might provide "best evidence" for "matters of fact," but it was unattainable by courts. Courts therefore relied on documents that recorded the actions or rights in question or on witnesses who had seen or heard the events in question. If courts were to employ witnesses, their testimony had to be believable and trustworthy. It was necessary to develop some way of thinking about which kinds of testimony were likely to be credible and which were not. There was an awareness that owing to the "imperfection of memory," the "rembrance of things fails and goes off" and men were likely to "entertain opinions in their stead."[21]

All early modern courts were dependent on testimony. Common, civil, and canon law developed rules of exclusion and evaluation, the second two more rule-bound than common law courts, where jurors assessed credibility and determined whether the "matter of fact" had been adequately proved. Legal procedures assumed jurors had sufficient intellectual ability and moral probity to assess witness credibility adequately and to reach verdicts of sufficient certitude to satisfy their consciences and the community at large. The law adopted an epistemology that put great faith both in witness observers and in jurors as "judges of fact." The common law courts provided a critical site for inquiry about facts.

Witness Competence

If decisions about credibility were made by juries, competency to testify was determined by the judge. Those guilty of certain crimes—for example, treason, felony, and *crimen falsi* such as perjury and forgery— were excluded, their oaths being "of no weight." Madmen, idiots, and children were excluded for "want of skill and discernment."[22] In civil cases those with a pecuniary interest were excluded from testifying.[23] There was controversy about accused co-conspirators, co-defendants, and acces-

The claims of those incompetent to
judge count for nothing.

sories who were most likely to have firsthand knowledge of the fact but also likely to lie. On the whole, such witnesses were treated as competent, leaving "it to the Jury what to believe."[24] Similar treatment was given to the testimony of those who had been convicted of a crime and later pardoned.[25]

Witness Credibility

Determination of witness credibility became central to the early modern trial, though technically decisions might be reached without any witnesses at all. Sir Francis Bacon, early in the seventeenth century, and Hale toward the end of it agreed that the law of England left "the discerning and credit of testimony wholly to the juries' consciences and understanding." As Hale put it, "It is one thing whether a witness be admissible to be heard, another thing, whether they are to be believed when heard." Jurors were "judges of the fact, and likewise of the probability or improbability, credibility or incredibility of the witnesses and the testimony."[26] There is, however little judicial writing on how such assessments should be made. It sometimes was asserted that witnesses should be considered "honeste, good and indifferent, till the contrary be shown," a view still echoed by Gilbert two centuries later.[27] Clearly, gender, property holding, social status, education, and expertise were part of the equation, as was the oath taken by witnesses and whether or not the testimony was hearsay. Juries were to judge the "Quality, Carriage, Age, Condition, Education and Place of Commorance of Witnesses" in giving "more or less Credit to their Testimony."[28]

The widely distributed manuals for justices of the peace contained credibility criteria to assist the justices in examining witnesses and persons accused of felonies. We do not know to what extent these manuals either echoed or were incorporated into jury instructions, although some of the "better sort" of jurors might have read them or heard them discussed before jury service.[29] William Lambarde's popular late-sixteenth-century handbook suggested that in the course of pretrial examinations justices of the peace must consider ancestry, education, occupation, and character. Post-1618 editions of Dalton's *Country Justice* added "two old verses" derived from the Romano-canon tradition indicating that those who examined witnesses should consider

> Conditio, sexus, aetas, discretio, fama,
> Et fortuna, fides: in testibus ista requires.[30]

The causes of suspicion, which resonated to Romano-canon law, were also to be found in Thomas Wilson's Ciceronian *Art of Rhetorique* (1553). Many of the same criteria were employed in assessing the guilt of the accused.[31]

The manuals for the justices of the peace, with their criteria for "suspicion" echoing both the Romano-canon tradition and English legal practice relating to arrest and pretrial examination, became absorbed into the general law and culture of evidence.[32] Gilbert's authoritative treatise on evidence, which summarized the practice of the early eighteenth century, thus indicated that there were a number of things that might "render a witness suspected." A party to a crime or one who swore "for his own safety or indemnity, or be a relation or friend to the party, or the like; or be of a profligate or wicked temper or disposition; and the weight of the probability lies thus; if you think the bias is so strong upon him, as would incline a man of his disposition, figure and rank in the world, to falsify, you are to disbelieve him; but if you think him a man of that credit and veracity, that, notwithstanding the bias upon him, would yet maintain a value for truth, and is under the force and obligation of his oath, he is to be believed."[33]

Hearsay Testimony

The formal exclusion of hearsay was a rather late development in English law, probably because of the late and rather gradual arrival of witnesses and of jurors as fact evaluators. Although hearsay was a familiar concept and hearsay evidence was clearly viewed as inferior, it does not appear to have been rigorously excluded until the mid-eighteenth century.[34] Quintilian's *Institutes of the Orator*, studied by schoolboys from the sixteenth century onward, examined how hearsay testimony could be used by the orator as a means of strengthening and undermining arguments. Polybius's critique of hearsay too was well known. Secondhand testimony was considered far less valuable than that received "from those that report of their own view." This statement by Hale is echoed by Lord Chief Justice Holt, who indicated in a 1691 case that witnesses had not presented "Evidence: unless they testified what they themselves knew or had heard from the accused." By the time Locke wrote at the end of the seventeenth century, it was already a truism "that any testimony, the further off it is from the original truth, the less force and proof it has. . . . A credible man vouching his knowledge of it is a good proof; but if another equally credible do witness it from his report, the Testimony is weaker, and the third that attests the hearsay of a hearsay is yet less considerable."[35]
Hearsay was clearly permissible under some circumstances. The principle that hearsay might be used to confirm or corroborate other testimony was employed in Raleigh's trial of 1603. In the early eighteenth century Gilbert wrote that "mere hearsay . . . may in corroboration of a witnesses' testimony, . . . shew that he affirmed the same thing before on other occasions, and that the witness is still consistent with himself."[36] The uncertain treatment of hearsay in the seventeenth and eighteenth centuries, and indeed in the twentieth, reflects the perennial epistemological

question whether poor evidence is better than no evidence. Indeed, hearsay is one of the few points at which legal theorists and historians confront problems of empirical knowing.

Indicia of Credibility

On the whole, women's testimony was probably trusted less than men's. The lesser value of women's testimony was embodied in the civil law. Although English women appeared as witnesses, they did not serve on juries.

A child's testimony was viewed as less credible than that of an adult, and the testimony of children under fourteen was generally excluded. The weak of mind and the insane too could not testify, for they like children lacked "skill and discernment."[37]

Reputation was also a factor in assessing witness credibility. Here again we can see a kind of translation from the justicing handbook directives concerning "suspicion" in pretrial examination to the criteria for jury assessment of witnesses. Only a generation or so after Lambarde and Dalton, Judges Hale and North echoed their criteria. North in particular mentioned the "inclinations" and the "education" of the witnesses. Those who have "habits of falshood and are Comon & Known lyars" and those who lived "open, vitious scandalous lives" could be heard in court, but their testimony could bind jurors "no farther" than they believed it in their conscience to be true.[38]

In criminal trials defendants often attempted to show that government witnesses were persons of low moral character, of "ill fame," or lacking in integrity. Thomas More, on trial for treason, attempted to show that Richard Rich had been notorious as a "common lyar" and a man of "no recommendable fame."[39] Cynthia Herrup's study of seventeenth-century criminal process also indicates that a reputation for good moral character substantially affected legal outcomes. The Popish Plot trials of the late seventeenth century often emphasized the low moral status and lack of integrity of crown witnesses. As Thomas Hobbes stated succinctly, the evaluation of testimony involved two considerations: "one of the saying of the man; the other of his virtue."[40]

Moral status and reputation blended into but were not identical to social and economic status. In the courtroom as elsewhere the testimony of independent property holders counted for more than that of dependents or the poor. We have noted references to "Quality" and "Condition" that first appeared in the justicing handbooks and reappeared in Hale's treatment of credible witnesses. In some instances the interests of servants were assumed to be that of their master, a situation roughly analogous to that of wives, whose interests were assumed to be identical to their husbands', and were thus seen as having "unity of persons."[41]

Assumptions about reliable testimony corresponded in a rough way to the existing social hierarchy in which noblemen and gentlemen were ranked above yeomen and merchants, and yeomen and merchants above poor husbandmen, servants, and the unemployed. But status considerations might be countered by others. As we noted earlier, those with a pecuniary interest were entirely excluded from testifying in civil cases regardless of status and wealth.

Religion played a role in assessing credibility of witnesses in a number of ways. One's reputation for piety was a relevant consideration, and those who were "atheistical and loose to oaths" were not to be given the same credit "as men of good manners and clear conversation."[42] Despite hostility to Roman Catholicism, the testimony of Roman Catholics was considered credible, at least in cases where religion was not involved.[43] In one of the Popish Plot trials, however, one judge indicated that slender credit should be given Catholic testimony in a "Papist Cause, and for a Papist."[44] In practice, questions of religion or irreligion shade into general questions of the moral character of witnesses or the issue of testimony under oath.

Jury consideration of the "quality and qualifications of witnesses" included the "manner of their Testimony." "Many times the Manner of a Witnesses's delivering his Testimony" provided "a probable indication whether he speaks truly or falsely."[45] Hale and others often stated that they preferred the English over the Continental process because of the superior opportunity to assess witness demeanor. Demeanor became a standard element in the evidentiary tradition: "An over-forward and hasty zeal on the part of the witness, . . . his exaggeration of circumstances, his reluctance in giving adverse evidence, his slowness in answering, his evasive replies, his affection of not hearing or not understanding the question . . . precipitancy in answering . . . his inability to detail any circumstances wherein, if his testimony were untrue, he would be open to contradiction, . . . are all to a greater or less extent obvious marks of insincerity."[46]

Expertise and Experts

Although expert witnesses are commonly found in the modern courtroom, they were less common in earlier centuries. In most matters the testimony of ordinary individuals was considered reliable. Yet expertise counted for something: "Discernment must arise from the skill, and will appear from the reasons and accounts they give of their knowledge." Those that give more "plain and evident marks of their knowledge" were thus deemed more credible.[47] These statements, however, seem to refer to greater experience and knowledge rather than to professional expertise.

Expert witnesses sometimes testified, though we know relatively little about their use and legal status. Physicians often testified in cases involving poisoning and witchcraft, and midwives in cases of infanticide or rape.[48]

Something akin to expert testimony also seems to come into play in cases involving the testimony of merchants on what constituted accepted and normal practice.

Multiple Witnesses

Unlike Continental and ecclesiastical courts, the English were not bound by the two-witness rule. English courts could reach verdicts without any witnesses at all. Hale and Locke state the normal preference for multiple witnesses, but numbers were not necessarily decisive. Refusals to indict or convict might occur in the face of the testimony of twenty or more witnesses.[49]

A recent study focusing on oaths suggests that the number of witnesses testifying on oath made a crucial difference and that credibility considerations counted for little.[50] This finding runs counter to all the contemporary statements concerning credibility assessments we have encountered. If it were correct, there would have been little point to a trial. Jurors would have just counted the number of witnesses testifying under oath and given their verdict. Yet Hale insisted that juries were entitled to "disbelieve what a Witness swear" and "may sometimes give Credit to one Witness, tho' opposed by more than one." One of the "Excellencies" of the jury trial was that the jury "upon Reasonable Circumstances, indicating a Blemish upon their credibility," might pronounce a "Verdict contrary to such Testimonies, the Truth where of they have just Cause to suspect, and may and do often pronounce their Verdict upon one single Testimony."[51]

Certainly the number of concurrent testimonies was thought to increase probability and make the evidence "more concludent." Gilbert would write, "The first and lowest proof is the oath of one witness only." A single witness required "great confidence in the integrity and veracity of the man." The testimony of two oaths was "higher" because, if they agreed "in every circumstance," they must be either "perjured or telling the truth."[52]

There were traces of the biblically derived two-witness rule in England. In treason cases the two-witness rule was often voiced, though the various treason statutes of the early modern period sometimes included it and sometimes did not until it was made permanent in 1696.[53] The two-witness rule is also to be found in connection with perjury. The still current requirement that wills be witnessed by two witnesses can be explained by the fact that until well into the nineteenth century wills were under the jurisdiction of the ecclesiastical courts.

Incredibility of the Fact

Prevailing common-sense beliefs also bore on questions of credibility. Francis North, Lord Guilford, chief justice of Common Pleas, indicated that the "Probability of [th]e Matter" was involved in assessing witness credibility.[54] The incredibility of the fact "overthrows" the testimony of a witness and "set[s] aside" his credit: "For if the fact be contrary to all manner of experience and observation," it was "too much" to receive on the oath of a single witness.[55] Multiple witnessing of incredible events, however, was more difficult to reject because the credibility of biblical miracles was defended on the basis of multiple witnesses.

Witchcraft provides an interesting example of a "fact" whose general credibility eroded over time. It came to be thought impossible by the majority of educated persons by the beginning of the eighteenth century. Although belief in witchcraft persisted among the uneducated, a 1712 jury acquitted the accused despite the testimony of numerous witnesses.

Contradiction and Consistency

Inconsistency of a witness "removes him from all credit, for things totally opposite cannot be believed from the attestation of any man." Enunciated by Gilbert in the early eighteenth century, this position had a long history. St. Germain expressed a similar view in the early sixteenth century. On discovering contradictions, juries were entitled to assume "lyghtness of mynde, hatred or corruption of money."[56] Justicing handbooks too indicated that if the tales of two persons varied, neither was to be credited. In a 1671 case a judge pointed out that the contradictions between the testimony of two witnesses "took off their Whole Testimony." Hale argued that when jurors could directly observe contradictory testimony, "great Opportunities" arose to gain "the true and clear Discovery of the Truth." Among elements for evaluating witness testimony, Locke too listed "the consistency of the parts, and circumstances of the relation" as well as "contrary testimonies."[57]

Cross-examination of witnesses by counsel as we currently know it did not exist in criminal cases. Something like it probably did in civil cases where both parties were represented by counsel. Even in criminal trials Hale noted that the jury, the parties, their counsel, and the judge could "propound occasional Questions, which beats and boults out the Truth." Oral questioning, he thought, was "the best Method of searching and sifting out the Truth."[58]

Oaths

The oath was a important feature of the early modern courtroom and was a part of legal proceedings long before rational approaches to fact finding came into being. Oaths predated the introduction of witnesses to the common law trial, and Anglo-Saxon oaths already invoked the language of fidelity and credibility that would later become hallmarks of witnesses. Although oaths had a longer history in the canon and civil law courts, the administration of oaths to witnesses must have been a relatively late addition to the common law trial. Witnesses swore to tell "the whole truth and nothing but the truth as near as God shall give you grace."[59] Yet it was obvious that both parties and witnesses might lie or fail to report all they knew of the facts. Writing at a time when witnesses were still relatively new to the common law trial, Thomas More noted that witnesses "myght swere false."[60] Perjury became a statutory crime during the same period in which witness testimony became routine.[61] The numerous discussions of credibility we have been examining do not suggest that credibility issues disappeared for testimony given under oath.[62] At most, it was probably true as Gilbert said that the law begins with the "benign and human" presumption that witnesses do "not falsify or prevaricate."[63]

In civil trials witnesses for both parties testified on oath. In such cases jurors were very likely to have heard conflicting testimony and could not have believed all the witnesses simply because they testified on oath. As noted earlier, it may be in practice that under such circumstances juries merely counted, but if so their practice ran counter to much contemporary scholarly and judicial commentary on credibility.[64] The situation was more complicated in criminal trials, where only prosecution witnesses testified on oath. The question here was whether those who testified under oath were automatically considered more credible than those who did not. Hale tells us that things "may blemish the credibility" of sworn testimony and that credibility assessments were left to the jury, "who are judges of the fact, and likewise of the probability or improbability of the witness and his testimony." "It is one thing, whether a witness be admissible to be heard, another thing, whether they are to be believed when heard." Judge North, Lord Guilford indicated that juries had "great Latitude" and "may say they beleev or doe not beleeve in any Case, & concerning any Witnesses." If juries were to evaluate credibility as Hale, North, and even Gilbert clearly suggest, what are we then to make of Gilbert's statement citing Coke that "every plain and honest man affirming the truth of any matter under the sanction and solemnities of an oath, is entitled to faith and credit"?[65] The actual relationship between the oath and the jury's duty to assess witness credibility remains problematic. Seventeenth-century juries probably received instructions looking both ways. Since prosecution witnesses testified under oath and the defendant and his witnesses could not, most cases would have left nothing for juries to decide if sworn testimony had been taken at face value. Yet we know that juries did acquit.

The tension between credibility and oath became especially apparent during the politically charged Popish Plot and Exclusion trial. Prosecutors asked jurors to believe Crown witnesses simply because they testified on oath. The defense insisted that jurors weigh the credibility of those wit-

istry emphasized the role of reason in making rational and moral decisions under conditions of less than perfect certainty. When the conscience of jurors reached a state of a "satisfied conscience" or "moral certainty," conviction was appropriate. When they entertained reasonable doubts, they were to acquit. Neither the satisfied conscience nor the moral certainty test was considered to have the same degree of certainty as demonstration or mathematical proofs.

According to Coke, the prosecution to be successful must be uncontradicted and unanswerable.[76] From the Restoration period onward we have more abundant evidence about the standard for jury verdicts. Edward Waterhouse wrote of verdicts reached "as they think in their Conscience: the truth of the facts after hearing the evidence . . . concerning the fact." Before reaching their verdict, the jurors were to recess "to consider their Evidence, . . . they are to weigh the Credibility of Witnesses, and the Force and Efficacy of their Testimonies."[77] "A great Weight, Value and Credit" could be given such verdicts because the "unanimous Suffrage and Opinion of Twelve Men, . . . carries in itself a much greater Weight and Preponderation to discover the Truth of a Fact, than any other Trial whatsoever."[78] Another judge noted that "in all cases [tha]t depend on . . . witnesses," jurors "are to . . . weigh all Circumstances, and as they in their consciences beleev concerning [th]e testimony so are they to give their verdict."[79] The "satisfied conscience" standard was synonymous with the term "moral certainty." Late-seventeenth-century judges often used expressions such as "if you are satisfied or not satisfied with the evidence" or "if you believe on the evidence." A juror swears "to what he can infer and conclude from the testimony . . . by the force of his understanding."[80] During the early eighteenth century there was increasing reference to the understanding of the juror. Jurors "were rational men and will determine according to your consciences, whether you believe those men guilty or not."[81] Understanding and conscience were concerned with the same mental processes.

Over time judges became increasingly likely to mention doubts on the part of the jury. From the mid-eighteenth century the now familiar "beyond reasonable doubt" terminology of modern Anglo-American law was added to its cognates, "satisfied conscience" and "moral certainty." The meaning of all these phrases was identical and they often were used together.

Jurors

Given our primary concern with "fact" and "fact finding," some attention must be paid to the character of juries. Coke describes jurors as "homines liberi et legales." Earlier in their history it was hoped that

knights and substantial freeholders would serve as jurors. By the late sixteenth century and early seventeenth century, however, it was rare for the
gentry to serve on trial juries. Grand jurors were on the whole of higher
status than petty jurors and during the late seventeenth and eighteenth
centuries were dominated by the gentry. The ideal grand jurors were
"grave and substantial gentlemen" and the "most sufficient freeholders in
the county."[82] Grand jurors on assize panels, however, were composed of
the lesser or parish, not county, gentry.

Assize jurors, that is, trial or petty jurors, were mostly drawn from the
yeoman class, and quarter sessions jurors tended to be lesser yeomen and
even husbandmen. Juries were composed of modestly propertied men of
the "middling classes" drawn from village elites and included artisans and
tradesmen as well as yeomen. They were the leaders of village society experienced in the administration of local government but not highly educated or sophisticated men.[83] Jury service, though prestigious, was time
consuming, and many sought to avoid it. Shortages meant that bystanders
were not infrequently added to jury panels. Although addressed in court
as "Gentlemen of the Jury," most jurors in civil and criminal cases were not
actually gentlemen.[84] To ensure independence, there was a property qualification for jury service, and women, servants, and the lowest ranks of society were excluded. Those of middling economic and social status were,
to use current parlance, treated as "epistemologically competent" to reach
judgments about legal "facts."

Jurors were assumed to have the qualities of mind necessary to make
judgments of matters of fact. They were intelligent enough to consider
whether the "fact" had actually occurred and who had been responsible for it. They were considered capable of evaluating the demeanor of
witnesses, comparing testimonies, spotting inconsistencies and contradictions, and evaluating the extent to which these factors affected the credibility of witnesses. Jurors were also expected to consider the moral qualities and lifestyle of those who testified.

English judges and juries were both idealized and criticized. Although
the common law was lauded for its employment of juries, there was
sufficient unease about juries to generate a special jurisdiction for Star
Chamber over jury corruption. It was often claimed that jurors were not of
sufficiently high status because inflation eroded whatever property requirements were instituted. If some, such as Interregnum law reformer
William Walwyn, praised juries for "justly and faithfully, judging the cause
of rich and poor without fear or favour, . . . without respect to persons,"
others yearned for juries of "twelve able understanding gentlemen" to re-
place the "weak and ignorant."[85] The Restoration Parliament and several
post-1660 writers expressed similar concerns, and periodically bills were
introduced to ensure "able and sufficient jurors."[86] Jurors were criticized

as "simple," "unlearned," or unsophisticated men who might be misled, and praised as capable, responsible, "of known integrity," that is, "good men and true."[87] The English governing classes praised juries, refused to serve on them, and sought means of ensuring their continued improvement. Jury composition did not change significantly, and fact determination in the common law courts continued to be the responsibility of the "middling" classes.

Social Status and Legal Facts

Legal fact finding is particularly relevant to Steven Shapin's emphasis on the importance of social status in connection with English empirical philosophy of the Restoration era. Shapin has suggested that aristocratic and courtier codes of the Renaissance, with their concerns with honor and civility, established a system of trust and trustworthiness that contributed in important ways to the construction of knowledge.[88] Although English society recognized a connection among birth, wealth, and virtue and exhibited greater inclination to trust the testimony of gentlemen than those of lower status, those assumptions alone did not determine fact finding in the courts. First of all, in England it was less clear than elsewhere who was and was not a gentleman, the gentlemanly class being a rather fluid one involving birth, wealth, and lifestyle, which to some degree were substitutable for one another.

Societal inclination to trust those of high status was undermined in a variety of ways in the legal setting. Although the justices of the peace were predominantly of the gentlemanly class, they were often criticized by assize judges for partiality.[89] Gentlemen themselves engaged in countless lawsuits that pitted the word of one gentleman against that of another. It was after all the upper classes who were most prone to litigate in the common law courts. Those with even the slightest financial interest in a civil case were excluded from testifying on the grounds of partiality and interest, gentleman or not. Gentle witnesses for both parties could not all be assumed to be telling the truth. Although one writer on the subject of "honor" indicated that "the testimony of a Gentleman ought to be received and more credited than the word of a common person,"[90] there were other considerations that sometimes modified that deference in the courtroom. Accusations of partiality and interest might be pitted against status claims. Upper-class criminal defendants no more than lower-class criminal defendants were permitted to testify on oath. In all cases testimony would be evaluated by those of the "middling classes." Even peers would be tried by ordinary juries in civil cases. On the other hand, the bias in favor of the upper classes was clearly present. Social status was one, but only one, factor in assessing witness credibility.

Although Shapin has suggested that the common people were perceived as "perceptually unreliable" during the early modern period, there is nothing in the legal literature to support such a claim. All normal men were deemed to be perceptually competent in the legal context, and there was no suggestion that either "sense" or memory, key elements in matter of fact, were less acute or accurate in those of lower status. Jurors, men of the middling classes, and legal professionals, many of whom were not quite gentlemen, were entrusted to evaluate witness testimony for reliability and credibility. Shapin also suggests that merchants in the seventeenth century were perceived to be deceitful and untruthful. Yet the law did not distinguish merchants from others. From titled aristocrat downward, all witnesses with pecuniary interests were excluded from testifying. "Interest" was not a function of social status.

No matter what their social status, some witnesses would lie and some were foolish, easily influenced, or partial or prone to self-contradictory testimony. No doubt the law incorporated general societal assumptions about trustworthiness into its own fact-finding machinery, but the law's fact finders were for the most part not gentlemen, nor were most of its testifiers as to facts. Nevertheless, in very high-stakes situations it managed to find facts accurately to its own satisfaction and to the satisfaction of sixteenth- and seventeenth-century Englishmen generally. Throughout this period social status was one factor among many to be taken into account in the assessment of the credibility of witnesses by a body of some gentle, but mostly nongentle, persons deemed fully capable at arriving at the truth of the facts.[91]

The Norm of Impartiality

Recent studies of early modern English natural philosophy have noted the emphasis on impartiality among the advocates of the new empiricism and attribute it either to humanist efforts to polish academic manners or to gentlemanly mores.[92] The legal system and its concern with establishing matters of fact may have been a greater influence. Efforts to ensure impartiality have always been at the heart of the legal enterprise. Both the Romano-canon and the common law systems attempted to ensure it by a variety of institutional forms. The common law attempted to reduce or eliminate partiality and bias in jurors, judges, and witnesses while assuming partiality in the litigating parties and their lawyers.

Jury Impartiality

The common law provided for juror challenges to prevent favoritism, corruption, and bias. Jurors "are not to be of the Kindred or Alliance of any of the Parties. And . . . Not to be such as are prepossessed or prejudiced before they hear their Evidence." Parties were to have "notice of the Jurors, and of their Sufficiency and Indifferency, that so they may make their Challenges . . . if there be just Cause." Those of insufficient freehold too were unfit to try causes. Only twelve "indifferent" judges of the fact were to be sworn. Star Chamber punished corrupt jurors for egregious violations and "false" verdicts, and jurors might be fined until 1670. Jurors as judges of the fact were often reminded of their duty to be impartial, and even defendants reminded jurors to "put on indifferent eyes."[93]

Judicial Impartiality

It would be difficult to find a Western legal system that did not emphasize the importance of judicial impartiality. The English judiciary quite naturally adopted the norm, which applied to judges, to jurors who were judges of fact, and to justices of the peace acting in their capacity as judges. Queen Elizabeth had enjoined judges "to administer the law and justice indifferently without respect of persons."[94] Similar statements about impartiality and the "indifference of the court" were made by William Lambarde and Sir Edward Coke.[95] "All those that have the Administration of Justice committed to them" were "to behave with all Equity and Impartiality."[96]

Such rules as not allowing judges to go on assize in their own counties were designed to increase impartiality. Hale insisted on the importance of judicial rulings on exceptions to competency and other evidentiary matters being made publicly so that any "Partiality, and Injustice will be evident to all By-standers."[97] The impartiality norm required that judges must not give their opinion before all the evidence had been heard.[98] Hale enjoined "an entire absence of affection and passion which will easily occasion a wresting of judgment." Judging required a "temperate mind totally abandoning all manner of passion, affection, and perturbation so that he may come to the business with clearness of understanding and judgment."[99] Isaac Barrow summarized the conventional wisdom: "For as he is a good judge, who after a full cognisance, and carefull discussion of the case . . . doth pronounce freely and fairly, being no way swayed either by his own inclination, or by temptation from without, who is not byassed by any previous affection or dislike, not drawn by favour, not daunted by fear, not bribed by profit, not charmed by flattery, not dazzled by specious appearance, not gulled by crafty insinuations, or by fine speech; not tired by solicitation or importunity, not seduced by precedents or custome."[100]

The norm of impartiality did not imply modern judicial behavior. Early in the seventeenth century imperious judges often gave "Light and Assistance" to the jurors by "weighing the evidence before them . . . and by shewing them his Opinion even in Matter of Fact, which is a great Advantage and Light to Lay-Men . . . in investigating and enlightning the Matter of Fact, whereof the Jury are Judges."[101] Judges were not reluctant to interfere with juries, and several legal historians have argued that juries took their lead from the bench throughout the period.[102] Judicial influence was perhaps most obvious when judges summed up the evidence, but we do not how common this practice was. A major jury defense against excessive judicial influence was the notion that jurors might have direct knowledge of fact and witness credibility quite apart from the testimony presented in court.[103] Essentially for political reasons, this idea persisted long after juries had become unlikely to have such direct knowledge. As Hale noted, "If the judge's opinion must rule the matter of fact, the trial by jury would be useless."[104] Standards of judicial behavior were modified over the course of the seventeenth century. The ideal of impartiality was a constant, but the hectoring and overbearing behavior of Sir Edward Coke would not have passed muster as an appropriate model of judicial behavior in the age of Judge Holt.

The norm of judicial impartiality, however, was not always practiced and certainly not always seen to be practiced. Judges could "never escape the imputation of partiality and injustice from some party."[105] Particular judges were felt to be less than disinterested, especially in cases where royal interests appeared to be pitted against the property rights of subjects, where political interests were at stake, or where judges were thought have been bribed or unduly influenced by one of the parties. But demands for judicial impartiality were not simply platitudes. The 1620s witnessed the impeachment of Francis Bacon, Lord Chancellor of England, for judicial corruption and other judicial misbehavior. At the outbreak of the civil war several of Charles I's judges lost their offices. Such removals, more often than not motivated by political considerations, were made in the guise of efforts to regain judicial disinterestedness and impartiality. The issue of judicial partisanship was again raised during the reigns of Charles II and James II as Whigs attacked "Tory" judges. Only in 1696 did judges become irremovable from office by the Crown except for violations of the standard of "good behavior."[106]

Thus in early modern England impartiality was neither an unexamined assumption nor a subject of value conflict but rather an ever present and hotly defended norm of judicial conduct. And this norm had been and continued to be central to legal discourse quite independently of humanist concerns and gentlemanly codes.

Impartial Witnesses

We have noted the ways in which the courts attempted to ensure that witnesses would be impartial. Clearly, the ideal witness was the impartial witness, and "that which is reported by persons disinterested" was preferable to "that which is reported by persons of whose interest it is to have the thing true, or believed to be true."[107] Witness were most credible when "wholly indifferent and unconcerned." Indeed, their credit was "to be taken from their perfect indifference to the point in question." When "a man who is interested in the Matter in Question would also prove it, 'tis rather a Ground for Distrust rather than belief; for men are generally so short-sighted as to look at their own private Benefit, which is near to them, rather than the Good of the World, that is more remote."[108]

The quest for the much-praised impartial and disinterested witness, however, resulted in unanticipated problems. For instance, exclusion of financially interested parties from testifying in civil suits meant that those best informed about the issue in question were not permitted to testify— even if their pecuniary interest was minute. Only in the late eighteenth century did judges begin to allow the testimony of financially interested parties and to let jurors decide whether or not it should be believed.[109]

Impartiality—Lawyers—Rhetoric

The English mixed respect for and hostility toward the legal profession. Lawyers were supposed to be partial because they represented the contesting parties in adversarial proceedings. Apprehension was expressed that the "learning, art, and eloquence" of the lawyers might "seduce the minds" of unsophisticated jurors.[110] Lambarde, Hale, and Isaac Barrow suggested that the rhetorical skills of the lawyers might undermine the impartiality of courts. Courtroom eloquence, Hale indicated, "bribes [the jury's] fancies and bias[es] their affections"; Barrow noted the dangers of "crafty insinuations" and "fine speech" that detracted from impartiality.[111] John Hawles, a Whig polemicist of the 1680s, suggested that the "best judicatures of the world . . . utterly reject the use of Rhetoric," implying that the "Art of Persuading" was little different than deceit. Sir George Berkeley was confident that on the Day of Judgment neither the "voluble Oratory" nor "subtile Law-distinctions" typical of the lawyer would in "any way avail."[112]

All the discourses of "fact" became suspicious of rhetoric and often voiced this suspicion in connection with announcing their dedication to the norm of impartiality. The disciplines of law and historiography, however, were somewhat ambivalent about rhetoric, decrying its dangers on the one hand and incorporating it on the other. The adversarial character of the common law was premised on the belief that contending, partial, and interested parties, with the help of contending lawyer advocates, could reach the truth of particular facts, or rather that judge and jury could reach it for them. Counsel were expected to use the available means to win their case, but what means were available was determined by legal rules.

The English legal system, like that of the Continent, was sensitive to the norm of impartiality. The norm was frequently stated with respect to both jurors and judges and in the rules relating to admissible witness testimony. If the norms with respect to prejudice, bias, and partiality were not always observed, they were constantly reiterated, and a variety of procedures existed to assist in achieving them. The English legal system attempted to create institutional settings and procedural mechanisms that would facilitate truthful judgments about past human events and actions. The legitimacy of the legal enterprise was built on the foundation of impartiality.

An Epistemological Conclusion

Now that we have examined the meaning of "fact" and the elements of fact determination in a legal setting and reviewed the various participants in that process, we turn to the epistemological aspects of legal fact finding. In doing so we consider the courtroom,[113] as others have considered the scientific experiment, as a site of knowledge making, that is, a setting where a variety of participants engage in creating or determining the "truth" of something by a set of site-specific rules. In the courts juries, judges, witnesses, and counsel participated in a process that was designed to produce "morally certain" verdicts in "matters of fact." By following certain procedures, using written documents of specified types, listening to witness testimony produced by certain kinds of persons and under certain conditions, and considering "circumstances," "judges of the fact" were able to produce just and true knowledge of "matters of fact." This practice was shaped in a number of ways by the norm of impartiality.

Courts were sites of epistemological inquiry, but they were also part of a larger political, administrative, and legal system and thus were sometimes sites of ideological conflict. Courts had a moral as well as an empirical function so that juries sometimes reached judgments clearly against the evidence in order to achieve what they felt to be a just result. The jury's primary function, however, was to make what society believed to be epistemologically sound findings about events or "facts" under conditions that were recognized to be imperfect. The security of life and property, deeply held cultural values, depended on these outcomes.

The common law made several epistemological assumptions that were not spelled out in great detail or in philosophical form and intermingled old and new learning. These were perhaps best summarized by Sir Geoffrey Gilbert, who emphasized that although firsthand sense data was the best source of knowledge, it was of limited usefulness to courts because the law dealt with "transient things" of no "constant being" that had to be retrieved by memory. When we "cannot see or hear any thing ourselves, and yet are obliged to make a judgment of it," it is necessary to "see and hear by report from others." It is reasonable to give "faith and credibility . . . to the honesty and integrity of credible and uninterested witnesses, attesting any fact under the solemnities and obligations of religion, and the dangers and penalties of perjury." When such conditions are met, the mind "equally acquiesces as on a knowledge by demonstration, for it cannot have any more reason to be doubted than if we ourselves had heard and seen it."[114]

Although Gilbert's formulation is more sophisticated than those of his predecessors, their assumptions and conclusions were roughly the same. They assumed that it was possible to arrive at sound judgments about facts, that is, events and deeds, though those events involved actions that could not be observed or replicated by those doing the fact finding. Sound judgments could be arrived at by examining the testimony of those who had seen or heard the events. In order to make such judgments it was necessary to examine the quality and quantity of testimony, to be suspicious of hearsay, and to consider any relevant "circumstances." Oaths were assumed to enhance the probability of testimonial truth but not to ensure it. It was also assumed that institutional arrangements and procedures, such as the right to challenge jurors or to exclude witnesses with financial interests, would help ensure just and truthful fact determination. Whatever their origins and evolution, such rules were perceived as ensuring accurate judgments of fact.

Some matters of fact might be considered "proved" and others doubtful or false. "Fact" in this context did not necessarily refer to an established truth but often to an issue of truth. Indeed, one of the great changes that occurred over the course of two centuries in some cultural arenas was the transformation of "fact" from something that had to be sufficiently proved by appropriate evidence to be considered worthy of belief to something for which appropriate verification had already taken place.

Litigation is not compatible with a skepticism so extreme that nothing can be known and no decision be worthy of acceptance. English law of the early modern era existed in an epistemological space of probability, reasonable doubt, and moral certainty in which decision making could not be delayed indefinitely on the grounds of insufficiently certain knowledge.

The fact-determination process of the common law was not quite one of "free proof." It was, however, far freer than that of the Romano-canon system with its rigid rules about numbers of witnesses. Juries were barred from exposure to some evidence by rules that excluded certain categories of persons from presenting evidence. Early modern juries were not yet prevented from hearing hearsay, though the tendency was in that direction. Until the early eighteenth century some testimony was given under oath and some was not.

During the sixteenth and seventeenth centuries there flourished a legal culture of fact built on the concept "matter of fact." The legal system was pervaded by the belief that ephemeral "facts" of human action could be established with a high degree of certitude and that ordinary persons had sufficient ability to evaluate testimony for credibility and documents for authenticity in order to arrive at impartial, truthful verdicts guided by their intelligence, reason, and conscience. Confidence in the jury system thus contributed to the general feeling that ordinary persons, if financially independent and if situated in institutional settings with the appropriate safeguards, were capable of determining matters of fact. Whatever the defects of the jury trial, the English preferred the common law fact-determination process to other varieties in other venues. That setting required empaneling impartial, disinterested fact evaluators and impartial, disinterested judges who operated in public rather than closed settings. Although actual judges and juries did not always meet these standards, the jury system was praised as the best means of finding the truth.

The legal concept "fact" and the epistemological assumptions and procedures associated with jury fact determination became well known to large numbers of Englishmen, not only to legal professionals but also to those who served on juries, potential jurors, frequenters of trials, justices of the peace, and grand jurors. The spate of published criminal trials, especially state trials, dating from the 1670s onward also made the evidentiary elements of the common law criminal trial familiar to a large number of general readers and the politically interested. A large proportion of the upper and "middling" classes, both urban and rural, had encountered the concept of fact and the common law approach to establishing "matters of fact." In this period references to legal fact finding were liberally scattered through the literatures of other disciplines.

Studying the process of knowledge making in the legal arena is obviously difficult, not only because of the lack of material but because the process involved institutions that were embedded in a larger political arena and were evolving over time. Despite the difficulties, it is important for cultural historians in general, and historians of science and philosophy in particular, to become more aware of a legal culture that established a widely admired mode of establishing correct beliefs in the world of "fact." During the early modern era the English legal system had produced a well-accepted epistemological framework and a method of implementing it that worked reasonably well in reaching judgments of "fact" necessary to making important social decisions. Much of this epistemology and method could be and was transferred to other sites of knowledge and other knowledge-making situations.

The remainder of this book is concerned with showing how legal concepts and practices related to fact finding were first extended into other disciplines that dealt with human actions and then to the "facts" of natural and divine phenomena. By the end of the seventeenth century the epistemological thinking characteristic of legal fact finding came to pervade English thought and culture. Legal modes of establishing appropriate belief played a larger role in the development of truth-establishing practices than has hitherto been recognized.

Not all aspects of the legal tradition would become relevant to other areas of learning. None of the other fields we survey made use of oaths or used adversarial institutional forms that required witnesses, juries, lawyers, and judges. And none was under the kind of pressure to reach immediate decisions on the facts that juries were. But to the extent that their concerns were with verifying events or actions, human, natural, or divine, they came to use many of the concepts embedded in the English legal system that we have been examining.

CHAPTER   TWO

"Fact" and History

The notion of "historical fact," a true statement about the past worthy of belief, is itself a historical development. The development is not, however, clear or straightforward, and tracking it requires us to look carefully at numerous aspects of the practice of historians and their associates.

As we have already noted, "fact" or "matter of fact" was used to mean an act or deed performed by a human agent. "Factum" was, of course, Latin and referred to deeds, feats, and events. The plays of Shakespeare and Ben Jonson used "fact" in referring to a variety of deeds,[1] and "in fact" and "in deed" appeared to have been used synonymously. Civil histories were accounts of the words and deeds ("de dictis et factis") of great men, and legal authorities similarly distinguished between "dictum" and "factum." In early usage facts and deeds might be either fictitious or real, "feat" was commonly used as a synonym for deed, and the words "history," "narrative," and "story" were often interchangeable. This conflation of meanings would diminish during the early modern period.

The Classical and Christian Heritages

The classical tradition of history writing was revived and imitated during the Renaissance.[2] One element of that revived tradition was the Aristotelian distinction between history and poetry, and thus between the real and the fictional, reemphasized in the writings of Sidney, Bacon, Davenant, and Hobbes.[3] Another element, however, was the classical concept of "historia," referring to particular happenings, events, and stories, which only sometimes distinguished real happenings from fictional ones. Classical historiography emphasized writing about what one had witnessed oneself, a concentration that tended to produce accounts of one's own lifetime and experience rather than of a more distant past. There was little concern with documentary evidence. Classical history focused primarily on politics, the state, and war. The best-qualified historian was the experienced statesman or military man who had been in a position to observe events. In addition to a firsthand, well-written account, the historian was to provide explanations and causal analysis of the events he narrated. Historiography was allied with rhetoric, and historians often provided praise or blame of their subjects' behavior. Rhetorically oriented historians invented speeches and events and transposed events in order to provide greater verisimilitude and more effectively instill appropriate lessons.

Cicero, Polybius, Lucian, and Tacitus were frequently cited. Cicero emphasized that history should be the witness of the past, the light shed on truth, the life-giving force to memory, and the guide to life, free of partiality and malice: "For who does not know history's first law to be that an author must not dare to tell anything but the truth? And its second that he must make bold to tell the whole truth?"[4] Yet Cicero, the orator par excellence, thought it permissible to manipulate historical material in order to make a point more convincingly.[5] Polybius and Lucian, often cited during the later part of the sixteenth century, underscored the truth-telling functions of the historian and the requirement of impartiality. The former opposed the eloquent style favored by Cicero, the latter distinguished between the rhetorician and the historian.[6] The adage "History is philosophy teaching by example" was often voiced by early modern historians. Historians were expected to provide examples of appropriate and inappropriate and moral and immoral behavior. Roman emphasis on the usefulness of history in moral and political education, or what has been called the "exemplar theory of history," predominated.[7]

Early modern historians were also heir to a Christian tradition that emphasized the role of God's Providence in shaping human affairs. They were concerned with the historical nature of the early church and committed to the truth of the central scriptural events. The early modern English historian was also the possessor of the lives of medieval saints, medieval chronicles and annals, and the fables and myths relating to ancient British history.

Historiography and the Legal Tradition

The traditions of legal "fact" determination would also play a role in the making of early modern "historical facts." The alliance between law and history appears to have developed first in France when historically oriented lawyers began to study the French constitutional past, to collect and critically evaluate documentary evidence, and to purge history of legend and fable. These lawyer-historians employed legal categories—for example, the distinction between eyewitness accounts (*testes*) and written authorities (*testimonia*)—preferred eyewitness accounts to hearsay, emphasized the importance of original documents over copies, and detected historical forgeries by the same means as lawyers did more recent ones.[8] The historian Pasquier treated documentary sources as "demonstrations oculaires," to be included with historical narratives so that readers could touch them personally "with their fingers."[9] Unimportant in Roman historiography, documentary sources were becoming significant as historical as well as legal evidence. Comparing the historian to a judge, Bodin noted the importance of sifting sources, diligent investigation, and eliminating interest and bias. "If the account is not true, it ought not even be called history."[10] French historians typically distinguished civil from natural history, that is, the world of man's making, *factum*, from that of God's making, *verum*. As we shall see shortly, that verbal distinction became blurred in England and eventually disappeared.

The intermingling of law and history was soon found in England as well. English historians also preferred politically experienced and firsthand witnesses, began to employ documentary evidence, and referred to historians as impartial witnesses and judges. Writing about history in the late sixteenth century, Thomas Blundeville used language redolent of law and "fact." History "bee made of deedes" by individuals or "public weals." "Every deede is done by some person, for some cause, in tyme, and place, with meanes and instruments." The historian should examine the historical actors' "power, skill, and industry. For these three things doe bring to effect the possibilitie, occasion, and successe, of the deed: For the power & ability of the doer, causeth the thing which is possible, to be done in deed. Against his skill, causeth him to take occasion when it is offered, and to use the meetest means to bring it to passe. Finally, hys industrie & earnest following of the matter, bringeth the successe of the deed to perfection."[11] Blundeville's language echoed that of contemporary justicing manuals dealing with the examination of witnesses accused of a crime. The language of witnessing was commonplace among historians, and most reiterated the importance of firsthand reports of knowledgeable witnesses. Many indicated their suspicion of hearsay as well as an awareness of the distinctions between rumor, fame, and truth.

Long part of the lawyer's domain, documents increasingly became a part of the historian's. In some kinds of historical investigation documentary analysis and interpretation would become more important than firsthand witnessing. Lawyers and historians examined charters, deeds, and legislation, acquiring the philological learning necessary to authenticate, date, and interpret these "testimonies" often in order to determine current rights and settle current disputes. Sir William Dugdale's *Monastican* was even admitted as evidence in the Westminster courts.[12] The concept of the ancient constitution too was important to both legal and historical communities. Lawyers added important elements to historical thinking, especially ways of thinking about and evaluating oral and written testimony.

Many of the most admired historians of the early modern era, including Thomas More and Francis Bacon, were lawyers, as were three prominent historians of the English civil war: Thomas May, Bulstrode Whitelocke, and Clarendon. Many lawyers belonged to the Society of Antiquaries, whose members engaged in historical and legal studies and often referred to credible witnesses and well-attested facts at their meetings. A substantial number of lawyer-historians frequented Sir Robert Cotton's famous library, the center of Jacobean antiquarian activity.[13] John Selden, the most learned of the lawyer-historians, took his terminology of historical proofs from the law and described the process of dealing with sources as "a kind of trial."[14] Both lawyers and historians were concerned with levels of certainty of factual knowledge.[15]

Categories, Definitions, and Varieties of History

There were several ways of categorizing history, each with somewhat different implications for the use and meaning of "fact." The first kind of "history" was related to "historia," which was distinguished from philosophy and poetry by its concern with the particular. Hobbes wrote that seeing "a fact done" and remembering it "done" together produced the "Register of Knowledge of Fact . . . called History."[16] For Hobbes and many others who adopted the tripartite classification of knowledge, there was no obvious way to bridge the gap between the particular facts of history and the universal principles of philosophy. "Facts" simply could not produce "philosophy."

"Perfect" and "imperfect" history were also distinguished. The most admired form throughout Europe from the Renaissance through the Enlightenment, "perfect history" consisted of extended narratives dealing with military matters and the affairs of state written by firsthand observers who were experienced men of public affairs. The perfect historian, however, did more than narrate "matters of fact." He also provided lessons and explanations and discussed the causes of the facts he narrated. For Bacon, "perfect history" focused on a period of time, a person worthy of mention, and an "action or exploit of the nobler sort."[17] Although perfect history was the model, few outside the classical exemplars—only Bacon and

Clarendon among the English—were thought to have achieved it. Historians therefore repeatedly expressed the view that the history of England had yet to be written. Bolingbroke expressed the conventional contempt for "naked facts without the causes that produced them" and the "want of imagination and judgment" that could render history the discipline "most proper to train us up to private and public virtue."[18]

Perfect history with its emphasis on firsthand witnesses was contemporary history, or what was often called "the history of one's own time." Document-oriented history dealing with long-past eras could not achieve the most exalted historiographical status. In the nature of things perfect history was as hard to produce as the epic poem. Some came to feel that the goals of perfect history and the "perfect historian" were as much a chimera as the "perfect Hero."[19] The classical model was wearing thin in both genres. Bacon labeled most of the history actually being produced "preparatives to history." Yet some historians and readers began to treat these "imperfect" memorials, diaries, reports, antiquities, and narrations as history itself.

"Memoirs" were often difficult to distinguish from "history." Both relied on firsthand observation and sometimes the testimony of other contemporaries. Gilbert Burnet thought the memoirist had the easier task. The historian must be well informed of all that passed on both sides and be able to open up secret causes and beginnings of great changes. Those who prepared "Memoires from a Collection of Papers," as Burnet himself did, had the more limited job of providing "a faithful account of such things as are in his Papers."[20] In some instances, however, the label "memoirs" might simply be the mark of modesty. Edmund Ludlow and Denzil Holles, both of whom entitled their works "memoirs" or "memorials," present evidence-based accounts of major events that go far beyond the personal and make claims to historical truth.[21] By the time Burnet wrote, "memoirs" too might include documentary support.

Most often, however, diaries or memorials were "accounted proper to furnish Materials" for the historian rather "than to pass for History themselves." The "particulars" of diaries kept "by persons of learning and curiosity . . . intimate with public affairs" would go "very far towards a Perfect History of those times."[22] The world should be "glad of collections and memorials" until "time can produce some Master Accomplish'd for so great a Performance." It was said of the memorialist Bulstrode Whitelocke that on some occasions he "writes up to the dignity of an historian" but on others only records "occurrences diarywise" without refining or improving them "to the perfection and true standard of an History."[23] Although there might be a loss of narrative line and an absence of how "things hang together" in the memoir form, what was read would be true and readers could make their own inferences from "simple matters of fact."[24] If not "perfect history," these memoirs provided the "Foundation for certainty in an Historian, as rarely any times have afforded."[25]

If memoirs were sometimes difficult to distinguish from history, they also merged imperceptibly with the autobiography, the diary, and the travel account. John Evelyn referred to his Diary as "Memoirs."[26] Robert Hooke planned a "History of my own Life" that would include "as many remarkable Passages, as I can remember of, collected out of such Memorialls as I have kept in Writing, or are in the Registers of the Royal Society, together with all my Inventions, Experiments . . . which I have made, the time when, the manner how, and means by which, with the success and effect of them, together with the State of my Health, my employments, and Studies, my good or bad Fortune, my Friends and Enemies."[27] His "history" would all "be the Truth of the Matter of Fact, so far as I can be inform'd by my Memorials or my own Memory, which Rule I resolve not to transgress."[28] "Annals" too were usually included among the imperfect genres. Yet Camden was greatly admired for his annals of the reign of Elizabeth modeled on the Tacitean annals, and Guicciardini, who like Camden employed the annalistic form, was sometimes included among the ranks of the perfect historians.

For Bacon and many others, "antiquities" was a species of imperfect history, which "like the spars of a shipwreck" might be used "to recover somewhat from the deluge of time."[29] Antiquarian investigations, like documentary scholarship, began to be called "history," though never "perfect history." Although memoirs, memorials, annals, and antiquities on the whole retained the Baconian sense of "preparatives," some productions so labeled were sliding into the category history itself.

The early modern understanding of "history" was thus unstable. Confusion might arise depending on whether the author was speaking of perfect history or something more like the much broader "historia." Much of what was recognized as the best contemporary historical work, for example that of Camden and Selden, was not "perfect history." All varieties, however, were contrasted with fiction and falsehood and highlighted truth telling, "fact," and impartiality. Although perfect history emphasized narrative skill, exemplarity, causal explanation, and utility, and the much broader "historia" did not, both increasingly used the legalistic language of witnesses, credibility, and "matters of fact."

A review of the writings of historians and about history reveals a number of major themes and tensions. There is increasing emphasis on history as truth. The word "fact," and cognates such as "feat," continue their resonance of deed or human doing, although many phenomena that are not facts in this sense come to be thought of as part of history. The classical emphasis on war, high policy, and great men continues. But lesser topics, including what we would now call social and economic history, and the lives of lesser men are pounding at the door.[30] Economic, architectural, and geographic data and "wonders" that are usually the province of topography, chorography, news, and annals sometimes appear in or at the edges of texts claiming to be histories. Documentary studies are too obviously a mode of discovering the truth of the past to be excluded from history.[31] A serious problematic of narrative continues. Annals that are exclusively year-by-year lists of events are not history, but annals with threads of narrative may be. History is about particular occurrences, but mere episodic accounts of some particulars are not quite history. Conversely, accounts of institutions and practices that persist over time rather than occurring as particular events may be history or included in histories.[32] Mere narrative accounts of facts without causal analysis are not history or not good history or not quite history. Antiquarian studies based on coins, medals, and monuments are or are not history.[33]

History, Truth, and Fiction

Whether the historian was engaged in the most elevated "perfect" history or any of its lesser forms, he had the duty of telling the truth. The historian's office was "to tell things as they were done without either augmenting or diminishing them, or swarving one iote from the truth," to write "nothing lesse than truth." Perfect history required "Truth, in sincerely relating, without having anything . . . foisted in by our owne invention, to smooth the passage of our story."[34] The lawyer-historian Selden insists, "I sought only Truth."[35] Historical "matter of fact" was sometimes contrasted with slander, libel, and lying. History and matter of fact also implied the rejection of fable, myth, and fiction. This emphasis on truth therefore tended to underline the differences between history and fiction.[36]

Yet at the beginning of our period or just before, history and what we might call fiction and contemporaries often called "poesy" were not clearly demarcated. Romances and Arthurian tales were often presented as if they were history. Mixtures of fact and fiction were also typical of humanist historiography such as Sir Thomas More's *Richard III*. In the late Elizabethan genre "poesie historical," a writer might "devise many historical matters of no veracity at all." Spenser, the model of the "poet historical," described the "antiquities of Faerie land." The historical drama of Shakespeare and others borrowed heavily from chronicles and histories that were considered to be accurate accounts but were not constrained by them. For Bacon, history might be real or "feigned." Sir Walter Raleigh wrote that historians borrowed "ornaments" and "somewhat of their substance" from poets.[37]

Yet the distinction between history and poetry was becoming sharper.

Himself a poet-historian, Samuel Daniel wrote that historians should not "introduce fiction of our own Imagination."[38] History and poetry were often said to derive from different sources, history from memory, poetry from the imagination. As history became separated from poesy it became more closely connected to discourses attempting to establish and narrate believable matters of fact. Fictional "facts" or "feats" would lose their status as "facts." The truth of poetry was thought to lie in its ability to capture universal moral truth and did not turn on epistemological questions of evidence, error, or partiality as the truth of history did. As more attention was placed on "matter of fact" and the evidence for matters of fact, imaginative forms were more clearly contrasted to history.

The first fictional element to be rejected was the invented speech. The practice of allowing the historian to put plausible but fictional words into the mouth of historical personages had a long history that derived from rhetorical techniques. Although the invented speech was still used by a few early-seventeenth-century historians, it was gradually excluded. Bacon still allowed himself to present the inner thoughts of historical actors, but that practice too became less acceptable. Increasingly, the words of historical actors had to be authentic. Thomas Blundeville in 1574 was already insisting that the historian must not "fayne any Orations nor any other thing, but truly to report every speach and deede, even as it was spoken, or done." Camden refused to report "Speeches and Orations, unless they be the very same verbatim, or else abbreviated." By the mid-seventeenth century when Margaret Cavendish promised there would be no "feigned Orations" in her biography of the duke of Newcastle, the promise was becoming conventional. Writing during the Restoration, Burnet indicates that invented speeches, once a common practice, were now "Universally distasteful." White Kennett contrasted his "Historical Register and Chronicle" to "feigned Orations, Poems, Apologies, personated Plays, . . . Romances, Novels, and every idle work."[39]

Historians also moved to eradicate fable and legend. The origins of the British and particularly the legend of the Trojan Brutus came under critical scrutiny. Camden would reject "fictions and fables" for "sincere and uncorrupted Monuments of Antiquity," and Selden "poetic fictions," "mythic reports," and "bardish hymns," noting that the British legends were no more historical than the stories of Ariosto, Rabelais, or Spenser.[40] Bacon wished historical learning to "supersede the fabulous accounts of the origins of nations." In the absence of firsthand reports of national origins, he recognized that historians must work with "things" of antiquity or fragmentary records.[41]

Similar concerns extended into the Restoration and eighteenth century. Brutus was thus a "meer Poetical Fiction," and historians must attempt to "observe the obscurity and fabulousness of Things." Fables, for

William Temple, were "idle Trash and Worth less Stuff." To Kennett pre-Conquest history looked "like Scenes of Fairyland." For Defoe, the lives of famous men often remained "drowned in Fable," so much so that that "Matters of Fact" were "handed down to Posterity with so little Certainty, that nothing is to be depended upon."[42] Over time the Trojan Brutus was excised and Lear, Cymbeline, and King Arthur routed from history.

The "matters of fact" of history were most often contrasted with "romance." For John Nalson, "History without Truth, or with a Mixture of Falsehood, degenerates into Romance." Robert Brady condemned those who perversely "Disguise Matter of Fact, and make History Romantic." Women and children might "dote upon Romances, and silly Legends, or listen with attentive admiration to the wars of the Pigmies, and Adventures of the Faiery Land. But men of sense expect solid Transactions, and such substantial Examples as may be advantage to improve their judgment in Civil Wisdom, and the necessary conduct of life." Thomas Sprat claimed that "the way of Romance is to be exploded" in both natural and civil history.[43] Eighteenth-century commentators continued to distinguish history from romance and denigrate the latter.

Historians emphasized their commitment to the truth of matter of fact over all fiction, whether "fabulous," "romantic," or "verisimilar." They also contrasted historical "matter of fact" with lies and deceit. John Rushworth emphasized his commitment to "Truth," noting that his collection of documents countered those who "busie . . . their Hands, forging Relations, building and bartering Castles in the Air, publishing Speeches as spoken in Parliament which were never spoken there; Printing Declarations which were never passed, relating Battles which were never fought." His collections enabled future historians to "separate Truth from Falsehood, things real from things fictitious or imaginary."[44]

"Fact" and History

Historians of the early modern era often referred to "facts." John Selden used the term "historical fact" and referred to history as that "which is only fact," describing his *Historie of Tithes* as a collection of "such things of fact" as had been previously dispersed in a wide range of records. John Rushworth and William Howel respectively characterized history as "bare Narration of matter of Fact" and "plain matters of fact." Others wrote that the faithful historian reports "nothing but fact" or promises a "true Accompt" of "Matter of Fact." After explaining his approach to history, Clarendon wrote, "And so we proceed to our matter of fact."[45]

Yet many thought history required something more than an account of fact. For Locke, history without chronology and geography produced "only a jumble of Matters of Fact, confusedly heaped together." Burnet criticized the chronicle, a medieval form, as "a String of meere Facts" lacking the "Account of the Springs and Motives" necessary for "History." Hume came to see history as a "collection of facts, . . . multiplying without end." For some, history combined well-established facts with orderly narration and explanation. They proposed first "to enter into a most serious examination of the matter of Fact itself" and then, "by tracing out the footsteps of Truth, see what a conclusion may be drawn out of it."[46]

Historical facts, like legal facts, required evidence if they were to be believable, and it was becoming the obligation of the historian to provide the evidence that would support belief. Authors spoke of "Evident and Visible Fact" or referred to evidence of "Matter of Fact" derived from their personal observations and the testimony of others. In representing the "plain Matter of Fact" of the Rye House Plot, Thomas Sprat insisted that the evidence for matters of fact must be presented in the "clearest Light and most Evident Proof." To avoid the reader's dependence on the "integrity and Faith of the Author, for the truth of things Related," Robert Brady cited documentary sources that were "matter of Fact laid down, and warranted, by such as lived in the very times when the Thing was done . . . or by sufficient Record." "Solid proofs" were necessary for "matter of fact." Occasionally, as in law, there is reference to "notorious facts," facts so well known to all that they required no additional proof.[47]

The language of the historian often echoed that of the law. Many early modern historians characterized themselves as witnesses who provided eyewitness testimony. They were often apologetic if they were not themselves eye or ear witnesses, had to rely on the reports of others, or offered as evidence the testimony of other historians. Reliance on the reports of other witnesses was sometimes but not always treated favorably. Defoe, for example, explained, the "Facts which he himself was not an Eye-witness of, he had taken from the authentick Relations of the Persons concerned in taking the Pyrates, as well as from the Mouths of the Pyrates themselves," and "living witnesses" could testify as to the truth of his account.[48]

Specifically legal language was sometimes invoked. Thomas Gumble, for example, suggested that the historian was on "Oath, (according to our English form)" to tell "the whole truth, and nothing but the truth," and to "assert the verity of all matters of Fact." For Thomas Fuller, "if the Witnesses be suborned, the Record falsified, or the Evidence wrested, neither posterity can Judge rightly of the Actions of the present time; or this time, give a certain Judgment of the Ages past."[49]

The language of "judgment" was a commonplace of the historical discourses, though it had multiple meanings. One resonated to the duty of juries, that is, to reach conclusions about the truthfulness of witnesses and belief in particular alleged matters of fact. Aubrey, for example, presented his archaeological findings as "evidence to a Jury." Yet the Society of Antiquaries, like the later Royal Society, was unwilling to reach "judyciall or fy-nall conclusion[s]" on its members' work. No courtlike body that collectively passed judgment emerged for the historical community, although Thomas Sprat made the interesting suggestion that the history of the English civil war be undertaken by one or two men and that an assembly, presumably along the lines of the Royal Society, "revise and correct it." Historical matters, according to Edward Stillingfleet, were "not to be decided in the Field, nor at the Bar, nor by a majority of voices, but depend upon the comparing of ancient Histories, the credibility of Testimonies, and the sagacity in search, and skill concerning them." Historical "judgment" thus required a "general skill in Antiquity and the best Authors," the ability to make suitable comparisons, and impartiality. References to the "judicious historian" were common. Historians required "exact Penetration and Severity of Judgment."[50] There were also many suggestions that judgments should be left "to the liberty and faculty of every man's judgment," that is, to the reader.[51]

Historians thus incorporated much of the legal language of "fact" and the witnessing and judgment that were a fundamental part of that language, although "judgment" sometimes implied something broader than determination of matters of fact and historical judgment might be less rigorous than legal.

"Dubious," "Uncertain," and "False" Facts

In instances where the evidence presented by the historian was thought to be insufficient or inadequate, the historical matter of fact in question might be doubted or even considered untrue. This raised the possibility of the "dubious," "uncertain," or even the "false fact,"[52] linguistic usage unfamiliar to the modern ear. Most historians suggested that they wrote only of true facts and that the duty of the historian was to "Learn out the Truth of the Fact."[53] The historian must know the "Verity of the Facts he recounts."[54]

In some instances, as in law, historians were unable, or were thought to have been unable, to provide adequate evidence. This meant that some "matters of fact" did not and could not command belief or assent. We thus find historians, like lawyers, referring to "real or supposed fact"[55] or suggesting how an account "differ[ed] from the truth of Fact."[56] Some referred to "undeniable Matter of Fact" and intimated that poor historians "deny or smother Matter of Fact." Some facts were mistaken and others misrepresented.[57] Brady suggested that "the Matter of Fact was not such as [Petyt] pretends and avers it to have been." Burnet mentioned "palpable Errors in Matters of Fact" and claimed that "scarce anybody" was "satisfied . . . with the Truth of Matters of Fact" relating to the civil war.[58]

Some historical facts, for Bolingbroke, were false, grossly improbable, or no longer tenable. Historians must establish "historical facts . . . on clear and unquestionable historical authority" and "reject candidly what cannot be thus established."[59]

Some facts, then, might be uncertain, dubious, improbable, or fictional, while others were "put beyond all doubt." One historian suggested that the matters of fact in question "seem'd not to be capable of clearer proof" and, in an echo of the legal maxim, of proof as clear "as the Sun is visible at noon, in a clear day."[60]

Historians sometimes were, and sometimes were not, "furnish'd with all the necessary Assurances to know the truth of the Fact." Some facts therefore could be labeled "indisputable Matters of Fact," and these "True Matters of Fact" contrasted with lies.[61] Roger North spoke of both deniable and "undeniable matters of fact": "For Facts may be contradicted, mistaken, or new Discoveries superinduced." Some failed in giving "precipitate Credit to Facts." "Facts" could be untrue.[62]

By the eighteenth century Bolingbroke defined "an historical fact, to be something which contains nothing that contradicts general experience, and our own observation, has already the appearance of probability; and if it be supported by the testimony of proper witnesses, it acquires all the appearances of truth, that is, it becomes really probable in the highest degree. . . . The degree of assent, which we give to history, may be settled, in proportion to the number, characters, and circumstances of the original witnesses."[63] Langlet de Fresnoy advised that "possibility" is "not sufficient reason to induce to believe that such a Fact is true." One must examine the "Internal" and "External" circumstances "attending any Fact to judge whether it be true or false." Employing a terminology of "spurious" or "improbable facts," he discussed the circumstances to be considered in deciding whether we should believe or not believe a fact and the conditions under which one should suspend judgment.[64]

For the historian, then, not all "facts" were believable. "False fact" was not an oxymoron for seventeenth- and early-eighteenth-century readers. Modern linguistic usage that equates "fact" with "truth" or "reality" had not yet become common, although the contrast between "fact" and "fiction" and the insistence on compelling evidence was leading in that direction.

Epistemological Assumptions

Historians, like lawyers, assumed it was possible to know something about events that had taken place in the past. The nature and logic of "historical faith," as it was called, seems to have been examined only in the sixteenth century as a response to the revival of skepticism. If not as susceptible to skepticism's corrosive effects as the French, some English thinkers adopted elements of the skeptical critique.[65] Bacon's "Idols" would emphasize the distortions and errors of custom and education as well as the fallibility of reason and the senses. Selden advised historians to avoid the "disputing Levitie" of the skeptics but to adopt their critical "Libertie of Inquiries."[66] Historians must negotiate the difficult path between skepticism and dogmatism on the one hand and between skepticism and credulity on the other.

History and law both were disciplines committed to determining the truth of past events. Both incorporated an epistemology characterized by faith in the ability of persons to arrive at a reasonable degree of certainty about past events combined with an awareness of human fallibility, that is, with recognition that the senses and memory fail or err and that distortions due to interest, bias, education, and partiality were ever present dangers. Believable statements in the field of history as in law were recognized to be different from the truths of logic and were by their very nature incapable of achieving mathematical certainty or metaphysical truth. Historians were convinced that it was possible to make statements about past events that were worthy of "belief." These events were characterized as "matters of fact" or true matters of fact when supported by appropriate evidence.

"Historical faith" was spelled out in some detail by Seth Ward in the middle of the seventeenth century. First he explained that the criteria of mathematical certainty and demonstration were inappropriate for matters of fact. Nor could one be expected to believe anything involving a "clear and evident contradiction to some natural principle." If, however, the history or relation was determined to be "within the bounds of evidence and certainty," one could safely move on to consider whether the author "had sufficient means of knowledge," whether he was "an eye or ear witness," and whether the things he reported were "publickly acted and known." One then considered "the qualities of the relators," their "Understanding" and "Will," and their "Sufficiency" and "Integrity," as well as possible bias or interest. The "faithful historian" is cast by Ward as an impartial witness who should be believed. Using this model, Ward argued that one could believe in a variety of events, places, and matters of fact one had not personally observed. The model provided for rational belief in the unbiased, firsthand, uncontradicted accounts of historians such as Julius Caesar's account of the war against the Gauls.[67] Thomas Hobbes, who rarely agreed with Ward, agreed on this point, accepting "belief" in facts that in many instances were "no less free from doubt, than perfect and manifest knowledge . . . there being many things which we receive from report of others, of which it is impossible to imagine any cause of doubt."[68] Historian Thomas Gale too indicated that his readers could arrive at "some moral certaintie or strong probabilities, touching the verities" of his assertions of fact. In history as in law, moral certainty was the highest certainty available for matters of fact.[69]

Historical Facts and Historical Evidence

Matters of historical fact, then, might be believable and accepted as truth, but they, like legal facts, required evidence. There were three kinds of historical evidence: firsthand observation, documentary evidence, and the evidence of "things."

Firsthand Observation and Witnessing

Firsthand observation was considered the most important type of evidence. Most historians not only emphasized firsthand witnessing in establishing historical "matters of fact" but, following classical historiography, continued to insist that the best history was written by participant observers, that is, "the history of one's own time." Time and time again we encounter historians claiming to write on the basis of firsthand knowledge or, if this was unavailable, on the basis of consultation with credible witnesses of the "facts." "Ministers and great officers . . . who have handled the helm of government and been acquainted with the difficulties and mysteries of state business" were best suited to become historians.[70] James Howell justified his historical effort by emphasizing that he had been a "Spectator" of some of the king's exploits, had received testimony from the cardinal, and had gathered his various pieces of evidence not "at the Porter's lodge, but above stairs, . . . from the Counsell Table, and Courts of Parliament." William Sanderson was described as especially capable of "penning the story" of Charles I because he was bred in the court, an "Eye and Ear Witnesse of most of those Transactions and Traverses of State" and an actor in them.[71]

A few, however, voiced the view that "ocular observation" was "not absolutely necessary." Insistence on firsthand observation would "extinguish the light of all Histories." Credible testimony could be derived from others as well as from "Matters of Record."[72] On the whole, however, it was felt to be "an unspeakable disadvantage" for the historian not to have been "a witness of the matters of fact, and know them but by papers and reports."[73] Justifying his historical qualifications, John Rushworth emphasized that he had "been on the Stage continually, and an Eye and Ear-witness of the greatest Transactions; imployed as an Agent in, and intrusted with Affairs of weightiest Concernment; Privy also to the Debates in Parliament, and to the most secret Results of Councils of War, in times of Action."[74] When Rushworth wrote of transactions he had not himself seen or heard, he would consult "Records" or confer "with Persons of un-questionable esteem."[75]

Restoration historians for the most part reiterated the need for first-hand observers with political and military experience. For Clarendon, contemporary history composed by firsthand observers was best. True history required not just the collection of records and documents but knowledge derived from "conversations and familiarity in the insides of courts and the most active and eminent persons in their government." "I knew most of the things myself which I mention, and therefore can answer for the truth of them; and other most important particulars, which were transacted in places very distant from me, were transmitted to me, by the king's immediate direction and order, . . . out of his own memorials and journals."[76] Burnet, though an avid user of documentary materials in his histories, similarly emphasized his "intimacy with all those who have had the chief conduct of affairs," which enabled him "to penetrate far into the true secrets of Counsels and designs."[77]

We hear little about the social status of the historian, a good deal about competence and experience, and a great deal about honesty, integrity, and fidelity. The emphasis on political and military experience meant that history writing, like poetry and natural philosophy, was assumed to be a male preserve.[78]

If preference for eyewitness testimony continued to be expressed long after the emergence of document-based history, we increasingly encounter historians combining firsthand observation with documentary evidence. Writing of the civil war some twenty years after the events, William Dugdale was not unusual in relying on his own experience and observations, credible authors, and the mercuries and other public licensed narratives.[79] Not a few found themselves in the position of Edmund Ludlow, who would "not strictly confine myself to a relation of such things in which I was personally concerned but also give the best account I can of such other memorable occurrences of those times as I have learned from persons well informed and of unsuspected fidelity."[80] Both Dugdale and Ludlow, however, were still writing a kind of contemporary history. Nevertheless, there was occasional reference to the disadvantages of writing the "history of one's own time," most of which revolved around the potential for partisanship and the limitations inherent in participant observation.[81]

The priority given firsthand observation blurred the line between history and the emerging forms of journalism. John Wilkins thus associated "matter of fact" with venues that included "diurnal," gazette, and chronicle as well as history. Roger L'Estrange, both historian and newsman, insisted that the "papers" on the Popish Plot printed in his weekly *Observator* were "the True History" and would provide "the Clearest Evidence [that] . . . the Matter of Fact is Evident, and Certain."[82]

Documents, History, and Matters of Fact

Cultural preferences for firsthand reporting and contemporary history reinforced by ancient models and legal practice, newer genres of "news" and travel reporting, and the developing empirical study of nature made it somewhat awkward to incorporate historical records into something labeled "history" and into "fact." Although documentary proof was familiar to courts, it was not immediately clear whether documents should be treated as evidence for historical "matters of fact" or were in some sense "facts" themselves. Emphasis on the historical participant-observer underlined the distinction between the more philological and document-based productions of antiquarians and first-person "history." For periods lacking eyewitness accounts, however, there was no alternative to seeking other varieties of evidence. Civil and ecclesiastical historians turned to public records and documents as "clear and undubitable Instances" that would help them place their "ancient constitutions" on a "firm and solid foundation."[83] "True Philologie," aided by "Curious Diligence and Watchfull Industrie," would reveal "many hidden Truths" in manuscripts and public records.[84]

Charters, public records, treaties, ancient authors, legislation, newsbooks, and pamphlets were preserved and collected by governments and such antiquaries or pamphlet collectors as Sir Robert Cotton and George Thomason. Elizabeth was petitioned to establish a national library for the "study of antiquities and history" to preserve "the matter of history of this realm, original charters and monuments."[85] The Society of Antiquaries put a great deal of emphasis on documents, and even nondocumentary historians emphasized the importance of "transcriptions" of "Laws, Orders, and Precepts . . . to personate the acts of men upon the Theater of this world."[86] Foxe produced his memorializing *Acts and Monuments* (1563).[87] Camden's *Annals* of the reign of Queen Elizabeth was undertaken at the suggestion of Lord Burghley and based on state records and correspondence. Although Camden also relied on his own observations and the reports of "credible persons which have been present at the handling of matters," he described himself as sitting among "great Piles and Heaps of Papers and Writings of all sorts."[88] His *Britannia*, a reconstruction of ancient Roman and Anglo-Saxon history and topography, used "the public records of the kingdom, ecclesiastical registers and libraries, and the acts, monuments and memorials of church and cities." He built on these "as infallible testimonies, and . . . [so] by such unquestioned evidences justice might be done to truth."[89]

Selden also treated documents as firsthand testimony, promising, "I vent to you nothing quoted at second hand, but ever loved the fountain, and, when I could come to it, used that medium only which could not at all, or least, deceive by refraction." The testimonies "were chosen by weight, not by number, . . . [and] never at second hand." For the Elizabethan lawyer-historian William Lambarde documentary evidence was preferable to firsthand accounts: "What need I to hang too long upon the credit of Historians, seeing from this time downward the Authenticke Records of the Parliaments themselves doe offer me present help." Dugdale proudly employed "publique Records, besides a multitude of Manuscripts, original Charters and Evidences."[90]

By 1625 the historical manuscripts and records relating to the period from the Conquest to the reign of Henry VIII were largely recovered and fairly available. Properly authenticated and well-ordered documents were "testimony" and "fountains" of past law, practice, and circumstances as well as anchors for political and ecclesiastical argument. Contemporary records were collected "whilst things were fresh in memory," making it possible to distinguish "Truth from Falsehood, things real from things fictional and or imaginary" and for "After-ages to ground a true History."[91] One collector described himself, as did some natural historians, as an "underworkman." Another suggested that Parliament record "the Matters of Fact of all affairs and occurrences" making them public only when all concerned were "gone off the Stage."[92]

Burnet marks the break from the classical view when he asserts that there are two groups of historians "best qualified for giving the world a true information of affairs," the traditional participant-historians and those with authentic documents at their disposal.[93] On the advice of Sir Robert Moray, he included documents of "Authentic Vouchers" in his *Memoires of . . . James and William, Dukes of Hamilton*, and an appendix of documents in his *History of the Reformation*. Records would provide the "full Evidence of the truth of the History."[94] Documentary evidence was thus becoming a kind of firsthand evidence. Burnet's practice of including documentary appendices or long extracts became quite common even for those writing the history of their own times.[95] Few document collectors thought of themselves as full-fledged historians. John Nalson refused to tie himself "strictly to the rules of a bare collector" but "indulged . . . in the liberty of an Historian, to tie up the loose and scattered Papers with the Circumstances, Causes, and Consequences of them," thus giving "Light . . . to the Matters of Fact." Even Clarendon inserted documents into his narrative.[96] The theoretical distinction between the antiquarian with his documentary orientation and the perfect historian writing contemporary history was in practice being eroded.

This erosion increased during the eighteenth century. For example, Thomas Madox insisted that Exchequer documents were "the foundation which sustain the whole Fabrick of this History." "Real History," for Defoe, meant "the Matters of Fact" were "upon Record." White Kennett, like

Selden before him, used the term "fact" in connection with documentary evidence: "Facts are stubborn Things." Historians were "stewards and Keepers of Account" who must present "the original Instruments and authentick Evidence" as "Vouchers for what they set down, if they would be found faithful."[97] John Oldmixon emphasized the growing expectation of documentary support except "when the Facts have not been of much consequence, or were so well known, that they attested themselves," and he contrasted the situation of the modern historian with that of the ancients, who had no need to provide support for their presentation of "facts." Critics' evaluations of historians often turned on their use of documentary evidence.[98]

Antiquities, History, and Fact

Thus historical studies were influenced by the antiquarian movement, which is seen sometimes as a part of history or as preparative to it and sometimes as an independent intellectual enterprise. Antiquarian production typically was not "history" and did not take narrative form. Examining and interpreting material objects such as coins or ruins, it usually did not concern itself with the kinds of deeds and events traditionally designated "facts." Antiquarian, however, was a term that covered both those dealing with documents and those studying material objects, such as medals and coins. It was nurtured by Renaissance philological studies, Reformation concerns with the nature of the early church, historical interest in the English past, and growing interest in chorography, topography, and geology. It was further stimulated by the English civil war, which produced a pervading sense of irreplaceable loss caused by iconoclasm and other destruction.[99]

Arnaldo Momigliano has suggested that history and antiquarian research were not integrated until the nineteenth century,[100] but antiquarian scholarship was increasingly seen as an important part of historical studies even though the antiquarian's written productions were not typically called "histories." New genres such as *The History and Antiquities of . . . X* suggest both kinship and the difference between them. In 1616 Richard Brathwaite admired the "laborious and judicious Antiquaries" and their benefit to historians.[101] A few decades later, discussing Britain's "most notable Antiquity," "Stone-heng," Inigo Jones commented that "history" dealt with more than great actions and extended to "the ruines of their Buildings; Demonstration, which obvious to sense, are even yet as so many eye-witnesses of their admir'd achievements."[102] While "things" or objects studied did not exactly yield "facts," like documentary remains they were increasingly analogized to the eyewitnesses required for establishing "matters of fact." "Things" were evidence. Aubrey wrote that "the Stones give

Evidence for themselves" and ancient barrows "would be evidence to a Jury." For White Kennett, inscriptions and other objects too gave "Testimony to Facts."[103]

We can see the growing overlap between history and antiquarianism in William Dugdale's work. His *Monasticon Anglicanum* bore the subtitle *The History of the Ancient Abbeys*.[104] His *History of Imbanking and Drayning of Diverse Fenns and Marshes* was based on "manuscripts, and other Authentick Testimonies,"[105] as was his *Origines Juridicales, or Historical Memorials of the English Laws, Courts of Justice*,[106] which contained "catalogues" of office-holders. Such histories were clearly far removed from "perfect history."[107] Historian White Kennett referred to himself as a "collector" of the "original and authentick" acts and records needed by historians. He registered the "chief Facts in Church and State" and recommended to others "honest Labours of the like kind." He praised the "public service" of those collecting and preserving England's antiquities, which allowed contemporaries to "understand the state of former Ages, [and] the Constitution of Governments,"[108] an understanding usually claimed by "historians," not antiquarian "collectors."

Because he dealt less with deeds and more with past practices and cultural conditions, the antiquarian-historian was somewhat less likely than the "perfect historian" to use the terminology of "fact," but usage was in the process of change. We have noted Selden's adoption of "historical facts" in connection with antiquarian materials. Kennett referred to his work on parish antiquities as "a faithful relation of matter of Fact."[109] Documentary historians and antiquarians were thus subtly expanding the "fact" from event or deed, that is, actions occurring at a particular moment in time, to cultural conditions, institutions, and practices that existed over lengthy periods and were not attributable to individual actors. To some extent, then, "historical facts" were losing their exclusive association with deeds and feats.

Those who examined artifacts and "things" sometimes wrote as if they thought such items produced good history. Aubrey, for example, wrote that the "vestiges of the Imperial Camps" allowed one to "trace-out the way of the victorious Roman Eagle took her Course," while Meric Casaubon thought visible antiquities could "represent . . . former times actually present, and in sight, as it were."[110] John Evelyn was convinced that coins and medals were "Vocal Monuments of Antiquity" that could transform historical knowledge. The "clear and perspicuous testimony" of medals were "pregnant of Matter of Fact. . . .We should need almost no other History" if we had a "perfect and uninterrupted Series of them."[111] The allusions to the eyewitness testimony so valued by lawyers and historians are noteworthy. For Joseph Addison, too, medals and coins supplied a "body of history" complementing and rivaling the authority of written texts. By the mid-eighteenth century Hans Sloane's collection of coins and medals could be characterized as one of the "lasting Monuments of historical facts."[112] Most historians dealt with "matter of fact," and those of an antiquarian bent were being drawn into the orbit of "fact" whether or not their studies were awarded the title "history."[113]

Explanation and Causal Analysis

There was disagreement within the early modern historical community as to whether historians should provide only a straightforward narrative of the facts or were obligated to consider the causes and explanations of the facts they narrated. Although the authors of "perfect history" were expected to explain as well as narrate, many historical practitioners were becoming reluctant to do so, preferring "bare narration" of "fact."

It was widely believed that history taught lessons and provided vicarious experience needed by those participating in government. Yet there was little discussion of the methods for drawing such lessons or agreement on their substance. In the sixteenth and seventeenth centuries such writers as Thomas Blundeville, Richard Brathwaite, and James Welwood argued for causal explanation in historical studies. In the early eighteenth century Lord Bolingbroke insisted that "naked facts, without the causes that produced them, and the circumstances that accompanied them, are not sufficient to characterize actions or counsels."[114]

Nevertheless, this view was not universally held. Thomas Hobbes was not alone in thinking that true causal explanation could never be derived from "fact." "Knowledge of fact, . . . a thing past and irrevocable," might result in prudence but not in a science that was the knowledge of consequences of "one fact upon another."[115] Most historians, however, did not seek the kind of causal analysis that could be labeled "science" but rather attempted something closer to what Hobbes called "prudence," sometimes along the lines of Machiavelli's maxims, which were said to be principles "illustrated, and conformed by Matter of Fact." Yet there was also criticism of Machiavelli's practice of "building Aphorism upon contingent Actions" and his drawing of "Rules of Policie from very uncertain premises."[116] Occasionally, historians used the language of cause and effect, presenting "facts" in the sense of events, as if they were the "effects" of some cause.[117]

The most common explanation for why events occurred remained providential. There were those who saw the hand of God in all human affairs, although distinctions between first and second causes were often drawn. Raleigh wrote, "There is not . . . the smallest accident . . . but that . . . is caused by God." "All second causes" were "but instruments, conduits, and pipes, which carry and disperse what they have received from the head and fountaine of the Universall." Puritan writers tended to emphasize providential explanations somewhat more than others. We find Oliver Cromwell complaining that historians too often provided only "narrations of matters of fact" and ignored the "strange windings and turnings of Providence and the Great appearances of God."[118]

Although providential explanations continued throughout the seventeenth century and beyond, they were sometimes rejected. Already in 1618 Edmund Bolton disparaged those who referred "all causes immediately to the Will of God" and neglected "to inform their readers in the ordinary means of carriage in human affairs."[119] Nonpolitical events such as comets and earthquakes, as well as political ones, might be discussed in terms of both God's displeasure and natural second causes. The view that God in most circumstances worked through second causes served historian and naturalist alike.

Most nonprovidential discussion of historical causation related to human motivation. Reference to the "springs" and "motions" of events was common. Blundeville and Bacon were not atypical in seeking explanations in the psychological makeup of the historical actors.[120] Clarendon insisted that the historian could not be satisfied with "bare relation of what was done" and must inquire into the "the causes of those effects." He looked to individual passions and characteristics, though he also thought the civil war was caused by "the same natural causes and means, which usually attended kingdoms swollen with long plenty." Other historians, however, disdained to "write in the usual form of the Historian, to pretend to have seen into the dark Closets of States-Men and Church-Men's Minds."[121]

Although the perfect history model required causal explanation, the ancient distinction between "historia" and "philosophy" made such explanation difficult. "Historia" dealt with particulars, philosophy with universal principles. It was never very clear whether the explanations and causes sought by the historian were expected be universal in character or whether they were to be peculiar to the particular circumstances and historical actors. If the first, how could the historian go from particulars to universals? Hobbes was not alone in thinking that principles could not be derived from "one fact upon another."[122] If the second, how would explanations derived from particular circumstances and individuals be applied to other circumstances and thus supply the desired lessons of history? Though charged with providing explanations and causal analysis, historians possessed no method for producing them. As a result, they either referred to Providence or particularized psychological and behavioral explanations—or ignored the problem and just narrated the "facts." It was only in the eighteenth century that we find historian-philosopher Hume arguing that the "chief use" of history was "to discover the constant and universal principles of human nature" and "the regular springs of human action and behavior."[123] When somewhat similar situations faced natural historians, many would turn to "hypothesis" as a means of linking particular matters of fact to convincing, if not certain, causal explanations.

Some seventeenth-century historians attempted to explain the causes of the English civil war, although more often than not this meant assigning moral responsibility according to partisan allegiance. Occasionally, historical parallels were offered, such as that between the English civil war and the barons' war or the French civil wars.[124] Sir William Temple, attempting to discern "the true Springs and Motions" of the wars between England and the Netherlands, attributed both the "rise" and "fall" of the Netherlands to trade.[125]

Attitudes were sharply divided about who should provide the explanations for historical facts. For some, that was the job of the historian. For others, such as John Rushworth, it was the reader who would discover his own "Prudence, Policy and Morality" and "find the Causes by the Effects," whereas he, the historian, would provide the reader only with "a true and simple Narrative of what was done, and by whom, and when." Readers would form "inductions from the particular Facts, to . . . understand the Designs then managed, and the Method propounded to Effect them." Still others, such as Gilbert Burnet, thought causal explanations might be "all Romance," resulting from the historian's "Imagination or Interest."[126] In all this debate a clear distinction was made between "fact" and "explanation."

Fact, Conjecture, Inference, Opinion, and Reflection

"Fact" was also distinguished from "conjecture," "inference," and "reflection." Of the three, conjecture was the most frequently used and typically was invoked in the absence of fact and evidence rather than as a means of explaining them. Historical conjectures were usually associated with speculation and even fiction. Yet Sir Walter Raleigh defended the historian's use of conjecture in the absence of historical records as neither "unlawful nor misbeseeing an historian," insisting, "He doth not fain that rehearseth probabilities as bare conjectures." Camden, far more circumspect, promised to be "cautious and frugal" with conjecture, and Selden castigated a scholar for relying on conjecture rather than documents. Bacon advised treating only limited time periods to avoid the "blanks and spaces" that the historian filled "out of his own wit and conjecture." Some, like Lambarde and Camden, occasionally offered multiple conjectures on the same matter.[127]

Those who wrote of the pre-Roman period used conjecture most freely and most often. Historians rarely adopted the language of "hypothesis" or "theory" that became commonplace among naturalists, though Sir Henry

Spelman used "theorem" in much the same way a naturalist would use "hypothesis." Thomas Gale sharply differentiated hypothesis and conjecture, indicating that his hypotheses offered "fuller evidence and convictive Arguments" that were "more than conjectural."[128]

Suspicious of conjecture or hypothesis arising from "mere fancy," Selden accepted "inference" and "liberty of interpretation." As in the legal sphere, inferences drawn from fact were viewed as less certain than the "facts" themselves. Others felt that the historian should not comment or add "unnecessary glosse" to his account or that mixing fact and reflection would "Pervert and Disguise Matter of Fact, and make History Romantic." Rushworth suggested it was the reader's, not the historian's, responsibility to make "reflections" on the matters of fact.[129]

The Faithful Historian

Telling the truth was the first and foremost requirement of the historian. The phrase "the faithful historian" was as much a commonplace as "the faithful witness" in the law. Probity, integrity, and honesty were all subsumed under the adjective "faithful." For Bacon, the historian not only must diligently examine but "freely and faithfully" report. Peter Heylyn insisted that "all things be laid down exactly, faithfully and without deviation from the truth in the least particular." Burnet promised to write "with all possible Fidelity and Diligence."[130] To be a historian required "Honesty, That he be a man of impartial Veracity, and firm Resolution to observe inviolable that prime Law of History. . . . Not to dare deliver any falsehood, nor conceal any Truth."[131] Fidelity implied disinterestedness and "sincere Affection to Truth"; its absence resulted in "Forsworn Narratives."[132]

Fidelity was frequently associated with reporting "matters of fact." The faithful historian follows the "rule of Writing nothing but Matter of Fact." A "true account" would "faithfully represent the plain Matter of Fact."[133] Kennett referred to his "faithful relation of . . . matter of Fact."[134] Like the reporters of "news" and the virtuosi who reported the "facts" of natural history, historians emphasized their commitment to faithful reporting.[135] Historical knowledge was thought to rely on the overlapping categories of faithful witness, faithful observer, and faithful historian.

The Norm of Impartiality and Problems of Partiality

Impartiality, so often mentioned in the legal arena, was, along with fidelity, the most frequently named attribute of the historian. The establishment of matters of fact, legal, historical, and natural, required impartial investigation, impartial reporting, and impartial judgment. Impartiality was both a methodological necessity and an essential rhetorical component of the "discourses of fact." Impartiality and "indifferency" were often claimed to be the "Glory of Historians."[136]

The impartiality norm of the historian had two sources. The first was that portion of the classical historiographical heritage that trumpeted the importance of nonpartisanship; the second was the legal tradition, with its emphasis on impartial witnessing and judgment. Peter Heylyn invoked the juridical analogue when he argued, "But in matter of fact, we put ourselves upon an ordinarie Jurie, not doubting, if the evidence prove fair, the Witnesses of faith unquestioned and the Records without suspicion of imposture, but they will doe their conscience and find for the Plaintiffe or Defendent, as the cause appears."[137]

While admitting the "strong Propensities in all mankind to join and adhere to one Side," another historian wrote that there were also such things as "Truth and honesty," and there "may be an impartial Historian as well as an impartial Judge in a Court, who can certainly give Sentence according to his Conscience and Judgment, tho' contrary to his Desires and Inclinations." Roger North analogized the historian to the impartial judge, suggesting that partiality and impartiality referred "to the will, and not to the Matter." It was the judge and witness, however, that were invoked, not the lawyer, and Burnet, not atypically, criticized the historian who wrote as "an Advocate that plead a Cause."[138]

The norm of impartiality was enunciated by the "perfect historian," by those inspired by the antiquarian and documentary traditions of scholarship, and by those who would report only "matters of fact." Statements of the historian's own impartiality and lack of bias were rhetorical commonplaces that accompanied most historical productions. "Verity and Indifference" were the "prime virtues" of the historian. The clearly partisan Clarendon claimed to be "free from any of those passions which naturally transport men with prejudice towards the persons they are obliged to mention, and whose actions they are at liberty to censure." Nathaniel Crouch, writing about the always controversial Cromwell, promised "an Impartial Account . . . Relating only matters of Fact without Reflection or Observation." The blatantly partisan Peter Heylyn insisted, "I am neither byassed by Love or Hatred, nor over-swayed by Partiality and corrupt Affections." Burnet and later historians similarly maintained that the biased historian "departs from the laws of an exact Historian," Burnet suggesting that he wrote "without regard to kindred or friends, to parties or interests" and at one point swearing to tell the truth.[139] But there was also recognition that the desired indifference was difficult, if not impossible, to achieve.[140]

One way to convince readers of the historian's impartiality was to present documentary evidence that would in some sense speak for itself. John Nalson told the reader that his points would be "plainly demonstrated by matters of undeniable Fact, drawn from the Records and Remains of those very men and Times." Brady insisted that the records would "shew and convince Men of Impartial and Unbiased Minds" in a way that "ordinary historians" could not. Some, however, recognized that documents could be presented in a partisan fashion. Rushworth was "a better Advocate than Historian" because he omitted and mutilated documents, and Kennett could write of "the apparition of Records" to justify historical arguments.[141]

Few, if any, historians writing on sensitive political and ecclesiastical topics were thought by their critics to have met the impartiality norm. Not surprisingly, those who wrote about the civil war were viewed as partisans, but so were the antiquarians who investigated the origins of Parliament and the early church. The work of one's historical opponents were partial and interested, sometimes even "malicious Calumnies,"[142] libels, or lies. Bolingbroke wrote of the danger of receiving "for true the history of any religion or nation, and much more than that of any sect or party, without having the means of confronting it with some other history. A reasonable man will . . . not establish the truth of history on a single, but on concurrent testimony. If there be none such, he will doubt absolutely; if there be a little such, he will proportion his assent or dissent accordingly."[143] Peter Whalley interestingly suggested a later sense of impartiality in the eighteenth century when he wrote that the historian's mind should resemble "a pure and polished Mirrour, which represents all Objects in the same form, Colour, and Dimensions which naturally belong to the Things themselves."[144] Impartiality here is no longer associated with the absence of partisanship or bias but rather with the idea of a wholly accurate portrayal of a past reality.

History, Rhetoric, and Style

Historians distinguished their work from that of the poet, the rhetorician, and the romancer and their truthful and impartial productions from those of the partisan advocate. There was a rhetoric of anti-rhetoric. Andrew Marvell's party-driven *Account of the Growth of Popery and Arbitrary Government* defended itself as a "naked narrative" unbiased by rhetoric. Walter Charleton and others insisted that history could be distinguished from pleading causes or from panegyric and invective. John Aubrey wrote that "the Offices of a Panegyrist & Historian, are much different," adding, "Pox take your orators and poets, they spoil lives and histories." Historians James Welwood, Gilbert Burnet, and Roger North too condemned panegyric and satire in historical works. Historians such as Selden and Burnet, who themselves invoked the impartiality norm, also found themselves accused of partisan advocacy.[145]

Historians wishing to reduce or eliminate the rhetorical encountered admiration of classical-era historians, themselves closely allied with rhetoric. There was also continuing insistence that historians provide moral instruction and examples of praise- and blameworthy behavior—functions deeply associated with rhetoric. The line between eulogy and biography was often blurred because historians were expected to memorialize worthy persons and events.[146]

The early modern English historian was thus torn between his obligation to award appropriate praise and blame and his obligation to record the truth of things and to narrate them without the deceptions associated with rhetoric. Brathwaite suggests the unresolved conflict. Historical examples were to "inflame the mind . . . unto valour and resolution," to "expresse the actions of good men with an Emphasis, to sollicite the Reader to the affecting the like means." Yet he denounced "making Histories meere Panegyrics" that "insinuate and winde themselves into the affection." Others insisted on history as a simple appeal to reason and at the same time recommended rhetorical flourishes in historical writing.[147]

Early modern English historians did not unanimously reject eloquence in historical writing. There were, however, countless statements rejecting rhetorical ornament. Rhetoric was often contrasted with "truth," and especially with the "naked" truth of matter of fact.[148] "Nakedness" was contrasted to artifice that disguised truth. History should not be "dressed up with gloss and artifice."[149] "Fact" was associated with a plain and naked style. The repudiation of rhetorical ornament became common among historians from the late sixteenth century onward and intensified during the seventeenth century. Post-Restoration historians and antiquarians in particular underlined the opposition between the simplicity associated with reality, truth, and matter of fact and the deceptions of rhetoric.[150] At the beginning of the eighteenth century, however, simplicity and elegance were less likely to be viewed as antagonistic. For Kennett, "Simplicity," the "principall Beauty in the style of an Historian," should have an "air of good sense and just Eloquence."[151]

Conclusion

From the beginning to end of the early modern era, "history" was associated with "fact," but during the course of the seventeenth century the meanings of both "history" and "fact" were modified. "History" sometimes referred to particularizing "historia" and was contrasted with universalizing poetry and philosophy. More frequently, however, "history" referred to the historiographical genre of "perfect history" produced by experienced firsthand observers writing about war and politics. "Perfect history" was contrasted to less than perfect "preparatives" such as memoirs, memorials, and antiquities. Over time the distinction between the perfect and less than perfect varieties eroded but did not disappear.

Although historians today often distinguish the antiquarian from the historian, we can see the interpenetration of the two modes in Selden's declaration that his antiquarian research was history. It may be useful to view the early modern historical enterprise as a continuum, with the "perfect" political historian being at one end and the sophisticated, erudite collector-critic of documentary evidence at the other, with a considerable number of historical practitioners falling somewhere in the middle. If the well-written narrative of politics, war, and state relations remained the ideal way to report the "facts" of history, it was increasingly necessary to provide supporting evidence in addition to the reports of the witness-observer-historian.

These changes interacted with the changing meaning of "fact." Initially, the deeds, actions, feats, or facts being recounted might be fictional or real. By the end of the seventeenth century the "facts" of history were "real," not imagined, and both history and fact were contrasted with the fictions of poetry and romance. "Fictional facts" were excised along with the invented speech, fable, myth, and romance. The historian's permission to invent was gradually withdrawn, and the playwright, even if he used historical materials, was treated as the creator of works of imagination, not "history." The decline of the early-seventeenth-century "poesie historical" was linked to the growing breach between "fact" and fiction. The development, however, was far from smooth, and it was only in the eighteenth century that dictionaries defined fact as something "really done."[152] Fact or matter of fact in the writing of history had come to include both real human actions and events known by firsthand observation and credible contemporary witnesses. It had also come to include knowledge of past events and practices that could be derived from documentary materials and ancient objects. Occasionally, we begin to hear of history as a "collection of facts."[153]

The treatment of history as "fact" might be used positively to indicate that nothing false or fictional was included or negatively to denigrate a collection of facts devoid of explanation or meaning. The distinction between history and fiction simultaneously sharpened the distinction between fact and fiction. We can trace the growing conceptual opposition between fact and fiction, history and poetry, and between fact and speculation or conjecture, but we should not take these contrasts to mean that the latter were necessarily deemed inferior. What seemed important was to ensure that the categories remained distinct. It became difficult to treat "poesy historical" as history, but not to admire both history and poetry.

As lawyers became involved in the practice of history, not only did the role of documentary materials become more important but the lawyer's language of "fact," evidence, and proof became part and parcel of the historian's vocabulary. A great deal of attention comes to be paid to witnessing in historical discourse and to legalistic criteria for judging the credibility of those witnesses. The appeal of fidelity, judgment, and impartiality became pronounced as legal terminology and methods reinforced the emphasis on experienced, firsthand witnessing and impartiality that was also the legacy of classical historiography.

In history as in law, not all "facts"—the lawyer would speak of "alleged facts"—were to be treated as true. Those without appropriate or sufficient proof would remain dubious and might even be rejected as false facts. Fact had not yet come to be synonymous with truth, though the distinction between "fact" and "fiction" and repeated emphasis on historical truth telling helped accelerate the process. The truth of the historian, no more than that of the lawyer, was not metaphysical or mathematical in character but instead implied reasonable belief in a variety of past acts.

If history was closely allied with "fact," it still did not consist solely of "matters of fact." It was to be a compound of believable matters of fact and explanation of or commentary on those facts. Causal analysis, reflections, and conjectures that might be included in histories were distinguished from "fact." If history was an account of "matter of fact," it was something more. That "something more" was difficult to define but had to do with the meaning or significance of past actions.

Early modern historians faced a number of problems stemming from competing notions of history, the addition of new subject matters and methods, and the role of fact. One, as we have seen, involved the difficulty of incorporating documentary evidence and material artifacts, given the classical preference for eyewitness reporting. Although the subject matter of history remained largely the story of states and rulers, some broadening occurred. As the subject matter broadened, so did the nature of "fact." Some of this expansion of subject matter resulted from antiquarian scholarship that dealt with ancient ecclesiastical and secular institutions and practices and the remains of Roman and pre-Roman Britain, but it also owed something to the older notion of "historia," which dealt with particulars of all kinds. We have, for example, noticed how new forms of collective biography were integrating accounts of learning and culture into "history." In a subsequent chapter we see how natural phenomena, also a kind of "historia," came to be treated as "facts." Documents and artifacts such as coins, great stone monoliths, funerary urns, and inscribed tombstones also helped erode the concept "fact" as human act. If King Arthur's deeds and actions ceased to be "fact," coins and medals might provide evidence for the "fact" of past battles and noteworthy events and deeds. But such coins and medals also might provide evidence of non-deeds, such as continuing political institutions and social practices. The expansion of the varieties of historical evidence is interlocked with the expansion of historical fact from deeds alone to any past phenomenon that reasonably can be believed to have existed on the basis of the range of evidence offered.

Another historiographical problem derived from the norm of impartiality, a norm so powerful yet so difficult to put into practice that it would be hard for early modern English history to embody it. The problem of impartiality was further complicated by the uncertain relationship between historiography and rhetoric. Many early modern historians contrasted the "truth" of the "matters of fact" of history with the blandishments and falsities of rhetoric. Yet they generally accepted the tasks of educating, memorializing, awarding praise and blame, and persuading, all associated with rhetoric, while rejecting partisan advocacy. In spite of much talk of impartiality and "naked truth," it was not clear to contemporaries how one could construct a meaningful persuasive narrative without rhetoric. This tension existed at the level not only of substance but of style. Perhaps because some respected classical historians favored an elevated style, the historical community remained somewhat ambivalent about the move in the direction of a plain and "naked" style. By the end of the seventeenth century the desire for a truthful, well-documented historical account of matters of fact existed side by side with the desire for an uplifting and flowing narrative of the English past.[154] Nevertheless, history had incorporated, or at least substantial portions of the historical community had incorporated, a scholarly tradition that valued accuracy and verification. History from the beginning to the end of our period dealt with "fact," but historical practitioners came to work much harder to ensure that the "facts" they wrote about were "real" and that they were supported by appropriate evidence. From the beginning of the eighteenth century we even encounter the plural "facts" in a context implying that those facts were assumed already to have been proved.

Discourses of Fact: Chorography, Description, and Travel Reporting

What began as a professional category for dealing with legally relevant events and became somewhat extended by historians was to be transformed into a common way of thinking about an increasingly wide range of events, occurrences, and things, human, natural, and divine. Here we examine the development of "fact" in chorography and travel literature, both of which describe places and report observations made during movement through geographic space. Although chorographies most often deal with local matters, and travel accounts are typically associated with far distant adventures, they share so many characteristics that often it is difficult to place a particular account in one or the other category. Both mixed accounts of hardships, dangers, escapes, and adventures with observations of the particularities of nature and rare objects. This and subsequent chapters repeatedly present us with the permeability and overlapping of the various discourses of fact. What may be an interesting curiosity or "matter of fact" for the traveler or chorographer thus might also be "intelligence" for the diplomat, a crucial find for the antiquarian, new information for a geographer, or an observation of a new species of plant or animal for the natural historian.

This chapter, then, takes us through several kinds of efforts to describe contemporary places, things, and cultural practices accurately. Such descriptions, which combined human and natural events and "things" with little conscious attention to the differences between them, played an important role in the expansion of the concept "fact" from human actions to natural phenomena and ultimately to the development of the notion "scientific fact."

Shared Characteristics

The chorographic and travel discourses shared a number of features indebted to the fact-finding methods of the English and European courts and to the historiographic tradition. Among these are insistence on truthful reports or narratives and the rejection of rumor, hearsay, falsehood, and fiction. Chorographic and travel reporters typically insisted that they truthfully reported "matters of fact." Whenever feasible they claimed to be "eye-witnesses" of honesty and good character. They appropriated the qualities of the ideal witness in the law court, pointing to their impartiality, lack of bias, or nonpartisanship. Secondhand reports were inferior although sometimes acceptable. When relying on others for information, writers were quick to insist that these reporters or witnesses too were reliable, unbiased, and honest, of the appropriate social status to inspire trust, or were by experience or training in a position to make their testimony about facts credible. Hearsay and rumor had to be identified as such. Products of the imagination rather than of the senses did not qualify as reports of "fact." As Henry Oldenburg wrote, what was wanted was "true matter of fact," not "fictions and ungrounded wonders."[1] When forced to rely on previous written accounts or histories, chorographers and travelers, like historians and newsmen, emphasized the quality, accuracy, and reliability of the accounts and records they drew on.

Chorographic and travel literature assumed that under favorable conditions ordinary persons were capable of reporting the facts accurately and ordinary readers could understand and evaluate their reports. In most instances it was not necessary to be learned or expert to state what one had observed or witnessed. Sea captains and travelers, both English and foreign, were considered capable of making accurate reports, although it was recognized that they did not always do so. As in the law courts, "matters of fact" might be adequately or inadequately reported. Partisanship, superstition, an inferior education, or human weakness might impair the ability of the observer to report properly. Christian teachings about human fallibility and the Baconian idols underscored this sensitivity to error in reporting "matters of fact." Some "matters of fact" thus might prove to be false. As in contemporary historical writing, there were references to "false fact." Readers of chorographies and travel literature became the judges of whether or not the "facts" presented were believable.

This stance suited an age that was abandoning Aristotelian authority and was familiar with but only partially accepting of the potent skeptical critique of the sixteenth century. Proponents of factual knowledge recognized the fallibility of the senses and distortions caused by partiality and superstition but rejected a thoroughgoing skepticism. The legal model proved useful to the newer discourses of fact because the law courts reached decisions under less than perfect conditions. The legal arena was not one that allowed lawyers, judges, or jurors the option of throwing up their hands in skeptical doubt. In law, decisions about "matters of fact" had to be made, and they had to be believable, sound, and practical, if not absolutely infallible. And outside the legal realm factual knowledge could be modified as more and better information was acquired. Factual knowledge about near and especially distant places might be erroneous or incomplete at any given moment, but it could improve over time as well-supported reports of geographic matters of fact multiplied.

Chorography and travel discourses typically adopted the first person: "I saw this," or "I encountered this or that." The chorographic or travel account either narrated events in the order observed or experienced, or employed a prescribed grid or set of chorographic categories such as soil and climate. Not infrequently, such accounts shifted between the first-person active and the third-person passive.

Travel experience was considered desirable particularly for gentlemen, but many were unable to do anything more than armchair traveling, benefiting vicariously from the experience of others.[2] Travel accounts were added to historical writing as a means of gaining the experience thought to be necessary for public life. Descriptive and travel publications were numerous and had a wide and rather varied audience. Some chorographical and travel accounts were produced to enhance local pride, or merely for entertainment. Others were written with an eye to public policy, as contributions to natural philosophy grounded on "matters of fact," or as a means of enhancing the educational opportunities of the political class.

Chorography

Chorography was a rather peculiar early modern genre that combined history, geography, topography, natural history, antiquities, and genealogy with socioeconomic, political, and cultural description of a particular region. Typically, it followed a preexisting pattern of topics that included soil, climate, agricultural products, manufactures, rarities, monuments, architecture, and remains of antiquity and thus tended to focus on the description of "things" available to the eye both of human and natural origin. Chorographers also might report on important families, trade, religion, manners, and other local cultural practices. Chorography and descriptive geography combined past and present "facts" as well as the human and natural "facts" of particular regions, just as cosmography combined them on a grander scale.[3] Although it tended to focus on the currently observable, chorography and descriptive geography also might be concerned with practices and "things" that had changed over time.

With its mixture of civil and natural history, chorography became an important vehicle through which the legally derived concepts of witnessing and evaluation of testimony were transmitted from human events and actions to natural phenomena, natural events, and experiment. The distinction between these two varieties of fact became blurred, and both were easily and naturally considered knowable by the same mental processes.

Like history, chorography and descriptive geography had ancient antecedents and were self-consciously revived during the Renaissance. Chorography was linked to a number of discourses of fact. It was treated as the companion of history, and histories of England were often accompanied by a chorographical description of the country. Chorographies were linked to natural history insofar as they described the plants, animals, and natural resources of a region. Many late-seventeenth-century publications devoted to particular regions were labeled "natural history." Antiquarian studies were often chorographic because antiquities were frequently discussed in the context of the region in which they were found. Some regional works focused primarily on antiquities, largely ignoring climatic or agricultural topics, either because the author was not interested in them or because he did not wish to duplicate the work of others.[4]

Chorography was also linked to Baconian and Royal Society–sponsored "histories of trade" that charted developments in trade, manufacturing, and agriculture. There were elements of cartography, surveying, and genealogy. Regional accounts often included sections devoted to political description and ethnography as well as materials to assist in gentlemanly touring. The line between the chorography and the travel account or traveler's handbook was often very thin or nonexistent. Bacon's direction for gentlemanly travel thus provided a list of "things to be seen and observed."[5]

Chorographical works included Camden's highly esteemed nationwide study, *The Britannia*, county histories, and description of towns such as Stowe's *Survey of London*. Although they might include more or fewer maps, genealogies, antiquities, items of natural history, or surveys of manufactures, all emphasized firsthand knowledge and reports from reliable witnesses and records.[6] Authors emphasized their own observations as they traveled through and recorded a particular geographical locale. Titles varied but often included the words "perambulation," "itinerary," "survey," "natural history," or "moral history."

In his *Survey of London* (1598) John Stowe employed every kind of data and evidence, observing the physical and documentary evidence at first hand. He critically examined the reliability and credibility of his witnesses and sought confirming evidence whenever possible. Echoing the lawyers and historians, Camden emphasized the role of the eyewitness. He noted, "One matter of fact faithfully and honestly deliver'd is worth a thousand Comments and Flourishes."[7] Like the scientific work of the Royal Society, chorography was a collective enterprise. In both endeavors "matters of fact" would be gradually accumulated and erroneously reported facts amended or excised to increase the store of knowledge.

The most widely practiced form of chorography in England was the county history, which was related to national and local patriotism as well as to the development of antiquarian studies and natural history. Some county histories focused on antiquities, others dealt equally with antiquities and physical characteristics, while still others emphasized natural history. Some thus exhibit greater kinship with the efforts of the short-lived Society of Antiquaries and others with those of the Royal Society. William Lambarde's *Perambulations of Kent* and Richard Carew's *Survey of Cornwall* are typical of the late sixteenth and early seventeenth centuries. William Dugdale's *Warwickshire* and Robert Thornton's *Nottinghamshire* leaned in the direction of legal antiquities, whereas the works of Robert Plot and John Aubrey gave greater emphasis to natural history.[8] The monoliths of Stonehenge and Avebury were of interest to both antiquarians and topographers.

Richard Carew's 1602 *Survey of Cornwall*, an early chorographical study self-consciously modeled on Strabo, adopted what would become the conventional arrangement of descriptive material. His categories—things above the earth, things below the earth, and things of the earth, the last of which was subdivided into things of life, growing, and things of life, feeling—were typical of his ancient predecessors and scientifically oriented successors such as Robert Boyle. Categories were not always rigidly followed. Carew's treatment of minerals included descriptions of the region's famous tinworks and its Stannery courts. Carew also provided information on the county's bridges and highways, its markets and fairs, its social divisions, its leading magistrates and officeholders, and its characteristic recreations. Such local histories or surveys might include information on almost any topic. Like larger-scale chorographies, county history was capable of nearly infinite subdivision, and Carew examined the county town by town and hundred by hundred. He hoped to cover all that could be seen by the eye of the careful observer and attempted to present his observations with the "sincerity" of a witness.

Lawyer William Burton's *Description of Leicestershire* similarly emphasized personal observation, noting that the arms on church windows and the inscriptions of the tombs he had "for the most part . . . taken by my own view and travell, . . . and may give testimony, proof." He proudly noted that his knowledge had even "been delivered in evidence to a Jury at the assizes."[9]

This tradition of English local description continued unabated into the eighteenth century, although over time the term "chorography" was replaced with the "natural history of X," the "Present State of Y," or sometimes the "Ancient and Present State of Z." Daniel Defoe characterized his *Tour Thro the Whole Island of Great Britain* as "a Description of the most flourishing and opulent country in the World" and "what he has been Eyewitness of himself" of "the Present State of the Country."[10]

Chorographical description required frequent revision since many of the "matters of fact" observed and described were subject to change. Although this was obviously not as true for topographical features or climate, cities, with their new buildings, places of interest, and economic endeavors, were constantly in flux. Harrison's *Description of England* was revised in 1587. James Howell's *Londonopolis* updated Stowe. Howell was in turn updated by others. Like many chorographers, Howell found that he could not rely entirely on his own observations but must "peruse many mouldred and motheaten Records, as so bring light as it were out of darkness, to inform the present World, what the former did, and make us see truth through our Ancestors' eyes."[11] Chorography, like historiography, thus might mix eyewitness reporting with the analysis of the written records of the past.

The changing London scene described by Stowe and then Howell soon attracted successor volumes, some very detailed, others small enough to pocket. Thomas De-Laune's 1681 *Present State of London*, a "Compendium" rather than a "voluminous History," contained "new things" that fell within his "own observation (or my Friends) respecting the Present State of this city." It described London's walls, towers, churches, monuments, and hospitals and included Westminster's courts and Parliament. It summarized London's governmental structure and described its trade, merchants, docks, and stagecoaches and even the fairs and stopping points of coaches, but it also provided an account of London's diseases, "accidents," and "rarities." Thus it was not only a chorography and a guidebook but a report of "news" and a participant in the tradition of writings on "wonders" and "rarities."[12]

Camden's *Britannia* quickly became dated, and at least two subsequent cooperative efforts were launched.[13] Perhaps the best example of continuous revision is Edward Chamberlayne's *Anglicae Noticia or the Present State of England*, a compendium of current information about England. Revisions recorded changes in what was currently observable, added new "matters of fact," and corrected errors. Chorographers, like historians and naturalists, frequently invited readers to contribute corrections and additional information. Defoe suggests that "A Compleat Account of Great Britain" must be the "Work of many Years" employing "many hands." "No description of Great Britain can be what we call a finished Account." It is "always altering with Time."[14] This sense of an ever growing and ever changing fund of information also was characteristic of those who collected and recorded other observed and experimental "matters of fact."

No more than historians and naturalists did chorographers limit themselves to description of their own country. Increasing attention was devoted to England's colonial possessions, Europe (especially its lesser-known regions), the Middle East, and the whole known world. Those focusing on the English colonies might combine description with business prospects,[15] while those dealing with the Middle East tended to give particular attention to English commercial and political interests. But even the colonial description most concerned with attracting investment capital and encouraging immigration adopted the language of witnessing and credible testimony. One work thus certified that its information was supported by "divers Letters from Virginia, by men of worth and credit there," its author insisting, "And let no man doubt of the truth of it, there be many in England, Land and Seamen that can beare witnesse of it."[16] Another writer apologized for the absence of "ocular proof" of eyewitnesses, relying on the "Credit and Reputation" of the "worthy Gentlemen" who had provided him with information. His faith in their description was as strong as his faith that "Jerusalem was in Palestine."[17]

Chorographers of Ireland covered a wide range of topics. Gerard Boate combined natural history with a description of Ireland's "Fashions, Laws, and Customs." Sir William Petty's *Political Anatomy of Ireland* (1691) emphasized historical development and contemporary social, political, and economic conditions, and Laurence Echard joined the "Chorographical and Modern" with the "Historical and Ancient."[18]

As the English began to describe other parts of the world, their accounts became indistinguishable from the travel report or descriptive geography. This chapter uses the term "chorography" largely in connection with Englishmen who traveled and described England and its colonial possessions and "travel report" when the author described non-English or distant locations, but the distinction is somewhat arbitrary. Was the Frenchman who described England a chorographer or a traveler? The term "chorography" gradually became obsolete as English and European travelers surveyed the familiar and unknown around the globe. Neither travel reporting nor chorography was peculiarly English, and the plethora of translations reminds us that the "discourses of fact" were neither an English preserve nor an English creation.

Travel and Voyage Reporting

Richard Hakluyt's *Principal Navigations, Voiages and Discoveries of the English Nation* (1589), largely official documents, personal letters, and firsthand accounts, was the first important travel collection, followed shortly by Samuel Purchas's similarly popular work.[19] Later examples include John Ray's *Observations Topographical and Physiological: Made in a Journey* (1673), Martin Lister's *Journey to Paris in the Year 1698* (1699), William Dampier's *New Voyage around the World* (1697), and Awnsham and John Churchill's vast *Collection of Voyages and Travels* (1704).

Travel writing tended to adopt two forms, sometimes blended in the same work. The first was the eyewitness report of a voyage or "adventure" in which the narrator proceeded chronologically, often beginning with the day his ship sailed. It recounted a variety of events, human and natural—storms, conflicts aboard ship, encounters with pirates or native inhabitants or foreign enemies, hardships, and other interesting sights and "adventures" along the way. Narratives might be continuous or a series of diary-like entries, or some combination of the two. These accounts were readily labeled "matters of fact" since they involved particular events or actions and merged easily with what might be called "contemporary history." Such first-person reports tended to exhibit clear beginnings, middles, and ends, the return of the voyager typically marking the end of the work.

The second variety was a descriptive-chorographic one that abandoned chronology for a cross-sectional description of a particular locale using some or all of the standard chorographical and travel topics or the later Royal Society articles of inquiry. The voyage or adventure mode involved movement and time, whereas the chorographic was more static, with the author suggesting that he was providing a "description" or "survey" of the locale being visited. The traveler was thus free to deal with chorographical topics such as climate, plants, agriculture, or local customs at the length or detail desired.

Corroboration by multiple credible witnesses, always at a premium in the discourses of fact, was often unavailable to the traveler. The "believability" of the travel account, therefore, relied on the credibility of the narrator and the plausibility of the account. Prefatory materials, often written by the author himself, friends, or associates, assured readers that the author was the kind of person whose observations were trustworthy. Character, status, and opportunity to observe were crucial to the credibility of his testimony. If the plausibility of the account seemed questionable, that issue too might be addressed. The widespread interest in and acceptance of the "strange but true," however, meant that reports of quite unlikely events, unusual or "marvelous" phenomena, strange customs, or "remarkable" adventures would not necessarily be viewed with the skepticism they are today. Early modern readers were often engaged by the rare and the "marvelous," and those who criticized the "credulous" in some contexts were quite prepared to believe "marvels" and "wonders" in others.[20] A cliché of the times was that the king of Siam did not believe reports of water becoming so hard it could be walked on though it had been witnessed by countless Europeans.

As in the other "discourses of fact," eyewitness testimony was preferred. Already in 1625 Samuel Purchas, like Richard Hakluyt a collector of travel accounts, noted, "What a World Travelers have by their own eyes observed ... each Traveler relating what ... he has seen."[21] The frequent lack of supporting testimony, however, meant that the travel account, more than any other discourses of fact, was not always accepted as a "true account of matter of fact." Travelers and travel writers had reputations for exaggeration and even dishonesty. Indeed, there existed a long tradition of what Percy Adams has called "travel liars."[22] Those traveler's tales that relied on an uncorroborated narrative were particularly suspect, even though larded with the conventions of proof for matters of fact and claims of true and impartial reporting, "sincerity," and "fidelity." The more exotic the place visited, the greater the problem of credibility.

Reader skepticism increased as the standards for evaluating "matters of fact" became more familiar. Perhaps for this reason, many post-Restoration travel writers associated their publications with the Royal Society or with respected diplomats with presumed knowledge of the locales described.

Credibility was not a problem for obviously fictional discourse, where invented elements were to be praised for wit, fancy, or imagination. These very praises, when contrasted with the frequent claims of and acclaim for truth in other bodies of writing, show the increasingly distinct boundary between the discourses of fact and those of fiction.

But the lines of demarcation between factual and fictional discourses, as we see in Chapter 8, were not always clear. When fiction writers adopted the conventions of factual reporting, it was not always easy for readers to distinguish the invented from the real. This problem occurred most often in travel accounts because corroborating witnesses were often unavailable. If early-eighteenth-century readers were provided with obvious clues to indicate that the adventures of Lemuel Gulliver were fictional, they could not so easily determine whether *Robinson Crusoe* was invented fiction or "matter of fact," as the author claimed. Most readers were probably fooled by George Psalmanazar's *Historical and Geographical Description of Formosa*, a blatant fraud that nevertheless promised to dispel the "Clouds of Fabulous Reports."[23] This and other collections of "Romantick Stories" or "magnificent Tales of Spectres and Illusions"[24] could not easily be distinguished from Knox's relation of Ceylon or William Lithgow's account of his nineteen years of travel based on his "own Eye-Sight and ocular experience."[25]

Joshua Childrey, Edmund Halley, and other writers took up the problem but could do little more than warn readers against uncritical acceptance or rejection. Childrey's *Britannia Baconia* instructed "the Vulgar . . . not to misbelieve or condemn for untruths all that seemes strange," since some "improbable" reports were true. Familiar locales were "easily examinable with little travel" or "hazard," but there was no foolproof method for verifying distant "rarities" and "adventures."[26] Readers were confronted with the king of Siam's problem. Rare plant, animal, and mineral specimens brought back by travelers could be directly observed, but there was no way to guarantee suitable verification for "adventures" or "strange practices" other than the trust placed in the reporter. Edmund Halley thus doubted a well-attested French report about a transsexual, his doubt stemming from the "bantring ridiculing humour of that light nation."[27] If nationality or religious affiliation influenced credibility, they could never become overwhelming considerations for those seeking a republic of letters or a universal knowledge grounded on "matters of fact." To greater or lesser extent the discourses of fact hovered between the poles of corrosive skepticism and reliance on authority and, for the most part, rested on the testimony of those deemed to be trustworthy and faithful witnesses.

Both the travel and chorographic genres were characterized by the adoption of what has been called the plain style as contrasted to a highly ornamented rhetorical one. Edward Chamberlayne's *Anglia notitia* was typical in its self-conscious avoidance of "all curious Flowers of Rhetoric."[28] Honesty in the factual genres required unadorned prose. Rhetorical fluency and highly ornamented and figurative language had connotations of deception and flattery.

Although an extensive description of the chorographic-travel genres is beyond the scope of this chapter, we must note that the efforts of travelers and chorographers resulted in a vast production of manuscript and printed material that increased as more and more parts of the world were explored. Here we focus on the promotional role of the Royal Society in order to show the interconnectedness among the growing number of discourses of fact.

The Royal Society and Travel Reporting

From the time of its inception the Royal Society, which frequently defined its mission as the development of a natural history on which to build a secure natural philosophy, promoted careful travel reporting.

Much of its effort was directed at reducing the variety and idiosyncrasy of this kind of reporting by promoting a more uniform and systematic mode of recording and organizing properly observed "matters of fact." The Society created and disseminated "articles of inquiry" that provided grids on which travelers might organize their observations. Although these categories stemmed from and overlapped with those of Renaissance chorographers, which in turn were descended from Strabo and the ancients, the Society's efforts are often viewed as having a "scientific" rather than a "humanistic" flavor. Such distinction, however, obscures the overlap between early modern natural history and humanistic enterprises.[29]

From the time of the Portuguese voyages, travelers became increasingly aware that many of the phenomena they described contradicted ancient authority or introduced matters of fact previously unknown. Bacon felt that "distant voyages and travels" were beginning to change natural philosophy and that all "regions of the material globe . . . have been in our time laid open widely and revealed."[30] By 1633 accounts of voyages were already being associated with the improvement of natural history.[31] Since human and natural "matters of fact" were mixed in the Royal Society reporting program, its efforts should be seen as contributing to the development of ethnography and political description as well as to the history of manufacturing and trade and, of course, to geography, topography, and natural history.

Although we first hear of the Royal Society's plans for a method for "inquiries for foreign parts" in 1661, its "General inquiries" were first drawn up in 1664 and printed in the *Philosophical Transactions* the following year.[32] By 1681 Robert Hooke wished to further regularize the collection of "matters of fact." Seaman and travelers needed instructions "to shew them what is pertinent and considerable to be observ'd . . . and how to make their Observations and Registers or Accounts of them." He noted the lack of "fit persons" to promote and disburse such instructions, to collect the returns and compose them into histories, "separating what is pertinent from what is not so, and to be Rejected." Even accurately recorded "matters of fact" would require expert sifting.[33] For Hooke, it had become obvious that the collection and accumulation of factual data without organization or classification was unwieldy.

Robert Boyle's *General Heads for the Natural History of a Country, Great or Small Drawn Out for the Use of Travellers and Navigators*[34] provided another revision of the Society's program. John Woodward's *Brief Instructions for Making Observations in all Parts of the World . . . For the Advancement of Knowledge both Natural and Civil* provided even more detailed instructions.[35] The Churchills' *Collection of Voyages and Travels* advised travelers to have "a Table-Book at hand to set down everything worth remembering, and then at night more methodically transcribe the Notes."[36] In 1713 the government ordered ambassadors, admirals, and officers to "receive directions and instructions from the R.S. for making enquiries relating to the improvement of natural philosophy."[37] Most post-Restoration travel accounts, chorographies, and natural histories approximated the prescribed format and arranged their "facts" according to it. Many post-Restoration travel publications identified themselves with the Royal Society's efforts.

Henry Oldenburg aggressively sought information from foreign sources to fill the Society's "philosophical storehouse." His correspondence is larded with requests for information on Italy, Spain, Portugal, France, Germany, Poland, and Hungary as well as Persia, Turkey, the West Indies, Brazil, and Mexico. An important part of his role as secretary was to gather "information in the completest and faithfullest manner" from "Ingenious and curious Men in all parts of the world."[38]

The well-reported observations, routinely labeled "matters of fact," of travelers or foreign residents thus provided crucial information for the virtuosi's research. Edmund Halley's "Historical Account of the Trade-Winds and Monsoons," an account composed of "matter of Fact," was based on conversations with experienced navigators. Its perfection would depend on future "Observations" by those knowledgeable about the nature of winds. Only a "multitude of Observers" could "bring together the Experience requisite to compose a perfect and complete History of these Winds."[39]

The Royal Society too was faced with the problem of witness credibility. Members received reports of "matters of fact" from a wide range of sources, not only gentlemen like so many of themselves but also ordinary seamen, merchants, and travelers. One set of directions was explicitly designed "to better capacitate" seamen so that observations might be "pertinent and suitable."[40] It was important to know the name of each reporter so the Society could assess "wth what cautions, his testimony is made use of, in ye following History." Reports thus were to be evaluated as well as received. Industrious and wise men must be "aroused to collect accurately, compile faithfully, and make public each the history of his own region."[41]

The virtuosi's conception of the ideal reporter of distant matters of fact is suggested by Hooke: "I conceive him to be no ways prejudiced or byassed by Interest, affection, hatred, fear or hopes, or the vain-glory of telling strange Things, so as to make him swarve from the truth of Matter of Fact."[42] Here again we see the emphasis on impartiality and absence of interest so much a part of the legal and historical traditions.

Clearly concerned with the skill of its informants, the Society nevertheless placed considerable faith in the ordinary traveler's ability to faithfully report "matters of fact" and appears to have put greater faith in such reports than its French counterpart, which expressed dissatisfaction with the ability of merchants and soldiers to provide accurate accounts. At times the virtuosi were forced to rely on the testimony of those who did not meet the Society's ideal standard. Sir William Petty's Interregnum Down Survey, a large-scale enterprise, used barely literate soldiers supplied with simple instruments, and John Graunt's pioneering demographic work was at least partially compiled by "Old-women searchers." As in the courtroom, distant matters of fact were established by eyewitnesses of varying status. A fair number of reports from distant locales received by the Royal Society were provided by seamen. A report on whale fishing on the Bermudas was "delivered by an understanding & hardy Seaman, who affirmed he had been at the killing work himself." While the reports of sea captains were undoubtedly preferable to those of ordinary seamen, both might be acceptable.[43]

Some Royal Society members themselves became travel reporters. John Ray's *Observations Topographical, Moral and Physiological: Made in a Journey* and his *Collection of Curious Travels and Voyages* are noteworthy examples. Like most travelers, Ray indicated, "Only what I write as of mine own knowledge is punctually and in all circumstances true, at least according to my apprehension and judgment. . . . And for what I write from the Relation of others, though I will not warrant it for certain, yet to me it is seemed most likely and probable."[44] The great natural historian of birds and fishes, Francis Willughby, traveled widely in Europe and planned a trip to the New World to "view and describe the several Species of Nature" at first hand.[45] Members frequently communicated factual reports when traveling. If most reported on natural "matters of fact," others, like Edmund Halley, also contributed antiquarian data.[46] Martin Lister commented on a wide range of nonscientific topics during his visit to France, as did Edward Browne.[47] The tradition of member-supplied travel accounts continued into the eighteenth century and beyond. Dr. Hans Sloane, secretary and later president of the Royal Society, contributed the "matter of fact" of his observations in *A Voyage to . . . Madera, . . . and Jamaica.*[48]

The Society received numerous reports of "matter of fact" from nonmember travelers, some concerned with plants and animals, some with mines and natural products, and still others with ethnographic topics. If the Society was reasonably confident about the ability of its own members to provide faithful reports on matters of fact, it sometimes expressed concern with the difficulties involved in relying on factual information provided by less well known informants. Like historians, the Royal Society had to rely on witnesses whose trustworthiness, impartiality, and accuracy were sometimes questionable or unknown. If natural philosophy was to be built on this foundation, reliable reporting of "matter of fact" was essential.

As Steven Shapin has recently shown, trust was an unspoken foundation for factual knowledge. Shapin, however, suggests that the community of reliable witnesses for scientific experiment was a rather closed one, bounded by those who could make claims to gentlemanly status.[49] While gentlemanly status may have a role for those engaged in creating experimental "facts," the community could not be so small for the "facts" of natural history gathered from distant climes. Many of those whose reports were received by the Royal Society were distinctly not gentlemen. The natural history sought by the Society necessarily included the testimony of those who could not be adequately cross-examined, whose observations could not be easily repeated, or whose credibility and social status could not be carefully scrutinized. For this reason, the "facts" of natural history, especially those reported for relatively untraveled or exotic locales, were, and would remain, something of an epistemological problem.

It is impossible here to indicate the range of the Society's worldwide fact-gathering interests and activities. Some members, of course, were more interested than others in its chorographic and travel endeavors, and at times the Society focused more on some areas of the world than others. As we have noted, the particular interest of individual members sometimes stimulated a line of inquiry. The accidents of members' itineraries also played a role. Robert Hooke and Christopher Wren, then president of the Royal Society, promoted seaman Robert Knox's *Historical Relation of the Island of Ceylon*, and several members were involved in sponsoring Richard Blome's ambitious *Geographical Description of the World*.[50] William Dampier's popular travel accounts were dedicated to the Royal Society, and the collections published by Awnsham and John Churchill had the assistance of Dr. Hans Sloane and John Locke. Dampier's *New Voyage Round the World* was written by a seaman, who indicated that the account "is only matter of fact being the several passages and transactions . . . which I am now going to describe."[51] The Royal Society's "noble design" in promoting chorographical investigation and travel reporting was widely known and admired.[52]

At times particular regions were of special interest. Oldenburg asked John Winthrop, also a member of the Society, to contribute "all the Observables both of Nature and Art" from New England. He wrote again in 1670 asking him to acquaint us "wth what particulars you know of the matter of fact in America."[53] John Josselyn's 1676 *Account of Two Voyages to New England*, dedicated to the Society, contained a description that included "natives," "creatures," and "remarkable passages."[54]

The Royal Society also promoted translations. What we have been treating as an English phenomenon was well developed in France and elsewhere. By the end of the seventeenth century, if not earlier, there was an almost insatiable taste for "facts" concerning European and more distant places.

Political Description

Although scholars have occasionally speculated as to why a more empirically oriented political science did not develop in the wake of scientific advances, they have, for the most part, continued to focus on issues of divine right, the ancient constitution, and the theoretical approaches of Hobbes, Harrington, or the Levellers and largely ignored the large, and admittedly amorphous and scattered, body of seventeenth- and early-eighteenth-century description dealing in whole or in part with the political arrangements and institutions of European and non-European states.[55] This material, often difficult to locate because embedded in the voyage and chorographical literature or contained in volumes bearing unfamiliar titles such as *The Present State of X* or *The Ancient and Present State of X* or *A Survey of X*, was an important part of the discourses of fact.

We briefly examine several examples to indicate the affinity of political reports with the "discourses of fact." We can trace an early, albeit rather undeveloped, stage of a kind of factually oriented "political science," or "social science," although no contemporary would have employed the term "science" for any descriptive treatment of human or natural phenomena or facts. "Science" was a term reserved for certain knowledge and causal explanation and was not applicable to the accumulation of even the most well established "matters of fact." Such "factual" political description might include first-person eyewitness accounts, the more or less reliable accounts of other contemporaries, and sometimes documentary or historical materials. As such it was subject to the same kind of evaluative criteria as other discourses of fact. Some political descriptions exhibit no obvious political agenda; others related to contemporary political controversy or matters of national interest.

Sir William Petty's unpublished "Method of Enquiring into the State of any Country" suggests the nature of the enterprise. Petty's concern with socioeconomic topics should be viewed as part of a larger enterprise, roughly comparable to Willughby's, Ray's, and Lister's concentration on fishes, birds, plants, and insects and in keeping with the Royal Society's articles of inquiry. Although for Petty the ideal political inquiry relied on firsthand observation assisted by the best maps and weights and measures, documentary materials such as chronicles and statutes were not to be neglected. The investigator was to inquire who held the legislative power and how the jurisdictions of the courts were distributed. It was necessary to examine economic matters such as highways, coach services, labor, agriculture, housing, population, rents, and prices. Observers were to report on money, interest rates, and banking arrangements as well as provisions for the sick and aged. Social and professional groups were to be described along with the most flourishing trades, typical recreations, and the pursuit of the arts and sciences. Attention was to be focused on the present prince, his strengths and weaknesses, and the nature of his friends and foes. State revenues and available military resources were of particular interest, as was information concerning who was feared and envied and what alliances and conflicts existed among powerful men. The observer-reporter was to record not only the names of the principal noble families and their aims but also to indicate the principal officers of state and reigning court beauties. What distinguishes Petty's scheme from others generated by the virtuosi was its "tilt" toward political and economic matters.[56] Many publications in the "survey" or "present state of X" format conformed roughly to Petty's "method," though few covered the full range of prescribed topics.

This kind of political description was of interest to Bacon and to Isaac Newton, who in 1668 recommended that travelers follow "general heads for inquiries and observations" along lines being promoted by the Royal Society.[57] Such directives were in keeping with the traditions of gentlemanly education. Both direct "experience" and vicarious experience provided by reading history were considered necessary for the politically engaged life. The general "experience" of the traveler, however, was not labeled "fact." Only when particular experiences were recounted to others did they become "matters of fact."

Edward Chamberlayne's frequently revised and often printed *Anglia notitia: or, The Present State of England*,[58] the most widely circulated collection of political "facts" in England, reveals the genre's distance from the later analysis of Montesquieu. A fellow of the Royal Society, Chamberlayne first considered the "ancient state" of England, relying heavily on legal writers from Glanvill, Bracton, Fortescue, and Stamford to Coke, Spelman, and Selden. His format for dealing with England's "present state" is the familiar chorographic model that provided a description of the current government and the courts of justice. His inclination, however, was to list officeholders rather than describe how particular offices or institutions functioned. This approach thus lacked the analytical or classificatory impulses characteristic of virtuosi reporting on natural phenomena. Analysis, comparison, and classification of natural phenomena, however, were typically done not by travelers themselves but by those such as Hooke, Boyle, or Ray, whose specialized interests or skills that allowed them to arrange "matters of fact" into larger analytical or classificatory schemes. Those engaged in political description exhibited few concerns beyond truthful reporting of "matters of fact."

Knowledge of European states was indebted to diplomatic reporting as well as chorographic and travel-related discourses. Machiavelli's reports to his Florentine superiors and the famous reports of the Venetian ambassadors provided important sixteenth-century examples. Political description, whether inspired by diplomacy, curiosity, or natural philosophy, advanced rapidly. By 1673 there already existed many works entitled "The Present State" of England, France, Italy, Holland, Venice, or Muscovy.[59] Nearly all such works included government as a standard topic.

Perhaps the most admired English practitioner of European political reporting was the diplomat Sir William Temple. His observations on the Netherlands (1673), which he described as an account of their "late Revolutions and Changes," was accompanied by the customary chorographic "Map of their State and Government."[60] Although France attracted some English attention, no notable descriptive work was produced by English observers.[61] The author of a fact-oriented political study of Italy typically noted, "Above all I must observe their Government, and if it be possible their mysteries of state, so I must endeavour to know the persons and qualifications of Princes and ministers of state." Because "first hand" information was best, he relied on his own "particular observations," that is, from "seeing and conversing" and only secondarily from reading.[62]

Descriptions of Denmark and Poland were often marked by contemporary concerns about the growth of royal absolutism and loss of "liberty." *The Present State of Denmark and Reflections upon the Ancient State Thereof*, which covered most of the standard chorographical topics, commented, "We are very much in the Dark as to the Government and Manners of those People."[63] In keeping with Petty's program, the author reported on royal revenues, the prerogative powers of the king, and the strength of the king and his armies. A la Chamberlayne, he included a catalog of principal families, royal officials, and councils.

Robert Molesworth's better-known *Account of Denmark*, though it adopted many elements of the chorographic survey, focused on Danish loss of liberty, the danger of recent French conquests, and the reprehensible doctrine of passive obedience.[64] Although Molesworth's "matters of fact" were collected from his "own Knowledge and Experience" or from "sensible grave Persons," one critic found him so biased that he concluded that Molesworth's "intention was to give us a Novel, . . . whereof of late years some have taken a priveledge to intermingle Truth with their own Inventions" rather than "a true and impartial Account of the present State of Denmark." Charges of fictionality implied that the work dealt not with "matters of fact" but with something closer to lies. Molesworth had not only ignored the examples of Temple and Burnet and the "rules of true History" but crossed the boundary from "fact" to the forbidden "fiction."[65]

Bernard Conner was a physician member of the Royal Society whose *History of Poland . . . [Its] Ancient and Present State* came somewhat closer to the approved model. A description of Poland was useful, Conner thought, "because the Form of Government . . . is in some respect like that of ours." Like Molesworth, Conner was concerned with the issues of royal absolutism and liberty. His account, he claimed, was gathered from what he had observed himself or from credible sources, those being "the most Intelligent Natives" and the "best Polish Authors." He discussed the forms of government, royal power, governmental revenues, and the court. Poland's famous elective kingship and its gentry are described as having "in time made a perfect Republic" in which ninety percent of the population were "no better than slaves to the gentry." The "unhappy State of Poland" was no model for England to follow.[66] Prescription and description were easily combined.

Most publications in the chorographical-descriptive mode treated governmental matters along with many others. Richard Blome's *Description of the World* (1670), sponsored by several members of the Royal Society, suggests the importance of political description in such multisubject accounts. Blome advised travelers to observe and record the types of law, their conformity to the nature of the people, who governs, the type of sovereign, and the mode of succession. Attention was also to be given to the character and aims of the ruler and his relations with his subjects, favorites, and the court as well as to state revenues and the strength of land and sea forces. Travelers were to compile information on the nature, causes, and success of wars, describe subordinate magistrates and the administration of state business, and record the chief officers of state, army, and navy. They should describe the criminal and civil legal system and the legal profession. Travelers were requested to keep a daily record of their observations and to report to friends regularly. Blome's instructions on governmental topics alone were so demanding that few would have had the time to complete his requirements.[67]

The reporter's "eyes and Senses" were to be his "guides and companions." "Reading and hear-say" were inferior. Political description served state policy because neither "Policy, or Management of the State" nor "Wars, Societies, or Leagues can be well made with a Foreign State or Kingdom" without "a perfect Knowledge of the disposition, Manners, Customs, Strength, etc of the Nation or People" in question.[68]

Some areas of the world were of greater political interest than others. Turkey, with its unique political and military traditions and strategic position, received attention throughout the seventeenth century. Sir Henry Blount's 1634 report, reprinted in 1669, promised to avoid the fictional methods of the "Utopians" who doted on "Phantastique supposals," and it reiterated the advantage of firsthand experience over secondhand or "book knowledge, . . . not dazled with any affectation, prejudicacy, or mist of education."[69] Paul Rycaut's *Present State of the Ottoman Empire* focused extensively, though not exclusively, on "Turkish Policy, Government, and Maxims of State." Rycaut, a member of the Royal Society, stressed his firsthand knowledge of Turkish politics, suggesting that his position as secretary to the Turkish ambassador positioned him "to penetrate farther into the Mysteries of this Politie" than others. His account of Turkish "maxims of state" was drawn from "the Mouth and Argument of considerable Ministers" or from his "own Experience and Considerations." Like most of those who participated in the discourses of fact, Rycaut promised to "deal truly and impartially, according to what I have seen and observed, and what hath been related to me by credible persons."[70] Rycaut's work, like that of Temple, was designed to be useful to the English government and was among the few that attempted to move from description to explanation.

Given the quantity of political description being accumulated, one might well ask why its practitioners so rarely engaged in the conjectures of historians or the classificatory efforts and hypotheses of the virtuosi. Part of the explanation may lie in satisfaction with preexisting classificatory systems. The ancient categories of monarchy, aristocracy, and democracy, in their good and perverted forms, as well as the category of mixed government and the distinction between absolute and limited monarchies, may have appeared adequate. Certainly the categories of classical political analysis were not subjected to the same kind of corrosive criticism as was ancient natural philosophy.

Other features of this genre also led away from analysis. Emphasis on recording particular matters of fact tended to yield lists of named officeholders. Such "directories" were no doubt useful, but they did not lend themselves to comparative, classificatory, or developmental treatment.[71] Another feature of the genre was its emphasis on unusual customs or institutions, a practice in keeping with the age's interest in "marvels" and "rarities." The intense focus on particular matters of fact thus had major weaknesses if viewed from the vantage point of later disciplinary development.

We should note that the intermingling of factual description and policy recommendations affected "natural history" as well as political description. John Evelyn's *Sylva* (1664), a pioneering work on forest trees which introduced forestry as a kind of science, advocated a conservation policy, and his *Fumifugium* (1661) described air pollution and offered measures to abate it. Descriptions of physical conditions of distant locales might be partnered with economic or political prescriptions. Increasingly, however, policy was discussed in the context of factual data. What we now call "economics" was clearly indebted to the newly elevated status of the factual. Sir William Petty and John Graunt, who were among the pioneers of economic and demographic analysis, were concerned with "matters of fact" relating to population, the coinage, trade, and public expenditures. These data were then used to produce statistical statements or placed in arguments concerning various political and economic projects. Policy recommendations were therefore sometimes treated as inferences from "matters of fact."[72]

This alliance between knowledge and policy was not unique to the new "factual" endeavors, however, having been repeatedly urged by Renaissance humanists. Humanist concern with useful knowledge was continued and elaborated by Bacon and his successors. But over time the "experience" referred to by Renaissance writers such as Machiavelli was given more precise meaning. Personal "experience" tended to become more specific and subject to verification. The accumulation of well-recorded "matters of fact" thus might provide the basis for sound policy.

Some "matters of fact" might be quantified. In Petty's *Political Arithmetick* sense-based matters of fact were expressed in "terms of number, weight and measure" and treated mathematically. Graunt's demographic findings were based on the recorded "bills of mortality."[73]

Ethnography

If well-reported "facts" were modifying the nature of political and economic knowledge, they also created a new body of knowledge dealing with the manners, customs, and religious practices of human populations, both foreign and domestic, familiar and exotic. Much of this information too was embedded in the chorographical-travel discourses. Here again we find ancient and Renaissance exemplars. It was the Spanish and Portuguese who led the way. Although ethnographic observation in England became closely connected to Baconian natural history and the efforts of the Royal Society, the tradition was also indebted to ambassadorial reports and to Hispanic accounts such as Joseph Acosta's *Naturall and Morall History of the East and West Indies*, which described the "Manners, Ceremonies, Lawes, Governments, . . . of the Indians."[74] Although the descriptions of Acosta and Bartolomé de las Casas emphasized what they saw with their own eyes,[75] Acosta was far more concerned than seventeenth-century English "ethnographers" with squaring his observations with Aristotelian and other ancient authority. The "moral history" terminology used by Acosta or the French "moeurs" to cover religion, superstition, customs, policy, and laws did not find an English cognate.[76] The absence of suitable terminology led to "matters of fact" concerned with cultural topics being subsumed under "natural history," "chorography," geography, travel, and works labeled the "Present State of. . . ." Because "natural history" later tended to exclude ethnography and the term "chorography" disappeared from common use, much early knowledge that might now be labeled anthropology or ethnography has until recently been largely ignored by later historians. Both descriptive anthropology and "political science" of a sort thus existed prior to their later "invention."[77]

Ethnographic description was a component of the "discourses of fact." Information on customary practices and religion was becoming as available, if not nearly as reliable, as "facts" of the plant and animal life, trade, and natural resources of an increasing number of European, Middle Eastern, Asian, and New World locales. The acquisition of ethnographic "matters of fact" was actively promoted by the Royal Society via its successive articles of inquiry. John Woodward, for example, instructed travelers to observe the "Tempers, Genius, Inclinations, Virtues, and Vices" of native inhabitants and to report on their traditions concerning the creation of the world and the Deluge. Inquiries must be made among local inhabitants as to beliefs about their origins as well as their religious doctrines and ceremonies. In addition, observers were to "get an account of their Laws, and Civil Government," language, learning, diet, agriculture, medicine, arts and sciences, manufactures, sports, weapons, that is, "all their Customs, Usages, both Religious, Civil and Military."[78]

This vast accumulation of data reported by English and European travelers, which lies scattered among the numerous and variously titled chorographic and travel accounts, has been relatively little studied. We do not as yet have an account of English contributions to cultural anthropology comparable either to the many analyses of the development of English natural history or to the anthropological work of sixteenth-century Spanish missionaries and explorers. Though there has recently been considerable interest in how colonial and exploited populations have been conceptualized, we still know remarkably little of the ethnographic studies of the early modern era or their role in multiplying the "discourses of fact."

Unlike the matters of fact concerning flora, fauna, and topography, ethnographic, religious, and cultural data available to late-seventeenth-century readers remained in its original form and was not subjected to analytic scrutiny. As we see shortly, comparison and analytic classification of plants and animals was not solely or even largely the work of the traveler-observer-explorer but was undertaken and refined by those who had become experts in one or another area of natural history. John Ray and Francis Willughby had become "experts" with respect to plants, birds, and fishes by using the observations and reports of others as well as their own. Robert Hooke did not personally observe earthquakes or volcanic eruptions, but his sustained interest and examination of well-established "facts" dealing with this category of natural phenomena made possible his contributions to "geology." Ethnographic "facts" found no English Willughby, Ray, Lister, or Hooke. The "grid" supplied by the ancient geographers and then by the Royal Society was being filled in for particular locales, but the cultural "facts," once collected and read, were largely ignored. Ethnographic reporters, unlike political writers, lacked an inherited classification system, although the categories Christian/non-

Christian, European/non-European, or perhaps the English and "other" provided minimal constructs. The emphasis on ethnographic "particulars" led neither to attempts at generalization nor to the sustained cumulative efforts characteristic of antiquarians, who frequently worked on the same artifacts over long periods of time. Although several modern disciplines in both the natural and human sciences shared a background in the seventeenth-century "discourses of fact," their later development did not always take a common path. Indeed, we should note that the tendency to focus on particulars and particular cultures continued even after the development of modern ethnography.

Conclusion

The discourses of fact, which encompassed both human and natural phenomena, past and present, were characterized by the belief that it was possible to establish reasonable belief in "matters of fact" when appropriate evidence and impartial witnesses were available. When the desired number of witnesses was unavailable, a situation not uncommon for travel reporters, it became even more necessary to rely on the character and honesty of a single, presumably impartial observer. What constituted the ideal observer during the seventeenth and early eighteenth centuries clearly involved visual acuity, social respectability and status, expertise, and lack of bias. Much depended on trust, but who was deemed trustworthy depended in part on circumstances.

Emphasis on "particular" things, practices, or events is characteristic of the discourses of fact. If the historian for the most part focused on the feats and actions of princes and military men and the virtuosi observed natural phenomena and experiments, the voyager and chorographer reported both human and natural "facts." The observations or experience they reported ideally were their own but in practice often relied in part on "credible relations." For those who could not travel themselves, the vicarious experience derived from travel accounts provided a valued, if imperfect, substitute, producing what Steven Shapin has called "virtual witnessing." Whatever authors claimed, the discourses of fact could not repudiate knowledge gained from books. After all, the reports of eyewitnesses were for the most part themselves delivered in written form and subsequently published. No one could have firsthand experience of everything.

Despite the possibility of error or deceit on the part of the chorographer and traveler, there was considerable, though not complete, confidence that matters of fact would be truly and faithfully reported and that it would, in most instances, be possible to distinguish matters of fact from fable and fiction, with respect to natural phenomena, human customs, and "adventures." Perhaps more than any of the other discourses of fact, travel reporting gave rise to elements of distrust. Thus travel reporting posed the greatest threat to the evolving discourses of fact. For if distrust was carried too far, all knowledge claims based on "matters of fact" would have become suspect and the disciplines of law, history, and the new empirical natural history might have disintegrated. The discourses of fact could not be sustained either by a thoroughgoing skepticism or by reference to infallible authorities. Nevertheless, chorographers and travel reporters seem to have earned a sufficient measure of that trust to have most, if not all, of their observations accepted as established "matters of fact."

Well-observed and well-reported matters of fact, however, led to quite different results in different disciplinary trajectories. Political and ethnographic description were not pursued as a means of laying the foundation for political science, moral philosophy, or anthropology in the same way as the Royal Society pursued the knowledge of natural "matters of fact" as the foundation for a new natural philosophy. "Facts" accumulated, and many were sorted into categories popularized by the Royal Society. Classificatory enterprises proved productive in some areas and less so in others. The classification schemes of the naturalists were built on the observations of many travelers over substantial periods of time as well as their own eyewitness observations. In the arena of "human facts" we see the collection of information unaccompanied by much desire to categorize or make use of these "facts" except in connection with immediate economic, diplomatic, or military policy.

What we have been observing is a vast enterprise devoted to the collection of "matters of fact" from all over the world. The desire for "facts" on an enormous range of topics grew rapidly, and the public avidly purchased the accounts of chorographers and travelers. Chorographical description and the reports of travelers, both close to home and far-flung, played a significant role in the creation of a "culture of fact," as travelers reported on a wide range of topics, physical and cultural. These rapidly expanding "discourses of fact," which intermixed reports of human and natural phenomena, thus played a significant role in the transfer of the category "fact," once solely applied to the domain of human action dealt with in the law courts or described in historical discourse, to the natural world, to natural events and things.

"News," "Marvels," "Wonders," and the Periodical Press

Having explored travel reporting and chorography, we turn to pamphlet "news" and the newspaper, genres that developed rapidly during the course of the seventeenth century.[1] I characterize "news" as still another "discourse of fact" of the early modern era and suggest how intellectual stances and modes of proof first associated with the law were assimilated into still another of the fact-oriented genres and disciplines. The emphasis on credible witnesses that developed in historiography, chorography, and travel writing is to be found in the news media as well. So are the emphasis on truth telling and impartiality, the rejection of fiction, and the distinction between a relation of matters of fact and commentary or conjecture on those facts. Another feature of "news" that we have encountered in other discourses is the emphasis on particulars. News involved an "event" or series of events, that is, particular occurrences rather than general experience. A news report might recount a battle but probably not a whole war. It might recount a crime or a trial but not examine the nature of murder or treason. Typically, "news" involved not only the recounting of a particular act or event but an unusual, strange, marvelous, important, or particularly interesting event. In 1621 Robert Burton indicated, "I hear new news every day, and those ordinary rumours of war, plagues, fires, inundations, thefts, murders, massacres, meteors, comets, spectrums, prodigies, apparitions, of towns taken, cities besieged in France, Germany, Turkey, . . . daily musters and preparations . . . which in these tempestuous times afford, battles fought, so many men slain, monomachies, shipwrecks, piracies and sea fights, peace, leagues, stratagems, and fresh alarums."[2]

The kind of facts that were most newsworthy were the political and military events of various wars, unusual human events such as heinous murders, and unusual natural occurrences such as comets, earthquakes, or great floods. More ordinary events might be reported, but they were not the staple of "news." The strange, the wondrous, or the consequential event, adequately evidenced by witnesses or suitable documentation, constituted the "news." The vogue for marvels, a Europe-wide phenomenon, influenced art, drama, and natural philosophy as well as the new news media. Both the "marvelous" and the "news" emphasized novelty and rarity, the bizarre and the strange.[3] The history of "news" and "facts" cannot be separated from the "wonders" and "marvels" of the age.

The English newspaper or newsbook was indebted to a variety of English and Continental predecessors. One of these was the diplomatic report. As we have seen, such reports shared characteristics with travel and chorographical accounts as well as the newly developing news genres. Private, handwritten newsletters dealing with diplomatic and economic information also developed in the sixteenth century. These newsletters, often carried by couriers, peddled "intelligence," that is, information concerning such recent events as the issuance of a papal indulgence, official proclamations, military feats, atrocities, and a variety of marvels and wonders.

Printed "news" appeared almost with the beginning of printing itself. The earliest English news pamphlet recounted the victory over the Scots on Flodden Field in 1513. The events of the Reformation whetted the appetite for news, and printing made for increasingly larger audiences. Heinrich Bullinger, the Zurich reformer, initiated the *Neue Zeitung*, compiled from his own correspondence. The development from letter to print was accomplished rather easily, although manuscript newsletters, which avoided formal licensing requirements, continued well into the eighteenth century. By 1589 the printed "Advertisements out of France" was providing information about royal and noble personages and military movements. In 1594 Cologne's *Mercurius Gallobelgicus* had an international audience.[4]

English news media initially lagged somewhat behind. Few printed news pamphlets emanated from England during the late sixteenth century, though occasional news pamphlets printed in London were to be found from about 1590. The Licensing Act prohibited all presses outside London, except at the universities, and required printed materials be published under a licensing system. Since foreign news was considered less disruptive than domestic, most early English news reporting concerned matters foreign. Even reports of extraordinary domestic occurrences such as the assassination of the duke of Buckingham were rarely printed.

Although English reports on recent occurrences often had designations or titles such as "Relation," "True Relation," or "True Report," the most frequent was "Newes." Many of these were translations providing "News from Rome," "News from Spain," or "News from France." Early English newsbooks frequently drew on foreign "corontos," which provided short accounts of foreign news, especially news of the Thirty Years War. Another forerunner of the mid-seventeenth-century newsbook was the "news" shouted or hawked by town criers and, after the development of printing, increasingly produced and distributed in broadside form. Largely non-political, broadsides tended to report the unusual, the "monstrous," and the sensational. Strange animals, unusual weather, "monstrous" human or animal births, criminal behavior, or accounts of witchcraft were among the most common items of broadside "news" hawked on the streets of London. Like the modern tabloid, these broadsides emphasized crime, violence, and wonderful cures. The sensational or "strange but true" were staples of broadside news and newsbooks.[5]

The appetite for "factual" accounts of the unusual or sensational seemed boundless. Even the briefest survey of early printed books reveals hundreds of titles like "Strange and miraculous news from . . . ," "Strange and terrible news from . . . ," "Strange and True news from . . . , "A Strange and Wonderful Account of . . . ," "Strange and wonderful news from . . . ," "A Strange but true Account of . . . ," A True Relation of . . . ," "A True Account of . . . ," "An Exact and True Account of . . . ," "An Exact and Faithful Relation of. . . ." Many of these newsworthy events were explicitly designated "matters of fact" and publications reported particular events and deeds supported in the ways that "facts" were supported in court or by the historiographer.

By the late sixteenth century broadside "news" was beginning to be characterized by the conventions for establishing "fact" or "matters of fact" that we have seen elsewhere. There was an emphasis on identifying the precise time and place of the event and on providing proof by credible witnesses. One early example, *A Most True and marvelous straunge wonder, the lyke hath seldom ben seene, of xvii Monstrous fisshes, taken from Suffolke, at Downame brydge, within myle of Pisidik. the xi day of October,* a 1558 broadside, not only provided great detail but the names of those who had caught the fish. Another, *The Description of a rare or rather most monstrous fish, taken on the East cost of Holand the XVII or November, Anno 1566,* included the names of the English witnesses and noted that the rare catch had been publicly displayed and thus witnessed by many. From the earliest news reporting we can already see the "who, how, what, where, and when" mentality associated with the modern newspaper story.

Reports of such unusual sightings and events were frequently embedded in a religious framework and used to illustrate God's Providence or provide timely warnings to the sinful. The "perfect and true description" of the Suffolk fish proclaimed the "strange and marvelous handye workes of the Lord," and *The Description of a monstrous Pig* (1562) suggested "strange and monstrous thinges" were sent by God.[6] Great storms, earthquakes, comets, and monstrous births continued to provide moral instruction throughout the seventeenth century.

"Strange News from" or "Strange and wonderful news from" here or there might also be treated as events of "natural history." The Great Plague of the Restoration era was simultaneously "news" reported in the press, a subject treated by scholars as part of the natural history of disease, and a sign of God's displeasure. News reports of natural phenomena came to share the conventions for establishing matters of fact found in writings on natural history.

John Wilkins explicitly listed a number of genres, including "Diary," "Diurnal," and "Gazet," among the numerous genres "relating to matter of fact."[7] Although most events constituting "news" were of human making or involved human beings, the news reports of unusual natural events were one of several vehicles that helped transfer the category "fact" from human events and actions to natural phenomena.

Many news stories were validated by claims of eyewitness reports and references to "credible" and eyewitness testimony. Many reports from the latter part of the seventeenth century were also accompanied by statements directing readers to repair to a particular place, typically an inn or coffeehouse, where they could meet with an eyewitness or view appropriate testimonials and documentation.

We are concerned here less with the single broadside or pamphlet and more with the serial newsbook, which attempted, on a fairly regular basis, to provide brief accounts of numerous miscellaneous events of interest. For our purposes, the most important feature of this genre is the claim to present true and impartial narrations of "matters of fact."

From its inception, printed news had a dual character. On the one hand, it claimed to present the truth of "fact" rather than unsubstantiated rumor, fiction, or outright lies. At the same time, editors and promoters, however much they proclaimed their loyalty to truth, more often than not were motivated by partisan political goals and commercial interests in the sensational. The serial newsbooks, which grew by leaps and bounds with the end of the government's ability to suppress unlicensed printing, were unambiguously political. It was never difficult to distinguish a Royalist from a Parliamentarian journal, or later a Whig from a Tory paper, despite repeated claims of impartiality. Because our concern here is with the development of the concept "fact" and the values and procedures surrounding it, we do not concern ourselves much with the genre's partisan aspects, concentrating instead on how journalists presented and organized their "news." We focus on claims to factuality, truth, and impartiality, realizing that these values were more often enunciated than realized. But these very claims helped create and develop an audience that desired "facts" concerning the "news" and appropriate evidence for confirming it.

The newsbook developed with extraordinary rapidity during the civil war and Interregnum era as government control of printing broke down and audiences anxiously awaited domestic, political, and military news. Newsbooks became a mainstay of the coffeehouse, itself an important institution for the transmission and discussion of both "news" and "rumour." The newsbooks of the era were ubiquitous, at least in London. By one count there were 320 serial publications between 1641 and 1655.[8] This rapidly growing appetite for news was satisfied by a sometimes bewildering proliferation of newsbooks that provided information on the activities of Parliament, the events in Scotland, the victories or defeats of Royalist and Parliamentarian armies, and the various religious and sectarian successes and failures. Although the number of newsbooks dropped off sharply as Cromwellian and then Restoration governments reasserted government controls, the civil war and Interregnum experience with this new genre played a significant role in familiarizing the English both with the concept of fact and with the physical and intellectual difficulties of providing what was considered adequate and impartial testimony of the facts purportedly presented to readers.

Nigel Smith has suggested that two different kinds of journalism emerged during this era, one that plainly expressed fact, the other a bantering, ridiculing, and polemic variety. He also suggests that the closing of the theaters deflected theatergoing audiences from viewing fictional actions and deeds to reading about the actual deeds of political and military actors,[9] thus encouraging interest and appreciation of "real" as opposed to "fictional" facts and underlining the distinction between the two. These developments help explain the expanding audience for the "discourses of fact" which characterized the revolutionary and subsequent generations. The political upheavals of the civil war and Interregnum decades provided the opportunity for a new kind of factually based news reporting and attracted a substantial readership whose appetite for such reporting would extend to other discourses of fact as well.

Here I attempt to characterize the goals and values expressed by the civil war and Interregnum press as well as to show that these aims are representative of the "discourses of fact" more generally. These values were most systematically enunciated in the periodical titles. The newsbooks claimed to be purveyors of "truth." Thus we have *A True and Perfect Informer*, *A True and Perfect Journal*, *True Diurnal Occurrences*, *A True Diurnal*, *A True Relation of the Affaires of Europe*, *An Exact and True Collection*, *An Exact and True Diurnal*, the *True Informer*, *A True Diurnall*, and *Mercurius Honestus. Or, Tom Tell-truth*.

One editor noted, "I intend . . . to encounter falsehood with the sword of truth. I will not endeavour to flatter the world into a belief of things that are not; but truly inform them of things that are." Another insisted he would represent things "as they really shall happen."[10] Richard Collings in 1644 noted, "I am resolved hereafter to give you an accompt (though briefly) of every particular thing of note. . . . it shall be [my purpose] to enlarge a Truth or confirme it where it is certain, as neer to the best and most certaine Intelligence can direct me."[11] Truth was not always easy to obtain. "There were never more pretenders to Truth than in this Age, nor ever fewer that obtained it. It is no easie matter in such of variety of actions and opinions to deliver exactly to the world the proceedings of these present times, which, . . . [require] sound judgment, . . . [and] extraordinary Intelligence."[12] Echoing the maxim frequently voiced by seventeenth-century naturalists and experimenters, one editor noted, "Truth is the daughter of Time. Relations of Battels, fights . . . and other passages and proceedings of concernment are not alwaies to be taken or credit at the first hand, for that many times they are uncertaine, and the truth doth not so conspicuously appear till a second or third relation. And hence it is that histories sometimes fall much short of the general expectations, and battles oftentimes prove but skirmishes, and great overthrowes related to be given to the enemy prove often times equal ballancing losse on both sides."[13] Truth was the goal, but it was not always easy or quick to obtain and sometimes required correction or revision. There was an emphasis on correction of error.

Fidelity in the reporter was crucial. We thus have the *Faithfull Intelligencer*, *Mercurius Fidelicus*, the *Faithful Post*, and the *Faithful Scout* as well as the *Kingdomes Faithfull and Impartiall Scout*. One newsbook would "truly and Faithfully represent" the activities of Parliament, another insisted on the "sincerity" of its reports and relations.[14] We have seen the same emphasis on fidelity and sincerity in witness testimony presented in the courtroom and in the code of the historian. We will encounter it again when we examine the norms of the natural historian. Faithful reporting was a constituent part of the discourses of fact.

Like all the discourses of fact, newspapers distinguished their offerings from fiction. The *Weekly Account* promised to present news "without any gilded glossings, invented fictions, or flattering Commentaries." The editor of the *Moderate Intelligencer* insisted, "I am no Romance-Monger to present the world with Tragi-Comedies of my own invention." Rivals were criticized for deluding readers with "stories or tales" and "fictionate observations" rather than "relations." "What more acceptable service could be done," queried the *London Courant*, a Restoration periodical, "then to rescue Truth . . . from the Pretensions of Supposition and Fictions." That paper would represent things "as they really shall happen."[15]

The faithful, the exact, the certain, and the perfect are also contrasted to rumor, common fame, and "hearsay," terms familiar to the courtroom and to the historian. John Wilkins contrasted narrations of matter of fact with rumor, hearsay, and common fame, all terms particularly associated with the law.[16] Some newspapers labeled rumors as such, others did not. One distinguished "Certain Intelligence" from rumor. Another noted that unconfirmed news was "begotten of ayre and some thinne appearances... like so many clouds which doe hang upon the evening of truth."[17] Robert Burton noted, "One rumor is expelled by another; every day almost comes new news unto our ears, as how the sun was eclipsed, meteors seen in the air, monsters born, prodigies, how the Turks were overthrown in Persia, and earthquake in Helvetia, Calabria, Japan, or China, an inundation in Holland. ... All of which we do hear at first with a kind of admiration, ... but by and by they are buried in silence."[18]

Because rumor was so common, many of the newsbooks advertised themselves as intending "To Prevent Misinformation."[19] In 1680 a government proclamation demanded that "all News Printed and Published to the People," both foreign and domestic, should be "agreeable to Truth, or at least Warranted by good Intelligence," so that the kings' subjects "may not be disturbed or amused by Lyes or vain Reports."[20]

Because editors and publishers were not themselves eyewitnesses to the events reported, they attempted to assure their readers that their accounts rested on reliable sources. "Our Letters from Madrid, bearing the date the 6th past, say ...," "From Cadiz they write ...," "By Letters from Tangier, we are given to understand ...," or "'Tis writ by a very good hand from Surat that ..." were some of the reassurances offered. Typical also are "Some letters from Warsaw ... confirm ...," "Our letters from Germany tell us ...," and "The newes ... was this day also verified and confirmed by some Letters ... with the additions of some particulars which before we had not, and the access of new occurrences which before we knew not." The *Intelligencer* noted of the activities of the Dutch in Newfoundland, "There has been a further inquiry made into particulars, which are formally attested by several credible persons that were upon the place and sensible witnesses of the whole story." Such phrasing, typical from the time of the earliest corontos, remained a characteristic feature of news reporting throughout the seventeenth and early eighteenth centuries. "I acquaint you with nothing but is extracted out of true and credible Originals, that is to say either Letters of justifiable information, or Corantos published in other Countries."[21]

Domestic news was similarly identified: for example, "From Reading it was this day certified ...," "It is advertised from London ...," or "This day it was confirmed for certaine, as before doubtfully reported, that ..." The *Perfect Diurnal* noted, "You may henceforth expect from this relator to be informed only of such things as are of credit, and of some part of the proceedings of one or both houses of Parliament fit to be divulged, or such other news as shall be certified by Letters from the Army, and other part, from persons of speciall trust. " *Mercurius Britanicus* at one point printed a letter as "a clear Evidence and Confirmer of the Truth."[22] Because the most frequent source for domestic news during the civil war years was Parliament, it was relatively easy to detect reporting errors. Several civil war and Interregnum newsbooks were largely devoted to reporting the "Weekly Passages" in Parliament.

Sometimes tentative language was employed. A printed report might be accompanied by a qualifying statement such as, "But the advice not coming from a constant hand, we must expect the certainty hereafter." One publication offered a second relation "more compleat than the former."[23] Tentativeness was often indicated simply by "'Tis said" or "It is reported." Occasionally, previously reported doubtful news was later "confirmed for certaine." Sources were summarized in the interest of brevity. Only rarely were they directly quoted. Richard Collings in 1644 promised, "I am resolved . . . to give you an accompt (though briefly) of every particular thing of noat. . . . it shall be [my purpose] to enlarge a Truth or confirme it where it is certain, as neare to the best and most certaine Intelligence can direct me."[24] Collings was sensitive to the difficulties in accurately reporting news. "And indeed in many Papers there have been such apparent contradictions and such a thwarting of the truth by an endeavour to inlarge the story, that whiles the Reader turns Sceptick and finds he hath reason to suspect, hee therefore doth draw often unto himself a wilde conclusion and will believe anything."[25] His reports, from "honest hands," were neither "defective or excessive."[26]

Some newsbooks emphasized their aggressiveness in searching out news. Adopting the midcentury familiarity with military scouts or spies, papers took titles such as the *Faithfull Scout*, the *Impartial Scout*, and the *Kingdoms Faithfull Scout*. Both "scout" and "spy" emphasize the discovery as well as the transmission of the matters of fact reported.[27]

Like others engaged in the discourses of fact, news reporters and editors insisted on impartiality. Here again titles are revealing. We have not only the *Impartial Intelligencer*, the *Impartial Scout*, and the extremely short-lived *Mercurius Impartialis* but the *Moderate. Impartially communicating martial affairs . . .* , the *Faithfull Scout, Impartially communicating . . .* as well as the *Faithful Post. Impartially communicating. . . .* Although the norm of impartiality was frequently voiced, distortion was common and the distinction between reporting and laying out a reformist program was sometimes blurred. The press, which reported "occurants" or "occurances," also transformed this term into the titles of newsbooks.

The repetitious and overlapping terminology to be found in the names of the newsbooks underscores the value placed on truthfulness, fact, exactitude, impartiality, and fidelity. The new news media reported political, diplomatic, and military facts in the sense of human actions and activities of the very recent past, but they also reported material facts such as fires, earthquakes, and natural anomalies. The development of new media both added to the growing repertoire of factual discourses and with chorography provided a bridge between the older notion of fact as a human action and the newer notion of fact as data about both human *and* natural phenomena.

The terms "Intelligence" and "Intelligencer" are frequently to be found in seventeenth-century periodical publications and provide another signpost of the linkages between "news" and the other discourses of fact.[28] "Intelligence" or information could be of many sorts, foreign or domestic, military or civil, or even philosophical. Reporting on his Swedish embassy, Sir Bulstrode Whitelocke used "intelligence" and "news" interchangeably.[29] Philosophic "intelligencers," Samuel Hartlib, Henry Oldenburg, and Sir Hans Sloane, gathered and distributed news and information about natural phenomena, manufacturing processes, and related topics. Oldenburg provided Robert Boyle with "weekly intelligence" of both state and philosophical news.[30]

The "intelligence" Oldenburg received from both foreign and domestic virtuosi was considered essential to building the foundation for natural history. Just as private news genres such as diplomatic reports had been transformed into public, printed, commercial forms, private philosophical "intelligence" was transmuted into a publicly sold, printed, commercial form. Oldenburg created the *Philosophical Transactions* out of his own intelligence network and the observations and experiments emanating from the newly founded Royal Society. Like other news provided in serial format, it was designed to disseminate "news" and provide income for its editor. The first issues contained digested news items similar to those of the newsbook. Only later did it expand to include authors' own reports and book reviews. Hobbes complained that natural philosophy was now being "learned out of their Gazets." The *Journal des Sçavans*, the publication of the French Academy of Science, too was labeled a "new sort of Gazette."[31]

If "intelligence" was the raw material, what emerged was typically labeled "reports," "relations," or "narrations," which were contrasted with "stories," "tales," or fictions. What was reported was sometimes called "Occurances," sometimes "news," and sometimes "matters of fact." In the eighteenth century "matter of fact" was commonly replaced by the more familiar "fact."[32]

The appropriate reporting style for news, like most discourses of fact, was to be plain and unadorned. Joseph Frank, the historian of the civil war and Interregnum press in England, has likened the style of the Interregnum newspaper to the plain style advocated by Thomas Sprat, the historian and apologist of the Royal Society. Many editors promised to avoid "tart language" and stick to "simply a narration of affairs," though, as anyone who has read these publications knows, most widely missed the mark. *Mercurius Civicus*, like many contemporary historians, emphasized the paper's intention of searching out the "naked Truth" and promised to avoid "Rhetoricall Flourishes."[33]

At least in principle, the news media distinguished reports of matters of fact from editorial comments on them. The earliest "Strange but true" broadsides distinguished the matter of fact report from the religious messages that might be inferred from those facts. The practice of segregating facts or news from commentary was formalized in the midcentury *Aulicus* and the *Mercurius Politicus*. The latter's "opinion" sections were chatty and blatantly partisan, more akin to the productions of the modern columnist than the reporter. Unlike the accounts of facts, these portions of the paper were loaded with pejorative adjectives and figurative language. For several months, the *Mercurius Politicus* explored the principles of political authority and obedience before presenting the news reports of the day. Although such commentary was indistinguishable from partisan pamphlet discussion of the same issues, the editor nevertheless attempted to segregate his witty, opinionated comments and theoretical musings from the news reports.[34] *A Modest Narrative of Intelligence Fitted for the Republique of England and Ireland* (1649) presented fairly straightforward factual accounts in some issues and opinionated discussions in others. The post-1688 *Present State of Europe: or the Historical and Political Mercury* was divided into "Advice," that is, news reports from particular foreign states, and "Reflections upon the Advice." The *Currant Intelligence*, a publication of the 1680s, promised to limit itself to foreign and domestic news "without any reflections upon either persons or things, giving only that are matter of fact." In 1702 the *Daily Courant* too promised not to "give any Comments or Conjectures" and "relate only Matter of Fact."[35]

We have already seen that historians were divided on the question whether or not it was appropriate to engage in both reporting facts and speculating on causes and explanations and distinguished "matter of fact" from "opinion," "reflections," and "inference." As we shall see shortly, natural historians too were divided as to how to relate matters of fact to speculation and hypotheses relating to "facts." Editors and readers of the "news" were familiar with the distinction between facts and commentary, and some editors, like some historians and some naturalists, tended to view going beyond the facts as legitimate while others did not.

Claims of truthfulness, credibility, accuracy, and impartiality were frequently contested—most commonly by competitors and political opponents. Claims of impartiality were ridiculed as party slogans, and proclaimed accuracy was scorned as inaccuracy or worse. Rivals were accused of relying on rumor and hearsay and departing from the truth by means of hyperbole, exaggeration, or outright lies. Some editors were said to have served up "frivolous fallacies related with intention to deceive," to have deluded the "ignorant and simple," or to have provided "redundancy of stories of tales" rather than truthful "relations." One was accused of encouraging the reader to "draw unto himself a wilde conclusion and believe anything."[36] Some editors roundly condemned others, often in picturesque and blatantly partial language. "But harke ye, thou mathematicall liar, that framest lies of all dimensions, long broad and profound lies, and then displyed the botcher, the quibling pricklouse every weeke in tacking and sticking them together. . . . thou art a knowne notorious odious forger. . . . This is the truth not railing."[37] If its rivals were accused of providing "a weekly cheat," the *Mercurius Aulicus* claimed it would "proceed with all truth and candor."[38] Competition and politics undermined the stated values of the news press from the beginning.

Censure and criticism came in a variety of forms. Mock journals satirized the media.[39] Ben Jonson's "Staple of News" satirized the inventions and falsehoods of the new news genre as early as 1625, and Royalist poet John Cleveland lambasted the parliamentary press in a series of "Characters." Focusing on deficiencies caused by the genre's brevity, he described the newspaper in relation to history as "a puny Chronicle, scarce pinfeather'd with the wings of time: It is a History in Sippet; the English Iliads in a Nutshell; . . . far remov'd from an Annal; for it is of Extract: onely of the younger House, like a Shrimp to a Lobster."[40] His comments nevertheless suggest the kinship of the compressed "news" and the more extended "history."[41] That kinship would remain as long as the model history was viewed as the product of firsthand observation.

A good deal of scholarly attention has been given to the newspaper of the civil war and Interregnum era, largely because that was the era of its creation and because it has been assumed that the post-Restoration press, again controlled by the government, is of less interest. Yet the newspapers of the latter portion of the century, and especially those published between 1679 and 1682, elaborated the themes of their progenitors and continued to cater to the appetite for news. Restoration newspapers continued to emphasize commitment to truth, credible sources, factuality, and impartiality, though most were arms of the government or partisan publications. Diplomatic and military reports from abroad were still prominently featured and were the staple of the official *Gazette*'s offerings.[42] These were presented as coming from reliable sources, and as earlier, there was frequent emphasis on the source and credibility of reported "matters of fact." "We are credibly informed that the Spanish Embassador is earnest in securing Flanders from invasion by the French King"; "By Letters from Tangier, we are given to understand. . . ." Also as earlier, the actual reporters were not usually identified.

Domestic news broadened somewhat to include routine and apolitical information such as lists of assize judges going on circuit and notices of who was preaching before the king. Occasionally, there are descriptions of public disturbances, such as a march of some eight hundred apprentices to destroy houses of ill fame.[43] Financial news became common in the late seventeenth century, and after 1695 the press routinely provided regular information on political, ecclesiastical, legal, naval, military, and civil appointments. Sensational crime news was common. Highway robbery, assaults, burglaries, murders, and suicides were becoming typical fare, as were the more routine crimes tried at the Old Bailey.[44] Like "marvels," such topics might be offered briefly or more extensively in broadside or short pamphlet. The *Account of the Proceedings to Judgment against Thomas Saxton* (Saxton was convicted of perjury against Lord Delemere) just as easily could have been carried as a news item in the periodical press. Reportage of the sensational murder of Sir Edmondberry Godfrey appeared both in brief newspaper format and in more extended accounts.[45] The ability to rapidly reproduce sensational and lurid reports expanded the production and diffusion of the discourses of fact.

Although the licensed press was generally chary of discussing domestic political news, dramatic trials, political and otherwise, were reported.[46] Grand jury proceedings against Shaftesbury and other Whigs during the height of the Exclusion crisis were well covered, as was the impeachment of Judge Scroggs. Trial accounts for treason and other crimes might be labeled *A True and Impartial Account of the Arraignment, Tryal, Examination, Confession and Condemnation of X* or *A True and Perfect Narrative of the Tryal and Acquitment of Y.* A good many of the treason trials were reported verbatim or close to it, eventually finding their way into the collection of state trials. One rather typical account claimed to have been "published impartially by an Earwitness, to quash false Reports."[47] Although forbidden to report parliamentary debates, the press printed Whig petitions directed at Parliament as well as the "Addresses" of their Tory opponents. However partisan the *Observator* might have been, it insisted that "the Matter of Fact" it reported was "Evident and Certain," claiming "the most shameless of [its] . . . Enemies, could never lay a Finger yet, upon any One Falseity of Fact." Roger L'Estrange, the author of this vituperative Tory publication, insisted that what was most "necessary was thus to Learn out the Truth of the Fact."[48] Presumably, some facts might prove false.

The Restoration press, like its predecessors, was anything but impartial, but it too enunciated and publicized the assumptions and rhetoric common to the discourses of fact. The editor of the *Loyal Protestant, and True Domestick Intelligencer* denounced false reporters and "Imposters" who "impudently obtrude upon the People."[49] Restoration-era newspapers too insisted on the truthfulness and impartiality of their accounts as well as the deceptiveness and partisanship of their rivals. The combination of factuality and partisanship was endemic in reporting political news.

The news media treated a wide range of events as "matters of fact" but also employed the legal sense of the term "fact." One account noted that the criminal had been condemned "to suffer for the Fact," that is, the deed or act he had committed. Another reported of a murder that "the Fact was done in a field." Still another report of a trial indicated that "the fact was excellently opened, was fully Prov'd," and "so soon as he had done the Fact, he fled, and a Hue and Cry" followed.[50] Newspapers thus familiarized readers with the "fact" as used in law at the same time they employed the concept "fact" in other contexts and with broader meanings.

The news broadside, news pamphlet, and periodical newspaper all continued to cultivate readers' appetites for sensational news. Reports of fires, shipwrecks, and piracy, the "last dying speeches" of criminals, and the bills of mortality all appeared in short and more extensive formats.

The boundaries between the various discourses of fact were often blurred. News and history overlap in such writings as *Sad and dreadful News from New-England, being a true Relation of the Barbarous cruelty lately committed by the Spaniards upon the English*, which treats of events occurring over a considerable period of time. In the typical fashion of factual reporting, it portrayed itself as "being an unquestionable Truth, attested before the magistrates of Boston in New England . . . impartially relate[d] matter of Fact." Dubious readers were advised to consult the named witnesses.[51] Such "matters of fact" were "verified" by multiple witnesses as they often were in the other discourses of fact. *Strange News from Virginia; being a full and True Account of the Life and Death of Nathanial Bacon . . . with a full Relation of all the Accidents which have happened in the late War there between the Christians and Indians* was another work lying between news and history.[52]

Titles beginning a "True History" or a "True Account" also alert us to the overlap between factually oriented history and "news." One periodical indicated the importance of "true Memorials of our present affairs to all succeeding generations," so that "Posteritie may see the truth of their forefathers actions."[53] John Rushworth, the author of *Historical Collections*, also published the *Perfect Diurnal*, an important civil war newsbook. Firsthand news reports were roughly equivalent to the historian's "memorials." The distinction between the news account and the historical account was often simply one of length. In this connection we might recall Cleveland's satirical depiction of news accounts as historical miniatures, in which the news was characterized as a shrimp compared to the historical lobster. In his *Portugal History: or, a Relation of the Troubles that happened in the Court of Portugal* Samuel Pepys noted that although his readers "cannot but have heard something of the Story from Reports or Public Gazetts," he would "more amply and truly ma[ke] known the whole Transaction of it."[54]

For others, however, history was not simply a longer or fuller account but a more elevated endeavor. As Laurence Eachard put it in 1725, "the Business of an Historian is not barely to tell his Reader a true and faithful Story, which is the Office of a Gazetteer and Journalist; but he ought withal insensibly to instruct him, . . . not so much to lead his Memory, as to enrich his Understanding, to elevate his Thoughts, and even to captivate his Affections."[55]

The "compleat Historian," whose "perfect Work" was "justly rank'd with the greatest of all Human Undertakings," was rarely to be found, and most who claimed the title of historian belonged to the "lower Class" of annalists, biographers, and authors of "particular Descriptions."[56] This "lower class" of historians seems to merge imperceptibly with that of the journalist.

Bills of mortality reporting weekly the deaths in and around London also could take on a historical dimension. John Graunt, suggesting that the bills constituted "news" for their original readers, collected and published all the bills for 1665 to form a statistical history of the plague year. C. John Sommerville suggests that the bills together with the periodical publication of commercial items such as commodity prices and exchange rates were important in establishing news as a discourse of "mundane factuality."[57]

We also see the blurring of disciplinary boundaries and the overlap among the discourses of fact when we put the news media's attention to unusual natural phenomena alongside the natural histories of the virtuosi and some of the writings of theologians. Contemporary wonders and marvels were news to the periodical publisher, providential events with moral implications to the preacher and theologian, and, to the virtuoso, the subject of reports offered to the Royal Society and in the *Philosophical Transactions*.

Unusual cloud formations, comets or blazing stars, storms, frosts, and other natural events continued to be newsworthy. A typical report was *Strange News from the West, being a true and perfect Account of several Miraculous Sights . . . on Thursday last, being the 21 day of this present March, by diverse persons of credit standing on London Bridge between 7 and 8 of the Clock at Night. Two great Armies marching forth of two Clouds, and encountering each other, but after a sharp dispute they suddenly vanished. . . .*[58] As so often in the discourses of fact, events were verified by the testimony of credible witnesses. Another report, *Strange News from Barkshire, or an Apparition of Several Ships in the Air, which seemed to be Fighting,* again emphasizes the particularities of time and place and suggests that readers might be "fully satisfied . . . of the truth" at the Sarazen's Head in Carter Lane. The practice of referring readers to witnesses or to corroborating documents retained at particular inns or coffeehouses was becoming increasingly common. Although the author refused to prognosticate on the meaning of the cloud formation, he insisted that his report was not the "fancy of a whimsical Brain." It was impossible for six persons in perfect health and sound memory to be erroneous in matters of this kind.[59] The language of "full satisfaction" was commonly utilized in both news accounts and jury instructions.

Verification by credible witnesses had become a practice common to all the discourses of fact. We thus have *A True and Perfect Account of a Strange and Dreadful Apparition which lately Infested and Sunk a Ship bound for Newcastle called the Hope-well of London*. This report, which emphasized the particularities of the occurrence, was "attested by nine men more, all belonging" to the ship.[60]

Many of these reports utilized the concept "fact" with its accompanying proof by witnesses. Thus the description of a comet, *The Wonderful Blazing Star: with the Dreadful Apparition of Two Armies in the Air*, emphasized the abundance of eyewitnesses.[61] Typical of the genre was *A True and Perfect Narrative of the Great and Dreadful Damages Susteyned . . . by the late Extraordinary Snows*, a report of two-pound hailstones.[62] The fairly cautious *True Protestant Mercury* reported:

> We had last Week an Account of a strange and terrible Apparition seen in the Air at Exeter, but being very cautious not to emit anything but matters of Truth and far from any intent to disturb people with a noise of fictitious Prodigies, we then forebore to mention; But hearing that the same is since confirmed and attested by persons of unquestionable Credit, we shall now give it the Reader in the very Words wherein it was communicated to us. . . . Tuesday night last, several Credible and Intelligent Persons, retir[ed] into a convenient place . . . to view the appearance of the Blazing Comet which very dreadfully dilated itself in the Western part of the Heavens. . . . As we were discoursing our several Conjectures upon its Portents, on the sudden we beheld very perspicuous in the Air two voluminous Clouds . . . plainly discovered itself to be an Army of Souldiers engaged in a terrible battle lasting half an hour. This strange sight caused in all of us Amazement and Astonishment: and I do not Write this as a rumour or Hear-say, but it was Visible to my self, and some hundreds of People besides. So that it can sufficiently be attested as being certainly True as Dreadful.[63]

Here we see the emphasis on firsthand observation, the corroboration of witnesses, and the rejection of hearsay that we have encountered in connection with the law and travel reporting and will encounter still again in the discourse of the scientific community.[64]

Daniel Defoe's *Storm, or, A collection of the most Remarkable Casualities and* disasters which happen'd in the Late Dreadful Tempest (1704) and A Wonderful History of all the Storms and Hirricanes, Earthquakes &c That have happen'd in England for above 500 Years Past (1704) show that a taste for this kind of material continued into the eighteenth century. Defoe explicitly associated these accounts with history, noting that it was the historian's duty to "convey matter of fact" with its "Vouchers" so that thus "confirm'd," it would "pass all manner of question." He would therefore "no where . . . Trespass upon Fact."[65]

Reports of great storms, hurricanes, and frosts also appeared in the *Philosophical Transactions*, itself a periodical news journal, and in the correspondence of its "intelligencer," Henry Oldenburg. Methods of substantiating those events were the same for the virtuoso and the newsman. If Robert Hooke complained that the *Gazette*'s report of an earthquake in the Antilles was too short, he nevertheless found it sufficient to "illustrate and confirm" his "Conjectures" on earthquakes. Earthquakes, for Hooke as well as for the news media, were "matters of fact."[66] Nathaniel Crouch and John Aubrey relied on the *Gazette* for facts on earthquakes, and Robert Boyle used accounts of barometric observations from "the late Gazettes" as scientific data.[67] At least some newspaper accounts were treated as trustworthy accounts of "matters of fact."

The recording of marvels and unusual natural phenomena was itself part of Bacon's natural history program and remained an aspect of the Royal Society's research program. Bacon's guidelines for the recording of marvels required the identification and evaluation of witnesses' testimony and the rejection of hearsay. Sir William Petty suggested that travelers to foreign locales report "monstrous or prodigious Productions and Accidents."[68]

Among post-Restoration news accounts we find "true Narration given under several persons Hands . . . of a most Strange and Prodigious Opening of the Earth" out of which arouse a dreadful apparition. "It is farther Credibly reported, as an Evidence of the truth of this Narrative," that several gentlemen as well as friends and neighbors corroborated the initial report. Dubious readers were advised to repair to a designated London bookseller who possessed the report.[69]

Monstrous births continued to be of interest both to newspaper readers and to the members of the Royal Society. Increasingly, such reports were supported with the witness proofs associated with matters of fact. When the *Mercurius Politicus* reported a monstrous birth in the Low Countries, it emphasized that it had been "attested by persons of quality and learning" whose "Names are Underwritten, Doctors of Physick, Surgeons, and Apothecaries." Those present at the dissection of the joined-together twins "do verifie the particulars of this Relation." Robert Boyle reported to Oldenburg about a case of joined triplets observed by a physician well known as "an Excellent Occulist." On receiving the news from Oldenburg, the Royal Society requested "double attestation" of two physicians.[70] Boyle kept lists of "Strange Reports" of natural wonders as well as an "Outlandish Book" of strange occurrences. For Boyle, "Matters of fact extraordinary" and "Prodigies," if attested "but by slight and ordinary Witnesses, . . . would be judg'd incredible," but he insisted that "we scruple not to believe them, when the Relations as attested with such Circumstances as make the Testimony as strong as the things attested are strange."[71]

Further overlap between news reporting and the scientific interest in the "marvelous" can be found in connection with the sensational and seemingly miraculous cures of Valentine Greatrakes, which were reported in the *Intelligencer* and also attracted serious attention from a considerable portion of the medical and scientific community.[72] If the category of the preternatural, of such great interest to the sixteenth century and to Bacon, once had been viewed as a special kind of nature, it was increasingly transformed to the merely unusual or the accidental, worth noticing and exploring but perhaps no longer a special type of nature itself.

The Royal Society investigated the "sport and extravagance" of nature as well as its more ordinary manifestations following Bacon's method of listing witnesses and the details of time, place, and circumstance. It collected information on monstrous births, unusual physical formations, and "rarities" and planned a collections of them for its "repository." These "wonders" and "rarities" were treated as "remarkable" but nevertheless "natural." Sprat's *History of the Royal Society* took up the issue of the marvelous, in part to counter arguments suggesting experimental philosophers denigrated prophecies and prodigies.[73] The "monstrous," the "strange," and the "marvelous" thus continued to be of considerable shared interest among naturalists and newsmen throughout the seventeenth century.[74] Very slowly over time, many if not all "marvelous" or "monstrous" matters of fact came to be viewed as having natural explanations. Whether classified as human, natural, preternatural, or supernatural in origin, they remained "matters of fact" that required substantiation by an appropriate number of credible witnesses. News reports of apparitions and mermaids were as filled with proofs for these matters of fact as were the accounts of the Royal Society. Even tongue-in-cheek reports were similarly surrounded with offers of proof. A midcentury "true relation" of a man-fish seen in the Thames carrying a "muscat" in one hand and a petition in the other was alleged to be credibly reported by six named sailors who spoke with him. Similarly verified was the reported sighting of a beautiful mermaid with comb in one hand and looking-glass in the other who unfortunately swam back out to sea.[75]

Even properly verified "marvelous" news events might be subject to different interpretations. John Edwards, for example, was distressed by Seth

Ward's treatment of comets as regular repeated natural appearances and insisted that comets were singular events portending political change or signaling God's displeasure.[76] The expectation of variety in interpretation or explanation was characteristic of many discourses of fact.

The experiments and investigations of the virtuosi were sometimes treated as newsworthy events by the popular media. The "Experiment" of Sir William Petty's double-bottomed ship and the difficulties it encountered during a "great storm" were reported. The *Royal Impartial Mercury* related Sir Samuel Morland's visit to France "to experiment his Invention in Waterworks." A news publication reported a new invention for "grinding Corn without wind or water" that might be viewed on the Bankside.[77] During the 1680s, the period in which Robert Hooke's *Philosophical Collections* was intermittently published, there was talk about introducing briefer and cheaper "philosophical gazettes" to "propagate natural philosophy."[78]

The *Athenian Gazette*, directed at a general audience, suggests how widely the concept of matter of fact and its proofs had been disseminated. The journal repeatedly advertised that "if any Person whatever will find in any New Experiment, or curious Instance, which they know to be truth, and matter of fact, circumstantiated with Time and Place, we will insert it in our Mercury." It would also include "the conferences and transactions" of the English virtuosi, whatever is "Curious and Remarkable, if well attested," and reports of any "curious Accident or remarkable Providence that's matter of Fact."[79] Though not in the class of the *Philosophical Transactions*, the *Athenian Gazette* played an important role in purveying natural information and news to a broad audience. If not always as scrupulous as it claimed to be in distinguishing well-substantiated "news" from the fanciful, it nevertheless attempted to base its information and its answers to readers' queries on well-verified "fact." To one rather incredible report it replied: "We must here, once for all, desire those Gentlemen who send in Questions of this nature, to be more particular in their Relations, and to specifie the places, where, and times when things happen'd, and what Evidence there is that they ever did so. . . . when we are satisfied in, and that we are not imposed upon. . . . As for the Case here mention'd . . . till we know how it's attested, we must take the liberty to doubt the Matter of Fact." Early in its history the typical article printed in the *Philosophical Transactions* took the form of a firsthand account in letter form.[80]

The question of what and whom to believe remained somewhat puzzling for contemporaries. Should one believe the ordinary and suspect the unusual, or were both equally believable if reported by a sufficient number of credible witnesses? What should be made of the *True Protestant Mercury*'s 1681 account of Pennsylvania that "the Climate thereof, . . . is near the same with Naples in Italy"?[81] The answer was not always what modern readers might expect. Obadiah Walker, for example, suggested, "When news comes from an uncertain Author, though probable and expected, yet suspend your belief: because men easily report what they desire to expect; but rather give heed to certain extravagant and unexpected Relations, as unlikelier to be invented."[82] Here the plausible and the expected were suspect, and the "extravagant and unexpected" more believable. If the reverse was more often thought to be appropriate, it was still difficult to find any completely satisfactory standard of belief in "factual reports," even those allegedly supported by respectable and experienced witnesses.

Conclusion

The news media, which began at the end of the sixteenth century and flourished in the seventeenth and eighteenth, played a vital part in the development of the discourses of fact. They purveyed a kind of culture of facts to a relatively wide range of Englishmen. Midcentury circumstances of civil war and political turmoil stimulated the desire for political and military "facts." The period from 1640 to 1660 thus had a significant role in the acculturation of the concept of fact. The news media, especially after the Restoration, treated both human affairs and natural phenomena as facts, thus fostering the shift of "fact" from the older legal and historical meaning of human deed to a newer, more encompassing meaning. They bolstered the concern for verifiability through such techniques as multiple witnessing that are to be found in the other discourses of fact. They linked the public more closely with the concerns of historians and lawyers. They reiterated the norm of impartiality. And, particularly in their treatment of the marvelous, the news media took the public into the realm of empirical verification, which concerned both theologians and natural philosophers.

The Facts of Nature I

D espite the common early use of "fact" in law, historiography, and news reporting, the concept is now most often associated with natural science. Indeed, the concept "fact" has become so closely identified with science that it is often assumed this association has always existed. Yet in England the concept "fact" had its principal origin in law and was initially limited to human actions and events. Only later would it acquire its association with a "true statement" about the natural world.

Until quite recently, the constituent concepts of early modern natural philosophy, concepts such as "experiment," "experience," "fact," "hypothesis," "theory," "cause," "probability," and the "laws of nature," have not been a central concern.[1] That situation is now changing. The pioneering work of Steven Shapin and Simon Schaffer on the conceptual elements in the competing natural philosophies of Robert Boyle and Thomas Hobbes has shown that "matter of fact" played a central role in the construction of Boyle's natural philosophy. Their work, to which we frequently make reference here, is characterized by a contextualism that focuses on short-term and localized English conditions and, therefore, does not concern itself with how "fact" or "matter of fact" evolved or was related to other intellectual traditions at home or abroad. Shapin's more recent work associates scientific fact finding with the social categories "courtier" and "gentleman." It takes a longer view but also ignores related traditions which pose major difficulties for the gentleman hypothesis. Peter Dear has described the subtle but crucial differences between "experience" and "experiment" in the work of certain late scholastic natural philosophers in the mathematico-physical tradition and in the empirical experimentalism of the Royal Society. Katherine Park and Lorraine Daston have connected the origin of the natural fact with descriptions of marvels and monsters. Like Dear, they contrast the "common experience" of traditional natural philosophy with the particularized "fact" of the natural historians and experimentalists of seventeenth-century England.[2]

The historical understanding of the concept "fact" has been somewhat obscured by Vico's "*verum-factum*," which expressed a distinction between the unknowable world that God made and the world human beings have made, which is knowable because they have made it. Paolo Rossi has utilized Vico's categories not to underline the differences between natural knowledge and human knowledge but to suggest the gradual acceptance of new ways of thinking about "knowing" and "doing," with respect to the natural world, in the work of magicians, alchemists, Paracelsians, and hermeticists. He emphasizes Francis Bacon's indebtedness to the tradition that connects making and doing, theory and practice, art and nature. Bacon's role in the human construction of natural knowledge is developed further by Antonio Perez-Ramos. Current emphasis on natural knowledge as a human construction runs counter to intellectual traditions that separate knowledge of the natural world and the world of human making.[3]

My treatment of the creation or construction of the "scientific fact" is both related to and somewhat different from this body of scholarship. It takes a longer chronological perspective and relates the "facts" of natural philosophy to a group of contemporary discourses that already had adopted, or were simultaneously adopting, the concept "fact." In this chapter I attempt to show how the legal concept "fact" or "matter of fact," which dealt with past human acts, was adopted and then adapted by natural historians and experimentalists to suit the new emphasis on observation of particular natural phenomena. Although my study does not emphasize the constructivist elements in the making of English natural philosophy, it should shed some light on the early modern mixtures of "understanding" and "doing" posited by Rossi, Perez-Ramos, and Hans Blumenberg.

The distinction between *verum* and *factum*, or the distinction between the work of God and the works of man, was a commonplace in the early modern world.[4] In this conceptualization of knowledge, natural phenomena were not handled under the rubric of "fact" or "factum," terms attached to the works of man. The innovation of Francis Bacon and his successors was to apply the techniques and conceptions developed to deal with human deeds to natural phenomena, that is, to the works of God and natural phenomena "made" by humans. Over time, the testimony of witnesses became crucial to establishing knowledge of natural phenomena, whether ordinary, unusual, marvelous, or experimental. With the introduction of "fact" into the realm of natural history and experimental philosophy, the distinction between *verum* and *factum* is eroded and the methodologies for establishing and verifying human actions and natural phenomena become almost, if not completely, identical. It is that process that we trace in this chapter.

The most prominent strand of English natural philosophy became a philosophy based on "fact," or, as contemporaries would have labeled it, "matter of fact." The English emphasis on "matter of fact," and efforts to link fact and hypothesis, gave English natural philosophy its most distinctive features. Although there was no unanimity within the English scientific community, and some comparable developments occurred elsewhere, the English scientific program and practice as exemplified in the work of the Royal Society was distinctive. A significant part of its distinctiveness resulted from its initial enthusiasm for the Baconian program of natural history and experiment grounded on well-proved "facts." The twin concepts "fact" and "hypothesis" proved central to the natural philosophy that came to characterize the Royal Society, the visible symbol of English natural philosophy during the late seventeenth century.

Francis Bacon and the "Facts" of Nature

Francis Bacon was a central agent in the transformation of "fact" from human to natural phenomena. Bacon not only insisted that properly verified "matters of fact" provided the foundation for natural philosophy but also extended natural history to include experiment. Of course, the translation of "fact" from human to natural phenomena was not achieved exclusively by Bacon's efforts. We have already examined the process by which cosmographers and topographers began to treat both human and natural objects and events as "matters of fact" and how unusual natural events were beginning to be somewhat similarly treated. The growing popularity of Baconian natural history, however, underlined the possibility and desirability of treating both natural and human history as rooted in "matters of fact" observed and recorded. Bacon is also central to the creation of the "experimental fact." Human agents created artificial, that is, humanly constructed natural events that could be observed and recorded just as were such ordinary and wondrous natural events or objects as comets, plants, and birds.

For Bacon, observations and experiments were to yield the "facts" that would be used to construct a new natural philosophy to succeed that of Aristotle. Aristotelian "experience" did not refer to a particular experience or to observations that occurred at particular times and places. Aristotelianism also maintained a clear distinction between nature and art. Thus, it was only with some difficulty that constructed experiments were incorporated into Aristotelian natural philosophy.[5]

Bacon was ideally situated to appropriate legal-historical methods to the cause of natural philosophy. He was an important legal practitioner and judge, familiar with common and civil law procedures as well as the hybrid procedure of Chancery over which he presided. He was a self-conscious reformer of *both* jurisprudence and natural philosophy as well as a historian. I am, of course, hardly the first to suggest the general connection between Bacon's legal thought and his natural philosophy.[6] My concern is not with the overall indebtedness of Bacon's science to law but with the particular origins and functions of "matter of fact" in his natural philosophy.

History, for Bacon, was divided into the two familiar varieties. Natural history "treats of the deeds and works of Nature, civil history those of men." The "deeds and works" of both were concerned with particulars "circumscribed by time and place."[7] Bacon found the current state of natural history deplorable. He castigated the traditional reliance on experience in which "rumour and vague fames" or the "gossip of the streets" were "allowed the weight of lawful evidence." Nothing was "duly investigated, nothing verified, nothing counted, weighed or measured."[8] His predecessors had given only a "glance or two upon facts and examples and experience" before invoking "their own spirits to give them oracles." "Dwelling purely and constantly among the facts of nature," Bacon would begin the program anew.[9]

Baconian natural history was to break from the Renaissance tradition of natural history, a tradition aptly characterized as an "emblematic world view" in which a mélange of symbols, correspondences, observations, proverbs, and fables formed a complex web of verbal and natural associations.[10] The breakdown of this tradition, facilitated and partly caused by the discovery of previously unknown New World species of flora and fauna, was dramatically embraced by Bacon, whose new natural philosophy was to be built on natural histories expunged of literary, mythical, and symbolic elements. Natural history, still neglected by scholars, would be reconstructed so that it would be based on well-established "facts," not literary allusion or traditional lore.[11]

The new Baconian natural history was to be compiled with "religious care, as if every particular were stated upon an oath."[12] Although initial information was provided by the senses, observations had to be sifted and examined in a variety of ways to discover error. Bacon warned that the "testimony and information of the sense has reference always to man, not to the universe, and it is a great error to assert that the sense is the measure of things." Yet, as in law, eyewitness testimony takes pride of place. Experiments would play a crucial role, being, Bacon thought, more subtle than immediate sense observation.[13] All depended on keeping the eye steadily fixed on the "facts of nature."[14] "Matters of fact," broadened by Bacon to include virtually all natural phenomena either observed or created experimentally, were to provide the basis for what he felt to be an entirely new natural philosophy.

Although Bacon recognized that there were dangers connected with "wonders," he nevertheless wished to record the unusual, the anomalous, and the accidental.[15] He also expanded the scope of traditional natural history by proposing that well-certified histories of trades be compiled. These, like experimental histories, combined natural materials and human intervention and construction. The credit of things both ordinary and anomalous must be evaluated as "certainly true, doubtful whether true or not, certainly not true." The doubtful must be reported in such tentative phrases as "it is reported," "they relate," or "I have heard from a person of credit," phraseology reminiscent of the news media. In important instances "the name of the author should be given, and not the name merely, but it should be mentioned withal whether he took it from report, oral or written, . . . or rather affirmed it of his own knowledge; also whether it was a thing which happened in his own time or earlier; and again whether it was a thing of which, if it really happened, there must needs have been many witnesses; and finally whether the author was a vain-speaking and light person or sober and severe; and the like points, which bear on the weight of the evidence."[16] These criteria, already part of the legal and historiographical traditions, would also become central to empirically based natural philosophy.

Bacon occasionally employed the phrase "the Facts of Nature" and he believed such facts could be firmly established.[17] Although natural history, or the "Facts of Nature," would "give light to the discovery of causes," it did not deal with causes.[18] Only after the facts and experiments were properly verified and recorded, with the same or perhaps even greater certainty than facts in the courtroom, would the *New Organon*, itself derived at least in part from legal interrogatories, be implemented by sophisticated professionals.[19] If Bacon's goal of acquiring knowledge of the Forms left him an essentialist at heart, the empirical foundation on which that essentialism was to be built was itself grounded in the nonessentialist traditions of legal fact determination.

Bacon's combination of the historico-legal "fact" of human action with the natural fact established by observation and experiment made it possible for his successors to apply a familiar legal technique of verifying events in the human world to natural phenomena. In natural history as in law, "matter of fact" could best be established by the testimony of a sufficient number of firsthand witnesses of appropriate credibility. The term "fact" or "matter of fact" implied, for most of the seventeenth century, not something already worthy of belief or true but rather a matter capable of proof, preferably by multiple eyewitness testimony.

The creation of the natural and experimental "fact" was, of course, only one component in the complex series of intellectual developments conventionally labeled the "scientific revolution." Nor was Bacon always first. Ancient and Renaissance astronomers had described seemingly singular nonrepeatable events long before Bacon, and those working in the alchemical tradition also employed witnesses.[20] If English natural philosophy of the seventeenth century contained important Baconian strands, it cannot simply be equated with Baconianism. However much the virtuosi of the Royal Society condemned Descartes for dogmatism and system making and scholastic Aristotelians for their outmoded and useless notions, a good many English virtuosi incorporated elements of Cartesianism or retained Aristotelian concepts. Many developments in mathematics, physics, astronomy, anatomy, and medicine can be explained with little or no reference to the Baconian program. Yet the innovative Baconian transformation of "fact" from the realms of law and history where human agents were exclusively involved to natural history and natural philosophy was crucial to the development of the natural and later "scientific fact."

While the scientific revolution is often characterized as occurring primarily in the realm of astronomy and physics, the bulk of activities carried on by the English scientific community during the decades following Bacon's death focused on natural history composed of "facts" derived from observation and experiment. By the mid-seventeenth century the combined influence of the Baconian appropriation of "fact" to natural history and the development of chorographic-intertwined descriptions of human and natural phenomena permitted the English to use the term "fact" or "matter of fact" in connection with both natural and civil history.

Thomas Hobbes, no admirer of the natural philosophy that would be developed by the Royal Society, thus treated natural history as "fact." For Hobbes, "the register of Knowledge of Fact is called History." Natural history was "the History of such Facts, or Effects of Nature . . . Such as the Histories of Metalls, Plants, Animals, Regions and the like. The other is Civil History, which [is] the History of the Voluntary Actions of Men in Commonwealths."[21] In both varieties "fact" was derived from "sense and memory" and characterized as "the knowledge required in a witness."[22] For Hobbes, however, "scientific" knowledge was dependent on reason, not observation or experiment, and his philosophic model was self-consciously borrowed from geometry, not the fact-establishing methods of the law. Hobbes's association of "fact" with the traditional language of the "effects of nature" is significant because this association facilitated the ability of empirically minded naturalists to assimilate the emphasis on particular events and experimental observations to established linguistic conventions of natural philosophy.[23]

The decades between Bacon and the founding of the Royal Society witnessed the physiological investigations of William Harvey, whose work combined traditional medical assumptions with the importance of firsthand sense observation. Harvey too adopted legal phraseology when he spoke of the "right verdict of the senses controlled by frequent observations and valid experiences" and called upon his readers to take nothing he said on trust. Their eyes would be his "witnesses" and "judges."[24]

Natural history based on careful observation and experiment in the Baconian and Harvean modes thus became the dominant, albeit not the exclusive, form of English scientific inquiry in the generations following Bacon's death. Some aspects of the new philosophy utilized experiment, without assuming that the principles of natural philosophy necessarily would be built on the foundation of natural history or natural "matters of fact." Although Bacon's natural philosophy did not easily incorporate mathematics, several Restoration naturalists would combine mathematics with observation and experiment. "Fact" and experiment would also be deployed by alchemical, chemical, and vitalist natural philosophers as well as mechanical ones.[25]

We use the term "empirical natural philosophy" to include both those who felt that a true knowledge of causes could be derived from observed "facts" and those who felt that causal explanations would always remain probable or hypothetical. Well-observed and experimentally produced "facts" would become central to both schools of thought. It was the shift in investigations of nature to the particular firsthand observation, that is, to natural and experimental history, that brought natural phenomena into the orbit of "fact."

While our attention will be focused largely on the Royal Society, we should take note of the civil war and Interregnum decades, when some Baconians were linked to millenarian and other projects and others were pursued by a group of scholars centered at Wadham College, Oxford. Although there was some overlap, Puritan projectors and educational and social reformers centered around Samuel Hartlib represent one strand of Baconian thought, and the efforts of the Oxford group, another. Many of the future leaders of the Royal Society gathered around John Wilkins, the warden of Wadham College, who was described as the "principall Reviver of Experimental Philosophy (secundum mentem Domini Bacon)." Here Wilkins, Seth Ward, John Wallis, William Neile, Ralph Bathurst, Jonathan Goddard, John Evelyn, Christopher and Matthew Wren, Thomas Willis, William Petty, and latecomers Robert Boyle and Robert Hooke pursued a wide variety of Baconian and non-Baconian projects orchestrated by

Wilkins. This "Embryo or First Conception of the Royal Society," which overlapped with the Oxford Harvean physiologists, engaged in astronomy, medical experiment, mathematical theorizing, practical inventions, and chemical experiments, without providing a public statement of their methods and goals. Seeking relief from the political and religious turmoil of the times, they worked quietly and privately until they again joined forces with their London-based Gresham College colleagues and returning Royalist exile virtuosi to form the Royal Society. Much work published in the early years of the Restoration was the fruit of Interregnum research.[26]

Matters of Fact and the Research Program of the Royal Society

Observed and experimentally produced "matters of fact" became central to the research agenda of the Royal Society. Like legal facts, "scientific facts" were established primarily by witnesses whose testimony would be evaluated on the basis of a set of legally derived criteria of credibility, such as opportunity, ability, probity, skill, fidelity, status, experience, and reputation. As we have seen, common law decisions on matters of fact were placed in the hands of lay jurors whose middling socioeconomic standing was deemed sufficient to render them capable of independent impartial decisions on matters of fact. We have also seen that similar criteria were invoked by historians to favor the testimony of politically experienced firsthand observers. These models, taken over by the naturalists when they adopted the concept of matter of fact, help explain the law-laden language of the virtuosi and their emphasis on witnessing, impartiality, and cautiousness about going beyond well-proved facts. Widespread previous familiarity in other disciplinary realms also helps explain why we find no justification or explanation by the virtuosi of their adoption of the usage "fact."

Apologists and Spokesmen: Thomas Sprat,
Joseph Glanvill, and Henry Oldenburg

Given their importance in communicating the research program and aspirations of the Royal Society, we begin with Thomas Sprat's and Joseph Glanvill's attempts to publicize and defend the Society and with Henry Oldenburg's vast correspondence undertaken as secretary of the Royal Society and his *Philosophical Transactions*. All three men insisted on observation and experiment as the core of the Society's early agenda. The "New" or "Experimental Philosophy" was described by Sprat as grounded on "matter of fact," that is, on a natural history based on observation and experiment. At one point Sprat suggested, with some exaggeration to be sure, that members of the Royal Society "only deal in matters of Fact." The Society preferred its "own Touch and Sight," privileging firsthand reports provided by the senses over hearsay or secondhand experience. Where firsthand observation was lacking, the Society, like the historian, was "forced to trust the reports of others." Sprat described the Royal Society's primary activity as "Directing, Judging, Conjecturing, Improving and Discoursing upon Experiments," with judgments to be based on "the matter of fact and repeated experiments." Witnessing by substantial numbers would give credence to the experiment observed, Sprat emphasizing in this connection that judgments on matters of fact coming before the Royal Society would be based on the "concurring testimonies" of its members: "In almost all other matters of Belief, or Opinion, or of Science: the assurance is nothing near so firm as this." Because membership ranged from about sixty to one hundred, conditions for reaching moral certitude were far better than in the law courts, where the testimony of two or three witnesses was sufficient in judgments on matters of life or estate. Sprat characterized members as impartial judges before whom reports were given and experiments made. Jury-like, they accepted or rejected proposed "matters of fact."[27]

Reports were to emphasize the firsthand observation and experience of the speaker, who typically used the first person as a means of giving credibility to the discrete occurrences described.[28] The use of the first-person active voice was precisely what was required of a witness describing an event to a jury or judge and was the preferred mode of the memoirist, chorographer, and traveler.

Joseph Glanvill, after Sprat perhaps the most vocal apologist for the Royal Society, also employed the terminology of "matter of fact" to describe the methods and procedures of the virtuosi. The Royal Society dealt with the "plain Objects of Sense" because it was in these, "if anywhere, there might be found Certainty." Similar certainty might arise from testimony, which under the best circumstances also provided "undubitable assent." These conditions were met when reporters were disinterested, their reports full, and acceptance general. Such reporters were to be found in the Royal Society, whose members were men of "wit and Fortune . . . where fondness of preconceived opinions, sordid Interests, or affectation of strange Relations, are not like to render . . . reports suspect or partial, nor want of Sagacity, Fortune, or Care, defective." The reports of their "Tryals" might thus be received as "undoubted Records of certain events." While error was always possible, "matters of fact well proved ought not be denied." It was necessary, of course, to proportion assent to the "degree of the evidence" and to be confident "only in those distinctly and clearly apprehended."[29] Like the common law jury, the Royal Society could determine the truth of "matters of fact."

Like lawyers and historians, Sprat and Glanvill distinguished between "matters of fact" and explanations or causes of those facts. Glanvill observed that, even if derived from careful observation of particulars, the best principles of natural knowledge remained "but hypotheses." Without the history of nature, "our Hypotheses are but Dreams and Romances, and our Science mere conjecture and opinion."[30]

Henry Oldenburg provided official statements of the Royal Society's goals and methods in his correspondence with domestic and foreign virtuosi and in his private periodical venture, the *Philosophical Transactions.* Oldenburg referred to the task of building a new natural philosophy from "a large and truthful natural history" obtained by "observing carefully and faithfully and exactly passing on whatever" was observed. Such a "faithful History" would "comprehend a competent stock of observations and Experiments, carefully made." This was a cooperative enterprise to be jointly undertaken by Society members and "the most philosophicall and curious persons" from "all parts of ye world." "Ingenious conceptions and philosophical matter of fact" contributed by the "learned and inquiring of the world" were crucial. After "comparing and considering" observations and experiments "all together," the Royal Society hoped to raise "a body of natural Philosophy, as may give a rational account of ye effects of nature." "Facts" thus were essential but not the final goal.[31] Like Sprat and Glanvill, Oldenburg used the phrase "matter of fact" easily without explaining its meaning or its rather novel application to physical phenomena. Presumably, the concept was already sufficiently familiar to their readers.[32]

If some scholars now reject the notion of a single scientific ideology characterizing the Royal Society,[33] its chief apologists and public spokesmen adopted a Baconian rhetoric of cooperative collection of "matters of fact" derived from careful observation and experiment. They anticipated that the resulting natural histories in time might result in natural philosophy. The collection and production of "matters of fact" was in many respects the enterprise that held the Society and its correspondents together, however much members might differ on the best means of dealing with or interpreting the "facts."

Natural History

For many years, Thomas Kuhn and Andre Koyre have accustomed us to think of the "scientific revolution" in terms of astronomy and physics. Historians have, therefore, underestimated the extent to which the Royal Society was devoted to "natural history," a term that currently has a more circumscribed meaning than it had in the seventeenth century. For most members of the Royal Society, the "new philosophy" would be grounded on a new and faithfully constructed natural history, that is, a collection of well-established "matters of fact," sometimes created experimentally, and personally observed or credibly reported. The range of what was to be covered by this natural history was enormous. Both Hooke's astronomical observations and Hevelius's *Selenographia* were treated as natural history. Natural history included topography, geology, climatology, botany, zoology, anatomy, and chemistry as well as human customs, manners, governmental structures, and trades. Virtually all the chorographical topics were included under the umbrella of natural history. But natural history also included aspects of physiology, anatomy, and medicine. All natural objects, occurrences, or experimental results capable of being observed might be "matters of fact" and thus part of natural history. These "facts" then might be utilized by those who adopted mechanical, atomist, vitalistic, or alchemical natural philosophies.[34]

Although one is not likely to think of Robert Hooke as a natural historian, natural history in the broadly conceived seventeenth-century sense was central to his conception of natural philosophy. Carefully observed information was to be transcribed in a special record book while still fresh in mind. Not every kind of observation and experiment would do, nor was "every observator fitt to be a collector." "Observations not rightly and accurately made" were "pernicious and Destructive" like "a rotten beam in a large edifice." The philosophical historian must be taught "what he ought to observe, how to examine it, how to preserve & and register it, How to range and order it." Ideally, this work was to be done by "a society of men . . . as have an eminency both of Parts and Fortune, & of such as have a will as well as abilities."[35]

Natural history for Hooke comprised "all kinds of Naturall and artificiall bodies and all kinds of Naturall and artificial motions or actions." Some were so obvious that they could not "scape the most negligent observer, others soe abstruse and hidden that they may elude the endeavors of the most Diligent inquirer." Experiment too was required. The philosophical historian "should Indeavour to be knowing & versed in all the various ways of examining & trying of matter or making experiments, trialls, . . . essayes on various kinds of substances."[36] Experiments should be "ranged in several orders of degrees: in every of which places they may stand like so many witnesses to give testimony of this truth or against that error. . . . And a most severe examination of these witnesses must be made before a jury can warrantably give their verdict or a judge pronounce sentence for branding one proposition or hypothesis as erroneous . . . or for establishing another for truth or axiom."[37] Although sense could not reach all of nature, there was no method as "certain and infallible," if "rightly and judiciously made use of." Not surprisingly, Hooke referred to his own experiments as "History and matter of Fact."[38]

As we have seen, Oldenburg solicited "matters of fact" from his worldwide correspondence network. "Matters of fact" were also solicited in the

Royal Society's queries of travelers. The term "matter of fact" also appeared frequently in connection with reports on particular aspects of natural history and in publications dealing with natural history topics as diverse as Humphrey Ridley's *Anatomy of the Brain* and Peter Wyche's description of the Nile. John Ray would "admit nothing for Matter of Fact or Experiment but what is undoubtedly true"; Francis Willughby's *Ornithology* would include only "particulars" that could be "warranted upon our knowledge and experience or where we have assurance by the testimony of Good Authors or sufficient Witnesses." John Evelyn employed "matter of fact" in connection with civil, geographical, and natural history; Martin Lister emphasized the importance of faithfully delivered "matters of fact"; and John Wallis referred to his experiments on Mercury as "matter of fact." In 1676 Isaac Newton wrote Oldenburg indicating that "the business" he was concerned with "being about matter of fact" was properly decided not by discussion but "by trying it before competent witnesses."[39]

The focus on fact continued into the latter part of the century as well, John Woodward claiming, "All parties so far agree" that "observations are the only sure Grounds . . . to build a lasting and substantial Philosophy." His natural history of the earth would, therefore, "be guided wholly by Matter of Fact; . . . [it is] of all hands to be the best and surest; and not to offer anything but what hath due warrant from observations; and those both carefully made, and faithfully related." Sir Hans Sloane, who succeeded Newton as president of the Royal Society, similarly asserted that "matters of fact" were the essentials of scientific knowledge and "that the Knowledge of Natural History, being Observations of Matter of Fact, is more certain than most Others . . . less subject to Mistake than Reasonings, Hypothesis and Deductions."[40] Yet many of these early modern invocations of "matters of fact" indicate that, as in law, facts remained in the realm of the provable rather than the proved. As Ray's statement suggests, not all facts were worthy of belief. Facts thus should be "candidly taken notice of and faithfully rectified or corrected."[41]

Robert Boyle

In recent years, Robert Boyle has become increasingly central to discussions of English natural philosophy, and several scholars have spotlighted his role as model virtuoso.[42] The most influential are Steven Shapin and Simon Schaffer. While noting Boyle's legalistic terminology relating to fact, they substantially underestimate the role of legal concepts not only in Boyle's natural philosophy but in shaping the epistemological foundations of English natural history and experimental science more generally. Placing Boyle's comments on witnessing, testimony, and matters of fact alongside those of his fellow virtuosi, we can see that Boyle's role in creating and publicizing the concept "matter of fact" in English natural philosophy has been overemphasized. The crucial transition from human to natural fact was made by Bacon and the chorographers and was enhanced by additional writing in the vernacular. Had the majority of English naturalists continued to communicate about natural phenomena and experiment in Latin, it is less likely that "matter of fact" or "factum" would have become so commonly used to refer to natural events. It was the English virtuosi collectively who made that transformation a fundamental part of the "new philosophy."[43]

Like Bacon, Hooke, and others, Boyle held that "Natural history, . . . the only sure Foundation of Natural Philosophy,"[44] was based on "matter of fact," that is, particular experiments and specific "Observations faithfully made and deliver'd." "Matters of fact" provided Boyle the epistemological basis of his philosophy, and he frequently used legal metaphors to describe them. He referred at one point to the "Testimony of nature," analogizing nature to a witness. At another, he referred to "judicious and illustrious witnesses" and at yet another suggested that "matters of fact ought to be brought to trial."[45] Both his outlook and his language with respect to "matters of fact" were little different from those of his virtuosi colleagues.

Knowledge of "matter of fact" was, for Boyle, derived from the senses and communicated to others by means of testimony. Experience, "the knowledge we have of any Matter of Fact," might be personal, that is, based on one's own sensation; historical, that is, known by the relation or testimony of someone else; or theological, that is, known by revelation.[46] The knowledge of matters of fact included past and present, the human, the natural, and the divine.

Nowhere did Boyle or his Restoration contemporaries suggest that they are introducing a novel concept to natural philosophy. And how could they have done so, given the use of "fact" or "matter of fact" in so many different fields of endeavor? One of the things that made their new natural history so readily acceptable was that it was to be established by familiar and respected methods and criteria. These were so well known that there was no need for explanation or comment. Although new to "natural history" and "natural philosophy," the concept of fact and appropriate means of establishing matters of fact were not new to English audiences.

Witnessing

Witnessing was an essential part of establishing matters of fact, and participants in the discourses of fact were well aware that witnesses might vary in number and be more or less reliable. We have encountered the criteria for credible witnessing in several disciplines and genres and noted the concern of the Royal Society with ensuring that the inquiries it pursued in distant locales were made by credible and well-qualified reporters. To the extent that the Royal Society cooperated with non-English observers, experimenters, and travelers, it enlarged the fact-gathering community far beyond the cluster of English virtuosi who resided in or near enough to London to participate in its experimental activities. Reliance on persons outside the London-Oxford community of investigators meant that nongentlemen and often relatively unknown reporters were deeply enmeshed in the Restoration fact-establishing network.

Although we often speak of the English scientific community as if it were one, there were in fact several involved in producing natural or scientific "matters of fact." Membership in some of these "fact"-establishing circles required little more than honesty, sharp eyes, and an ability to describe or illustrate what had been viewed. In others it required medical or anatomical knowledge, a sophisticated knowledge of mathematics and physics, chemical knowledge and experience, or familiarity with particular scientific instruments. Some members of each of these subcommunities might be personally known to the nucleus of Royal Society members, others would have been known only by reputation, and still others not at all before their initial reports.

While the "matters of fact" being assembled by the Royal Society were so various and came from so many different individuals and venues, some qualifications were considered necessary or desirable in all those who contributed observations and experimental reports. Shapin has argued that the social status of gentleman provided the necessary and sufficient guarantee of credibility. The criteria of credibility, however, were more specific and more varied and were substantially the same as those of the courtroom and the other contemporaneous realms of fact. Credibility was assessed on the basis of a range of considerations that included social status but also the experience, skill, fidelity, and impartiality of the observer and the number of supporting observers.

The social aspects of scientific witnessing have been recently highlighted by Shapin's attention to the issue of whose word was trustworthy in Restoration society and his contention that the model of aristocrat and gentleman was central in shaping the ideal type of "scientist."[47] In this connection we would do well to recall that social class *and* experience played a role in the legal arena and that opportunity for firsthand observation of the fact in question had a crucial role in creating legal credibility. The mere status of gentleman could hardly be decisive in the courtroom where one gentleman might well be contending against another and where witnesses of several classes might appear on both sides. I suggest that the scientific community adopted important elements of legal witnessing as constituent elements in the construction of the ideal scientific observer and reporter rather than relying on the courtier-aristocratic model. To be sure, institutional and technological differences between the English legal system and English natural philosophy resulted in some differentiation in how the two disciplines attempted to verify "facts." We therefore point both to the virtuosi's adoption of the methods of legal fact determination and to modifications engendered by differing disciplinary circumstances.

Eyewitnesses and "Ocular" Testimony

In their search for well-established facts, virtuosi, like lawyers and judges, expressed the need for eyewitness testimony. They too preferred the visual over other senses, and well-established facts over inferences that might be drawn from them. And both expressed a distaste for, if not a complete rejection of, secondhand or hearsay evidence, although the naturalists, like historians and news reporters, also recognized that circumstances sometimes required them to rely on the reports of others when dealing with nonreplicable or far-distant events. In both law and natural philosophy, emphasis on the particular meant that the testimony of a reliable witness was the best evidence available.

If, unlike the courts, the Royal Society had neither the power nor the desire to compel the attendance of witnesses, reference to eyewitness testimony became a commonplace of the English naturalists. Boyle, for example, emphasized that "the bulk of the matters of fact I deliver should consist of things, whereof I was myself an actor or an eye-witness." Yet he recognized that he would often have to depend on the reports of others. In such instances he would believe only reports that had been delivered "upon" the author's "own particular knowledge, or with peculiar circumstances."[48] Robert Plot would mention only what he had "seen himself, or has received unquestionable Testimony for it." Walter Pope insisted he "would make no hearsays in this true relation." John Ray wished for "Assurances from Eye-witnesses of Credit," being "loath to put in anything on uncertain Rumour."[49] The uncertainty of rumor, hearsay, or common fame, as in the courts, was contrasted to eyewitness testimony. Rechecking a report of a "rain of wheat," the Royal Society asked the author to write the bailiff of the town, requesting the ministers and the physicians who had witnessed it to send a further account of the "matter of fact." Microscopic studies, Hooke insisted, required "a sincere Hand, and a faithful eye" to examine and record "the things themselves as they appear." Sir Matthew Hale favored a natural philosophy that began with the senses, which "examine particular Matters of fact, how they are, or fall out, search into Experiments and visible Trials."[50]

Recognizing that the Royal Society's policy of "receiving all credible accounts" might result in some "hazard, and uncertainty," Sprat argued that this danger was removed because the Society reduced "such matters of hearsay and information, into real, and impartial Trials, perform'd by their Experiments," capable of "exactness, variation, and accurate repetition."[51]

Naturalists routinely referred to "ocularly manifest" observations or to "ocular demonstration[s] . . . of matter of fact."[52] Harvey's circulation of the blood, for example, was characterized as "an Ocular Demonstration." Royal Society members witnessed Valentine Greatrakes's inexplicable cures in order to "have an ocular Testimony of Truth" as "eyewitnesses of what was done." Sir Robert Moray consulted those who learned by "ocular inspection and Experiment or by the relation of trustworthy persons."[53]

Eager to expand its data base, and without the material interests of conflicting parties who were affected by what was "let in," the Royal Society was actually far less hostile to secondhand testimony than the courts. The Society often had to make do with reports that merely claimed to be based on eyewitness testimony. Yet emphasis on the eyewitness testimony behind the secondary reports reflects the same rejection of common knowledge. And, where possible, members sought to convert hearsay or single-witness testimony into a record established by multiple eyewitnesses. Experiments first done in private often would be repeated before the assembled members rather than simply reported to it. It is noteworthy that in such instances, where the Society might have relied on the word of gentlemen experimenters, it preferred eyewitness corroboration.

The Social Status of Witnesses:
Travelers, Seamen, and Tradesmen

In considering the problem of scientific witnessing, we must refer to Chapter 3's description of the Royal Society's efforts to obtain natural history materials from all over the world. Because members were unlikely to be found in all the desired venues, Oldenburg solicited reports from English diplomats, travelers, virtuosi, sea captains, and ordinary seamen, emphasizing that the Society drew on the "learned and skillful in every country" to assist in establishing "a true history of nature."[54] John Winthrop of Massachusetts was asked to contribute not only the "Observables" made by his own "ingenuity, experience and veracity" but also what he might "learne from observing and credible navigators." Moray requested of the duke of York that all ships be required to make observations and perform experiments for Society use. Hooke referred to the reports of Erasmus Bartholine, "a person of known Abilitys in Mathematical and Physical Learning," and noted that Bartholine and Picart "wanted neither skill nor Instruments." Edmund Halley's account of the trade winds relied on navigators and others "acquainted with all parts of India, and having liv'd a considerable Time between the Tropickes."[55] In these instances knowledge and experience counted for more than social status.

The Royal Society thus depended both on well-known and trusted individuals and on unfamiliar persons whose credibility could not be easily determined. Here again structural difference between legal and scientific institutions come into play. The Society could afford to take a somewhat looser view of evidence because it could engage in incremental correction of its findings of fact over time, something a court, bound by *res judicata*, could not do.

We should recall, too, that Boyle's *General Heads for the Natural History of a Country, Great or Small Drawn Out for the Use of Travellers and Navigators* as well as Hooke's and Rooke's instructions, relied on travelers and seamen whose social status and reliability were often unknown. The Society was thus dependent on accounts such as one on the Peak of Teneriff "received from some considerable Merchants and Men Worthy of Credit." Henry Stubbe attacked the Royal Society precisely because it made use of "Narratives picked up from negligent, or unaccurate Merchants and Seamen . . . men of no reading."[56]

Although the Royal Society might have preferred the testimony of members to nonmembers and gentlemen to sea captains, ordinary seamen, and traveling merchants, it had to rely on those with the opportunity to observe the desired natural phenomena. Hooke's statements concerning the need to filter and assess reports and Boyle's attempts to interview travelers personally suggest awareness of credibility problems involving both gentlemanly and nongentlemanly reporters.[57]

Reluctance to define the credibility issue in terms of social class is reflected in *The History of the Royal Society*, some portions of which emphasized the role of the gentleman, while others insisted that philosophy necessitated participation by the "vulgar." "Sound Senses and Truth" was "sufficient Qualification," there being enough variety in the Society's work to include those with "the most ordinary capacities." "Noble Rarities" were presented "not only by the hands of Learned and profess'd Philosophers; but from the Shops of Mechanicks; from the Voyages of Merchants; from the Ploughs of Husbandmen; from the Sports, the Fishponds, the Parks, the Gardens of Gentlemen." The Royal Society required "plain, diligent and laborious observers" who, though lacking scholarly knowledge, "yet bring their hands, and their eyes uncorrupted."[58]

Experience, Skill, and Expertise

Clearly, experience, skill, expertise, and opportunity to observe provided counterweights to gentle status. The Royal Society received its "intelligence" from "the constant and unerring use of experienc'd Men of the most unaffected, and most unartificial kinds of life." Those who pursued the history of trades were dependent on craftsmen and tradesmen, who combined relatively low social status with craft knowledge and expertise. Hooke could thus stress both the importance of learning from workmen and the danger of being manipulated by them. Glanvill was not unusual in sending information on mining from "some very experienced Minemen."[59]

Skill and experience were important criteria. Oldenburg emphasized the "skill and faithfulness" of those who make "tryalls and take observations," and Hooke, skills in mathematics and mechanics, the ability to draw well, and willingness to work cooperatively. Without appropriate skills it would "be almost impossible to Anser many very essential quaeries with sufficient accurateness & certainty and consequently they will become very lame & useless." Those "not skilful in the History of Nature" were "apt to impose upon themselves and others."[60]

Robert Boyle provides the centerpiece for the arguments both of Shapin and Schaffer and of Rose-Mary Sargent, the former two emphasizing Boyle's commitment to the norm of gentlemanly credibility, the latter underscoring the role of experience and expertise in Restoration natural investigations.[61] The evidence with respect to Boyle is mixed. On one occasion Boyle thought an account credible precisely because it was not written by "a Philosopher to . . . serve an Hypothesis, but by a Merchant or Factor for his Superiors, to give them an account of matter of fact."[62] In another he obtained "credible relations" from both masons and a gentleman of his acquaintance.[63] He also accepted as credible a report from a "rich and judicious" merchant, adding, however, that he was "more addicted to letters than is usual to men of his calling."[64] On the other hand, he was troubled by the fact that so few tradesmen were versed in natural philosophy or could "give . . . a clear account of their own practices." In another mood, however, Boyle indicated that much could be learned from craftsmen and tradesmen, precisely because they were "were diligent about the particular things they handle."[65]

Boyle sometimes underlined the capabilities of ordinary persons. When observing "obvious phaenomenon of nature, and those things, which are almost in everybody's power to know, (if he pleases but seriously to heed them), . . . that attention alone might quickly furnish us with one half of the history of nature." Here ordinary but careful individuals were suitable scientific witnesses, little different from witnesses who provided testimony to the courts. Experimental work and more difficult observations, Boyle wrote, required a different kind of observer, it being very difficult "to make and relate an observation and faithfully enough for a naturalist to rely on."[66]

"Humane Testimony," for Boyle, was "of great and almost necessary use" in natural philosophy. Like the testimony of witnesses in the courtroom, that testimony might be "Insufficient for want of moral qualifications in him that gives them . . . [or] insufficient if the Matter of Fact require Skill in the Relator."[67] Boyle made it clear that "the better qualified a witness is, in the capacity of a witness, the stronger Assent his Testimony deserves . . . for the two grand requisites of a Witness [are] the knowledge he has of the things he delivers, and his faithfulness in truly delivering what he knows."[68] Here again the attributes that weigh most heavily are skill and the moral approbation of the reporter, neither of which was associated exclusively with gentlemen.

Shapin has contrasted the moral and epistemological competence of gentlemen with the doubtful cognitive competence of skillful technicians, underlining the epistemic differences between gentlemanly observations and those of mechanic laborers. Yet Hooke was not a gentleman, and much of the Royal Society's experimental program was dependent on his skill at experimental design. Without Hooke, who mixed easily with gentlemen, high-ranking government officials, clergymen, and even the king despite his lack of gentlemanly status, the Society's knowledge-making capacities would have been seriously impaired. Hooke's contributions to natural history and natural philosophy were widely known and respected. As Hooke himself put it, natural history was to be the work of "a society of men of the most accomplished abilities, of such as have an eminency both of Parts and Fortune, & of such as have a will as well as abilities."[69]

Fidelity

References to the fidelity and integrity of witnesses figure as prominently in the writings of naturalists as they do in historical and legal publications.[70] The expression "a faithful history" became a commonplace of natural history. When Henry More criticized Boyle's position on an experimental matter of fact, he nevertheless indicated that Boyle's testimony was so faithful that his reports of natural phenomena would themselves serve as "the judicature of nature herself." The *Philosophical Transactions* contained an attempt to calculate credibility mathematically, in which the credibility of the reporter was rated by both "his Ability" and his "Integrity or Fidelity."[71]

Given the prominence of religious polemic and the Protestant antipathy and distrust of Catholicism, it is noteworthy that religious affiliation was not important in assessing the fidelity of the scientific witness. The Royal Society had several Roman Catholic members, communicated regularly with continental Roman Catholic virtuosi, and at one point sought information from "curious and philosophically given" Roman Catholic missionaries.[72]

Multiple Witnesses and Concurrent Testimony

The virtuosi adopted the legal preference for multiple witnesses. Although often enunciated, this preference could not always be satisfied, particularly where travelers' reports or testimony about singular events were involved.[73] Hooke insisted on recording the number and names of those who had observed experiments. Ideally, two or three persons should be present to observe and judge experiments before they were registered.[74] Boyle too emphasized that the number of concurring witnesses to a fact substantially increased its credibility, explicitly invoking the legal analogy. He notes that in murder and other criminal causes in England "it is thought reasonable to suppose, that, though each Testimony single be but probable, yet a concurrence of such Probabilities (which ought in Reason to be attributed to the Truth of what they jointly tend to prove) may well amount to a Moral certainty, such a certainty as may warrant the Judge [in a murder proceeding] to proceed to the sentence of death against the Indicted party."[75]

Boyle's position is remarkably similar to that of Judge Hale, who insisted "that which is reported by many Eye-witnesses hath greater motives of credibility than that which reported by few."[76] The replication of experiments first done in private before the assembled Royal Society is illustrative of the influence of legal procedures. Where later natural philosophy treated replicability as part of a peculiarly scientific method in which one individual investigator checked on another, the Society often treated replication as a mode of creating multiple witnesses whose testimony could be employed to prove a past event.

Judgment on Facts

Although portions of Sprat's *History* suggest that the Royal Society would, jury-like, make judgments on matters of fact, and other members such as Sir William Neile argued that those fittest to make the experiments were fittest to judge them,[77] this was not a responsibility that members readily assumed. There were no juries of naturalists who reached final judgments on the facts or, for that matter, naturalist judges who made authoritative findings of law.[78] While there are a good many statements from the virtuosi that suggest that some matters of fact might reach the status of moral certainty, there were no institutional arrangements for determining when they had done so. Allowing any individual or group to pronounce authoritative judgments about the principles of nature also violated the virtuosi's antiauthoritarian principles. Legal systems require means of establishing authoritative statements of both facts and law. The natural philosophers did not.

Witness Fallibility and Human Weakness

Testimony concerning natural phenomena and experiment was thought to be impaired by human fallibility. If the senses were faulty, how could matters of fact based on observation and experiment reach the desired status of moral certainty, which engendered belief beyond reasonable doubt? From the time of Bacon onward it was suggested that such problems might be mitigated by the use of scientific instruments and the testing of sense by reason and reason by sense. Faulty memory was also recognized as a problem. The imperfections of memory led Hooke and others to insist on the immediate recording of observations.

The sense of fallibility was also related to the Christian sense of original sin and the vast differences between human knowledge and divine omniscience. The question of how far human weakness impaired human knowledge was a topic of considerable discussion during the Restoration as rational theologians and latitudinarian divines attempted to expand the uses of reason in religion without denying human fallibility. Both Restoration virtuosi and latitudinarian theologians emphasized the possibility of morally certain facts while denying one could know the ultimate principles that governed God's Creation.[79]

The testimony of witnesses, though crucial, was imperfect. It was weakened when witnesses were partial, unfaithful, or dishonest, defects that might result in "falsities in matter of Fact."[80] Matters of fact thus might be inadequately supported or even untrue. In short, in natural philosophy as in law, "matter of fact" had more connotation of issue and less connotation of settled knowledge than the word "fact" later acquired. Only those facts proved to a "moral certainty" could be confidently believed.

Conflicting Witnesses and Controversies about Matters of Fact

Although the virtuosi were disinclined to consider the epistemologically troublesome problem of conflicting testimony, they encountered it on those occasions when well-respected observers differed in their observations. In such cases the Royal Society faced the choice of reaching a "judgment" on the facts, much in the same way that a jury might, or of evading decision.[81]

Three kinds of problems surfaced. The first involved differing observations of the same phenomenon made by seemingly reliable witnesses. The second arose when the matter of fact did not seem possible or the reporter credible. The third occurred when claims were made that the conclusions drawn from suitably recorded facts were as certain as the facts themselves.

If Royal Society spokesmen and members often analogized the role of the Society to that of the law court, in practice they avoided making collective judgments about matters of fact, even when judgment was sought by disputing parties. One of the most dramatic disagreements causing embarrassment for the Society concerned the 1664–65 comet observations of Adrien Auzout, a well-regarded French astronomer, and Hevelius, the respected author of *Selenographia* (1647), a Baconian "history of the moon."[82] Their dispute was referred to the Royal Society for adjudication, and the participants quickly adopted legalistic language. Because their differences concerned "matters of fact," Viscount Brouncker thought "authority, number and reputation of other Observers" should "cast the Ballence."[83] The testimony of other astronomers who had observed the comet supported Auzout, and the *Philosophical Transactions* noted that "unanimous consent" had been established. Echoing Brouncker, it reported that the "Controversie being about matter of fact, wherein Authority, Number, and Reputation must cast the Ballance, Mons. Hevelius, who is as well known for his ingenuity, as learning, will joyne and acquiesce that sentiment."[84] Hevelius, who continued to characterize fellow members of the Royal Society as "skilled and impartial judges," replied that he would "acquiesce in their judgment" but expressed hope that they "would not pass judgment . . . because of the plaintiff's importunity, . . . before I offer my just proofs and defense." What he "depicted with great care" was what he had seen "together with other notable persons."[85] He and Auzout thus both invoked multiple supporting witnesses.

Moray, continuing to employ legal language, suggested that the Society "give Hevelius his doom" but recommended that a few members, rather than the whole Society, respond. Oldenburg was to inform Hevelius of "his doom concerning his mistake" as well as the fact that the astronomical experts "consent against him." Feeling himself to have been "condemned without a hearing," Hevelius requested one "as truth and equity demand." He asked the Royal Society, which he characterized as "free from prejudice and self interest," to "rigorously investigate, examine, compare . . . [and] then declare their judgment." Oldenburg insisted that there had been no condemnation. But "since controversies of that kind" could be settled only "by weighing the number and qualities of the observations," he suggested Hevelius abandon his position.[86]

The matter, however, did not rest there. The possibility of two comets was explored as a way of evading the embarrassing problem. John Wallis wrote Oldenburg, "I see not why wee should disbelieve him in matter of fact," since Hevelius had used the best instruments and there was no reason to suspect that either astronomer "would willingly falsify an observation." He preferred "to suspend judgment" rather "than determine anything concerning it."[87] In seeking to resolve this conflict the participants referred to the consensus of skilled astronomical experts rather than the social status of the observers.

When a "controversy about matter of Fact or Experiment" developed between Fabri and Borelli, Wallis suggested further experiments as a solution.[88] Fortunately, major disputes over matters of fact seem to have occurred mostly among foreigners, who were unlikely to experience unpleasant face-to-face contact in London.

In other instances, the problem was the credibility of a report of an individual or group of individuals. Boyle recognized that the credibility of "wonderful" reports might be questionable.[89] The epistemological issue was not directly faced, and the most common response to difficult-to-believe testimony, like that of conflicting testimony, was silence rather than outright denial. Outright denial of incredible testimony provided by seemingly credible witnesses would have undermined the concept "fact" and the disciplines that were founded on it.

Although the Royal Society appropriated the legal language of credible witnesses and often employed other legalistic language, its members were unwilling to adopt either the adversarial role of lawyers or the role of juries as judge of facts. The virtuosi operated in a different institutional and cultural arena. Legal institutions exist to settle disputes authoritatively, not evade them, and to impose state power to enforce their decisions. The Royal Society was primarily investigative in character and discussion-like in discourse, not a decision-making body. It avoided making decisions between contending parties which would undermine collegial enterprise, raise the specter of authority, and perhaps threaten the whole basis of a fact-establishing natural and experimental history.

Scientific Instruments and Natural Facts

The new natural and experimental history relied on sense observation but recognized the weaknesses of the unassisted senses. These weaknesses were, it was believed, at least partially correctable. Baconians as well as non-Baconians such as Galileo and Descartes made good use of sense-enhancing scientific instruments.[90] The advent of the microscope and other instruments modified observational possibilities and thus the nature of witnessing. New and improved instruments permitted previously unknown or barely known phenomena to be observed and more accurately measured.[91] "By the help of telescopes there is nothing so far distant but may be represented to our view; and by the help of Microscopes, there is nothing so small, as to escape our inquiry; hence there is a new visible World discovered to the understanding. . . . the Earth itself . . . shews quite a new thing to us, and in every little particle of its matter, we now behold almost as great a variety of Creatures, as we [are] able before to reckon up in the whole Universe itself."[92] The demand for multiple witnessing and replication increasingly referred to microscopic or telescopic observations. Anatomy, embryology, and pathology were transformed by the microscope,[93] and other instruments, such as Hooke's air pumps, enabled Boyle's experiments to go forward.

Because instruments enhanced perception, greater credibility was assigned to instrument-based testimony.[94] Those using telescopes were better witnesses than those without them, and those with the best telescopes became more reliable witnesses than those with simpler ones. Legal and historical witnessing remained dependent on the visual acuity of the average person. Here legal and scientific witnessing began to diverge. The virtuosi adopted legal concepts but modified them to suit different investigative conditions. In time, scientific instrumentation and the ability to construct repeatable experiments were to generate in observers of natural phenomena a sense of superior expertise.

The observation of natural occurrences, however, was treated somewhat differently than the reporting of experimentally produced facts. Sir Matthew Hale reminded readers that although the telescope enabled the senses to perceive stars or other objects impossible without it, the "Stars in the Milky-way" were not "in the Heavens . . . because the Telescope hath discovered them, for they were there before." Telescopic observation did "not make the thing to be, but evidence them to be."[95]

Experiment added a new dimension to witnessing, because it typically involved equipment, making it possible to manufacture "matters of fact." The virtuosi's involvement in experimental knowledge-making eroded the traditional distinctions between theory and practice and between art and nature. The possibility of replication differentiated the experimental witness from the legal or historical witness of past events and from the witness of one-time natural events.

Instrumentation and experiment distinguished the virtuoso from the ordinary observer, but they did not eliminate the need for "witnessing" itself. "Fact," for the seventeenth century, required a human presence. Without witnesses, "facts" could not be established and in some sense did not exist as "facts." Given an approach to natural philosophy that made natural history its foundation, it was essential that the "matters of fact" on which that philosophy was to be built be secured with as much certainty as humanly possible. Every effort had to be made to ensure the credibility of the scientific observer. The prior acceptance of witness testimony for legal and historical matters of fact helps explain the relative lack of concern among the virtuosi about the proper method of establishing the natural history foundation on which natural philosophy would eventually rest.

Problems: "Things" and Witnesses, Fact and Classification, Fact and Illustration, Circumstances

The introduction of the "fact" into the realm of natural philosophy brought a number of difficulties, some of which were recognized and others ignored. From an epistemological standpoint the largest problem was the faith placed in observation and experiment. If "facts" thus established were not secure, neither were the new natural and experimental histories on which the new philosophy was to be based. On the one hand, it was argued that facts might be established to a moral certainty or beyond reasonable doubt. On the other hand, it was recognized that not all matters of fact could be established with that level of certainty. The senses by which facts were established were capable of error. While error might be reduced by multiple witnessing and the use of sense-enhancing instruments, consciousness of human fallibility remained a fundamental assumption of early modern culture. Instruments, after all, might introduce distortion or result in differing interpretations of what had been seen. That there was so little thoroughgoing skepticism in England, however, meant that the awareness of human weakness did not run deeply enough to undermine a faith in a highly probable, if not certain, factual knowledge even when difficulties were acknowledged.

Experimental results, for instance, were "often various, and inconstant, not only in the hands of different, but even of the same Triers." The proper response to such difficulties was repetition and "jealous and exact Inquiry" to ensure that precisely the same ingredients be used in the same way "and the same circumstances be punctually observ'd." Then, Sprat maintained confidently, "the effect without all question will be the same." Sprat also recognized that the Royal Society's acceptance of accounts that might "seem expos'd to overmuch hazard, and uncertainty" was a problem. But the Society could reduce "such matters of hear-say and information, into real, and impartial Trials."[96]

If one of the most common uses of "fact" involved the observation and description of natural events and "things," there was occasional confusion between "fact" and "thing." Although "fact" required the observation of human witnesses to particular events and experiments, "objects," "things," or "specimens" sometimes became so closely associated with "matters of fact" that they were occasionally referred to as "silent witnesses" or testimonies capable of producing "fact." The traditional distinction between "things" and "words," or *res* and *verba*, also confused matters. "Facts" were neither *res* nor *verba*.

Nature itself, then, might in some sense provide "testimony." Boyle was said to appeal "to the Testimony of Nature, to verify his Doctrine." Yet for Boyle, "things" and inanimate bodies, which had the advantage of being without bias, did not literally speak for themselves.[97] Those who dug up fossils or other objects occasionally did call such things "Witnesses for themselves."[98] For antiquarians, Roman remains were similarly objects that "do abundantly witness."[99] For Hooke, shells and other natural objects were "the Medals, Urnes, or Monuments of Nature whose Relievoes, Impressions, . . . are much more plain and discoverable to any unbiassed Person, and therefore he has no reason to scruple his assent. . . . These are the greatest and most lasting Monuments of Antiquity, which in, all probability antidate the very pyramids, Obeliks, . . . and Coins, and will afford more information in Natural History, than those other put altogether will in Civil."[100] The Royal Society members prided themselves on dealing with *res* or "things" rather than *verba*, but they did not clarify the relationship between *res* and "fact." Moreover, since verbal narratives or description by observers remained the standard mode of establishing matters of fact, the contrast drawn between *res* and *verba* was not as clear as it sometimes appeared to be.

Nor was it always clear whether experiments themselves yielded "testimony" or whether human beings were necessary to "witness" and report the observed experimental events. At one point Boyle suggested that the pressure of water in his experiments had "manifest effects" on "inanimate bodies" and that these experiments did not suffer the weaknesses of human witnesses, being incapable of "prepossessions, or giving us partial informations."[101] There appears to have been a silent process at work in which the "scientific fact" based on witnessing was being elided so that the "thing" or experiment itself took on the functions of human reporting of fact.

Problems relating to "fact" were also created by new classification systems, such as that of John Wilkins, which aspired to include all categories of things and concepts. Could such prearranged and preconceived systems be satisfactorily linked to the observed "facts" of natural history? What was to be done when observed matters of facts did not fit the categories? We find John Ray complaining that Wilkins's system, on which Ray himself had worked, did not, in all respects, conform to his observations of plants.[102] Here "fact" and "classification" are at odds. On the other hand, Martin Lister emphasized that thanks to his "extremely minute but extremely faithful observations" of spiders, his classifications were "not arbitrarily or artificially imposed on the facts, but inspired by the particular features of the animals themselves."[103] The arrangement of particular "facts" into categories and classifications was important to some but not all naturalists. The relation of the particular to the general was, of course, a problem felt beyond the boundaries of classification systems.

Similar vaguely perceived and unresolved problems were encountered about scientific illustrations, representations that were neither the "things" themselves nor verbal testimony about them. Their status was complicated by the fact that they were often prepared by persons other than eyewitnesses. There was talk of the value of illustrations but little examination of their epistemological status.[104]

Naturalists often wrote of the need to record the "circumstances" surrounding the primary facts they described. Shapin has called this practice "virtual witnessing," since it was designed to reproduce in the reader the experience of the eyewitness.[105] Virtuosi such as Boyle and Hooke used the term "circumstances" in connection with "matters of fact," but they, no more than the lawyers and judges who employed the term, really defined its meaning.[106] The epistemological status of the "circumstances" surrounding matters of fact was left unexamined, and it is not clear whether they were to be included to increase "verity" or "verisimilitude." The addition of "fact" to the realm of natural philosophy both modified and confused the epistemological terrain.

Judging and Judgment

The words "judging" and "judgment" had many uses and a variety of related meanings. Judging was, of course, central to courts. Juries exercised their rational faculties on the materials provided by sense and testimony and attempted to reach sound judgments on the matters of fact before them. "Judgment" was also used to characterize many activities outside the courtroom, often, however, retaining a somewhat legal cast. Historians, as we have seen, either reached "judgments" themselves or turned over that function to readers who considered the evidence presented to them. Moral judgment, which was at the heart of casuistry and moral philosophy, was well known. Casuists frequently analogized moral judgment to that of the courts. "Judgment" combined, conflated, and/or confused empirical, logical, and normative conclusions.

Natural philosophy was also enmeshed in the language of judgment. Judgments might be reached with respect to matters of fact or, as we see shortly, hypotheses and theories. If the Royal Society evaded institutional "judgments," individuals often made assessments of the testimony they heard. Sprat wrote of the Royal Society, "There will be always many sincere witnesses standing by, whom self-love will not persuade to report falsely, nor heat of invention carry to swallow a deceit too soon; as having themselves no hand in the making of the Experiment, but onely in the Inspection. So cautious ought men to be, in pronouncing even upon Matters of Fact."[107] Such judgments were not to be placed in the hands of a single person or a company of like-minded individuals but to be made by the Royal Society's "men of various studies."[108]

Good judgments about matters of fact, whether in natural philosophy or elsewhere, required evidence from experienced, skillful, impartial, disinterested observers of good moral character with appropriate opportunity to observe. Multiple witnessing and access to sense-enhancing instruments and experimental equipment too entered into "judgments" about the truth of matters of fact.[109]

The Norm of Impartiality

The norm of the impartial investigator, so fundamental to modern scientific ideology, became an integral feature of Restoration empirical philosophy when it adopted the concept "fact." The norm of impartiality was particularly indebted to the legal tradition, where the very notion of "justice" implied impartiality, lack of bias, and avoidance of partisanship. Judges, juries, and witnesses who prejudged or were "prejudiced" were thought to undermine or contaminate the legal process. Both the common and civil law provided institutional safeguards to prevent interested witnesses and thus biased judgments. The common law prohibited various kinds of interested witnesses, provided for jury challenges, and imposed property qualifications on jurors to help ensure impartial outcomes. Historians, too, donned the mantle of impartiality, claiming to make unbiased judgments or requesting that the impartial reader do so. The "news" media and travelers also promised "true and impartial relations." The norm was common to all the discourses of fact.

The norm of impartiality quickly became part of the fact-oriented empiricism of the Royal Society. Members frequently reiterated their emphasis on lack of interest and bias.[110] Boyle saw himself as cultivating "chemistry with a disinterested mind; neither seeking nor scarce caring for" any "personal advantages" from it. He also emphasized the impartiality of experimental data. In discussing the Hevelius controversy, Wallis stressed the need for "disinterested, and unbiased persons to judge." And impartiality and lack of prejudice were sometimes imputed to the reader in natural as well as historical reporting.[111] The writings of the English virtuosi are suffused with statements about the need for impartiality as well as with the difficulties of attaining it.

Virtuosi were far less likely than were historians and newsmen to accuse fellow investigators of partiality and prejudice. Faulty reports or judgments were more apt to be ascribed to observational error, lack of experience, or the absence of suitable instruments or apparatus. Adoption of the Baconian cooperative vision, relative freedom from the "idols" generated by conscious and unconscious partisanship, and rejection of the adversarial model of courts may well have reinforced the disinclination of the virtuosi to denigrate the judgments of others.

The Witnessing of Nature and the English Culture of Fact

The role of witnessing in natural matters of fact was part and parcel of a larger system of knowledge, which initially dealt with human and, in some instances, divine testimony. That system, at least the outlines of which were of medieval origin, developed rapidly in England during the second half of the seventeenth century, culminating in Locke's *Essay on Human Understanding* (1690).[112] Most English thinkers concerned with issues of probability and certainty emphasized "matters of fact." Precisely because the new scientific community sought proofs beyond a reasonable doubt, it sought to build a new natural philosophy on the basis of a sound natural history. The witnessing of natural and experimental matters of fact could provide a basis of proof beyond reasonable doubt. This approach was promising because the category "matter of fact" and the method of establishing facts to a moral certainty that is beyond reasonable doubt were already well-established parts of English experience. The desired attributes of testimony first worked out in detail by lay and clerical lawyers became integral components of a common European culture. Ultimately, these ideas were most developed in England, in part because they had become a constituent element of English empirical natural philosophy. The widely known Lockean generalization of this approach would make "fact" an even more important feature of the English intellectual landscape.

Geographical Diffusion: The Case of France

Given our focus on English culture, we have had little to say about comparable developments elsewhere. Although the expansion of the concept "fact" from human to natural events and phenomena occurred first in England, the "natural" or "scientific" fact did not remain an English preserve. If Baconian-style natural and experimental histories came to play a role in France, more traditional styles of natural philosophy, with their emphasis on general experience rather than particularities, had a more prominent place and a somewhat longer life there.[113] More influential in France than England, Cartesian natural philosophy did not accord the "facts" of observation and experiment as central a place as they had in the English empirical tradition. Although Descartes himself was involved with observation and experiment, they remained subordinate to a science of causes. Neither the Aristotelians nor the Cartesians appear to have used "fait." Nor does Gassendi's more observationally and experimentally grounded probabilistic natural philosophy appear to have made use of "fait" or "factum" in connection with natural phenomena. Those writing in Latin, as we noted early, were less likely to use "factum" for natural phe-

nomena. The connection between the language of "fact" and a probabilistic empiricism such as Gassendi's was not a necessary one. The practice of natural history took hold in France as elsewhere, and experiment
was integrated into both traditional and Cartesian natural philosophies.
The circles around Peiresc and Mersenne included natural historians and
experimentalists but do not seem to have used "fact" or "fait" in connection with their activities. Although "fait" was widely used in French law and
historiography, it does not appear to have been used in connection with
natural phenomena or experimentation during the first half of the seventeenth century.[114]

The term "fait" appears to have been adopted in France by natural historians associated with the Académie de Sciences in the 1660s. Like the
English, they distinguished between descriptive natural history (*l'histoire*)
and natural philosophy (*physique*) as well as between history and explanation. A Baconian style of natural history was an early item on the agenda
of the Royal Academy of Sciences. It seems likely that the "natural fact" was
introduced in France in connection with the Academy's natural history
program.[115]

Claude Perrault's *Memoirs for a Natural History of Animals . . . dissected by
the Royal Academy* employs "fact" (*fait*) in applying a distinction already
common in civil history to natural history. All history, Perrault commented, is written in one of two ways: "General history" relates "all the
things which have at several times been collected, and which do belong to
the Subject it Treats of." Alternatively, "we are confined to the Narrative of
some particular Acts, of which the Writer has a certain knowledge." The
latter form, labeled commentaries by the Romans and memoirs by the
French, contained only the "Elements" of history and lacked "the Majesty
found in that which is general." If the historian was "exact and sincere,"
however, memoirs had the "Advantage" of "certainty and Truth." "General
Histories of Animals" were characterized by inexact and unfaithful "Descriptions" laid on "sandy Foundations."

The natural historical "memoirs" provide "unblemishable evidence of a
certain and acknowledged Verity." These were "not the work of single person, . . . overly fond of his work and who less considers the truth of the
Facts [*la vérité des faits*], which are not his own Production." They contained "only Matters of Fact verified by a whole Society" (*que ne contiennent
point de faits que n'aient est vérifiez par toute une compagnie*), composed of men
well qualified "to see these sorts of things . . .; who study not so much to
find out Novelties, as carefully to examine those pretended to be found;
and to whom even the Assurance of being deceived in any Observation,
being no less satisfaction than a curious and important discovery; So much
the Love of Certainty prevails in their spirit above all other things."[116] The
Academy, unlike the Royal Society, did not seek to enlist merchants, trav-

elers, and sea captains, who in its view were insufficiently "indowed with [the] Spirit . . . [of] Philosophy and Patience" to provide the necessary sound foundation for natural philosophy.[117]

Like the members of the Royal Society, the academicians sometimes went beyond reported matters of fact but would not pretend "to put a value on our Conjectures, farther than particular Facts [*faits singulars*] can prove them." "Facts" had priority because philosophy "ought to be grounded on the knowledge of all particular things [*toutes les choses partic-ulières*]." Thus instead of saying bears have fifty-two kidneys on each side, they would say only that the particular bear they had dissected had such a conformation.[118]

The academicians would not place "over much reliance on the Reason, which we have intermixt amongst our Experiments, and that it will easily be judged, that we pretend only to answer some matters of Fact which we advance." "Facts [*faits*] are the sole Powers" to prevail against traditional authority. Yet the academicians, like members of the Royal Society, would not limit themselves to memoirs, since it was "impossible to Philosophize without making some general Propositions." These must be "grounded on the knowledge of all particular things [*Ces faits sont le seules forces . . .*]." Carefully verified matters of fact would provide the foundation of their natural history.[119]

A number of French naturalists were in frequent contact with their English counterparts. Huygens, who lived in France, corresponded regularly with Sir Robert Moray, as did Auzout, Justel, and Duhamel with Oldenburg. Oldenburg suggested the possibility of a philosophical alliance between England and France, and Sprat, who thought France "next to England" in its zeal for the promotion of experiments, emphasized the Royal Society's "perpetual intercourse" with French philosophers and the value of reports from "their most Judicious Travellers."[120]

Fontenelle's 1699 *Memoirs of the Royal Academy of Science* echoed Perrault in emphasizing the particularity of "facts" and the distinction between fact and conjecture. The Royal Academy would produce collections "composed of separate Fragments, independent of one another: whereof every one who is the Author, warrants the Facts and the Experiments."[121]

Our sketchy evidence for France suggests that the concept "fact" migrated from law and history to natural history and that particular observations and experiments played a significant role in that migration. Although Lorraine Daston has suggested that the French use of "fait" was less firm than the English "matter of fact," "fact" or "fait" had become part of the vocabulary of French naturalists.[122] Daston's contrast may be somewhat overdrawn, because English use of "fact" also referred to both morally certain facts *and* "matters of fact" insufficiently supported by credible witnesses.

We know even less of the history of "fact" in other European locales. It was Iberian encounters with unknown parts of the world that led observers to depart from the authority of traditional natural history texts. Garcia d'Orta, the first European to provide accurate descriptions of Indian plants and medicines, Bartolomé de las Casas, Gonsálo Fernández de Oviedo, and Francisco Hernández emphasized the value of eyewitness testimony. Although such ventures produced greater descriptive accuracy, more accurate mapmaking, and the importation of exotic flora and fauna from Brazil, Africa, and India, we do not yet know how and when "fact" (*hecho*), already part of the Spanish legal terminology, entered the Iberian natural history vocabulary.[123]

The Spanish Crown certainly encouraged acquisition of what we today would call factual information. The Council of the Indies created the office of cosmographer-chronicler and produced printed questionnaires for distribution in Spain's American possessions in order to compile useful topographical, navigational, and natural history data. This effort, larger in scale than that of the Royal Society a century later, was of much the same character. While the Royal Society was self-consciously engaged in gathering well-supported "facts," we do not yet know whether the Spanish effort was characterized as "fact" collection. One might speculate that the transition from human acts and deeds to natural phenomena took place rather late in Spain because of the decline of Spanish natural philosophy at the end of the sixteenth century and Spain's lengthy adherence to Aristotelian science.

In the Netherlands, as elsewhere, "matter of fact" in law (*het feit*) was the companion of "matter of law" and was used in a number of law-related contexts. For most of the seventeenth century, it appears that "feit" was used only in connection with human occurrences and events.[124] There were, of course, significant Dutch contributions to detailed natural history, microscopic observation and experiment, exact description of physical objects and locales, and medicine, cosmography, and the collection and cataloging of specimens from the far-flung parts of the globe. All these were areas where "fact" was deployed by the English. One would expect that the Netherlands would have provided fertile ground for development and/or acceptance of the concept of fact in relation to natural phenomena.[125]

All European countries adopted the legal distinction between question or matter of fact and question or matter of law and employed "fact" in the context of historical work. If the English were the first to make "fact" central to natural history and natural philosophy, there remains much to learn about how and when that process was extended to other national cultures.

Conclusion

At the beginning of the seventeenth century what today we would call the "scientific fact" did not exist. With the Restoration, well-supported "matters of fact," whether alone or in the company of "hypothesis," played a major role in the research program of the Royal Society and in the English natural history and natural philosophy community more generally. This chapter has attempted to show how a concept initially employed to deal with human actions and deeds was self-consciously adopted by empirically oriented naturalists. Bacon, we have suggested, played a pioneering role in transforming the "human fact" into the "natural fact" by applying the legal witnessing criteria to particular natural events and experiments. His role was supplemented by an English descriptive chorographic tradition in which human and natural "things" and "phenomena" were observed and recorded by the same procedures and mental processes as those employed by historians of human events.

We have also seen that the language and practice of the Royal Society, like all the "discourses of fact," exhibited features derived from the legal arena—emphasis on witnesses, preference for multiple witnesses, the rejection of hearsay, criteria for evaluating witnesses, and a concern for the degree of certainty to be attributed to witnessed matters of fact. In law, "moral certainty" or "belief beyond reasonable doubt" was the highest possible certainty. The natural realm could claim a unique capacity for achieving such certainty because some of its observed facts and many of its experimentally created ones could be replicated before multiple, impartial, skilled, and often instrument-employing witnesses whose testimony could be presented in a nonadversarial setting.

This chapter has continued to trace a group of related characteristics and values that link the varieties of fact finding in a number of seventeenth-century disciplines. The most characteristic feature of the discourses of fact was witnessing, preferably eye-witnessing. Ideally, witnesses were of medium or high social status, independent, and of good moral character, all qualities that enhanced the credibility of their testimony. Although matters of fact involved both the senses and memory, the former was given greater attention. The "ocular" was favored over all others. Another important concern that natural philosophy took over from the legal sphere and the other discourses of fact was impartiality. We have come to see that the conception of the ideal investigator of natural phenomena overlapped with the ideal juror, judge, historian, travel reporter, and newsman.

Although legal concepts did not shape all aspects of English natural philosophy or absolutely determine any of them, the role of the legal tradition in the creation of the "scientific fact" is central. Yet law must be seen as primus inter pares among a number of parallel intellectual developments that collectively composed a culture of fact. We have noted, for example, how "strange but true" natural phenomena became "news" and how closely the conventions of news reporting paralleled the reporting norms of the naturalists, no matter how much less careful in practice journalists were in assessing the "facts" they reported. Our discussion of chorography, voyage reporting, and "moral history" also reveals striking similarities between their descriptive traditions and the discourse of natural history.

We have similarly traced a group of related values connecting the varieties of fact finding we have considered thus far. The most important were the linked values of impartiality and lack of prejudice, values first enunciated by the legal profession and then adopted by historians, travel reporters, and journalists as well as by observers of natural and experimental phenomena. The ideal scientific witness resembled the ideal legal witness, although the former's testimony might be enhanced by the employment of sense-enhancing instruments and experiment.

There are a number of things that remain somewhat elusive about the development of the scientific or natural fact. "Matter of fact" initially referred to a category of things that had to be adequately evidenced and witnessed to be believed. Appropriate testimony was required to substantiate satisfactorily the matter of fact if belief was to reach the level of "moral certainty." Many matters of fact failed the test, making some matters of fact more believable than others and some not believable at all. We thus encountered statements mentioning the possibility of error or mistake in "matters of fact."[126] Boyle, in discussing a "Design for a natural history," even suggested that an appendix where errors of fact could be recorded should be part of the design.[127] Some matters of fact thus were unsuitable to be believed by rational persons, although the notion of untrue, nonbelievable, improbable, or even false facts is alien to modern usage.[128] If we recall the legal origin of the concept "fact," we are less surprised at the notion of false, erroneous, or insufficiently substantiated matters of fact. In the adversarial legal context, "matters of fact" are really "issues of fact" to be pled and proved by one side against contrary pleadings and proofs by the other. One side or the other's matters of fact must be false or insufficiently proved. The process by which matter of fact became the modern "fact," with its association with "truth," is itself part of a historical process in which legal discourse is transposed into other disciplines and, in the process, transmuted.

CHAPTER SIX

The Facts of Nature II

The Gentlemanly Thesis

The "gentlemanly thesis" was first explored by Steven Shapin and Simon Schaffer in their pathbreaking *Leviathan and the Air Pump* and later extended and elaborated by Shapin in *The Social History of Truth*.[1] These books have focused attention on the shaping of knowledge and knowledge claims by social values and social hierarchies. In the first study the authors were especially struck by Boyle's emphasis on the social status of those who witnessed experiments. They contrast Boyle's experimental method and his reliance on "matter of fact" with the method of Thomas Hobbes, who found his model in geometry and emphasized a deductive mode that gave relatively little attention to experiment and observation of particulars. Shapin and Schaffer also suggest that Restoration methods of constructing "matters of fact" reproduced existing societal hierarchies.

More recently, Shapin has argued that the aristocratic and gentlemanly norms derived from Italian Renaissance aristocratic courtesy manuals were transferred to the ideal scientific investigator. He calls particular attention to the role of trust in scientific endeavor and argues that the societal convention of trust in a gentleman's word was adopted by the Royal Society. Shapin also suggests that English emphasis on social hierarchy led to the treatment of technicians, who lacked gentlemanly status, as servants. The contrast between Robert Hooke, the employed technician, and Robert Boyle, the high-status experimenter, is sharply drawn. It is Boyle, the embodiment of the gentleman-aristocrat, whom Shapin sees as giving shape to the scientific norms of the Restoration era.[2]

We have seen that the reliability of witnesses was a crucial issue in all the discourses of fact, including law, history, and natural history. In all of them social status was one but not the sole criterion of reliability. Expertise, experience, opportunity, number, disinterest, and impartiality were other criteria. When scientific witnessing is placed in the context of the common culture of witnessing of the time, gentlemanly trust recedes to one of a number of bases for trust.

It is doubtful that the clergymen, government officials, and physicians who were members of the Royal Society would have been considered gentlemen by Shapin's exemplar, Robert Boyle, or by Restoration social norms generally.[3] In fact, the social status of those in what we now call the professions was ambiguous. When a clergyman became a bishop and a barrister a judge, their gentle status might be confirmed, but only in the eyes of some. Sir Matthew Hale, a leading judge, renowned legal scholar, and sometime naturalist, was the son of a clothier and raised in a modest yeoman family. The prominence of the professions in fact-finding endeavors and the decisive role of middling-rank jurors in legal fact finding suggest that attention to "middling" social status ought not be too rapidly jettisoned.

As we noted earlier, the Royal Society aggressively sought reports of "matter of fact" from seamen and travelers. Had Boyle been wedded to the notion that only gentleman were worthy of credit, his efforts to cultivate such reporting would have made little sense. Robert Hooke certainly did not possess the social status of Boyle, but his observations, experimental findings, microscopic studies, and observations of comets, all of which were to be found under the rubric "matter of fact," were highly respected by fellow virtuosi.[4] Sprat did report that most Royal Society members were gentlemen "free and unconfined." He also noted the king himself brought tradesman John Graunt to the Society's attention and wrote "that if they found any more such Tradesmen, they should be sure to admit them all." Sprat urged the Society to have "careful regard" for "all sorts of Mechanick Artists."[5]

The contrast between the social status and ethos of scholars and gentlemen also is drawn too sharply by Shapin and Schaffer. To be sure, there was a substantial difference between the traditional scholastic disputation and the model of discourse adopted by the Royal Society, but a good many of the most prominent Royal Society figures—Wilkins, Ward, Petty, Bathurst, Barrow, Goddard, Wren, Willis, and Newton, among others—were, or had been, academics, and the Society's behavioral norms had been worked out at Wadham College, Oxford, and in the earlier 1645 group at Gresham College.[6] There were a good many English institutions in addition to the universities where those of high and middling status mingled. Government offices, trading companies, religious institutions, the law courts, and the Royal Society itself provide examples.

In short, the culture of fact was as much a culture of professional success as of gentle courtesy. And the realm of professional success is one of competence and expertise. In natural philosophy as in law, social status bore on credibility, but so did expertise and competence. That expertise about nature was largely generated, as it was in most areas of human endeavor, by the opportunity for observation or learning by experience. In natural philosophy, experiments and instruments, and the increased observational specialization that came with them, redefined expertise. Such an invigorated expertise tended to undercut claims of social status. Ray may not have been quite a gentleman because of his dependent status, but his reports on plants were far more credible than those of an untutored squire.

As sense-enhancing instruments such as microscopes and measuring devices became more accurate and sophisticated, social status would matter less. The Auzout-Hevelius controversy presented grave difficulties to the scientific community not because of issues of social status but because astronomical instruments had so enhanced observational potential. The microscopic observations of Leeuwenhoek were doubted less because of his low social status than his reluctance to share his instruments.

We have seen the role of social status in assessing the credibility of witnesses in common law courts where social status was only one among a complex of *indicia* of credibility. Anyone who had seen and heard was a better witness than anyone who had not. Hearsay from a high-status source remained hearsay, and the credibility criteria developed in the context of canon and civil law predated the Renaissance courtier tradition. The fact that yeomen staffed most juries and determined "matters of fact" at common law suggests that the epistemologically significant line of social demarcation was lower than that of gentleman though perhaps higher than the "vulgar." Shapin and Schaffer are certainly correct in insisting that "matter of fact" was a social as well as an epistemological category, but that social category was being transferred from one kind of institutional setting to another—from the courts to scientific inquiry—and modified to meet the needs of the naturalists. It was the language of the law and the analogy to legal processes and criteria of truth, not the language of the courtesy manuals, that was constantly in the mouths of the virtuosi. And though the law took account of social status sometimes and for some purposes, it was most certainly not a realm of gentle courtesy.

Common law courts, however, employed an adversarial procedure engaged in by highly self-interested parties. When "matters of fact" are transposed to a self-recruited scientific community composed of persons with common interests, it is not that a special climate of trust must be established by reference to gentle courtesy but rather that the special climate of mistrust and antagonism found in litigation is sloughed off. Shapin notes that Boyle insisted that experiments had to be actually witnessed by an appropriate number of suitable persons in a suitable physical space. That most of the witnesses might be gentlemen may have been comforting, but more important was a social setting in which, quite unlike the law courts, the experimenters and the witnesses were engaged in a mutual endeavor in which no participant had a strong material interest in falsifying facts. The problem the naturalists faced was error, not falsification.

In emphasizing Boyle's literary technique of "virtual witnessing," Shapin provides another form of the gentlemanly thesis. The reader will put his trust in Boyle's account because Boyle is a gentleman.[7] But juries, no more than readers of Boyle's texts, could literally see the events narrated. They too received witness testimony and reports of "circumstances." They thus engaged in a kind of "virtual witnessing," as did the readers of newsbooks, which Nigel Smith has suggested sought to create the illusion that the reader himself was witnessing the action.[8] Something akin to Boyle's "virtual witnessing" was shared by several, if not all, early modern "discourses of fact."[9]

As treated by Shapin and Schaffer, "matter of fact" is associated particularly with Boyle, and his predecessors and contemporaries are largely ignored. Without the Baconian insistence on natural and experimental histories based on firsthand experience, however, "facts" would not have become central to the Restoration scientific community. The crucial change that made possible the "scientific fact" was the application of the modes of proof of fact finding about particular human actions to particular natural and experimentally produced phenomena. In this application the gentle status of the investigator was a plus but was not decisive. And, of course, this adoption was characteristic not only of Boyle but of his many naturalist contemporaries in the Royal Society.[10] Even if Boyle was seen at the time as the embodiment of gentlemanly courtesy, there is little evidence that his predecessors and contemporaries were obsessed with gentility. Being in the class of gentleman obviously counted for a great deal in Restoration England, but it does not provide a sufficient guide to the creation and construction of the "scientific fact."

If the aristocratic and gentlemanly cultural ideal made prominent the attributes of honor, politeness, trustworthiness, and civility, we must also note the less desirable traits associated with that culture. Pride, arrogance, self-regard, and what Hobbes called "vainglory" were as much a part of aristocratic, gentlemanly culture as honor, politeness, and civility. If the

Renaissance court fostered civility, it was also the scene of fierce interpersonal competition and the "rhetoric of social combat." The courtly model was more competitive than cooperative, and the success of one aristocrat or gentleman was, more often than not, at the expense of another.[11] All this was a far cry from the deliberately low-keyed collaborative endeavors of the Royal Society.

Although Restoration society was preoccupied with social hierarchy and social status, England was less preoccupied than France, Spain, or Italy. One would therefore expect to find a greater role for socially based epistemological categories in those locales. Yet these countries were not in the forefront in constructing an intellectual category of natural "matter of fact" conforming to the socially dominant classes. Nor do we find that the more bourgeois Netherlands adopted a different set of socially influenced epistemological distinctions.

The relationship between those who exercise epistemological power and those who exercise political and social power in a socially stratified hierarchical society is a complex one that confronts students of medieval scholasticism and Renaissance humanism as much as it does those of Restoration natural philosophy.[12] The issues of knowledge and power discussed by Shapin and Schaffer are immensely important, but an extension of the narrow context in which they consider those issues suggests that a number of other social and intellectual forces were as important, if not more so, as the tradition of gentlemanly courtesy in establishing a culture of fact.

"Fact" and "Hypothesis"

Having explored the origins and development of the "scientific fact," we now turn to the question of what Restoration virtuosi thought was to be done with the appropriately verified "matters of fact" that constituted the natural history research program. Natural history, after all, was not natural philosophy. How might one move from "facts" to the explanations of those facts and to the discovery of the principles of natural philosophy?

If there was a consensus on how to establish facts, there was less agreement on how to develop natural philosophy.[13] Since relatively few members of the English scientific community in the pre-Newtonian era expressed confidence that their explanations and axioms could ever be as certain as the facts on which they rested, what was the relation between fact and explanation or generalization? Most Restoration virtuosi might have agreed that "rude heaps of unpolish'd and unshap'd materials" would not automatically yield philosophical principles. Most, however, did not adopt the method outlined in Bacon's *New Organon*. Even Sprat admitted that Bacon had been too inclined "to take all that comes, rather, then to choose; and to heap, rather, then to register." [14] Few were attracted to the forms of experimentalism adopted by the Jesuit scientific community or to Hobbes, whose natural philosophy provided little role for facts. Relatively few were committed to Cartesian natural philosophy.

The majority of the members of the Royal Society and the English naturalist community more generally, though often castigating overly speculative hypothesizing, were led to conjecture, hypothesis, and theory as a means of linking well-proved facts to some kind of generalization. The English scientific community was somewhat ambivalent about the employment of hypotheses, and few were ready to consider such conjectures, hypotheses, or theories as capable of the same degree of certainty as matters of fact. One might be "unquestionably sure" of the existence of many things but on uncertain ground in explaining "the nature of them." No man "in his wits could doubt" well-established facts, yet, once found, many "remained inexplicable." [15]

Some were content simply to accumulate facts, believing that explanations and principles could be put off, at least for the time being. Others, like Newton, felt that true principles or theory could be "deduced" from the facts. The most common, but never the sole, approach of the Restoration era was to link "fact" to "hypothesis."

"Hypothesis" had a long history in natural philosophy, mathematics, and mathematical astronomy before the introduction of the new natural history with its concept "fact." It had acquired a considerable range of meanings by the Restoration era. Naturalists were familiar with rival Copernican and Tychonic hypotheses. Hypothesis also played a considerable role in Cartesian physics, typically being offered as plausible or possible explanations that might be false. [16] Bacon discussed but was not sympathetic to hypothesis. [17]

The language of "theory," "hypothesis," and "conjecture" was rather unstable. [18] "Theory," like hypothesis, had mathematical associations and was sometimes used interchangeably with hypothesis, though for many virtuosi "theory" implied greater certainty than hypothesis. Many natural philosophers who referred to or employed hypotheses insisted that well-established matters of fact provided the appropriate evidence for the hypothesis in question. The same might be true for "theory," though this term was most often adopted when natural phenomena were described mathematically. "Conjecture" too was employed, most frequently in the context of "conjecturing on the causes" of some phenomenon or set of facts. In natural philosophy conjecture might be used as a synonym for hypothesis, especially by those unwilling to make strong statements in behalf of their explanatory claims, but, unlike "theory," it was sometimes associated with guessing.

Despite the variations in terminology, the joining of "fact" to "hypothesis" was a crucial development in Restoration natural philosophy. If some naturalists associated hypotheses with "fiction," "romance," and "mere speculation," the more prevalent view was that particular hypotheses attained higher or lower degrees of probability depending on how well supported they were by well-established matters of fact. There was disagreement over whether all hypotheses should be treated as equally probable, whether some hypotheses might be so certain as to be treated as laws of nature, the relationship between hypotheses and experiment, the role of reason in the construction and evaluation of hypotheses, and the importance of hypothesis formulation and testing for the construction of principles of natural philosophy. A clear distinction between the "hypothesis" as a tentative, causal statement derived from empirical observation and disconfirmable by further empirical observation and the more traditional usage of "hypothetical" as merely asserted and unconfirmed had not yet fully emerged. In the process of groping toward that distinction, the writings of the virtuosi often seem simultaneously to condemn and commend "hypotheses."

We explore the treatment of some of these issues by examining the views of Sprat and Glanvill, spokesmen and apologists for the new philosophy, and by sampling the views of several virtuosi, in particular those of Robert Hooke, Robert Boyle, and John Wallis, all of whom treated hypothesis rather extensively, if not always consistently. We conclude with Isaac Newton, who, whatever his actual practice, seemed to offer a radically different position on hypothesis.

Apologists and Spokesmen

We begin with Sprat's *History of the Royal Society*. Given that he was a hired publicist, selected by and writing largely under the supervision of John Wilkins, Sprat may be viewed as Wilkins's mouthpiece and thus as having an adequate understanding of Royal Society practice.[19] The *History*'s sometimes ambiguous and even inconsistent statements about hypothesis may be explained either as an attempt to comprehend a number of contradictory views or as expressing the Society's own ambivalence and uncertainty concerning "hypothesis."

Sprat often referred to hypothesis and conjecture rather suspiciously, but he also treated them positively when they were based on "matters of fact." Though the Royal Society refused to concern itself with general principles, these being "a kind of metaphysics," it was willing to conjecture on the causes of natural facts. But it insisted on circumspection, modesty, and wariness in order to avoid the "disguised Lies" and the "deceitful fancies" of "catching at" explanations "too soon." Continued experiments would prevent "overhasty and precipitant concluding upon causes." Sprat provided numerous examples of hypotheses presented and discussed at Society meetings which dealt with astronomy, pendulums, fire, the air, filtration, earthquakes, petrification, the lodestone, tempering steel, light, colors, and fluidity. Some readers might "imagine that" hypothesis "consists not so well with their Method," which was "chiefly bent upon the Operative, rather than the Theoretical Philosophy," but Sprat emphasized that "by affirming, that whatever Principles, and Speculations they now raise from things, they do not rely upon them as the absolute end, but only use them as a means of farther knowledge." Hypotheses and "Doctrines of causes" served "to promote our Experimenting; but they would rather obscure, than illumine the mind, if" made "the perpetual Objects of our Contemplation."[20]

Sprat sometimes used "theory" interchangeably with "hypothesis." In writing of Wren, Sprat spoke of "theory"; Wren himself used "hypothesis."[21] Sprat treated "theory" positively in speaking of Wren, critically when he wrote of Descartes. He condemned those who disputed about the "Nature and Causes of Motion in general" without "prosecute[ing] it through all particular Bodies" and expressed reservations about virtuosi "a little too forward to conclude upon Axioms, from what they have found out, in some particular Body."[22]

Sprat selected Christopher Wren as the exemplar of the Royal Society and associated him with observation, hypothesis, and theory. His "Doctrine of Motion . . . the most considerable of all others for establishing the first Principles of Philosophy, by Geometrical Demonstration," is compared favorably to that of Descartes, who made "some Experiments of this kind upon Conjecture, and made them the first Foundation of his whole System of Nature." Wren, in contrast, had demonstrated "the true Theories, after they had been confirm'd by hundreds of experiments."[23] Wren himself wrote that a "hypothesis" confirmed by observed facts might be "true."[24]

Sprat's treatment of the Society's attitude toward hypothesis did not differ substantially from one of 1686 in which the Society was characterized as concerned not only with performing experiments "but also with useful Discourses concerning Physical, Mathematical, and Mechanical Theory or Observations."[25]

Similar terminological laxity characterized Oldenburg's massive correspondence, which was liberally sprinkled with references to hypotheses, theories, and laws without much by way of distinction between the terms.[26] At times there is a utilitarian Baconian vision with relatively little place for hypothesis. On one occasion Oldenburg changed his terminology from "hypothesis" to "theory" to conform to Newton's insistence that his report on colors had been erroneously characterized as a "hypothesis."[27] Statutes governing the Royal Society indicated that members would discuss their experiments and observations as well as consider "what may be deduced from them." The Society would not commit itself to any particular hypothesis, but individual members often offered their views for discussion. Well-founded hypotheses were taken seriously.[28]

For Royal Society apologist Glanvill, hypotheses without a "history of Nature" were "but Dreams." If "we frame Schemes of things, without consulting the Phenomena, we do but . . . describe an Imaginary World of our own making." Hypotheses without facts were fictions, but they were useful when based on "events and sensible appearances." Given the current inadequacies and incompleteness of natural history, however, it was difficult to develop hypotheses and advance "natural Theory . . . much less, to fix certain Laws and prescribe Methods to Nature in her Actings."[29]

In some moods and on some occasions Glanvill took the position that "all we can hope for, as yet, is . . . the History of Things," the establishment of "general Axioms," and the making of hypotheses to be "the happy privilege of Succeeding Ages." "We have as yet no such thing as Natural Philosophy; Natural History is all we can pretend to"[30]—Glanvill's more frequently stated position was not quite so pessimistic though it emphasized the probabilistic quality of even the best hypotheses.[31]

The Virtuosi

Given the use of hypotheses in astronomy and in Cartesian physics,[32] it would have been difficult for English virtuosi, some of whom were influenced by Descartes, to avoid hypotheses entirely. Atomism and corpuscularism required hypotheses because minute particles, being invisible to the senses, had in some sense to be hypothesized. But it was the linkage of observed and experimentally produced "matters of fact" with hypothesis that most characterized the practice of the English Restoration community.

Henry Power noted that "real Experiment or Observation" was necessary to avoid error in hypotheses and conjectures and indicated that empirical work would both suggest and test hypotheses.[33] Samuel Parker, an early defender of the new philosophy, commended the Society for rejecting "all particular hypotheses" in favor of "true and exact Histories"; nevertheless, he believed that the new natural history would in time "lay firm and solid foundations to erect Hypotheses." Matters of fact might be "exact and certain," but hypotheses were "conjectures" having "uncertain (though probable) applications." Lord Brouncker's experiments on gun recoil "commanded" by the Society aimed at the "discovery of the cause thereof." Ralph Bohun, Robert Plot, and John Beale wrote of speculation, conjecture, theory, opinion, and principles to be tested by matters of fact, experience, and experiments.[34] Causal analysis was obviously part of the Royal Society's mission from its early years.[35]

Though the distinction between fact and hypothesis and fact and causal analysis was clear, the distinction between hypothesis and theory was not. Sometimes theory implied greater certainty, sometimes it did not. Sometimes theory implied a connection with mathematics, sometimes it did not. It is thus difficult to know how to interpret John Evelyn's 1663 comment that the goal of the Royal Society was to produce "real and useful Theorie." Walter Charleton referred to the "great evidence and certainty" of Harvey's hypothesis dealing with the circulation of the blood, indicating he was "well satisfied" with its "Verity." He noted the "singular probability" of the Copernican hypothesis, which was accepted "upon grounds of as much certainty and clearness, as the sublime and remote nature of the subject seems capable of."[36] Not all hypotheses were as certain as Harvey's or as probable as that of Copernicus. Charleton, for example, felt that his investigation of the passions would not allow him to hope for "certain and demonstrable Knowledge" but thought it was "so plausible, at least, as to form an Hypothesis."[37]

Natural historians who at some times were content merely to collect and classify data, at others engaged in linking "fact" and "hypothesis." Nehemiah Grew described the philosophy of the Royal Society as "Reasoning grounded upon Experiment, and the common notions of Sense, the former being, without the latter, too subtle and intangible, the latter without the former, too gross and unmanagable." Though it was necessary to "subjoin Experiment to conjecture," much caution was required in making and "passing a Judgment" on the latter.[38] On another occasion Grew told Oldenburg, "I think I have not only conjectur'd but demonstrated many things. And if I were convinced, That those things I have said . . . , were only bare ingenuitys, I would immediately burn them."[39] There was a general, if not unanimous, understanding that facts could and should serve as bases for generating causal explanations and that various and contradictory hypotheses could be generated from the same facts.

Although the language of the "laws of nature" was not widely or frequently employed in the pre-Newtonian era by natural philosophers when referring to natural phenomena or natural facts, "law" was occasionally employed, as was "true hypothesis and "true principle."[40] In 1662, referring to hypotheses of Wren and Boyle, Huygens, a regular correspondent of Moray, wrote that hypotheses exhibited "many degrees of Probable, some nearer Truth than others." "The highest degree of probability existed when the Principles that have assumed to correspond perfectly to the phenomena which experiment has brought under observation, and further, principally, when one can imagine and foresee new phenomena which ought to follow from the hypothesis which one employs, and when one finds therein the fact corresponds to our prevision."[41]

Mathematician William Neile seems to have envisioned a full cycle of initial fact collection followed by hypothesis formulation and then hypothesis testing as a guide to further empirical research. He proposed that committees of the Royal Society consider the "possible cause or causes" of experimental results, arguing that those best qualified to do the experiments should also "steer their judgments and reason to the indagation of the causes." Experiments would shed light on the causes, and the "forming of causes" would help discover "new and unthought effects," a position not so far from that expressed by Sprat.[42]

Sir Joseph Williamson suggested that it was best to "proceed synthetically by first making the proposition what was designed to be proved, and then proceed with the experiments to make the proof." Sir William Petty, on the other hand, felt experiments were "more faithfully made and delivered, if not made to help out a theory, because that might prepossess and bias the experimenter."[43] In their disdain for earlier natural philosophy, some members moved to a crude empiricism in which facts should be piled up now with theory deferred until later, seeing premature hypotheses as creating a threat of biased experimentation. Others envisioned programs of experiment guided by hypothesis as superior to ambitious but random fact collection.[44]

Although it is clear that the Royal Society combined fact and hypothesis, neither its members nor its apologists and leadership had reached a consensus on precisely how the two should be linked. A somewhat closer examination of the views of three major Restoration virtuosi, all of whom were active in the Royal Society's affairs, underlines both the desire to link "fact" with "hypothesis" or "theory" and the uncertainty as to the nature of the linkage.

Robert Hooke

One of the most active and prolific members of the Restoration scientific community, Robert Hooke worked in a dazzling array of fields. He was involved with planetary observation, theoretical astronomy, microscopic studies, and geology as well as a host of practical inventions. Hooke is often considered a Baconian, and in some sense he was. Although he spoke of the "Incomparable Verulum,"[45] he abandoned the Baconian distrust of hypotheses, writing that even natural historians primarily concerned with compiling the facts of nature must be "acquainted with all sorts of hypotheses & theories by which the phaenomena of Nature have been Indeavored to be solv'd."[46]

Hooke distinguished between matter of fact and "philosophical conjectures on the causes" or "reasons of . . . phenomena," viewing both as vital to the Society's activities.[47] Like Sprat, Hooke noted that though the Society had "seem'd to avoid and prohibit pre-conceived Theories and Deductions from particular, and seemingly accidental Experiments," these "if knowingly and judiciously made are Matters of the greatest Importance, as giving a Characteristick of the Aim, Use and Significancy thereof." Without hypotheses, "many and possibly the most considerable Particulars" would be passed over "without Regard and Observations."[48] The business of the Royal Society should, in fact, include "examination of all Hypotheses and Doctrines that have hitherto been published and for trying how Consonant they are with their own assertions and experi[ments] and in what they are good & in what Defective where they have asserted truth and where falsehood and what part of them is worthy to be retained and what is absolutely false & absurd & and to be rejected, and what is of a middle nature & and deserves to be farther considered."[49]

Hooke's *Micrographia* (1665) praised the Royal Society for rejecting any "hypothesis not sufficiently grounded and confirm'd by Experiments" and lauded its efforts to "correct all Hypotheses by Sense." His own hypotheses were to be treated "only as Conjectures and Quaeries," and his discussions of "causes of things" observed were not to be viewed as "unquestionable Conclusions, or matters of confutable Science." Readers were not to expect "Infallible Deductions, or certainty of Axioms."[50]

Yet Hooke disparaged experimenters who "make no use at all of their reason and employ nothing but their senses in taking notice of matter of fact." Indeed, it was "a little below the name and dignity of Philosophers to sitt still with the bare registering of effects without an inquiry into their causes."[51] Hooke favored a procedure that began with observation, continued according to reason, and then returned to the "Hands and Eyes" in a "continual passage round from one Faculty to another." In the process, Hooke hoped "true Hypotheses" would result.[52] Some causal explanations, however, would remain merely "probable" because insufficiently supported "by Observation . . . to conclude anything positive or negative." Employing the judicial analogy, he noted that experiments "may stand like so many witnesses to give testimony of this truth or against that error. And a most severe examination of these witnesses must be made before a jury can warrantably give their verdict or a judge pronounce sentence, for branding one proposition or hypothesis as erroneous and absurd or for establishing another for a truth or axiom."[53]

Some kinds of hypotheses, however, were not even eligible for such a trial, among them speculations that could not be supported by matters of fact.[54] Hooke's *Cometa* took up the problem of dealing with competing hypotheses when needed facts or data were lacking. Here he suggested that whatever was not built on careful observation was nothing but "conjecture" and "hypothesis."[55]

Hooke also employed "hypothesis" in connection with astronomy and physics, where he spoke of both "a true hypothesis" and "probable arguments."[56] He sometimes contemplated the possibility of a fact-based, mathematical, empirical philosophy that would yield a certainty roughly equivalent to that of "mathematical certainty."[57] His statement that the goal of natural philosophy was to "discover the nature and properties of bodies as well as the true causes of natural philosophy"[58] is difficult to reconcile with his more probabilistic pronouncements. In these partial contradictions Hooke represents the Restoration mainstream that connected the Baconian fact to hypothesis but remained somewhat uncertain as to the nature of the connection and divided over the certainty of the results. He was quite capable of using the word "hypothesis" pejoratively, to apply to mere speculation neither empirically derived nor tenable, or to use it to refer to an empirically derived and testable causal proposition or in connection with a mathematical theorem and proof.

Robert Boyle

Although Boyle recognized the difficulty of building "an accurate hypothesis" on "an incompleat history" of nature,[59] he was ready to develop hypotheses on the basis of the available factual data, it being "sometimes conducive to the discovery of truth, to permit the understanding to make an hypothesis . . . by examining how far the phaenomena are, or not, capable of being solved by that hypothesis." If "built upon a more competent number of particulars," hypotheses were freed from "imputation of barrenness."[60] He and his associates should "forbear to establish any theory, till they have consulted with . . . a considerable number of experiments, in proportion to the comprehensiveness of the theory to be erected on them."[61]

Boyle developed hypotheses in a many different contexts. His work on the consistency of gems, which resulted in a "Conjectural hypothesis," would first show that his hypothesis was possible and then "set down some particulars to make it very Probable." His "explication" was to be judged according to how well it fit the factual data.[62] His "Origine of Forms and Qualities" had both "historical" and "speculative" parts.[63] Boyle also indicated that hypotheses could "render an intelligible account of the causes of the effects, or phaenomena proposed, without crossing the laws of nature, or other phaenomena; the more numerous, the more various the particles are, whereof some are explicable by the assisted hypothesis, and some are agreeable to it, or, at least are not dissonant from it, the more valuable is the hypothesis, and the more likely to be true."[64] Although many atomists, corpuscularians, and other naturalists "presume to know the true and genuine causes of the things they attempt to explicate," the "utmost they can attain to, in their explications, is, that the explicated phenomena may be produced in such a manner, . . . but not that they really are so."[65] Boyle also considered the "Requisites of a Good Hypothesis." Among them were consistency with observations and the laws of nature. An "excellent hypothesis" had additional requirements, including being the simplest one, the only one capable of explicating the phenomena, and the ability to predict future phenomena.[66]

Boyle's views on sense and reason help explain how "matter of fact" and hypothesis were linked. Reason, the "superior faculty," judged what conclusions could and could not be "safely grounded on the information of the senses, and the testimony of Experience."[67] Explanation and hypothesis required that reason be "duly exercised" on "matters of fact." Only in this way could one hope to gain knowledge of "unobservable truths."[68] When reason judged which of "two disagreeing opinions" was "most rational," it "ought to sentence" what is "preferred" by reason, "furnished, either with all the evidence requisite or advantageous to make it give a right judgement . . . , or, when that cannot be had, with the best and fullest information, that it can procure."[69] Experience was therefore "but an assistant to reason . . . the understanding remains still the judge, and has the power or right to examine and make use of the testimonies presented to it. . . . This prompts me to illustrate the use of reason by comparing her to an able judge who comes to hear and decide cases. . . . When an authentick and sufficient testimony has cleared things to him, he then pronounces according to the light of reason he is master of; to which the witnesses did but give information, though that subsequent information may have obliged him to lay aside some prejudicate opinions he had entertained before he received it."[70]

Boyle's terminology was not consistent. Sometime he spoke of hypotheses, at others of "theory," "conjecture," "explication," or even "conjectural hypothesis." Hypotheses might refer to large-scale systems of natural philosophy, such as the Peripatetic, Cartesian or Epicurean, or to some facet of his own or others' experimentally based work.[71] Boyle occasionally employed the language of "theory" but made it clear that such "superstructure[s]" ought to be "looked upon only as temporary ones; which though they may be preferred before any others, as being the best in their kind that we have, yet they are not entirely to be acquiesced in, as absolutely perfect, or uncapable of improving alterations."[72] Given his belief that the generalizations of natural philosophy were probable and always subject to modification, Boyle, like Sprat and Hooke, insisted on not being overly forward in establishing general principles and universal axioms.[73] In view of both the limitations and strengths of the human mind and the way in which reason operated on sense data and matters of fact, all theories, generalizations, or hypotheses were necessarily probabilistic.[74]

Boyle's experimental philosophy included both confident belief in "matters of fact" and the deployment of hypotheses of varying degrees of probability. Like many other Restoration-era naturalists, he was led in the direction of nonessentialist natural philosophy, for hypotheses and explanations, however well grounded, remained probable and tentative.

John Wallis

Mathematician John Wallis, Savilian Professor of Geometry at Oxford and a founding member of the Royal Society, like most English virtuosi wished the Royal Society to "contribute . . . conjectures, advice, and reasoning" as well as observations and experiments. Experiment would both furnish "the matter to determine ye Hypothesis" and "be the best judge" of the hypothesis in question.[75]

When Wallis presented his "hypothesis about the flux and reflux of the Sea," he promised to discuss it modestly "as a conjecture to be examined, and upon that examination rectified if there be occasion, or rejected if it will not hold water." He contrived experiments "to illustrate" the hypothesis but emphasized that the "clearest evidence" would come from celestial observations. His "discourse" was therefore to be considered "only as an Essay of the general Hypothesis," which would be "adjusted" as the still wanting "General History of Tides" developed. He would therefore not insist on "the certainty of it." His hypothesis would eventually "stand or fall, as it shall be found to answer matter of fact." "For where the Matter of Fact well agreed on, it is not likely that several Hypothesis should so far differ." Although Wallis used "hypothesis" most frequently in connection with his work on tides, he also spoke of that work as "surmise," "conjecture," and "essay." Oldenburg labeled it a "theory."[76]

Wallis also discussed hypothesis when requested to comment on Leibniz's *Hypothesis physica nova*. He responded evasively, suggesting delay in assenting to new hypotheses, even those "proved by the evidence of the eyes," until there was time to assess arguments on both sides. The truth of hypotheses emerged slowly. The Leibniz hypothesis, not yet proved "by ocular inspection nor by certain demonstration," would, if "founded on true reasoning . . . at last . . . find a place in the minds of those who philosophize freely."[77] For the most part, Wallis seems to treat hypothesis in terms of empirical confirmation but probably did not entirely distinguish empirical support from mathematical or other rational proofs.

In seventeenth-century English natural philosophy some real conceptual confusion seems to have remained between hypothesis as empirically derived and empirically disconfirmable, probabilistic, causal statement and hypothesis as mathematical proposition subject to mathematical proofs. Most of the confusion, however, was linguistic rather than conceptual. In one sentence hypothesis was fiction or at least conjecture, neither empirically derived nor tested. In another it meant roughly what scientists today mean. Yet behind the verbal confusion is a fairly clear understanding of what constitutes a scientifically appropriate hypothesis and of its probabilistic nature. There was, however, some genuine disagreement about whether particular areas of empirical inquiry were yet ready for treatment by hypotheses. And there was fear of premature acceptance of or excessive dependence on newly proposed hypotheses. There was also marked distrust of large systems of hypotheses or universal theories as running far beyond existing fact-gathering and processing resources. Although the English scientific community was neither unanimous nor consistent in its expressed attitudes toward hypothesis, the combination of "fact" and "hypothesis" became the most characteristic feature of Restoration scientific practice.[78]

Newton and the Newtonian Era

Boyle and Hooke combined Baconian natural history based on morally certain "matters of fact" with more or less probable hypotheses. Although Newton shared their Baconian insistence on well-observed and well-recorded experimentally produced phenomena, he frequently rejected hypotheses as "suppositions," instead attempting to employ mathematically structured arguments to produce what he took to be universally valid statements. Newton claimed that his conclusions, which he often labeled "theories," enjoyed a certitude greater than that of hypotheses because directly derived from experimental facts. From one vantage point we may view Newton as more Baconian than Boyle or Hooke; from another he participated in the mathematical physics of Galileo and his successors and in the physico-mathematical tradition of mixed mathematics.[79] In any event, his successes in deducing "theory" from facts (he used the term "phenomena"), facts now treated mathematically, played an important role in the transformation of English natural philosophy. Here we focus on those instances where he appeared to differ most from his English contemporaries.

We begin with Newton's defense of his 1672 "theory" of colors. Although Newton, his critics, and his supporters were equally wedded to experimental "facts," there was considerable disagreement on the relationship of the "facts" to his "theory" as well as on how to characterize his results. "You know the proper method for inquiring after the properties of things is to deduce them from experiments; and I told you that the theory, which I propounded, was evinced to me, not by inferring 'tis thus because not otherwise, that is, not be deducing it only from a confutation of contrary suppositions, but deriving it from experiments concluding positively and directly. The way therefore to examine it is by considering whether the experiments . . . do prove those parts of the theory, to which they are applied, or by prosecuting other experiments, which the theory may suggest for its examination."[80]

Newton's most vocal critic, Hooke, rejected Newton's claims of certitude, suggesting that his own hypothesis on light explained the experimental facts equally well. Newton was insulted when his "theory" was labeled a "hypothesis," insisting that he had presented "nothing else than certain properties of light." He preferred the Royal Society to have "rejected them as vain and empty speculation" rather than have acknowledged them as "hypotheses." If the "possibility of hypotheses" were the "test of truth and reality of things, I see not how certainty can be obtained in any science."[81]

Yet for Huygens, too, Newton's theory of colors was a hypothesis, though a "very probable" one, in which the "experimentum crucis" "confirms it very well." Huygens wrote Oldenburg, "What you have put in your late Journals from Mr. Newton confirms still further his doctrine of colors. Nevertheless the thing could very well be otherwise, and it seems to me that he ought to content himself if what he has advanced is accepted as a very likely hypothesis."[82] Oldenburg, who began by calling Newton's proposition a "hypothesis," changed to "theory."[83] If for some natural philosophers, such as Boyle, terms such as "theory," hypothesis," and conjecture" might be used interchangeably, for Newton they could not. Newton remained angry at attempts to offer "an hypothesis to explain my theory." However labeled, Newton's experiments, according to James Gregory, would "cause great changes throughout all the body of natural philosophy, by all appearances, if the matter of fact be true, which I have no ground to question."[84]

In the *Principia* (1687) Newton elaborated the view that the principles of natural philosophy and scientific facts were inseparably bound together. He proclaimed even more emphatically, "Hypothesis non fingo." He would "frame" or "feign" no "hypotheses."[85] Whatever was "not deduced from the phenomena" was "an hypothesis" and had "no place in experimental philosophy." Particular propositions were inferred from the phenomena or observed facts and afterward rendered general by induction. Gravitation was not a hypothesis because its principles had been deduced from observed facts. A hypothesis was simply "whatever is not deduced from the phenomena" and, for Newton, it had a very low status indeed.[86]

What Newton had "deduced" from the body of "facts" itself took on the quality of "fact" and became connected to universal truths and the laws of nature. With Newton, fact and theory were so closely connected that the conclusions or "theories" drawn from "facts" were treated as true. The association was further accentuated by Newton's mathematical approach. As Newton's mathematical representation replaced verbal description, it diminished the sense of human fallibility. Newton's *Principia* over time produced a change in scientific sensibility. The mathematization of nature contributed to a decline in courtroom analogies in dealing with matters of fact and a corresponding increase in the language of the physical laws.[87] The development of a discourse of the laws of nature in the Newtonian sense did not displace a discourse about facts. Rather, the discourse became more refined as philosophers and experimenters came to talk about facts, theories, hypotheses, and laws in more nuanced ways.

The quarrel over "hypothesis" between Newton and his contemporaries was in one sense simply linguistic. Newton sought to preserve the older meaning of the word, synonymous with supposition or conjecture, for propositions about empirical matters that were not themselves derived from or confirmable by factual observations or experiments. He reserved "theory" for those propositions that were properly, that is factually, derived and confirmed, propositions that others were now calling hypotheses in the newer sense. He also put special emphasis on the care needed in hypotheses or theory construction, that is, on the need to lay a careful factual foundation at the induction stage, but Hooke and others had made that point as well. Along this dimension the seeming disagreements between Newton and others are largely illusory or are arguments about whether rival hypotheses have been equally persuasively induced and/or confirmed.

Along another dimension, however, the disagreement is more serious. Newton may well be taken as claiming that both theories in his sense and factual findings can rise to something comparable to mathematical certainty, that is, to true and invariable laws of nature. Alternatively, it might be argued that Newton was insisting that at any given time the natural philosophy program should be limited to investigating those realms of fact in which quantification or measurement was possible.

Newton's stunning achievement had an enormous impact. Even Locke, whose probabilistic empiricism resembled Boyle's, viewed Newton's achievements as extraordinary. "Mr. Newton has shown, how far mathematics, applied to some parts of nature, may, upon principles that matter of fact can justify, carry us to the knowledge of some . . . particular provinces of the incomprehensible universe." If others could provide "so good and clear an account of other parts of nature . . . we might in time hope to be furnished with more true and certain knowledge."[88] For the most part, however, Locke was content to link matters of fact to less certain hypotheses. Few were expected to accomplish what the "incomparable Mr. Newton" had done.

Newtonians changed natural philosophy by joining observed and experimentally derived facts with mathematical physics. The "laws of nature" became indissolubly linked to "facts," and these, in part because they were expressed in mathematical form, took on some of the certitude associated with mathematics. Mathematics and mathematical physics had always been a concern of the Royal Society and the English scientific community more generally, but their prestige was now enhanced. Experimental facts expressed mathematically were seen as having produced laws of great certitude and universality. John Keill emphasized the application of mathematics to natural philosophy, "which is founded upon observations and calculations, both which are undoubtedly the most certain principles, that a Philosopher can build upon . . . for without observation we can never know the appearances and force of nature, and without Geometry & Arithmetick we can never discover, whether the causes we assign are proportional to the effects we pretend to explain."[89] Newton's achievements set the standard of what had been and what might be accomplished by natural philosophers.

Newton's success in mathematizing nature did not diminish English enthusiasm for natural history. Fact gathering by observers, explorers, travelers, and experimenters continued, and facts were collected, classified, and situated in hypotheses of varying degrees of probability. In many respects, the Royal Society in the eighteenth century continued in much the same path as it had in the seventeenth, practicing a Baconian empirical science that emphasized facts. Many members would have agreed with Hans Sloane, president of the Society, who insisted that "Knowledge of Natural-History, being Observations of Matters of Fact, is more certain than most Others, and . . . less subject to Mistakes than Reasonings, Hypotheses, and Deduction are. . . . These things we are sure of, so far as our Senses are not fallible." "These matters of Fact being certainly laid down" might "perhaps afford some Hints for the more clear Reasonings and Deduction of better heads."[90] For Sloane, hypotheses and deductions remained less certain than properly observed fact. The ambivalent and sometimes hostile attitude to some types of hypotheses continued, perhaps reinforced by Newton's pronouncements. The English way of "philosophizing" was described as "not to sit down in one's study, and form an hypothesis, and then strive to wrest all nature to it, but to look abroad into the world, and see how nature works; and then to build upon certain matters of fact."[91] In the Royal Society much attention continued to be given to the facts of mixed mathematics, that is, the facts of astronomy, geography, and hydrography, which were being communicated to it from all over the globe. As in the past, optics, pneumatics, and meteorological experiments were of great importance. General philosophical speculation remained outside the Society's activities. Instrument improvement continued apace, making possible growing quantification in physics. As the Society's early members had forecast, new and better instruments were responsible for the development of previously unknown and previously unknowable "facts." Richard Sorrenson has even suggested that the eighteenth-century Royal Society was characterized by a "worship of facts."[92]

This is not to say that nothing had changed. Some natural historians modified their language in the post-Newtonian decades. John Woodward, for example, claimed that his "reflections" were "founded entirely upon those Circumstances, Phaenomena, and Experiments" and were "in truth so many Deductions from them." They were "therefore as much Matter of Fact" as "those are, and to be rely'd upon with equal Certainty." For Woodward, there were two kinds of proofs, "those which [are] only probable and which we have some reasonable intimations, but not absolute and demonstrative certainty," and "those whereof we have a plain and undeniable Certainty; those which flow directly and immediately from the Observations."[93] His own, he thought, were of the second variety and therefore as certain as "facts." Employing the beyond-reasonable-doubt language associated with suitably substantiated matters of fact, he found his deductions to be "so incontestible, as to leave no Room for a Man of Understanding to doubt of it."[94] A rather cantankerous naturalist, Woodward suggested that those who refused to draw conclusions from observed facts "might well be reputed very fantastic and extravagant."[95]

For many post-Newtonians, generalizations from fact were becoming so closely enmeshed with the "matters of fact" from which they had been "deduced" that they too might be accepted as "facts" or "truth." The "facts" of Boyle, Hooke, Glanvill, Sprat, and Oldenburg, which had been largely deployed in probabilistic hypotheses, now might be found associated with universal "laws of nature," to which a greater certainty was ascribed than most seventeenth-century virtuosi would have ascribed to even the best-crafted hypotheses.[96]

Some of these changes are exemplified in the works of Ephraim Chambers, author of the *Cyclopedia or An Universal Dictionary of the Arts and Sciences*, and Oliver Goldsmith, the author of a popular survey of experimental philosophy. Chambers wrote, "The latest and best Writers are for excluding Hypotheses and standing wholly on Observation and Experiment." Citing Newton, he noted, "Whatever is not deduc'd from Phaenomena, . . . is a Hypothesis" and has no place in "Experimental Philosophy."[97]

Goldsmith constantly used expressions such as the "observation of facts" and the "facts of nature." "Facts" are taken as givens, as true without the need to examine whether or not they were well founded. There was, therefore, less need constantly to refer to witnesses and credibility. Newton is seen as having ushered in a new era, effecting "what his predecessors . . . aimed at; namely the application of geometry to Nature, and by uniting experiments with mathematical calculations, discovered new laws of Nature, in a manner at once precise, profound, and amazing."[98]

Eighteenth-century language typically implied a divine legislator who had established "laws," inviolable except by divine abrogation. Agreed-on experimental "facts" could sometimes be treated mathematically in order to comprehend at least some of these "laws." Natural facts, which earlier had been evidence for the being and existence of the deity, now also became linked to his mode of operation. In the hands of Newton, the "facts of nature" were linked to God's universal laws.

At this point facts had come to play several roles.[99] Particular, well-evidenced facts might be related to hypotheses or suppositions of varying degrees of probability, might be simply collected and perhaps cataloged and classified, or might result in principles or laws of universal validity. The language of theory and hypothesis did not stabilize. For some, theory and hypothesis remained interchangeable; for others, theory implied something more certain. Perhaps we can speak of a continuum, from conjecture, to hypothesis, to theory, axioms, and laws of nature. "Hypothesis," the term most frequently used in the late seventeenth century by those hoping to derive principles, whether probabilistic or certain, from "fact," is partially replaced in the eighteenth century by "theory" or "law."

Harvey Wheeler and Rose-Mary Sargent suggest that scientific principles and legal principles were developed by similar procedures. They argue that lawyers culled cases to arrive at legal principles in much the same way that naturalists derived the principles of natural philosophy.[100] It is true that the virtuosi quickly adopted legal notions of how facts might be determined. But jurors, the fact finders in law, were not given a role in enunciating legal principles. Judges were to declare legal principles from the cases, but "cases" were not facts. The methodology used by judges in deriving these principles does not appear to be related to the forms of empirical hypothesis or theory construction we have encountered in the study of nature. Judges certainly did not think of themselves as going *from* fact *to* law or as confirming laws by empirical inquiry. Rather, they saw precedents as particular normative pronouncements from which the more general normative principles of the English people lying behind them might be teased out by reason. It is thus difficult to see how Coke's distinction between the artificial reason of the law, accessible only to judges and lawyers of long experience, can be harmonized with Boyle's and the virtuosi's use of reason as a tool of empirical inquiry. The laws or principles of nature were precisely natural, not manmade, and thus the same throughout nature. With the exception of those whose legal thinking was particularly shaped by natural law, seventeenth-century lawyers recognized that different nations operated according to different legal principles. Sir Matthew Hale distinguished the unchanging laws of nature from the mutable laws of man.[101] The judge's job was indeed to induce, but to induce the moral rules the English had chosen to enact into judicially enforceable statements. Although the virtuosi derived their methods of establishing matters of fact from the law, they did not regard themselves as engaged in enunciating authoritative or normative principles. The "laws of nature" appear to have been derived from Christian and mathematical heritages rather than a legal one.

The most commonly practiced form of natural philosophy in England during the Restoration era and beyond dealt in matters of fact and hypotheses of varying degrees of probability and believability. "Fact" had become a constituent part of the vocabulary of natural philosophy and has remained central to scientific vocabulary and practice. The combination of facts established by observation and experiment with probable hypotheses was a significant factor in moving English natural philosophy in an empirical direction. The introduction of the category "fact" as a central and constituent part of Restoration scientific endeavor and practice resulted in a readjustment of "conjecture," "hypothesis," and "theory" in English natural philosophy. This readjustment, however, was unstable. The concept "fact" proved compatible with a variety of positions on the nature and function of hypothesis and theory.

The Language of Natural Philosophy

Although naturalists did not always practice what they preached, we must take seriously their frequent statements against ornamentation and in favor of a plain and undogmatic style.[102] They attacked scholastic language, appropriating and elaborating the humanist critique of scholasticism. The linguistic practices of the alchemists and the philological, etymological, emblematic, and fabulous embedded in traditional natural history were also targets. Still another was the copious and highly ornamented language associated with Renaissance poetry and rhetoric.

In this period rhetoric was conceptualized in two quite different ways. The first, associated with Aristotle and Cicero, separated logic from rhetoric. The second, derived from the reorganizations of Agricola, Melanchthon, Ramus, and others, reshuffled traditional material to distinguish "rhetoric" from "dialectic," to produce a kind of rhetoricized logic. In the reformulated schemes, invention and disposition and thus argumentation were assigned to "dialectic," leaving rhetoric as little more than figures of speech. Because the two positions existed side by side, it is difficult to know whether critics of rhetoric were attacking the larger conception of rhetoric as argument and style or only excesses of style.[103]

Although the Restoration naturalists did not originate the factual style, they were emphatic and persistent in their stylistic pronouncements. Their severest attacks focused on rhetoric defined as style rather than "invention" or "judgment," now comfortably ensconced in "dialectic." The "facts" of the naturalist, no less than the facts of the lawyer, the historian, and the chorographer, were to be described in unadorned English. The naturalists, however, pushed that ideal considerably further than other advocates of the plain style, arguing that language describing nature should be brought "back again to our very Senses from whence it was first derived to our understandings."[104] Sprat proclaimed that the Royal Society "indeavor'd to separate the knowledge of Nature, from the colours of Rhetoric . . . this vicious abundance of Phrase, this trick of Metaphor, this volubility of Tongue." The remedy was "a close, naked, natural way of speaking; positive expressions; clear senses; a native easiness, bringing all things as near to Mathematical plainness as they can; and preferring the Language of Artisans, Countrymen, and Merchants, before that of Wits, or Scholars."[105]

Sprat's statements were underlined in the Royal Society's statutes, which required, "In all Reports of Experiments to be brought into the Society, the Matter of Fact shall be barely stated, without any Prefaces, Apologies, or Rhetorical Flourishes."[106] The facts of natural history must be recorded without "superfluousness in the Words. In the Choice of which, there ought to be great Care and Circumspection, that they be such as are shortest and express the Matter with the least Ambiguity, and the greatest Plainness and Significancy, not augmenting the Matter by Superlatives, nor abating it by Diminuitives, . . . avoiding all kinds of Rhetorical Flourishes, or Oratorical Garnishes, and all sorts of Periphrases or Circumlocutions."[107] John Ray, John Wilkins, Robert Boyle, Sir William Petty, Joseph Glanvill, John Ray, and Francis Willughby were among the many naturalist advocates of a plain unadorned style.[108] All the "discourses of fact" favored "perspicuity" and "plainness." Embellished language was, more often than not, associated with lies and deception and/or fiction and romance or with rhetorical excess. Highly ornamented language obscured matters of fact by intentionally or unintentionally insinuating falsehood or error.

Another feature of fact-oriented scientific discourse was the preference for first-person reporting.[109] Immediacy and vividness too were among the desired characteristics of observations and experimental reports, that is, of the language of "facts." As we have seen, suspicion of secondhand or hearsay reports was characteristic of all the discourses of fact. A focus on the particular time, place, opportunity to observe, and circumstances of a specific event characterized the scientific report of natural facts as well as the reliable news report, the description of a historical event, and the testimony of a faithful witness in a law court.[110]

Yet the virtuosi did not entirely discount the skills of persuasion. Sprat was hired to write an account of the Royal Society primarily because of his literary skill, and he himself noted its apologetic as well as its historical character. Oldenburg counseled New England members "to instill the nobleness of this institution and work with your best Logicke and Oratory, into the minds of all your friends and acquaintances there."[111] Rhetoric might legitimately and profitably be used to promote the goals of natural philosophy but marred accurate statements of "fact."

Hypothesis, Language, and Discourse

Hypotheses and other forms of causal explanation played a role in the language of natural philosophy. In contrast to matters of fact, hypotheses emphasized probability and, therefore, tentative language. Hooke insisted hypotheses must not be dogmatically stated. Since "demonstration" was unattainable in physics, there must always be "room for differences of opinion." Hypotheses therefore should not be delivered with "full confidence."[112] When Newton insisted that his "theory" of colors was no hypothesis, fellow virtuosi had difficulty accommodating to his assertive language.

The marriage of "fact" and "hypothesis" and their epistemological status generated a set of linguistic norms. The firsthand simple language of fact was expected to lead to agreement beyond reasonable doubt. The language of hypothesis should lead to the polite expression of differences over what could not be certain. The virtuosi rejected the academic tradition of formal, scholastic disputation and the forms of rhetorical debate introduced in the universities during the sixteenth century, although academicians who adopted the new discourses of fact were welcomed by the scientific community and played a substantial role in creating it. It was thus not the scholar but the disputation and other conflictual modes of discourse that were rejected. The norms of plainness and tentativeness were linked respectively to the adoption of "fact" and "hypothesis." The impact of the epistemology of fact and hypothesis on scientific language and decorum must be taken into account in evaluating the influence of humanist, courtly, and gentlemanly conventions.[113]

We have already noted that expertise and opportunity to observe were important to the Royal Society. Deference to rank that was so much a part of the Italian court-oriented scientific environment was largely, if not completely, absent from English scientific circles. Absence of a substantial royal and explicitly aristocratic presence at Royal Society meetings meant that it was unnecessary to defer to the opinions or research interests of the most socially prominent.[114]

Aristocratic and courtly life was immersed in the language of subservience and flattery. The tradition of the courtesy manual, central to Shapin and Schaffer's conception of normative scientific behavior, emphasized the need for courtiers to beguile with "salutary deception," creating a "veil of pleasure" by adorning language with "shady fronds and strewing it pretty flowers."[115] Linguistic reticence, circumlocution, ambiguous and embellished language, and the suppression of criticism and information so as to maintain aristocratic honor, though constant features of court life, were not admired or adopted by the virtuosi. Success in courtly civil society required "sprezzatura," a practiced but artificial virtuosity that appeared natural and required mastery of the rhetorical skills necessary to fashion oneself into a number of guises as the situation required. There was little that was straightforward about the language of the gentleman-aristocrat as embodied in the courtier manuals, and Sir Robert Moray, himself a courtier, made it very clear that the languages of the courtier and the philosopher were quite different.[116] It is true, however, that the literary academies that sprang up in Italy and elsewhere during the sixteenth and seventeenth centuries provided a nonacademic venue where scholarly and intellectual topics were cultivated in an atmosphere that prized civility. These no doubt played a role in providing a linguistic and behavioral norm for the newer scientific society.

The language of the virtuosi also probably owes something to the concept of the "Republic of Letters" fostered by seventeenth-century scholars of differing nationalities, religions, and political persuasions.[117] It was recognized early that scientific progress would require avoidance of the most divisive religious issues. The 1645 group, the Wadham group, and the Royal Society all excluded religious and political topics.[118] Influenced by the international traditions of humanism and antiquarianism and a vision of natural philosophy as transcending partisan political and religious differences, the English scientific community adopted a style of writing and discourse that fostered the broadest possible communication.

English latitudinarian religious views, as I have suggested elsewhere, also contributed substantially to and overlapped with the norms of Restoration scientific discourse.[119] For the latitudinarian, two types of speech and behavior were to be avoided. The first was that of the dogmatist, sure of his opinions and willing to force them on others; the second, the language of the "enthusiast," whose religious experiences and inspiration led to language couched in mystery and inspired by a certainty not amenable to reason or evidence. Reaction to these linguistic styles, prominent during the civil war and Interregnum years, resulted in the articulation of an alternative norm for religious discourse, promoted primarily by those desiring a less persecuting and less dogmatic church and a more rational approach to religion. This movement came to fruition during the Restoration. Latitudinarians, relatively feeble politically during the Restoration, came to control the established church after 1688.

Arguing that most religious doctrines were only probable and therefore open to doubt, the latitudinarians, who were mostly Anglicans, espoused polite and tentative language for expressing religious disagreement. Some of the most vociferous of the latitudinarians were to be found among the founding members of the Royal Society.[120]

The connection between Restoration natural philosophy and latitudinarianism was noted and applauded by Glanvill and Sprat, who emphasized the mutually reinforcing aspects of their epistemologies and modes of discourse. Glanvill even suggested that natural inquiries were a remedy for religious dissension because such inquiries "dispos'd mens Spirits to more calmness and Modesty, Charity, and Prudence in differences of Religion, and even silence disputes there."[121] Sprat announced that the new philosophy bred men "invincibly armed" against the "enchantments of enthusiasm." For John Wilkins, latitudinarian and virtuoso, polite discourse was essential, "it being utterly impossible . . . that we should always agree in the same apprehension of things. If upon every difference men should think themselves obliged to prosecute matters to the utmost height and rigour, such eager persons may easily from hence be induced to have recourse to Arms . . . and . . . it will be impossible to end their differences. . . . And thus would men grow wild and savage, the benefits of Society would be lost, and mankind destroyed out of the world."[122]

The Restoration naturalist, like the latitudinarian, was envisaged as possessing Christian humility and recognition of mankind's limited abilities. In the scientific realm, matters of fact might reach the level of moral certainty. So would the basic principles of natural religion and the central Christian doctrines. But other claims could not be substantiated with sufficient certainty to make authoritative and dogmatic pronouncements. Whether religious or scientific, probabilistic conclusions required probabilistic language and polite discourse.[123] All opinions and hypotheses should be heard and examined. Individuals rather than an authoritative collectivity should make judgments about them. The Royal Society made no official pronouncements even in the case of the Copernican hypothesis, on which most members agreed. The "Character of a True Philosopher" required "men, whose minds are so large, are in a far better way, than the Bold, and haughty Assertors." The "plain, industrious Man" made a better philosopher than "high, earnest, insulting Wits, who can neither bear partnership, nor opposition." Dogmatists were "satisfied, too soon . . . they love not a long and a tedious doubting, though it brings them at last to a real certainty." Royal Society naturalists, in contrast, were "well practis'd in all the modest, humble, friendly Vertues; should be willing to be taught, and to give way to the judgment of others."[124] The norms of scientific and latitudinarian discourse clearly were interdependent.

The model scientific discourse of the Restoration era was thus a compound of languages thought appropriate to "fact" and to "hypothesis." It was reinforced by hostility to the adversarial practices of scholastic discourse, a distrust of rhetorical and poetic language, and adoption of some elements of the gentlemanly norm and the traditions of humanist academies and the "republic of letters." It was informed as well by the latitudinarian response to the intense and destructive religious experience of previous decades.

Conclusion

At the beginning of seventeenth century the "scientific fact" did not exist. With the Restoration, well-supported "matters of fact," whether alone or in the company of "hypothesis," played a major role in the research program of the Royal Society. By the beginning of the eighteenth century facts had become central to English natural philosophy and even held out the promise of providing a basis for comprehension of the "laws of nature."

Initially employed to deal with human actions and deeds, "fact" was self-consciously adopted to the study of nature first by Bacon and subsequently by the new empirically oriented philosophers. Bacon's role in transforming the "human fact" into the "scientific fact" was supplemented by an English-language, descriptive, chorographic tradition in which human and natural "things" and "phenomena" were observed and recorded together using the same procedures and mental processes as those employed by other fact-oriented disciplines and genres.

Royal Society discourse concerning natural "matters of fact" shared with the other "discourses of fact" features derived from their legal origin—the focus on witnesses, the rejection of hearsay, the criteria for evaluating witnesses, and the aim of achieving the probabilistic truth of well-witnessed events. There was an emphasis on particular events and occurrences, whether ordinary or marvelous, observed or manmade. Breaking down the distinction between art and nature, naturalists seeking the truth of natural facts might create and repeatedly observe facts by experiment.

The recent work of Simon Schaffer and especially of Steven Shapin on the social history of truth has required special attention because their emphasis on the role of the code of the aristocrat and gentleman in the making of the Restoration scientific ideal is somewhat at odds with my own. In connection with the concept "fact" or "matter of fact," I have stressed the shared features of Restoration natural philosophy and other preexisting and contemporaneous discourses of fact, especially that of the law, rather than the uniqueness of natural investigation or aristocratic norms within natural philosophy. Although not denying that social status played a role in knowledge making, I suggest that a somewhat lower social threshold than gentleman was epistemologically significant in the production of believable facts. Skill and experience played a greater role in the creation of the model of the scientific investigator than birth, and mutual trust and civility among investigators increased once fact moved beyond the contentious, self-interested setting of the court. Indeed, the work of Lawrence Klein on the development of "politeness" in the eighteenth century should alert us to the potential conflict between gentlemanly and scientific culture.[125]

In natural history and natural philosophy, as in other discourses of fact, fact was opposed to "fiction," romance, and the imaginary. Natural philosophers contrasted "facts" sufficiently evidenced by credible witnesses with speculation, whether labeled "hypothesis," "conjecture," or "inference." Naturalists remained somewhat ambivalent, or at least not completely united, about the value and nature of hypothesis. Most virtuosi favored its use, though some considered it premature. Increasingly, hypothesis became the constant companion of "fact," and the combination of fact and hypothesis became the dominant mode of English natural philosophers of the late seventeenth century. Some argued that facts were probabilistically true and thus believable but that hypotheses remained speculative and therefore tinged with fiction. Others viewed hypotheses as securely based on or deduced from facts rather than fictional. Hypotheses, however, were subject to confirmation and might be wrong or incomplete. In some instances the conclusions drawn from facts might be labeled "theory" or even "laws of nature" rather than "hypothesis." Unlike "fact," the concept "hypothesis" was not linked to legal traditions of thought. It owed much to long-standing astronomical and other scientific practice. The concept "law of nature," which Newton associated with experimental fact, was indebted both to mathematical traditions and to Christian concepts.

The linguistic standards of scientific discourse were shaped by new concerns for "fact" and "hypothesis." The discourses of fact moved in the direction of a relatively unembellished prose style. The felt need for a language appropriate to the presentation of necessarily uncertain hypotheses, along with such other features of Restoration life as latitudinarianism and the idea of a "republic of letters," shaped the discourse of the Royal Society, a discourse different from the strategic elegance prescribed by the manuals of courtesy and the contentiousness of the scholastic disputation and humanist debate.

"Matter of fact" first meant a category of allegations subject to proof by adequate witness testimony. The evidence for a matter of fact might or might not support "moral certainty" of that fact. Many matters of fact failed that test—which made some matters of fact more believable than others. Contrary to modern usage, in the seventeenth century there might be true, false, or relatively uncertain facts or matters of fact. By the early eighteenth century, however, we begin to find two diverging usages. The first, the one we have just described, treats "fact" or "matter of fact" as a matter at issue subject to empirical proof; the second implies that anything appropriately labeled "fact" was already established as true. In this second usage the notion of a fact subject to reasonable doubt or a "false fact" became a contradiction in terms. Over time, facts, at least in the realm of nature, were becoming "true facts." During much of the seventeenth century the "facts" of the naturalists were not very different from those of other discourses. As the new philosophy gained prestige, so did the "facts" on which it was built. "Matters of fact" as issues turned into "facts" as outcomes.

The elements that brought about this change can be seen developing in the seventeenth century. Centrally involved are the increasing emphasis on the investigation of concrete, particular events, the importance of eyewitness testimony, the critical role of evaluation of such witnesses and their testimony, the open or public character of inquiry, and the development of a reporting language. Enhanced observational and measurement technologies were also significant. In all these matters natural philosophers may well have enjoyed one crucial advantage. The experiment allowed the controlled enactment of a particular matter of fact at a chosen time and place in the presence of a number of high-quality witnesses whose collective testimony could be recorded immediately and subjected to subsequent reconfirmation.

There is little doubt that the creation of the "scientific fact" marked a fundamental change in English natural philosophy. Yet it is important to keep in mind that science was only one of the "discourses of fact." Natural philosophy both "borrowed" from other disciplines and in turn influenced them. If natural philosophy assimilated the well-known and culturally legitimate category "fact" from the human sciences of law and history and used that concept to legitimize a new kind of natural philosophy, in time it was the "scientific fact" that would further legitimate the increased use of facts outside the natural sciences. In the hands of John Locke, "fact" would provide one of the foundations of all empirical knowledge. By the early eighteenth century "fact" was so widely deployed in so many diverse enterprises—legal, historical, religious, and scientific—that we can reasonably speak of England as a "culture of fact."

CHAPTER SEVEN

Facts of Religion

The concept "fact" or "matter of fact," with its commitment to credible witnesses and impartial judgment, was employed extensively in the context of religion. Restoration rational theologians and polemicists, particularly those with interests in natural philosophy and of a latitudinarian persuasion, found the concept "matter of fact" useful in a number of ways, the most important of which was to provide rational proofs for belief in the central events of the New Testament. "Fact" also proved useful in supporting several principles of natural religion, in bolstering the credibility of Old Testament accounts of Creation and the Flood, and in proving the existence of "spirit" in the world. The concept "fact" was also used by ecclesiastical historians exploring the history and character of the English church.

By the end of the seventeenth century a substantial part of the English Protestant edifice was anchored by the concept "fact." If not all English Protestants were as bound to arguments from "fact" as the rationalizing strand of the Church of England, arguments from fact were not rejected by either dissenting Protestants or High Churchmen. English Protestant Christianity would integrate the legal concept "fact" and legal language of establishing "facts" into its very fabric, thus deepening the impact of fact on English culture.

"Matter of Fact" and the Truth of Christianity

For many generations the truth of the Christian religion and of Scripture was unproblematic. The religious issues and conflicts of the sixteenth and seventeenth centuries brought epistemological issues to the fore. The use of "fact" or "matter of fact" to support the fundamental truths of Scripture was grounded on an approach to knowledge that distinguished various kinds of knowledge, each characterized by different kinds of proof that resulted in varying degrees and kinds of certainty or probability.[1] The establishment of legal and historical "facts," deeds, or events might allow the truths of religion to reach the level of moral certainty, if not the certainty of mathematical demonstration. As we have seen in connection with law, historiography, and natural history, credible witnesses played a crucial role in achieving moral certainty.

Although the distinction between demonstration and the moral certainty that could be achieved through the collection of current sense data had medieval and scholastic antecedents, it began to play an important role in religious thought beginning roughly with the publications of Hugo Grotius, the internationally esteemed Dutch jurist whose *Truth of the Christian Religion* characterized Christianity as a historical religion resting on "matter of fact." Though incapable of either direct sense experience or mathematical demonstration, seemingly impossible events such as those reported in Scripture could be established as true, Grotius argued, if "testified by . . . sufficient Witnesses living in the time when they came to pass."[2]

William Chillingworth adopted the Grotian line of argument in 1638 with his *Religion of Protestants: A Safe Way to Salvation*, designed to refute Roman Catholic insistence on an authoritative judge of Scripture. Although civil and criminal cases required an outside authority or judge, Scripture, where plain, did not. Scripture, however, was not itself a judge but rather provided the rule by which rational individuals could judge or evaluate religious truth. After consideration of all the available evidence, Chillingworth argued, a reasonable person would believe the truths of Scripture to a moral certainty or beyond reasonable doubt. Although Chillingworth did not spell out the relationships among credible witnesses, "matter of fact," moral certainty, and rational belief, he initiated a mode of argument that came to play an important role in the development of English religious thought.[3]

This cluster of ideas was elaborated in Seth Ward's 1654 rational defense of Scripture against radical claims of personal revelation. Ward, at that time Savilian Professor of Astronomy at Oxford, a member of John Wilkins's scientific group at Wadham College, and a committed Anglican, centered his argument on the nature of evidence and proof for "matters of fact." When events reported "were improbable," as were the central events of the New Testament, it was essential to critically examine the witnesses and the way they related their reports. One considered whether the event in question was knowable, whether the witnesses had the means to obtain the information, whether they were "eye or ear" witnesses, and whether the events were "publically acted and known."[4]

Ward's criteria for belief in the accounts of scriptural reporters were virtually identical to the criteria for ideal witness testimony in the courts. Ward also made ample use of historical analogs, for instance employing the conventional argument that belief in the existence of cities such as Rome or Paris was reasonable even for those who had not visited them. Historical accounts were believable if the reporters had the opportunity to observe the places and events they recorded and no contradictory evidence had been offered. Invoking the impartiality norm, Ward concluded, "No impartial person, could reasonably doubt the truthfulness of the matters of fact reported in the History of Holy Scripture."[5] Ward's appropriation of legal and historical criteria for proofs of "matters of fact" comes, it should be noted, before the natural philosophers' wholesale appropriation of those criteria in the 1660s.

It was in the period between 1660 and 1700, however, that arguments from "fact" were most frequently used to buttress the truth of Scripture. Now arguments from "matters of fact" were less likely to be directed at sectaries claiming direct access to divine revelation than at skeptics who expressed doubt as to the truth of Scripture and Roman Catholics who emphasized the doctrine of infallibility and the superiority of oral tradition. It was largely, though not exclusively, a group of latitudinarian laymen and clerics, many of whom were involved in or sympathetic to the new empirical natural philosophy, who deployed the concept "matter of fact" most extensively and most effectively in these decades. Because the fate of Protestantism and indeed Christianity itself appeared to be at stake, a great deal hinged on the success of the arguments based on the believability of "facts." By the 1670s, to be convincing to most literate English audiences, religious arguments had to be rational, not claims based on authority or divine inspiration. A well-known and well-established legal tradition for reaching rational belief in "matters of fact" was readily adopted by rational theologians such as Edward Stillingfleet, John Tillotson, Robert Boyle, and Gilbert Burnet.

Stillingfleet's *Origines Sacrae, or a Rational Account of the Christian Faith, as to the Truth and Divine Authority of the Scriptures* attempted to provide a "rational account of the grounds, why we are to believe those several persons . . . imployed to reveal the mind of God to the world." Stillingfleet did not seek to bring matters of fact to mathematical demonstration, because moral certainty was sufficient, not only in matters of this kind but also for "titles to estates derived from Ancestors." It was not reasonable to rely solely on one's own senses and "question the truth of every matter of fact which he doth not see himself." Yet steps had to be taken to ensure "the undoubted certainty of the matter of fact, or the truth of the History," and to ascertain that "such persons were existent, and did either do or record the things we speak of." It was necessary, for example, to show that "the certainty of the matter of fact, that the records under the name of Moses were undoubtedly his," as well as to show that he was a person of "more than ordinary judgment, wisdom and knowledge" with "sufficient information" of "the things he undertakes to write of." Given Moses' impeccable qualifications, as well as his fidelity and integrity, his "History is undoubtedly true."[6]

Stillingfleet used a similar approach in connection with the testimony of the Apostles and the miracles of the New Testament. "Where the truth of a doctrine depends upon a matter of fact, the truth of the doctrine is sufficiently manifested, if the matter of fact is evidently proved in the highest way it is capable of."[7] The facts of Scripture, like all others, were dependent on witnesses. "The greatest evidence which can be given to a matter of fact, is the attesting of it by those persons who were eye-witnesses of it. This is the Foundation whereupon the firmest assent is built, as to any matter of fact." While one might reasonably suspect "the truth of a story" conveyed by "uncertain fame and tradition," if that story is "attested by a sufficient number of credible persons who profess themselves the eye-witnesses of it, it is accounted an unreasonable thing to distrust any longer the truth of it; especially in these two cases. 1. When the matter they bear witness to is a thing which might be easily and clearly perceived. 2. When many witnesses exactly agree in the same Testimony."[8] The Apostles were obviously credible since they had "no motive to lie and lacked Mean or vulgar motives." Christ's miracles were visible, and no illusion of sense was possible, for many saw him raise a man from the dead, and many witnessed his Resurrection. Although counterwitnesses might "disparage" testimony, when "all witnesses fully agree not only in the substance, but in all material circumstances of the story, what ground or reason can there be to suspect a forgery or design in it." There had been no dissent as to the birth, miracles, life, death, or resurrection of Jesus Christ. Though they had written in different places and on different occasions, all witnesses had concurred.[9]

Like the lawyers, Stillingfleet emphasized the nature of the testimony. The Apostles had delivered "their Testimony with the greatest particularity as to all circumstances. They do not change or alter any of them upon different examination before several persons, they all agree in the greatest constancy to themselves and uniformity with each other."[10] These qualities were precisely those that justices of the peace were advised to look for when examining criminal suspects and witnesses and that jurors were to consider in reaching their verdicts.

Echoing the language of Sprat in connection with desirable and undesirable scientific language and the discourses of fact more generally, Stillingfleet argued that only those who wished to impose on the credibility of others employed ambiguity, fables, "cloudy and insignificant expressions," or obscure terms. The Apostles, however, laid aside "all affected obscurity, ambiguous expressions, and Philosophical terms." The Apostles spoke with the "greatest plainness and simplicity of speech" in a style appropriate to the "discourses of fact."[11]

In a work designed to shore up Protestant belief in Scripture against Roman Catholic oral tradition, John Tillotson, another rationalizing theologian, also adopted legal approaches to evidence and assent to issues relating to "faith." Faith "supposeth honesty among men; and that for Matters of Fact and plain Objects of Sense the generall and uncontrolled Testimony of Mankind is to be credited." The position taken by opponents would make it "impossible . . . to be certain about [the] History of any ancient matter of fact," including the existence of Caesar or William the Conqueror. Although matters of fact were incapable of demonstration, belief in history was reasonable when historians relied on secure grounds rather than "bare hear-say." The best evidence, he admitted, was immediate sense perception, which he, like the virtuosi, sometimes labeled "ocular demonstration." Next came the evidence of witnesses, applicable to both religious and secular events and acts. As was the case in the courtroom, all witnesses were not equal and had to possess sufficient mental capacity and impartiality before their testimony could reach the level of moral certainty. As early as 1671, using language similar to that of Stillingfleet and Tillotson, John Locke was writing of the appropriate number, credit, and conditions of witnesses.[12] Arguments from "matter of fact" were becoming crucial in securing belief in Scripture.

The year 1675 witnessed an outburst of publications employing the concept "fact" and "credible witnesses" to secure rational belief in Scripture. John Wilkins, a leading latitudinarian cleric, noted that evidence from testimony "depends on the credit and authority of the Witnesses," which might be "qualified as to their ability and fidelity." When these criteria had been met, "a man must be a fantastical incredulous fool to make any doubt of them." "As for matter of fact, concerning Times, Places, Persons, Actions, which depended on story and the relation of others, things are not capable of being proved" by mathematical demonstration. Instead, one must apply the "best evidence" rule.[13]

A leading latitudinarian layman, Robert Boyle, was similarly committed to showing what kinds of "Probation" or evidence "may reasonably be thought sufficient to make the Christian religion fit to be embraced."

Moral certainty, which governed "the practice of our Courts of Justice here in England," provided the appropriate model. In criminal cases, he argued, though the testimony of more than one witness of itself was not more credible than that of a single witness, a concurrence of testimonies might amount to a moral certainty.[14] The "Articles of the Christian religion" could be similarly proved by a moral, though not by a metaphysical or physical, demonstration and could "without any blemish to a man's reason, be assented to." Moral certainty depended on testimony about matters of fact. Though some things of "unquestionable Truth" might appear incredible if attested by "slight and ordinary Witnesses," "we scruple not to believe them, when the Relations are attested with such Circumstances, as make the Testimony as strong as the things attested are strange." A thing contrary to reason should not be disbelieved "provided there be competent proof that it is true."[15]

Some years later, in the course of refuting Roman Catholic claims to infallibility and claims that Protestants were guilty of schism, heresy, and apostasy, Boyle again embraced the argument from "fact." Most knowledge, for Boyle, was dependent on the senses, either immediate or "vicarious," the latter being the primary evidence for matters of fact. By testimony "we know, that there were such men as Julius Caesar and William the Conqueror, as well as that Joseph knew that Pharaoh had a dream."[16] Believable testimony must be provided by witnesses of good moral character who possessed firsthand knowledge of the things or events about which they testified.[17] The fundamental truths of the Christian religion and its chief mysteries, such as the existence of Christ in the World and his Passion, Death, Resurrection, and Ascension, were based on "eye-witnesses to all those things, which if nobody had seen, nobody now would believe."[18]

Yet another 1675 contribution was Gilbert Burnet's *Rational Method for proving the Truth of the Christian Religion*. Burnet, like Wilkins and Stillingfleet a latitudinarian cleric, insisted that biblical miracles were "matters of fact . . . positively attested by . . . many eye-witnesses . . . of great probity." Like his friend Boyle, he explicitly pointed to the standards of the law courts. The Apostles "were men, who upon the strictest tryal of Law must be admitted as competent witnesses; they were well informed of what they heard, . . . they were plain simple men who could not in reason be suspect of deep designs or contrivances; they in the testimonies they gave do not only vouch private stories that were transacted in corners, but publick matters seen and known by many hundreds; they all agreed in their testimony. . . . Their testimonies, if false, might have been easily disproved, the chief power being in the hands of enemies, who neither wanted power, cunning nor malice."[19] Like a lawyer summing up at the end of a trial, Burnet concluded that "it is as evident as is possibly any matter of fact can be, that their testimony was true."[20]

Religious utilization of the concept "fact," however, required some adjustment in the standard for what constituted an ideal witness because it was forced to rely on the evidence of "simple plain men." Although justices of the peace and lawyers sometimes emphasized "ability" and "fidelity" and often relied on the testimony of ordinary persons, they were nevertheless inclined to assign somewhat greater credibility to those of high social status. Natural philosophers, we should recall, sometimes emphasized expert qualifications and sometimes the gentlemanly status of observers, while in other circumstances they were satisfied with the reports of ordinary men. Although they too emphasized fidelity, historians preferred to rely on politically experienced witnesses. Those adopting a stance of factual inquiry toward the truth of Scripture were not in a position to stress either the high social status or the experience of their witnesses. These standards were turned on their heads as they capitalized on the simplicity and lack of sophistication of the Apostles, which appeared to render them incapable of orchestrating collective misrepresentation of the facts.

Although latitudinarians dominated the discourse on rational proofs of Scripture, they did not monopolize it. Neither Seth Ward nor Richard Allestree was a latitudinarian. Arguing against those insisting on mathematical demonstration or direct sense experience as the sole standards of truth, Allestree noted that the great factual events of Scripture could "be done but once; he could not be incarnated, and born, and live and preach, and dye, and rise again . . . every day, of every age, in every place, to convince everyman by his senses, to all those that did not see the matter of fact."[21] Faith in such events must be "made by Witnesses." "If we can be sure the witnesses that do assert a fact understand it exactly, if the things be palpable, . . . we can be sure too, that they are sincere, will not affirm that which they do not know, and do not lye, then testimony of it must be most infallible."[22]

There was sporadic publication in this vein for several decades.[23] Another flurry of activity came in the 1690s when the attacks of deists and skeptics on the need for and reliability of Revelation elicited a series of fierce defenses of the truth of Revelation and of scriptural miracles. Many of the defenses were mounted by nonlatitudinarians. John Edwards, a Calvinist minister, harnessed the proofs associated with matters of fact as well as those from presumption and notoriety. The writings of Edwards, a man hostile to Locke's *Reasonableness of Christianity*, suggest how widespread the arguments from "matter of fact" had become in rationalizing belief in the New Testament. Discussion was now taking place in periodicals such as the *Athenian Mercury*, whose editor defied "the Enemies and Blasphemers of the Sacred Books, to produce me one Instance of matter of Fact attested by the concurrent tradition of all places and ages that is not true."[24]

If discussion concerning the truth of the "facts" of Scripture had become commonplace before the end of the century, the problem of the accuracy of transmission of those facts remained worrisome, attracting the attention of not only theologians but even the Royal Society. In 1699 the *Philosophical Transactions* published "A Calculation of the Credibility of Human Testimony," which mathematically calculated credibility in such a way as to support the Protestant defense of the moral certainty of scriptural "matters of fact." After mathematically calculating the probabilities of error in the transmission of oral and written testimony, the author found written testimony to be far more credible than the oral tradition favored by the Roman Catholics. Mathematical logic had proved that the Scripture of the Protestants was virtually error-free.[25] By the end of the seventeenth century proofs of the truth of Scripture based on appropriately verified matter of fact were widely accepted by nonclerical media and non-latitudinarian writers.

Natural Theology and Matter of Fact

Proofs for the principles of natural theology, that is, the existence of the deity, his attributes, the immortality of the soul, and the existence of future rewards and punishments, also made use of arguments from "matters of fact," although these were less central than they were to the proofs of scriptural events. "Facts" could not directly prove the existence of a deity, because "spirit" could not be observed. "Facts" could be used, however, to infer the existence and attributes of the Creator and to infer the existence of spirit in much the same way as "signs" and "circumstances" might be used to infer guilt in certain kinds of crimes unlikely to be witnessed. When used in connection with natural religion, "facts" were sometimes treated synonymously with the observable "effects" of nature. As we have noted earlier in connection with Hobbes, from the mid-seventeenth century on, the practice of treating the effects of nature and natural "facts" as synonymous had been increasing. In the religious context this approach might be used to infer the existence and attributes of the Creator. "Effects" included ordinary natural events or phenomena observed by simple or sophisticated naturalists as well as extraordinary events and the "marvels" that attracted the interest of natural historians, newsmen, and ordinary persons. Although the language of the "effects of nature" was not unknown in theological circles during the first half of the seventeenth century, during the Restoration that language became firmly joined to earlier, more general arguments from design. It also seems likely that the use of the language of fact, with its association with actions and deeds, may have underscored the notion of a voluntaristic God, an artificer who had "made" the world.[26]

The development of a new natural history based on carefully observed "facts," which replaced the emblematic natural history of previous generations, led to a different kind of union of natural theology and natural history, a union so distinctive that it acquired the label "physico-theology."[27] John Ray's popular *Wisdom of God Manifested in the Works of Creation* went furthest in elaborating the argument that well-established natural "facts" demonstrated the existence and wisdom of the deity. A leading latitudinarian and a much admired botanist, Ray promised readers, "I have been careful to admit nothing for Matter of Fact or Experiment but what is undoubtedly true, lest I should build upon a Sandy and Ruinous Foundation; and by the Admixture of what is False render that which is True Suspicious."[28] The "facts" or observed "effects" of nature were offered as a basis from which to infer the wisdom of the deity.[29]

Many English virtuosi shared Ray's outlook and mode of argument. John Evelyn argued that the natural knowledge produced by the Royal Society "would lead men to the knowledge, and Admiration of the Great Creator." Nehemiah Grew characterized nature as "the Handmaid of Divine Wisdom." Boyle, a friend of Tillotson and Stillingfleet, frequently inferred God's existence, wisdom, and beneficence from nature. For Boyle, natural philosophers were peculiarly alert to the religious implications of natural facts because they were more likely than others to discover "tokens and effects of divine artifice in the hidden and innermost recesses of them." Divine artifice was not discoverable "by perfunctory looks of . . . unskillful beholders . . . but require[d] . . . the most attentive and prying inspection of inquisitive and well-instructed considerers."[30] Newly known "facts" revealed by means of instruments such as the microscope were also added to the arsenal of proofs of God's existence from observed "matters of fact." Hooke's *Micrographia* thus attempted to show how microscopically observed "facts" pointed to the wisdom of the Creator.[31]

The argument from design, of course, was a very ancient one but had not in the past employed the concept "fact." The contribution of Restoration theologians and naturalists was to emphasize that "matters of fact," now known with greater accuracy and precision, allowed one to observe more accurately the results of God's handiwork and thus to better appreciate his existence, attributes, and intelligent design. Characterization of the deity as the Divine Craftsman and Divine Artificer[32] may have increased the virtuosi's inclination to treat his Creation as a vast panorama of "matters of fact."

If rational theology had long relied on the "effects" of nature to provide evidence for God's existence, his Providence, and the immortality of the soul, in the post-Newtonian era theologians such as Samuel Clarke attempted to provide the rational proofs of Christianity by following a method as close to mathematics as possible, adopting what appeared to be Newton's "deductions" from fact rather than the inferential approach of

John Ray and his predecessors.[33] In both instances "fact" could support revealed and natural religion.

Mosaic Accounts of Creation, the Origin of Mankind, and the Deluge

Arguments based on "matter of fact" also played a role in the Restoration campaign against "atheists" and skeptics who repudiated the biblical accounts of Creation and the Deluge. Such arguments were difficult to make because of the absence of human witnesses. Nor did the "facts" from which inferences might be drawn seem as conclusive as they appeared to be in inferring divine design.

The Restoration era witnessed a multifaceted campaign to show that the scriptural accounts of the Creation and the Flood were accurate. The jurist Matthew Hale entered the fray to refute the "Atheistical Spirit that denies or questions the truth of the Fact" delivered in Scripture. In this context, using language with a striking parallel to his own legal writings, he discussed the nature of witness testimony and the need to consider the "credible and authentic witnesses." Firsthand testimony was preferable to hearsay, and the testimony of disinterested witnesses preferable to that of interested parties.[34]

Hale was unable to build his case exclusively on human testimony because the history with which he was concerned did not focus on particular acts or deeds associated with proofs from matters of fact. After a long and complex treatment of the nature of proofs available in "matters of fact" Hale turned to the "Origination of Man." He not only cited several "Instance[s] of Fact" to show that mankind had a beginning in time but presented eight "Evidence[s] of Fact" to show the "reasonableness of the Divine Hypothesis touching the origination of the world and particularly of Men." Admitting that each of his eight varieties of "fact" taken "singly and apart . . . possibly may not be so weighty," he argued that the "concurrence and coincidence" of "many Evidences" carries "a great weight, even as to the point of Fact; it is not probable that Supposition should be false which hath so many concurrent Testimonies bearing witnesses to it." He conceded that in arguments like the one he was trying to prove "which is touching a matter of fact that Evidences of Fact can be no more than topical and probable." He nevertheless insisted, "In these Evidences of Fact, . . . it is sufficient that they be probable and indicative of Credibility, though not of Science or Infallibility." He then provided "probable" evidence that would collectively prove the truth of the Mosaic account of the origin of man, an event that had taken place "near six thousand years" earlier. The concurrent evidences of a variety of natural and human "facts" for Hale proved the reasonableness, if not the certitude, of the "Divine Hypothesis."[35] Hale's use of the term "hypothesis" is interesting here. Natural philosophers often deployed facts in relation to hypotheses in a similar way. Lawyers, as we have seen, also used "signs" or "circumstantial evidence" to reach legal decisions in instances for which human testimony was unavailable. Hale's treatise was part of an attempt to achieve a unified chronology that would comprehend biblical, human, and natural history. Human history and the history of the earth were bound together both theologically and historically.

Although the biblical accounts of Creation and the Deluge were on the whole accepted as believable, some observed "matters of fact" proved difficult to square with scriptural accounts. There followed a variety of efforts, mostly couched in the form of hypotheses, to connect the biblical Deluge and observed matters of fact. The most troublesome were fossil forms of seashells, often called "formed stones," frequently found on mountaintops. Were these the remains of actual sea creatures or simply "sports" or "jokes" of nature, perhaps designed by the deity simply "to entertain and gratifie" man's curiosity?[36] This view was easier to square with Scripture but did not satisfy those who saw little or no difference between fossil and current forms of shellfish. Such concerns stemming from observed matters of fact stimulated religious debate and led to theorizing about whether changes in the earth's surface could be related to the Deluge.

Physico-theological speculation attracted a substantial number of naturalist-theologians and theologian-naturalists. Nicolas Steno and Robert Hooke argued for the organic origin of fossils. Much respected by members of the Royal Society, Steno carefully distinguished his observations from his "conjectures." Hooke, who turned his microscope on fossilized wood, suggested that earthquakes rather than the Deluge better explained the distribution of fossil shells.[37]

Thomas Burnet's *Sacred Theory of the Earth* (1681) initiated a discussion that lasted well into the next century. Most participants accepted the veracity of the biblical account of the Deluge and attempted to square their respective theories, explanations, or hypotheses both with the "facts" of the Old Testament and the "facts" of natural history. Most would have agreed with Burnet's view that the Mosaic account was "a true piece of Natural History" and with John Ray's view that Moses had provided "the History and Description of the Creation."[38] They disagreed as to how the observed "facts" could be rendered consistent with the biblical account. John Woodward, for example, hypothesized that the Deluge had involved total dissolution of the earth and was followed by its reconstitution into the currently visible geological layers. His theory, he thought, adequately explained the puzzling locations of fossil remains.[39] Woodward, writing in the post-Newtonian era, attempted to broaden the meaning of "fact" from the well-evidenced observations of natural and human phenomena to the deductions made from those facts. He thus insisted that the deductions made from observations and experiments were "as much Matter of Fact as the observations and experiments; and so to be rely'd upon with equal Certainty."[40]

Physico-theology was also linked to a variety of physical observations of and hypotheses about earthquakes and the origin of mountains. Here again observations of natural facts made by credible witnesses provided the basis for hypotheses designed to achieve consistency with biblical accounts. Because there were no human witnesses who provided testimony as to the Flood or the genesis of mountains, there were only "signs," "effects," "circumstances," or currently observable "facts" on which to base inferences or hypotheses.[41] These were roughly analogous to legal arguments from presumption and circumstantial evidence.

If the "rational" in rational theology of the period was not dependent solely on arguments from "fact," the appropriation of the language of "fact," witnessing, and circumstantial evidence provided a substantial support for rationalist religious arguments.

Witchcraft, Spiritual Phenomena, and Prodigies

But were supernatural events always to be believed when supported by the testimony of seemingly credible witnesses? If the method of proving matters of fact by credible witnesses was appropriate for the law courts, for historians, for the naturalists of the Royal Society, and for proofs of Scripture, why should it not be similarly employed to validate contemporary instances of supernatural phenomena? Arguments from matter of fact and credible witnesses had long figured prominently in cases of witchcraft. Witchcraft was a crime and thus like other crimes was a deed or "matter of fact" to be proved in court to the satisfaction of a jury. Witchcraft and the language of "fact" were thus intertwined quite early and remained intertwined long after prosecutions for the crime had abated.[42] Witnesses provided the most desirable form of proof for this crime as for others. Courts also allowed indirect testimony or circumstantial evidence because witchcraft was one of the class of *crimen exceptum* in which witnesses were unlikely. When witnesses were available, the quality and quantity of their testimony was crucial. Early in the seventeenth century John Cotta indicated that if the "witnesses of the manifest magical and supernatural act, be . . . sufficient, able to judge, free from exception of malice, partialities, distraction, folly, and if . . . there bee justly deemed no deception of sense, mistaking of reason or imagination," the accused should be tried. Richard Bernard similarly advised grand juries to inquire into the "wisdom," "discretion," and credibility of the witnesses.[43]

Few people entirely disbelieved in witchcraft. Yet as early as 1594 Reginald Scot suggested that a jury would be wrong to convict if a man were seen in London the same day as a murder he was alleged to have committed in Berwick, even if he confessed and others deposed the same thing. For Scot, arguments from impossibility trumped even those of credible witnesses and could not be defeated by appeals to the supernatural.[44]

This emphasis on credible witnesses also characterized the views of Restoration clerics such as Meric Casaubon, Henry More, and Joseph Glanvill, who applied the proof of fact to establish the existence of spiritual phenomena. Their concern was fueled not by a zeal to prosecute witches but by an aspiration to show the existence of spirit to an age that appeared to them overly attracted to mechanism and materialism. The denial of the existence of spirit would make it difficult to sustain a belief in the soul and in the existence of God. Their claims were grounded on the familiar concept "matter of fact" and the associated testimony of credible witnesses.

The challenge of atheistical and skeptical thought led Meric Casaubon to consider how the category "matter of fact," so often used in connection with "things Natural, or Civil," could be used to support religion. Like many Royal Society naturalists and rational theologians, he argued that it was often possible to produce "firm assent" based on observation without knowing the causes of the events observed. Many of "Nature's Wonders" could not be comprehended or explained. It followed that "upon good attestation, . . . so many strange effects of the power . . . of Devils and Spirits" were similarly believable. Faced with reports of "strange things, however, it was necessary to know the temper of the relator, if it can be known; and what interest he had, or might probably be supposed to have, had in the relation, to have it believed. Again, whether he profess to have seen it himself, or take it upon the credit of others; and whether a man by his profession, [is] in a capacity probable, to judge the truth of those things, to which he doth bear witness."[45]

The senses might sometimes deceive, but on the whole one could trust them. And though it was sometimes reasonable to suspect the relation of a single person, the testimony of two or three should be sufficient if there was "no just exceptation against the witnesses." After all, Casaubon argued, that was all that was required in courts of law. No more should be required to witness the truth of supernatural operations "by Devils and Spirits." To deny such operations simply because imposture was possible was "the way to deny all truth." We constantly depend on our own experience or that of others, "whether the relations are private e.g. of friends or travellers, or public as of historians of the present or past ages."[46] Casaubon noted he had lived only in England but had acquired a great deal of what he knew from those living elsewhere. Knowledge of an enormous range of things relied on accepting the testimony of others. Casaubon thus applied the familiar components of proofs from matters of fact to support belief in supernatural agents. He saw supernatural, human, and natural events as established by the same logic of proof. His work helps us understand how "news," "marvels," "prodigies," and apparitions all came to be subsumed under the category "matter of fact."

Joseph Glanvill, a latitudinarian defender of the Royal Society, was the most prominent figure to employ the proof from "facts" to defend the possibility of witchcraft and the existence and activity of spirit in the world. The defense of witchcraft should not seem surprising in an advocate of the "new philosophy," since Bacon had suggested that witchcraft cases be collected as part of a "History of Marvels," "marvels" defined as instances where there is "an assurance and clear evidence of the fact."[47] Leading Cambridge Platonist Henry More also was anxious to prove the existence of spirit as a means of combating atheism and materialism. The two collaborated in collecting witchcraft and apparition narratives to prove that spiritual phenomena existed. Whether or not "there have been and are unlawful confederacies with evil spirits" was simply a "Matter of Fact" capable of the "evidence of authority and sense"; like other "facts," it could be proved only "by immediate sense or the Testimony of Others." History had provided "attestations of thousands of eye and ear witnesses, and those not only of the easily deceived but of wise and gravely discerning persons of whom no interest could oblige them to agree together in a common Lye."[48] Although melancholy or imagination might produce false testimony, Glanvill refused to believe that "All the Circumstances of Fact, which we find in well-attested relations," resulted from deceived imaginations. For Glanvill, too, "Matters of fact well proved ought not to be denied" simply "because we cannot conceive how they can be performed." We must "judge of the action by the evidence, and not the evidence by our fancies about the action." Investigation was necessary since "the Land of Spirit" remained a "kind of America" standing "on the Map of the humane Science like unknown Tracts."[49]

Glanvill hoped the Royal Society would investigate the "World of Spirits," and he asked for Boyle's help in gathering "some modern well attested relations of fact, to prove the existence of witches and apparitions." In 1668 Glanvill began collecting experiments and reports for a "Cautious and Faithful History" based on "clear evidence of the fact."[50]

The dissenting clergyman Richard Baxter produced a similar collection of "proofs of invisible powers or spirits." He too insisted that "proved Matters of fact must not be denied," despite the possibility of fraud or inability to "expound the Causes." Worried about the growth of disbelief, Baxter thought many London skeptics would change their views if they could be certain of spirits, apparitions, witchcraft, and miracles.[51] The readers of the *Athenian Mercury* too were assured that "there are Witches" and that the proof of witchcraft "being matter of Fact, we must rely wholly on the credibility of the Evidence."[52]

John Webster argued the other side. The number of persons believing in witchcraft was not satisfactory proof because few were suitably qualified. Webster attacked the proofs provided by witnesses, charging that they involved hearsay, self-interest, deficient observation, and superstition. All known reports were "too light" to be accepted. John Wagstaffe went even further, entirely rejecting proofs from matters of fact in connection with witchcraft and spiritual phenomena. "Matters of fact," he insisted, necessarily involved the senses. Since spirits were too fine to be perceived by the senses, they were not amenable to proof of fact.[53]

Perhaps the most commonly held view at least by the early decades of the eighteenth century was expressed by Addison, who believed "that there is, and have been such a thing as Witchcraft" but could "give no Credit to any particular Instance of it."[54] Prosecutions and convictions for witchcraft became rarer as grand jurors, jurors, and judges became increasingly dubious of the evidence presented to them. In 1717 a grand jury threw out an indictment despite the testimony of twenty-five witnesses.[55] The campaign of Causabon, More, Glanvill, and Baxter largely failed to prolong earlier beliefs in witchcraft by appeal to "matters of fact."

As the efforts of Glanvill and others suggest, the line between the natural and supernatural was not always easy to draw. One of the most interesting episodes in this connection was the puzzling and fascinating career of Valentine Greatrakes, whom we encountered earlier in connection with "wonders." Greatrakes performed seemingly miraculous medical cures in Ireland and London by "stroking" his patients. In order to clear himself of charges of fraud, he invited credible eyewitnesses to join the throngs attracted by his cures. He labeled his experiments "matters of fact" and provided testimonials, with appropriate dates and locations, from well-known virtuosi, physicians, and clergymen such as Robert Boyle, Daniel Cox, and John Wilkins. The seemingly miraculous cures were also observed by such Cambridge Platonists as Benjamin Whichcote, Ralph Cudworth, and George Rust, a group with strong interests in proving the existence of "spirit." Rust testified that Greatrakes was honest and upright, having no "design of faction or interest." He had witnessed "the matter of fact, which is testified to be true by me." Greatrakes especially thanked the "honourable Gentlemen of Gresham Colledge" who witnessed his cures. Such "strange" and possibly nonmaterial phenomena relevant to the existence of "spirit" were deemed worthy of close and repeated observation by naturalists and theologians.[56]

There was another class of "facts," classified by some as natural and by others as preternatural, that played a role in religious, or rather politico-religious, discussion. As we noted earlier in connection with "news," unusual phenomena, such as comets, monstrous births, rains of blood, and unusual cloud formations, were newsworthy events, of interest both to the populace at large and to natural philosophers. For many generations, political and religious commentators had sought to infer their meaning, most frequently as divine warnings or expressions of divine displeasure. Efforts to find religious meaning in such events were commonplace during the civil war and Interregnum years but were increasingly, though by no means unanimously, rejected during the Restoration. One of the most vociferous in denying religious or political inference from "fact" was John Spencer, a latitudinarian scholar, who insisted that God's intention could not be inferred from natural or preternatural events. "Prodigy mongers" seized on every "strange accident," although most could be explained naturally. Facts they certainly were, but facts could not be used as "signs" to predict future political events or to fathom divine intention.[57] By the end of the seventeenth century many commentators were becoming less confident about the religious inferences that might be drawn from marvels, accidents, and prodigies. The distinction between fact and inference from fact was widely noted in many fields. Whether labeled "hypothesis," "conjecture," or "inference," inferences were to be treated as far less certain than the "facts" on which they rested.

Ecclesiastical History

The utilization of "fact" in ecclesiastical history can best be understood in the context of the changing norms of civil history outlined earlier and the increased use of "fact" in religious discourse. For this reason our treatment would be equally at home here or in our discussion of historiography. Certainly the concept "matter of fact" was a thoroughly familiar one to post-Restoration clerics who investigated the origins of British Christianity and the nature of the English Reformation. These historical issues were crucial because they bore on the much disputed relationship of the English church to Rome, on church-state relations, and on the independence of the clergy. Ecclesiastical historians investigated the early English clergy, the origin and nature of episcopacy, and the history of Convocation for similar reasons.[58] Making "matters of fact" a central feature of ecclesiastical history modified historical investigation but did not reduce its polemic involvement.

In the strictest sense "fact" did not play an overwhelming role in these investigations because "matters of fact" required the testimony of reliable witnesses, and "witnesses" were not always available for the historical issues being examined. Like civil historians and lawyers, ecclesiastical historians relied heavily on "records," occasionally even making use of the legal distinction between "matters of fact" and "matters of record." Here too records were required to be original and copies accurately transcribed and translated. Errors of omission and commission relating to the handling of the documentary record were becoming serious historical defects. Not infrequently, however, categories became confounded, as "records" were sometimes assimilated into "facts," and witnessed "matters of fact" treated as "records." As the distinction between document and witness blurred, the concept "fact" expanded to comprehend both record and witness testimony.

Anglican churchmen from John Jewel onward engaged in scholarly efforts to recover a primitive Protestant church independent from Rome and organized on an episcopal basis. There had long been debates over whether episcopacy or presbytery had characterized the early church. Historical investigation of the church was not a creation of the civil war or Restoration eras.[59] "Fact," however, does not seem to have played a prominent role in early discussions. Among the most prominent Restoration historians to rely heavily on the concept were several whom we have encountered earlier in other contexts, particularly latitudinarians William Lloyd, Edward Stillingfleet, and Gilbert Burnet. Their sermons, tracts, and histories vindicated Anglican claims against Roman Catholic versions of the English Reformation and High Church claims of clerical independence from secular control. When High Churchman sought historical validation for the church's independence, they too would resort to "fact." William Lloyd, bishop of St. Asaph, an associate of Stillingfleet and Tillotson, and a protégé of John Wilkins, produced his *Historical Account of Church Government as it was in Great Britain and Ireland* to show that the church had always been episcopally governed.[60] Stillingfleet's *Origines Britannicae, or, the Antiquities of the British Churches*, which aimed at demonstrating the Church of England's independence from Rome, was to provide as "clear and distinct a view" of the early church "as could be had at so great a distance." Building on the research of Ussher and Spelman and based on documents and charters, his study would rescue church history "from those fabulous Antiquities which had so much debased the Value and eclipsed the Glory of it." Because he was often unable to marshal the historical matters of fact on which he would have preferred to rely, Stillingfleet provided "probable" arguments, implying a kind of tentativeness akin to the virtuoso's hypothesis or to the civil historian's conjecture. "I hope to make it appear from very good and sufficient Evidence, that there was a Christian Church planted in Britain during the Apostles Times. And such Evidence ought to be allowed in this matter which is built on the Testimony of Ancient and Credible Writers and . . . a concurrent Probability of Circumstances."[61] Stillingfleet's "ancient testimonies" were documentary evidence. *The Origines*, one of the most important works in ecclesiastical history between the time of Ussher and the nineteenth century, played a major role in assimilating documentary records into the category "fact."

Despite the efforts his predecessors, Gilbert Burnet felt England still lacked an adequate history of the Reformation. Aided by patrons such as Robert Boyle, Burnet initiated a massive investigation of public and privately held records, benefiting not only from Stillingfleet's manuscripts but from those collected by means of newspaper advertisements. Material garnered from books published at the time of the Reformation yielded "considerable things of matters of Fact" as well as the arguments on which the controversies of the time turned. In his *History of the Reformation* Burnet repeatedly emphasized his evidence. "I shall vouch my warrants for what I say and tell where they are to be found." Manuscript material and copies of records were included in full in the original language so readers would receive "full Evidence of the truth of the History" and would be able to judge it at first not "second hand."[62]

Burnet's second volume, published two years later, particularly noted the "Records and Authentick Papers" that confirmed "the more remarkable and doubtful parts of the History." He corrected errors, especially where in "some particulars my vouchers were not good, and in others I had mistaken my Authors." His "design" from the start was "to discover the Truth and to deliver it down impartially." Thanking his friends Lloyd, Tillotson, and Stillingfleet for reviewing his work and his patrons for financial assistance, Burnet particularly insisted on the historian's commitment to impartiality. He warned that a historian or judge might be "secretly possessed, with such impressions of Persons and Things, as may biass his thoughts," especially in religious matters, where it was all too common to be more preoccupied with "what is good and honest in the abstracting Ideas than concerning matters of Fact."[63]

Burnet's volumes led to a storm of controversy lasting until the end of the century and beyond. Both his claim to impartiality and his scholarly competence were questioned, particularly by Henry Wharton, a chaplain of Archbishop Sancroft, who countered Burnet's assessments by referring to records unmentioned by Burnet and by noting errors both of omission and in the transmission of relevant documents. Wharton did not treat the documents themselves as "facts" but suggested that a proper reading of documents would prove matters of fact. On the basis of documents, he concluded, "So then the Matter of Fact is put beyond all doubt, that all the Bishops, Abbots and Priors sate in the upper House of Convocation." Other critics contrasted Burnet's "defamations" with books containing "matter of Fact and Argument." Simon Lowth insisted that his "method," unlike Burnet's, would relate "naked history" and "bare matter of fact."[64]

When a fellow Whig historian, Humphrey Hody, appealed to the "phenomenon of history," Burnet defended Hody's "facts." "Dr Hody has fully ended the argument that he had begun from the practice of the Church; and that in so convincing a manner, the matter of fact seemed no capable of a clearer proof. . . . Men may wrangel on eternally in points of speculations; but matters of fact are severe things, and so not admit of all that sophistry."[65] As the rancorous debate continued, "facts" were deployed and manuscript and other documentary evidence compared and evaluated to establish the "facts." Over time the manuscript records themselves seemed to become "approved facts."

Much of the Convocation and related controversies of the late seventeenth century thus turned on "matter of fact." In 1694 a High Church historian repudiated Burnet's and Tillotson's views on the Convocation issue by challenging their claim that "matters of fact seem'd not to be capable of a clearer proof." He provided contrary views "wherein the judicious Reader will find the Truths which I shall set down . . . to be as plain and legible in the following Collections, as the Sun is visible at noon, in a clear day."[66] Burnet's "matters of fact" were challenged here by the familiar legal criteria of "notoriety" and "manifest proof" and in the traditional legal metaphor of the noonday sun. In 1714 Thomas Salmon was still criticizing Burnet, asserting that "Little Justice" could be expected from him given his "little Regard to the Truth of any Fact he relates."[67]

Rival ecclesiastical historians, like rival newsmen and civil historians, accused one another of bias, interest, and erroneous statements of "fact." Such attacks were rarer among natural philosophers, who were perhaps less likely to dispute "facts" because many observations and experiments might be replicated. The Hevelius-Auzout controversy, however, reminds us that there might also be disputes about natural "facts." Yet the High Churchmen who disputed the accuracy of latitudinarian and Whig treatments of the facts of ecclesiastical history did not dispute their fact-oriented methods.

J. A. I. Champion suggests that historians have been misguided in treating scholarly developments in ecclesiastical history in a Whiggish mode that traces a historiographical advance from a Renaissance rhetorically oriented history to a more modern and more "scientific" history. He proposes that the new emphasis on "matters of fact" in ecclesiastical history should be viewed not as the mark of a more scientific history but instead as evidence of continued commitment to Renaissance humanistic history characterized by a rhetorical orientation and concern for moral lessons. For Champion, who views English historiography as virtually unchanged for two hundred years, the deployment of matters of fact and claims to impartial fact finding were nothing more than ammunition in the historiographer's rhetorical arsenal.[68]

Certainly no one examining the texts of ecclesiastical history would discount polemical and partisan intent. Even Burnet admitted that his readers might "find an Apology for the Reformation, interwoven with its History."[69] But one does not have to adopt a Whiggish stance to recognize the growing importance of "matters of fact" in late-seventeenth-century ecclesiastical historiography or its contribution to English medieval studies.[70] What may have begun as the rhetorical borrowing of persuasive phrases from civil history and other discourses became a defining disciplinary obligation. History without facts became "fancy," "fable," "romance," or "fiction," all associated with literary genres that no longer counted as "history." "Facts" may have been deployed for polemical purposes, but they had become essential to the practice of ecclesiastical as well as civil history. However polemical that history might be, the absence of well-proved "matters of fact" and documentation resulted in loss of the claim to be designated "history." Historical argument increasingly turned on the examination of sources and the proper dating, translation, and understanding of documents. "Facts" were marshaled against "facts" and document against document.

That one scholar's facts, or the inferences drawn from them, were challenged by another hardly shows that the discourse of fact employed by ecclesiastical historians was purely rhetorical. Rather, it tends to indicate that they took facts seriously. Disagreement over matters of fact and the inferences made from them was hardly unique to ecclesiastical historians. Natural philosophers too used agreed-on "matters of fact" to support quite different hypothesis and often constructed probable arguments to be evaluated by the extent to which facts supported them. Likewise, competing lawyers might use agreed-on "matters of fact" to construct arguments with different outcomes. Lawyers made their cases by means of rhetorically constructed arguments, but success rested on their deployment of both disputed and undisputed "matters of fact" and "matters of record" as well as rhetorical skill. In the legal arena both documentary "record" and witness testimony provided the basis for legal decision making. Surely no one would assert that because opposing counsel disputed one another's factual proofs, the courts' expressed concern for facts was merely rhetorical. Although historical documents were sometimes analogous to legal documents, the larger variety and the frequently unofficial status of many historical records made judgments about them more difficult. As historical research came to deal more with documents and manuscript materials and less with supposed eyewitness accounts, historical practice became more complex and the concept of historical "fact" broadened to more or less comfortably include the authenticated documents themselves.

In many respects, ecclesiastical historians were little different from "civil" historians who marshaled "matters of fact" into conflicting historical positions of contemporary political and constitutional relevance. As long as claims to the legitimacy of both church and state rested on their "original" condition, ecclesiastical and secular historical studies would remain partisan. Nevertheless, increasing reliance on testimonial and documentary remains and the assimilation of both into the concept "fact" modified the character of the historical enterprises. While recent investigations have pointed to the rhetorical features embedded in the historical enterprise itself, the presence of rhetorical elements and the deployment of rhetorically based forms should not be taken to mean that the historiography of the late seventeenth century was identical to its Renaissance predecessor.[71]

The late-seventeenth-century emphasis on "fact" did not bring an end to either historical polemic or rhetorical construction, but it altered the nature of what constituted an effective argument. However much the "facts" and especially the inferences from these facts might be disputed, they had become an integral part of historiographical discourse. The work of late-seventeenth-century ecclesiastical historians did much to create the view that history without well-established or believable "facts" was simply not history.

Conclusion

As one reviews the areas where proofs from matters of fact were employed in the religious sphere during the latter half of the seventeenth century, it is clear that "facts" provided an important support for religious belief. "Fact" was used in the construction of a rational belief in Scripture and the superiority of Protestant scriptural Christianity over Roman Catholic authority and oral tradition. It was employed to counter the dangers of skepticism and atheism. "Fact" played a role, albeit a lesser one, in establishing the principles of natural religion. The "facts of nature" were used to prove the existence of God and to support the Mosaic accounts of Creation and the Deluge. Efforts to prove the existence of "spirit" in the forms of witchcraft, possession, and "cures" turned on "matters of fact." And ecclesiastical historians, like their secular counterparts, increasingly based their histories on "matters of fact."

If the rationalistic arguments based on "matter of fact" offered by the latitudinarians in the early years of the Restoration were something of a novelty, by the end of the century they had become conventional wisdom. While the rational features of Enlightenment religion in England also were indebted to the natural law tradition, a substantial part of the religious rationalism that came to pervade English religion was based on "fact" and arguments derived from "matter of fact." As English religion incorporated "fact" into its arsenal, the category "fact" became more deeply embedded in English culture. To the extent English cultural assumptions at the end of the century were bound up with Protestant Christianity of a somewhat rationalizing bent, that culture became permeated by "fact." Religious applications joined the legal, historical, and scientific in creating a "culture of fact."

Cultural Elaboration of "Fact"

.

T his chapter deals with several aspects of the process of cultural elaboration of "fact." My purpose here is not to cover eighteenth-century developments exhaustively but to indicate some of the ways in which "fact" was further diffused and elaborated and to suggest some of the modifications that were taking place.

Locke and the Generalization of "Fact"

Locke's *Essay on Human Understanding* (1690) played a central role in generalizing the concept of fact and giving it philosophical form and status. Because of his familiarity with the many strands of English intellectual culture, Locke was ideally placed to generalize its epistemological assumptions and in particular the concept "fact." His position on faith and belief exhibits kinship with that of Wilkins, Tillotson, Boyle, and other rational theologians, and his *Reasonableness of Christianity* (1695) attempted to show that reason would certify Christian revelation. He was associated with latitudinarianism, although he eventually abandoned latitudinarian comprehension, adopting toleration as the best means of solving the problems of the Dissenters.[1] And as Locke himself pointed out, the *Essay on Human Understanding* had its origin in the religious discussions of the 1670s, a decade of substantial publication concerning rational proofs for religion.

Although Locke himself did not write history, he described his *Essay* as using "the plain historical method" and emphasized the importance of civil history for gentlemen. Without chronology and geography, however, history remained "only a jumble of Matters of Fact confusedly heaped together."[2] Locke owned a large collection of travel accounts, recommended them to others, and assisted in the Churchills' *Collection of Voyages and Travels.*

Locke was also part of the intellectual community of the Royal Society and a particular friend of Robert Boyle.[3] Like many of his naturalist contemporaries, he distinguished between probability and certainty, although he drew the line between these slightly differently than his contemporaries.[4] The "moral certainty" that some naturalists and theologians labeled a species of certainty remained, for Locke, in the sphere of probability. Nevertheless, "some propositions border so near upon Certainty, that we make no doubt at all about them: but assent to them as firmly, and act, according to that Assent, as resolutely, as if they were infallibly demonstrated."[5] Most of these were "matters of fact."

There were thus degrees within probability from "the very neighborhood of Certainty and Demonstration, . . . quite down to Conjecture, Doubt, and Distrust."[6] The grounds of probability were twofold, "the conformity . . . with our own Knowledge, Observation and Experience and the Testimony of Others vouching their Observation and Experience." Following the now familiar language employed by lawyers, judges, historians, naturalists, and natural theologians in dealing with "matters of fact," evaluation was to consider "1. The Number. 2. The Integrity, 3. The Skill of the Witnesses. 4 The Design of the author, where it a testimony out of a book cited. 5. The Consistency of the Parts and Circumstances of the Relation 6. Contrary Testimonies. . . . [As] the Relators are more in number, and of more Credit, and have no Interest to speak contrary to the Truth: so that *matter of Fact* is like to find more or less belief" (my emphasis).[7] Social status is not offered as a criterion for witness credibility. Knowledge depended on "the certainty of Observations, . . . the frequency and constancy of Experience, and the number and credibility of Testimonies." The judgelike evaluator then "casts up" or "summs up" "upon the whole evidence." For Locke, "Inducements of Probability" concerned either "some particular Existence," commonly termed "matter of fact which falling under Observation, is capable of human Testimony," or "Things beyond the discovery of Sense, and thus incapable of testimony."[8]

Locke's discussion reflects the disinclination of jurists, historians, and virtuosi to make strong assertions about matter incapable of sense experience or testimony. When a particular matter of fact is "consonant to the constant Observation of ourselves and others, in the like case, comes attested by the concurrent Reports of all that mention it, we receive it as easily, and build as firmly upon it, as if it were knowledge: and we reason and act thereupon with as little doubt, as if it were perfect demonstration."[9]

Difficulties occurred when testimony contradicted common experience or when reports clashed with the ordinary course of nature or with one another. Although Locke, like the jurists, was unable to offer precise rules for giving assent, he insisted it must be apportioned according to evidence and probability, and, echoing judicial summing-up, he stressed conclusions based "upon the whole matter."[10] He referred to the legal rule rejecting unattested copies of record and copies of copies, suggesting that the rule was equally suited to "our inquiry after material Truths." Legal practice and concepts clearly had philosophical application. Alluding still again to the practice of the courts, he noted "that any Testimony, the farther off it is from the original truth, the less force and proof it has. . . . A credible Man vouching his Knowledge of it, is a good proof; But if another equally credible do witness it from his Report, the Testimony is weaker; and a third that attests the Hearsay of an Hearsay, is yet less considerable."[11]

Locke, like so many of his contemporaries, was also concerned with the unobservable, ranging from "beings" such as angels or devils to "the means of operation . . . in most parts of the works of Nature, where we see the sensible Effects, but do not know their causes." Echoing Glanvill, Wilkins, and Boyle, Locke noted that one could "only guess and probably conjecture" about causes that were more or less probable.[12]

For this reason, Locke's faith in well-attested matters of fact was, like that of so many English naturalists, accompanied by both a suspicion of hypotheses and a commitment to employing those derived from "sensible experience."[13] General theories were "a sort of waking Dreams." To begin with theory was to begin "at the Wrong End, when Men lay the foundations in their own Fancies, and endeavour to suit the Phenomenon." Instead, one should "Nicely observe the History of diseases, in all their Changes in Circumstances." With an "establish'd History of Diseases, Hypotheses might with less Danger be erected." As useful as well-grounded hypotheses might be, they remained "suppositions" and were "not to be rely'd on as Foundations of Reasoning, or Verities to be contended for."[14]

Hypotheses thus "might be rely'd on" as "artificial Helps" and "not as Philosophical Truth to a Naturalist."[15] One must build a "hypothesis on matter of fact and make it out by sensible experience, and not presume on matter of fact because of his hypothesis." Natural philosophy was "not capable of being made a science."[16]

There were nevertheless a few hypotheses that Locke treated as true or very probably true—Boyle's corpuscular hypothesis on the nature of matter, the Copernican hypothesis, and Newton's theory of gravitation.[17] "The incomparable Mr. Newton" had "shown how far the Mathematicks, applied to some parts of Nature, may upon Principles that matter of fact justifie, carry us into the knowledge of some, as I may call them, particular Provinces of the incomprehensible Universe." Newton inspired Locke to believe that "we might in time hope to be furnished with more true and certain knowledge in several Parts of this stupendous Machine, than hitherto we could have expected."[18]

Locke's *Conduct of the Understanding* perhaps provides the best summary of my argument for the appropriation of legal and historical fact determination by the virtuosi, for there Locke noted, "Particular matters of fact are the undoubted foundation on which our *civil and natural* knowledge is built" (my emphasis).[19] The former was that "of voluntary agents, more especially the actions of men in society"; the latter, of "natural agents, observable in the ordinary operations of bodies themselves or in experiments made by men." There could be no clearer statement that "facts," "particular facts," as Locke at one point calls them,[20] which first were the province of lawyers, judges, and juries, and then historians, dealing with human acts and deeds, now unequivocally comprehended natural facts as well.

Locke both drew on the traditions of fact finding we have been tracing and himself played a central part in their development. Some of those discourses had placed the concept of fact in the context of hypothesis and conjecture, a crucial step toward Locke's construction of a nonessentialist philosophy. Locke's key contribution to the discourses of fact was to elevate the discussion from particular disciplines and genres to a plane of generality. It is Locke who most clearly brings the category "fact" to "philosophy." Locke, more than any other single figure, helped give the legal and Baconian "fact" philosophical legitimacy and general currency.[21]

By the eighteenth century "facts" were a constituent part of many British intellectual enterprises. It is possible only to touch on these developments here, but we can note the impact of Lockean empirical philosophy on the first legal treatise on evidence and the growing importance of "fact" in philosophical writing, the impact of "fact" on Newtonian natural philosophy, the implication of the change in usage from "matter of fact" to "facts," and the influence of "fact" on literary genres and literary development. "Fact" continued to be ubiquitous in many aspects of law, religion, historiography, and natural philosophy. If anything, its use expanded in the eighteenth century, but, in some instances, it again changed its character.

Facts, Law, and Philosophy

Locke's influence in a number of areas is notable. The first legal treatise on evidence appeared in 1754. It was written by Sir Geoffrey

Gilbert, also the author of an abstract of Locke's *Essay*, and introduced the English law of evidence in the context of Lockean epistemology. During the seventeenth century legal concepts played an important role in shaping empirical philosophy. Now empirical philosophy as formulated by Locke and his successors came to influence legal writing, creating a symbiosis between epistemology and the law of evidence. The rules of evidence did not change substantially with Gilbert. Instead of appearing as a series of ad hoc professional norms, however, they are now presented as built on a sound and systematic epistemological foundation.[22] Gilbert and his successors increasingly felt it necessary to place the rules of legal fact finding on a philosophical basis, drawing on the formulations of Locke and his philosophical successors, such as Isaac Watts, David Hartley, and Thomas Reid.

The intellectual relationship connecting epistemology, the law of evidence, and "fact finding," a close and even symbiotic one throughout the eighteenth and nineteenth centuries, further enhanced the reputation and role of "fact." While the evidence treatises drew on Locke's generalized approach to fact finding, specifically legalistic approaches were also incorporated into more general philosophical works.[23]

Isaac Watts's *Logick, or the Right use of Reason in the Inquiry after Truth* (1724), written for young gentlemen and scholars, provides an early-eighteenth-century example of the interaction of epistemology and law, particularly with respect to "fact." Dependence on legal practices is evident Watts's in treatment of "the Principles and Rules of Judgment in Matters of Human Testimony" and in his efforts to show that one might gain a moral certainty of some "Matters of Fact." His rules, like those we have met with in previous chapters, prescribed consideration of whether the thing reported was "possible," for "if not, it can never be credible, whosoever relates it." Its "probability" too was to be examined by asking whether there were "concurring Circumstances to prove it," in addition to the "mere Testimony of the Person that relates it." If not, "stronger Testimony" was required. One had to consider "whether the Person who relates . . . a Nice Appearance in Nature, or some curious Experiment in Philosophy . . . be capable of knowing the Truth: Whether he be a skillful Judge in such Matters." If the report concerned a "mere Occurrence in Life, a plain, sensible Matter of fact," skill was irrelevant, it being "enough to inquire whether he who relates it were an Eye or Ear-Witness, or whether he himself had it only by Hearsay." In other instances the narrator must be honest, faithful, and skillful. Invoking the familiar impartiality norm, Watt insisted witnesses must be disinterested and have no temptation to prevaricate or misrepresent. Like the lawyers, he advised consideration of whether several persons might have combined "in a Falsehood." The principles described by Watts covered natural and divine "matters of fact past and present," and in all instances assent was be given in the "exact proportion to the different degrees of evidence."[24] Logic for gentlemen followed the logic of legal fact finding.

From Gilbert's time onward the legal evidence treatise and works dealing with epistemology and reasoning become inextricably intertwined. Those writing in the post-Newtonian environment, however, were more confident about what could be known about the natural world. For Watts, the "course of nature" was "a settled order of causes, effects, antecedents, concomitant, consequences." Because these were "necessarily connected with each other," it was possible "to infer the causes from the effects, and effects from causes, the antecedents from the consequent, as well as consequent from the antecedents."[25] Some portions of natural philosophy had become more certain than those concerning human actions, though both relied on "facts." Human and natural facts were to be established in roughly the same way and according to the same criteria, but natural philosophers dealing with causes and effects were, at least in some circumstances, able to establish more certain principles. Increasingly, natural philosophy came to be viewed as being more capable of reaching causal knowledge. The human fact that had engendered the "scientific fact" thus came to be seen as having less potential for understanding causes than the "facts" of nature.

This development can be found in David Hartley's mid-eighteenth-century *Observations on Man.* Hartley was confident that, armed with Newton's "Method," natural philosophers could "discover and establish the general Laws of Action affecting the subject under Consideration, from select, well defined, and well attested Phenomena, and then to explain and predict the other Phenomena by these Laws."[26] The "laws of nature" linked to well-observed natural facts had by this time become part of the vocabulary of many post-Newtonian philosophical thinkers. "Facts" and the "laws of nature" discovered by natural scientists had been drawn closer and closer together.

Hartley's discussion of the senses, of assent and dissent, and of their relation to facts was not particularly novel. Following the pattern of Locke and Watts, he dealt with "fact" and belief in general philosophical terms, giving special attention to the role of "fact" in proving the truths of Christianity. Belief in Christianity and the concept "fact" were bound together for many eighteenth-century thinkers.

Writing in the 1760s, Thomas Reid followed a similar path. His treatment of belief and judgment is replete with the language of the law. There are degrees of belief or standards of proof, which range from the slightest suspicion to the fullest assurance. "Every man of understanding," he argued, was capable of judging belief correctly "when the evidence is fairly laid before him," when "his mind [is] free from prejudice," and when the proper circumstances concur. "The analogy between a tribunal of justice and this inward tribunal of the mind" came easily to Reid. Most human knowledge as well as the work "of solemn tribunals" was dependent on testimony.[27] Given the legal language and assumptions that pervaded Locke's, Watts's, Hartley's, and Reid's treatment of the principles of sound belief and judgment, it not surprising that their work finds its way back into the legal treatises.[28]

Reid's widely read works also suggest the changing nature of the "scientific fact." For Reid, "observation and experiment" were the only way to knowledge of "nature's works." Bacon and especially Newton had shown the way "to trace particular facts and observations to general rules, and to apply such general rules to account for other effects, or to direct us in the production of them." This procedure, familiar "to all in the common affairs of life," was "the only one by which any real discovery in philosophy can be made."[29] Everyone therefore should "try every opinion by the touchstone of fact and experience. What can fairly be deduced from facts duly observed, or sufficiently attested, is genuine and pure; it is the voice of God, and no fiction of human imagination."[30] Reid speaks no longer of "matter of fact" but of "facts," which are now elevated and linked to the "voice of God." Few, if any, pre-Newtonian thinkers would have made that statement.

Unlike most pre-Newtonian naturalists, Reid was confident that the laws of nature were knowable. Mechanics, astronomy, and optics were "really sciences, built upon laws of nature which universally obtain."[31] Even if no one knew why bodies put in motion continue to move or why they gravitate toward the earth with the same force, "these are facts confirmed by universal experience." Although their causes were unknown, there were "laws of Nature,"[32] rules "by which the Supreme Being governs the world. We deduce them only from facts that fall within our own observation, or are properly attested by those who have observed them." Some laws of nature were known to all, others only to philosophers. But both were "matters of fact, attested by sense, memory and testimony." The conclusions of philosophers were therefore built on the same grounds as those of the simple rustic who concluded that the sun will rise tomorrow. "Facts reduced to general rules, and the consequences of the general rules," are all that could be known of the material world.[33]

If the laws of nature were derived from facts, both were distinguished from conjecture, hypothesis, and theory, all of which were but "the creatures of man."[34] Philosophy "in all ages" had been "adulterated by hypotheses; that is, by systems built partly on facts, and much upon conjecture." "Just induction alone" should "govern our belief."[35] In Reid's account the laws of nature and hypotheses were quite different things. The laws of nature were now so closely tied to "facts" that they had become "facts."

Changing Usage and New Attitudes toward "Fact"

In earlier chapters we noted the legal and more general cultural preference for particular "facts" over inferences or conjectures based on those facts. In the post-Newtonian era of Watts, Hartley, and Reid, though fact was still contrasted to conjecture and hypothesis, fact and the "laws of nature" were becoming bound together. This connection gave "facts" a different and more elevated role in relation to the principles of natural philosophy.

During the eighteenth century we also begin to hear maxims such as "Facts don't lie" being used to support a preference for circumstantial evidence over the direct testimony of witnesses.[36] Only in the early nineteenth century did legal thinkers begin to suggest that "circumstances" did not speak for themselves and that circumstantial evidence too had to be established by witnesses. Maxims such as "Facts don't lie" also signal another important change in the cultural usage of "fact." For most of the sixteenth and seventeenth centuries, we encounter the expression "matter of fact," which suggests an action or event that then had to be substantiated with appropriate witness testimony. From roughly the beginning of the eighteenth century writers in a variety of intellectual disciplines began to use the plural "facts." This new usage is employed in such a way that speakers no longer implied that matters of fact are a kind of thing or event that must be satisfactorily substantiated by convincing evidence; rather, they indicate actions, things, or events that have *already* been satisfactorily proved or verified. A sixteenth-century "matter of fact" was not necessarily "truth" or something worthy of belief until the appropriate evidence had been presented. Now, instead of having to establish the "Truth of the Fact," the term "fact" or "facts" sometimes implied that satisfactory evidence had already been produced and thus that facts were not open to question. This usage, which increasingly identifies "fact" and "truth," corresponds more closely to modern usage. When eighteenth- and nineteenth-century writers referred to "facts," they were far less likely immediately to offer supporting evidence than their seventeenth-century counterparts. The need for credible witnesses was not rejected but was less frequently mentioned. Generalizations, especially those referring to natural phenomena, were commonly called "the laws of nature." The statement "Birds fly," which would never have been called a fact in the seventeenth century, in the eighteenth might have been labeled a "law of nature" or a "fact." New linguistic patterns, however, did not mean that older meanings and locutions disappeared. The centuries-old legal distinction between matters of law and matters of fact continues to this day, as do the legal expressions "before the fact" and "after the fact." For lawyers, "after the fact" even now is never about whether water freezes at 32 degrees Fahrenheit. The "fact" in "after the fact" can be a fact only in the oldest Latin meaning of the word, a human doing or making or act. New usage is layered above old.

When "matter of fact" initially came to be used in connection with the natural world as well as human action, those who adopted the term were still very conscious of the problems of judicial fact finding and frequently referred to the quality and quantity of the observers and experimenters as a means of enhancing the credibility of their testimony. Over time, many of these qualifiers disappeared, at least in common use. "Facts" took on a greater aura of objectivity and were less likely to be seen as the products of fallible human testimony. They increasingly came to be treated as unbiased objective statements of truth rather than reports provided by a spectrum of poor, good, and excellent observers.

Dictionaries too suggest the changes undergone by "fact." Most seventeenth-century English dictionaries do not even mention fact in connection with natural phenomena. That was not true of their eighteenth-century counterparts, several of which emphasize that "fact" related to "reality."[37]

"Fact," "Fiction," and Literature

Given our concerns with the development and diffusion of the concept "fact" and the relationship between "fact" and "fiction," some attention must be paid to "literature" and the genres most closely identified with fiction. We must return, if only briefly, to sixteenth-century discussions of "poetry" and "truth," the differentiation of poesy and history, and the adoption of "fact" by early English novelists. These topics, for several decades the focus of literary study,[38] have become more complex and elusive in recent years as literary theorists and philosophers have eroded the familiar fact-fiction dichotomy.

The Sixteenth Century

Although there had been a lengthy and complex tradition distinguishing between fiction and truth before the sixteenth century, the distinction between fact and fiction had not been much elaborated. "Fact" typically meant event or deed and could refer to either real or fictional ones. The deeds or feats of giants or fabulous characters might be referred to as facts just as in France "fait" often referred to the deeds of fictional characters. Some aspects of the distinction between truth and fiction were indebted to Plato, whose distrust of the fictionality of poetry was expressed not in the distinction between fact and fiction but rather in that between the real and the false, reality being conceived in abstract, not ephemeral or factual, terms. The Platonic notion that poetry was the father of lies was frequently accompanied by comments on the waste of time devoted to poetry and its fictions, time that might better be spent on religion or utilitarian pursuits.[39] The well-known distinctions of Cicero came somewhat closer to the fact-fiction dichotomy because he distinguished poetry from the "kind of truthfulness expected of a witness in court,"[40] but the distinction between the truthfulness of history and the "falsehoods" of fiction was not central to the classical world. The ancients, we should recall, treated history as a rhetorical genre that might properly include plausible speeches that had never occurred. History and fiction were not entirely separable for the ancients or many of their Renaissance admirers and imitators. The same could be said about classical and Renaissance natural history, consisting as it did of a mélange of actual and fabulous plant and animal species.

Poetry, the model fictional category, was particularly praised for its role as ethical instructor. Poetry was clearly fictional, and debate within critical circles during the Renaissance tended to revolve around such issues as whether the poet's fictions must be limited to the verisimilar or might include the fabulous. English neoclassical theory, as exemplified in Sir Philip Sidney, Ben Jonson, and their successors, derived much of its literary theory from Aristotle. It distinguished between history and poetry in a way that suggests something very much like the distinction between fact and fiction. Both poesy and history offered truth, but of different kinds. The first offered ethical truth, the latter the truth of particular events. In practice the contrast was not as sharp as Sidney's writings suggest, however, because many historians in the late sixteenth century still felt free to include invented materials. Sidney favored poetry over history, because the former, being completely invented, could be made to conform to desired ethical norms. Sidney's defense of poesy included the whole of what we would call imaginative literature or fiction, not just verse productions.[41]

As we saw earlier, seventeenth-century historians were becoming increasingly reluctant to allow the fabulous or the fictional into historiography. The gap between poetry and history was growing, though no chasm yet separated them. If on the one hand we can point to William Camden's emphatic rejection of "fabulous fictions" in history, we also must note the popularity of "poesie historical," which, as George Puttenham pointed out, need not adhere very closely to the facts of the past and might "devise many historicall matters of no veracity at all." "Poesie historical" occupied the as yet ill-defined region between fact and fiction.[42] The history plays of Shakespeare, which utilized the historical sources as they were then known as well as the resources of the poet's imagination, blurred the distinction between history and poetry. The historical drama and "poesie historicall" that confounded "fact" and "fiction" proved culturally satisfying for the decades straddling the late sixteenth and early seventeenth centuries. Increasing respect for historical "fact" may have been one of the causes of its decline. As long as historians felt somewhat free to modify historical "facts," the distinctions between history and poesy remained partially blurred.

The Seventeenth Century

Attacks on the superior moral claims of poetry and on the highly ornamented language of Renaissance prose and poetry became common during the course of the seventeenth century. Demands for stylistic simplification were often accompanied by critiques of romance and other forms of poetic fictionality. We have noted these developments in connection with history, travel accounts, natural history, and natural philosophy. Statements about the need to bring *res* and *verba*, things and words, closer together became frequent.[43] A clearer demarcation between history and fiction developed. Historians and their readers came to demand verity, not verisimilitude, and to expect a history based on documentary evidence and the testimony of credible witnesses. Thus, as William Nelson has pointed out, there came to be two kinds of story, one truthful, one not. Verisimilitude was becoming the standard for the fiction writer and poet, as they too were advised to jettison the fabulous and romantic. The vista opened of creating prose fiction modeled on the newly popular factual discourses. To some degree, it was the factual discourses that would provide the models for fiction.

As we saw in earlier chapters, "discourses of fact" became increasingly popular in the seventeenth century. Travel literature was an extremely successful genre, and "news" and factual accounts of various kinds began to appear in publications solely or largely devoted to them. The growth of pamphlet and serial news that characterized the war and Interregnum years promoted the appetite for factual and ostensibly factual genres, and the closing of the theaters cut off an important fictional mode. Publications increasingly bore factually oriented titles and labels associated with news, narration, report, account, intelligence, relation, or history, trumpeting their truthfulness, fidelity, and impartiality.

Those with literary aspirations became less and less likely to find subject matter in fable or myth. William Davenant, Abraham Cowley, and Thomas Sprat offered a poetics that jettisoned the superstitious paraphernalia of gods and goddesses. Cowley proclaimed himself the poet of natural philosophy, who "no longer pretends to create worlds transcending this one but rather reports on the material facts of this world," and Sprat voiced the hope that poets would draw their subject matter from history, Scripture, and the natural world, that is, from the familiar or "real."[44]

During the course of the seventeenth century the pride of place occupied by poetry waned in some circles and was replaced by distrust. Truth, and especially "the naked truth," was a watchword. From the second half of the century onward a simplified prose suitable for the presentation of "matters of fact" was praised and sometimes practiced. Truth and fact were associated with plain speaking; rhetorical ostentation, with dissimulation or worse. The neoclassic prose of the Restoration and eighteenth centuries became less ornamented than its Renaissance predecessors. Wit and good writing for Dryden required "deep thought in common language." The best writing exhibited a mean between "ostentation and rusticity."[45] Sprat and Tillotson, both advocates of a simplified, direct style, were considered models of superior writing. Sprat's attack on the use of metaphor and other figures of speech in natural history and natural philosophy was a particularly strong expression of this movement.[46]

The distinction between fact and fiction thus might seem to have been quite straight-forward by the Restoration, but it was not. News media reports of highwaymen, criminals, and rogues were sometimes compounds of fact and fiction, as were travel accounts. Scholars investigating the development of the novel have pointed out how news, travel writing, and "factual" accounts were linked to the growth of new forms of fiction. Yet even if there was an overlap between fact and fiction in some genres, it also seems clear that the discourses of fact were gaining in prestige.

Travel and Literature

Fact-oriented travel reports, surveys, and descriptions became so familiar that literary men began to create fictional matters of fact in imitation of real narratives or mixed such reports with invented materials. Over time, as such reports became more accurate and readers less gullible, some travel writers moved in the nonfictional direction of geography and natural history while others produced adventures filled with colorful native inhabitants and pirates who were more or less real.

Yet feigned and real travel accounts were sometimes difficult to distinguish, especially in instances without witnesses to confirm or deny the account. If some voyages, like those to the moon, Utopia, or Lilliput, were not designed to fool anyone, others were realistic enough to deceive. William Sympson's *New Voyage the Indies* seems to have been largely a fabrication, and George Psalmanazar's *Historical and Geographical Description of Formosa* (1704), which claimed to dispel "Clouds of Fabulous Reports" by providing materials on laws, history, religion, language, and customs, was a "blatant fraud."[47] In describing his voyage to Guiana, Sir Walter Raleigh reported on men with eyes in their shoulders and mouths in their chests, though he admitted he had not himself seen them.[48] Ambivalence as well as the potential for fictionality can also be seen in the *Tatler's* comment that "there are no Books which I more delight in than Travels, especially those that describe remote countries, and give the writer an Opportunity of showing his Parts without incurring any Danger of being examined or Contradicted."[49]

Later in the century the *Athenian Gazette* led a discussion as to whether the letters and stories of the Turkish Spy were "Fiction or Reality," noting with some ambivalence that "if All is a Fiction, as we are not inclinable to believe, 'tis yet so handsomely manag'd that one may rather suspect than prove it so. Whosoever writ it, . . . was exquisitely acquainted with the Oriental Customs and Languages; . . . and has a valuable Collection of History by Him."[50] It is not entirely clear whether the editors were refusing to reject the narrative of the Turkish Spy as a lie or praising its literary value.

Satire, Fiction, and the Discourses of Fact

Although several literary forms may be used for satirical purposes, the "discourses of fact," travel and chorography, seem particularly to have lent themselves to criticism of contemporary mores. The best-known example of pseudochorography was Thomas More's early-sixteenth-century *Utopia*, which combined the traveler's report with the geographical model of Strabo to provide moral and political insights. More adopted the conventions of chorography, suggesting that his delay in writing was inexcusable because he had only to record, not invent.[51] More's sophisticated Latin readers would have had no difficulty identifying the fictionality of "no place." Bacon's *New Atlantis*, though not a satire, also took the form of the travel account, describing an obviously fictional place to present the author's new natural philosophy program.

The Present State of Betty-Land features a continent ruled by the planet Venus, "having Island of Man wholly under its Jurisdiction." The "great City of Lipstick" is described, along with the soil and crops, which featured bachelor buttons. Its history and antiquities are detailed, as was its peculiar custom, matrimony. There was also the *Present State of Fairy-land*, a political satire written in the form of letters from a citizen of "Fickle-borough" to the king of "Slave-onia."[52]

The fictional Captain Lemuel Gulliver's *Travels into Several Remote Nations of the World*[53] links its narrative to "his cousin" Dampier's *Voyage Round the World* and incorporates material from the *Philosophical Transactions* to describe remote places, with the aim of contrasting them with contemporary life and practices. The author's and reader's mutual familiarity with travel reports is exploited fully. Swift's readers are provided with maps and calculations of distance of the kind offered by Dampier and others as well as descriptions of physical characteristics and mores of the Lilliputians and Brobdingnagians. Gulliver concludes his report of "plain facts" with the conventional insistence that he has "given a faithful history" of his travels of sixteen years and seven months, "wherein I have not been so studious of ornament as truth." Instead of astonishing readers "with strange improbable tales," he "related plain matter of fact in the simplest manner and style; because my principal design was to inform, and not to amuse thee."[54]

Though the travel genre was perhaps the most common form of "fictionalized fact," newspapers and periodicals too might be mimicked for satirical effect. The *Transactioneer* ridiculed the style and subject matter of the *Philosophical Transactions*. It mocked the journal's claim to be "exact in relating Matter of Fact" in its reports of Chinese curiosities such as ear- and tooth-pickers, comparisons of fish tongues, monstrous births, and the martial discipline of grasshoppers.[55] Familiarity with the conventions of the *Philosophical Transactions* was essential if such satires were to be successful.

Factual forms and language might be employed for other varieties of fiction as well. Novelist and playwright Aphra Behn used the language of fact, often with tongue in cheek, sometimes not. As playwright, she insisted, "I was myself an eye-witness" to what is "here set down; and what I could not be witness of I received from the mouth of the chief actor in this history, the hero himself." Her story, however, referred to a meeting with the protagonist of a new London play—a play written by Behn herself.[56] Her *Fair Jilt: or, The History of Prince Tarquin and Miranda* (1696) insists, "This is Reality, and Matter of Fact. . . . [Portions of this history] I had from the Mouth of this unhappy Great man [Tarquin], and was an Eye-Witness to the rest."[57] Of her *Oroonoko or, The Royal Slave: A True History*, Behn wrote: "I do not pretend here to entertain you with a feign'd story, or anything piec'd together with Romantick Accidents; but every Circumstance, to a Tittle, is Truth. To a great part of the Main, I myself was an Eye witness; and what I did not see, was confirmed by Actors in the Intrigue."[58] Although her story defies almost any reader's sense of plausibility, the narrative is interspersed with careful descriptions of plant and animal life and the customs and manners of the inhabitants. Detailed naturalistic settings of exotic places thus might be found in both fiction and nonfiction. Behn's playful use of the conventions of the discourses of fact suggests that the language of well-reported "fact" was so much a part of the cultural landscape that it could be satirized with the complicity of London playgoers and readers.[59]

Defoe and the Origins of the Novel

Among the origins of the novel are the real and imaginary "news" reports of rogues and criminals and travelers' tales, both of which sometimes blurred "fact" and "fiction." Some scholars have emphasized efforts to give the new genre an air of "reality" by presenting the story in the documentary form of letters, pseudo-eyewitness accounts, memoirs, or autobiography. Still others have emphasized the role of Lockean individualism.[60]

No doubt all these played a role. But it must be emphasized that without a strong preexisting reader preoccupation with facts and the conventions of factual reporting, a fiction of purported "facts" could not have been successful. When such new fictions were modeled on personal memoirs, "news," or travel accounts, they willy-nilly adopted the conventions of proof for matters of fact. Novelists often adopted the familiar requirements of the honest, impartial, credible witness and documentary or epistolary evidence reported by a truthful, faithful, and impartial reporter devoid of personal interest. As fictions became grounded in "fictional facts," the technology of proof required for legal and other "facts" found its way into the new fictional genre.

A brief examination of Daniel Defoe, whose career combined journalism, travel writing, and the novel, illustrates the tangled relationship between the "discourses of fact" and the early stages of the novel, and the embeddedness of both in a "culture of fact." Even Defoe's most factual works—*A Tour Thro' the Whole Island of Great Britain, A Journal of the Plague Year,* the *History of the Pyrates,* and *The Storm*—are now thought by scholars to contain fictional elements. Like most chorographical writing, *A Tour* promised to describe the "Genius and Constitution of the Inhabitants . . . Their customs and Manners; their Natural History, Mindes, Commodities . . . With Useful Observations." Utilizing the conventions of "The Present and Past State of a Country," Defoe focused on the "present State of Things, as near as can be." He would provide a "true and impartial Description" of the soil, products, manufacturing, and "rarities of Art, or Nature" of each county, most of which he claimed to have seen himself. All his information is treated as "Matter of Fact."[61]

A Journal of the Plague Year being, Observations or Memorials of . . . 1665, which purports to have been written by an eyewitness who remained in London during the 1665 plague, was written in 1722 when the plague had again become topical. This supposedly firsthand report (Defoe was born c. 1660) actually combined a variety of sources, including official documents.[62]

His *General History of the Robberies and Murders of the most notorious Pyrates,* and Also Their Policies, Disciplines and Government From the first Rise . . . to the present Year combined news, travel reporting, recent history, and fiction. His stated goal, of course, was "Truth," and "those Facts which he himself was not an eyewitness of, he had from the authentick Relations of the Persons concern'd in taking the Pyrates, as well as from the Mouths of the Pyrates themselves. . . . No man can produce better Testimonies to support the Credit of any History."[63] He had "living witnesses enough to justify" his account of two female pirates which might, at first glance, appear "Extravagant."[64] Volume 2 contained a history "intermix'd with a Description" of the "laws, manners, customs, government and Religion of Ethiopia," in familiar chorographical form. If some portions of both volumes were taken from witness testimony and contemporary broadsides, his description of a radical community on Madagascar appears to have been pure invention.[65] *Madagascar: or, Robert Drury's Journal, during Fifteen Years of Captivity on that Island* may be an entirely fictional work and may or may not have been written by Defoe. Or it may actually be an authentic journal written by a real Robert Drury. It takes the form of a preface by one William Mackett, a narrator's account, and a cut-down version of the supposed journal itself. Mackett certifies that Drury was redeemed from slavery and that Mackett himself brought him back to London, where he now resides. Drury is characterized as "an honest, industrious Man, of good Reputation," and his journal, which some might take for "another Romance as Robinson Cruso," was "a plain, honest Narrative of Matter of fact."[66] The narrator, whose identity is unclear, emphasizes the "strong Proofs . . . by concurring Testimony, and the Nature of the Thing," reiterates Mackett's statement on the credibility and good character of Drury, and indicates that a William Pruser "knew Mr. Drury there, and was an Eye-Witness" to events. Every effort is taken to show that there is "no Reason to doubt his [Drury's] Veracity in any material Circumstance." Though some might suspect that the description of the Madagascarian religion was invented, the account "is Fact." The transcriber altered no "Facts, or added any Fiction of his own." The narrator, who claims, "My Design, in the ensuing History, is to give a plain and honest Narrative of Matters of Fact," like many "news" reporters offers firsthand confirmation. "I am every Day to be spoken with at Old Tom's Coffee-house in Birchin-Lane; . . . to gratify any Gentleman with a further Account of any Thing herein contain'd to stand the strictest Examination, or to confirm those Things which to some may seem doubtful."[67]

If the Drury account was allied to the travel report, *The Storm: or, A Collection of the most Remarkable Casualities and Disasters which happen'd in the Late Dreadful Tempest* is linked to "news" reports of great storms and other natural disasters. Like them it draws moral inferences from the events reported. But Defoe also insisted it was "the Duty of an Historian" "to convey matter of fact upon its legitimate Authority, and no other; . . . where the Story is vouch'd to him with sufficient Authority, he ought to give the World the special Testimony of its proper Voucher, . . . and where it comes without such sufficient Authority, he ought to say so."[68] We might well have included Defoe's statement in our treatment of historiography. The same can be said of his suggestion that much of ancient history was "meer Romance" and that the lives of many of its famous men were "drowned in Fable." Though many "Matters of Fact are handed down to Posterity with so little Certainty, that nothing is to be depended upon," Defoe promised "no where to Trespass upon Fact."[69]

Those works of Defoe's that are clearly novels similarly adopt the conventions of the "discourses of fact." They often contain figures drawn from the real criminal world as well as more obviously fictional characters. *The Life, Adventures and Pyracies of Captain Singleton* used the literature of travel and pirate and privateer accounts, combining factual materials with themes of morality, sin, and redemption.[70] His *Memoirs of Captain George Carleton* described Spanish cities as well as manners and customs and provided a family history of the "memoirist" to enhance verisimilitude. *The History and Remarkable Life of Colonel Jack* takes the form of an autobiographical account, and *Memoirs of a Cavalier* is alleged to be an accidentally retrieved manuscript found in the closet of one of King William's secretaries of state. In this "memoir" "almost all the Facts" were confirmed by "the Writers of those Times."[71]

Defoe's novel, or rather "history," as he calls it, *The Fortunate Mistress: or, A History of the Life and Vast Variety of Fortunes of Mademoiselle de Beleau . . . Being the Person known by the name of Lady Roxanna* (1724), is replete with the language of factual discourse. The "author" insists "That the Foundation of this is laid in truth of Fact; and so the Work is not a Story, but a History." "The Facts" could be "trac'd back too plainly by the many People yet living." The writer, who claimed acquaintance with the woman's first husband, knew the "first Part of the Story to be Truth," and this knowledge, he hoped, would serve by way of "A Pledge for the Credit of the rest."[72]

Similar devices borrowed from the discourses of fact are employed in *The Fortunes and Misfortunes of the Famous Moll Flanders, . . . Written from her own Memorandums* (1721), a fictional account in which the "author" insists, "The World is so taken up of late with Novels and Romances, that it will be hard for a private History to be taken for Genuine, where the Names and other Circumstances are concealed."[73] Defoe insists that he is merely the editor of *The Wonderful Life and Surprizing Adventures of Robinson Crusoe . . . Written by Himself*, described as "a just History of Fact: nor is their any Appearance of fiction in it."[74] This fiction too was obviously closely related to both memoir and travel account.

Other early novelists also resorted to supposedly credible eyewitnesses and "authentick" documents such as letters, firsthand reports, and diaries. Samuel Richardson's use of fictional letters in *Pamela* is an obvious example. The 1744 preface to Eliza Heywood's *Fortunate Foundlings* even notes, "The many Fictions which have been lately imposed upon the World, under the specious Titles of secret Histories, Memoirs, etc., have given but too much room to question the Veracity of every thing that has the least Tendency that way." Her readers, however, would "find nothing in the following sheets, but what have been collected from Original Letters, Private Memorandums, and the Accounts we have been favoured with from the mouths of Persons too deeply concerned in many of the chief Transactions not to be perfectly acquainted with the Truth, and of too much Honor and Integrity to put any false Colours upon it."[75]

Alexander Welsh recently has suggested that the mid- to late-eighteenth-century preference for circumstantial evidence over direct or witness testimony in criminal law cases was adopted by novelists such as Henry Fielding, who replaced the earlier devices of witness-narrators, editor-narrators, or letters with the creation of a web of "circumstances." The "factual fictions" based on supposed eyewitness accounts and documents that eclipsed fabulous stories and the romance were in turn replaced by the circumstantially formulated realistic novel.[76]

The factlike fictions of the early eighteenth century not only were closely linked to the "discourses of fact" but provide further evidence for a developing "culture of fact." Only when "fact" had become part of the cultural vocabulary of the reading public could it be satirized or fictionalized. "Matter of Fact" was then turned on its head to create a new kind of realistic or verisimilar factlike fiction. The dichotomy between the truth of history and the fictions of poetry enunciated in the late sixteenth and early seventeenth centuries to enhance poetry was elaborated during the seventeenth century by the many discourses of fact that sought to eliminate fables, romance, and invented materials. Then that dichotomy was eroded by novelists seeking a new kind of verisimilitude. In the early eighteenth century "facts" and the ubiquitous methods of proving them provided a mechanism for the creation of a new kind of fiction.[77]

Those attempting to relate or report "matters of fact," fictional or nonfictional, were not aiming at mimesis. "Verification" of particular things reported, not "mirroring" a whole event, was the goal. For the most part, the evidence of reliable witnesses, and to a lesser extent documentary evidence, was used to provide that verification. Most authors distinguished their reports from interpretation, reflection, or explanation of the events. The discourses of fact, fictional and otherwise, attempted to record and report particular events credibly and without error to a third party, whether that party was a jury, the Royal Society, a consumer of periodical "news," or a reader of travel accounts, cosmographies, chorographies, histories, or novels. Early novelists such as Defoe claimed not to be reproducing reality "as it really was" but to be reporting "truth," as opposed to "fictions" or "romance." In the process they created a new form of "fiction."

Conclusion

In the seventeenth century the concept "fact" was given a kind of philosophical imprimatur by John Locke, the most influential English philosopher of his age. While Locke's philosophical views were modified and challenged during the eighteenth century by several English and Scottish philosophers, "fact" remained a central feature of their epistemology. In addition, our small foray into the eighteenth century indicates not only that the concept "fact" became more pervasive but that the meaning and deployment of the concept began to shift. As the decades passed, "matter of fact," which initially required the narrator, observer, historian, or lawyer to parade his evidence and examine his witnesses for impartiality and credibility, was being replaced at least in some circles by a usage of "fact" or "the facts" which assumed that satisfactory proofs had *already* been provided. This seemingly slight linguistic modification gave "fact" a greater air of certainty. Although I have not encountered the expression "hard fact" or "hard facts," one can easily see how it might develop out of early-eighteenth-century usage.

We have seen too that the changing nature of eighteenth-century natural philosophy altered the way the concept was deployed, particularly as a result of the post-Newtonian inclination to link "facts" to the "laws of nature." "Fact" moved further and further away from the original legal usage of a human deed toward references to natural phenomena. The early-eighteenth-century novel highlighted the role of credible witnesses in fictional fact finding to a greater extent than the philosophers concerned with "real" facts. The history of "fact" in the eighteenth and nineteenth centuries, however, remains largely unexplored territory that requires a great deal more investigation if we are to understand how both the professional and lay faith in "facts" came to predominate and how the recent erosion of that faith developed among contemporary philosophers and literary critics.[78] This chapter points the way for further research into a concept that came to dominate many aspects of British, American, and European culture for several centuries.

Conclusion

A t the beginning of the sixteenth century "fact" was a term of fairly limited use found primarily in the law courts and occasionally in historical writing. "Matters of fact," which were distinguished from both "matters of law" and "matters of record," played a prominent role in the major European legal systems. Although historians have recognized that various aspects of Roman law, medieval canon law, and English common law are intertwined with early modern political thought, legal concepts have not typically been treated as central to intellectual culture.[1] This book has given legal concepts a larger role in cultural development than is customary because the evidence suggests that they were significant in the development of an empirical natural science and more generally in the construction of a general culture of fact.

Legal systems that treat fact finding as a rational rather than ritualistic process or invocation of divine intervention require methods of fact determination comprehensible to litigants and to the culture as a whole. They possess, whether clearly articulated or not, an underlying epistemology, that is, a set of beliefs as to human ability to arrive at "true" and "just" decisions. Fact finding in the legal context requires making decisions about events that are no longer present to either the disputants or the judges. It requires faith in the possibility of reaching adequate and reasonable belief about such events and a mode of thinking about what is knowable, who can know it, and under what conditions it is knowable, as well as institutional arrangements and processes for knowing.

How societies structure institutions and procedures that encapsulate this belief, of course, varies. By the mid-sixteenth century most European states entrusted this function to professional judges and had elaborated a procedure in which two witnesses or confession was treated as suitable proof. The English produced another institutional arrangement, the jury. One of the major themes of this book has been that the absorption and spread of "fact" in England was facilitated by widespread familiarity with and esteem for lay fact finding by juries. Efforts by naturalists, historians, rationalizing theologians, and even novelists to rely on the credible testimony of firsthand witnesses thus built on and were assisted by an already existing, legitimate, widely shared, often glorified cultural practice.

This knowledge of, or rather belief in, "fact," however, was not thought to be perfect. Both English and Continental legal systems recognized that human error was always possible and that incorrect judgments might be reached. They attempted to provide institutional and procedural means as well as norms to reduce opportunities for error and willful distortion. The English system, like the Continental, developed distinctions between testimonial and documentary evidence and between these forms of evidence and circumstantial evidence and presumption. It recognized inference and made a distinction between firsthand observation and hearsay accounts. Over time the common law system developed criteria for knowing that were variously designated by the terms "satisfied conscience," "satisfied understanding," "moral certainty," and "belief beyond reasonable doubt."

The substitution of the jury for ordeals, combined with the introduction of witnesses, generated a kind of practical epistemology that could be understood by participants and observers and that on the whole proved satisfactory to those using the legal system. The early modern English legal fact-finding process did not lead to claims of demonstrative or absolutely certain knowledge. Early modern English facts, legal and nonlegal, remained in the realm of probability, though that probability might be extremely high when impartial witnesses observed carefully and reported clearly. This legal approach to fact became part and parcel of the generally held habits of thought characteristic of late-seventeenth- and early-eighteenth-century English culture.

Given its early meaning as human act or deed, "fact," not surprisingly, was an integral part of Renaissance historiography. Our historiographical survey underlined the historian's use of legal concepts such as credible witnesses and how the legacy of classical historiography with its emphasis on firsthand observers coalesced with the legal inheritance. The increased use of documents and material remains by antiquarian scholars broadened the historical enterprise's concern for "fact." If "matters of record" and "matters of fact" were quite distinct in law, these categories would lose their sharp edges in historiography as "fact" hesitantly began to assimilate documents. Our discussion of historiography also traced the widening gap between history and fiction and, more generally, fact and fiction. Historiography, which at one time had permitted a variety of fictional elements including the fictional feats of mythical kings, now attempted to excise them, heightening the factual and the truthful in history. During this period multiple and even conflicting meanings of "fact" were entertained by those writing history.

In "news," too, "fact" initially had referred to human actions. Although "news" focused primarily on human acts and human events, natural events were added so that "fact" came to include "marvels," divine signs, or warnings, and other, less wonder-producing natural phenomena. Newsworthy events were reported in new media that absorbed the norms of legal and historical "fact" production. "Fact" was also gradually absorbed by English chorographers and travel writers, who similarly began to treat both human and natural phenomena as "matters of fact." Widening application of "fact" appears to have been encouraged when human and natural events were treated in the same media and when those producing factual discourses used the vernacular rather than Latin, a language that employed separate terminology for human and natural acts.

The transformation of matters of fact to include both human and natural events was completed by Baconian natural historians and Restoration natural philosophers. Although I have emphasized the role of Baconian-style natural history with its emphasis on particular observation and experiment, the pronouncements of Bacon alone were not sufficient to accomplish this transition, particularly because when he wrote in Latin he did not always use "factum." The later movement into the vernacular appears to have underlined the use of "fact." "Fact" could accommodate both passively observed and experimentally produced natural phenomena because English did not distinguish between human and natural acts.

A bundle of familiar assumptions relating to witness testimony, impartial procedure, and the possibility of morally certain findings of fact came to permeate the new natural history and experimental philosophy. This shift of legal perspectives to natural occurrences and experimentally produced events was crucial to the establishment of English natural philosophy. The development of an empirical natural philosophy grounded on carefully monitored observation and experiment conducted in an impartial, unbiased environment echoed the norms and practices of fact finding found elsewhere. The English legal tradition provided a respected, ready-made technology of fact finding. That technology could be, and was, employed by naturalists and others seeking to legitimize empirical observation and experiment and give observed and experimentally derived natural matters of fact the status of "knowledge," if not "scientia." Naturalists did not have to explain or justify their use of "matter of fact" because it was already a well-established cultural category.

Legal, historical, and even scientific practice, however, cannot fully account for the high status of "fact" by the beginning of the eighteenth century. We must not underestimate the importance of religious and ecclesiastical uses of "fact." There were divine "facts" as well as human and natural ones. God's actions in the world, wondrous events as well as ordinary natural phenomena, were increasingly treated as "matters of fact." The central events of Christianity became "matters of fact" to be substantiated by the same methods as those by which one proved a criminal act, a historical event, an earthquake, or a scientific experiment. By the late seventeenth century the most deeply held truths of Protestant Christianity and the epistemological viability of Protestantism against the claims of Roman Catholicism were supported by arguments from "matters of fact." These truths could be believed to a moral certainty and were therefore "beyond reasonable doubt." "Fact" and arguments from "matter of fact" reinforced English Protestant Christianity, which in turn reinforced the legitimacy of "fact" and fact-determination procedures.

As the concept of fact spread from the law courts, it carried with it the legal concern with witnesses, evidence, and impartial judgment. All the fact-oriented disciplines exhibited a preference for personal observation and a belief that the testimony of credible witnesses under optimum conditions could yield believable, even morally certain "facts." It favored first-person accounts that made vivid the experience of the "facts" described.

In all the disciplines and genres we have examined we have noticed a distinction between "fact" or "matter of fact" and some other category or categories. In law the most common opposition was that of "matter of fact" and "matter of law," although we also hear of the distinctions between "matter of deed" and "matter of record," between fact and presumption, and between fact and circumstances. In history and the reporting of news we encountered distinctions between fact and fiction, between fact and explanation, and between fact and conjecture, reflection, or opinion. In natural philosophy the observations, experiments, and descriptions of human practices that were natural history led to "facts." As "fact" came into its own, the virtuosi distinguished between matters of fact on the one hand and conjecture, hypothesis, and theory on the other. Though modern scholars may concern themselves with the interpenetration of fact and theory, and the difficulty if not impossibility of separating factual and fictional narratives, such concerns were not characteristic of the early modern era, which saw itself as having established quite clear boundaries between fact and other matters.

All the discourses of fact emphasized the quest for evidence of facts sufficient to reach "moral certainty." Yet the seventeenth century essentially maintained the legal usage that a matter of fact was an assertion to be more or less fully proved rather than a statement of something already proved. The assertion that something was fact raised rather than foreclosed issues of belief, truth, and relative levels of certainty. With Locke fact was given philosophical form and treated as "knowledge." Only in the eighteenth century does fact sometimes come to refer to something that has already been sufficiently proved to count as "true." The categories "fact" and "truth" thus were slowly becoming one. Even the newly emerging novel began to appropriate many of the forms and locutions associated with "matter of fact," although in this medium fact is about verisimilitude rather than truth. Over the course of a century and a half, "fact" had become an important feature of English culture.

In the process, sense-based information and experience, particularly what was visually acquired, was elevated in epistemological status. Accompanying this respect for sense-based belief, however, was an awareness that distortions in observation and reporting were always possible and that partiality, superstition, poor education, and "interest" might impair the ability to report accurately. The Christian contrast between divine omniscience and human fallibility and the skeptical critique of both senses and reason are reflected in Bacon's idols and in the many statements that echoed his pronouncements.

The discourses of fact distinguished "fact" from the products of passion, imagination, and reason. Boyle, Hooke, and other naturalists applied "reason" to observed "facts," and historians and others attempted explanations of the facts. Inference, reflection, hypothesis, and causal analysis all involved applying reason and sometimes imagination to established facts. Some naturalists treated hypothesis as reasoning on the basis of facts; others associated it with imagination stimulated by fact. For still others, "laws" might be derived from "fact."

Efforts to separate fact from opinion, reflection, inference, and hypothesis were not entirely successful and were evaluated quite differently by different audiences. What counted as facts and what as inference from those facts was difficult to determine, especially in areas where partisan differences were powerfully expressed. Natural philosophers were divided about the nature and value of hypothesis. Even the relationship between fact and fiction was not always entirely clear. Some travel accounts blurred the categories, and new fictional productions such as the novel were sometimes taken to be "fact."

The discourses of fact were particularly concerned about distortions caused by language. They rejected highly ornamented language and scholastic forms of discourse and were suspicious of rhetoric. Fact was to be reported in a plain, clear, unadorned manner, preferably in first-person accounts.

Values prominent in legal discourse were applied in a growing number of other areas. The most often enunciated was impartiality. Typically, narrators and reporters describing matters of fact presented themselves or other witnesses as impartial and stressed the need for impartial judgment by those who evaluated or reached decisions on the basis of their testimony. Readers are frequently requested to put themselves in the position of the impartial judge. The norm of impartiality was a characteristic feature of all the discourses of fact. It was neither original nor exclusive to the English scientific community, although in practice the virtuosi violated it less often and less obviously than historians or newsmen.

The discourses of fact tended to straddle class divisions, or at least the gentle-nongentle boundary. They included an audience broader than the classically learned or university trained. Social criteria were relevant to assessing the credibility of witnesses and reporters of fact, but so were such considerations as expertise, opportunity to observe, honesty, and impartiality. Both the giving and receiving ends of the discourses of fact were populated by many who were not gentlemen, but also by many who were. In this connection we have emphasized the widespread participation of juries and the widely diffused knowledge of their obligations to make judgments on matters of fact as well as faith in their capacity to do so. We have also drawn attention to the enormous expansion of the "fact"-purveying media during the revolutionary era. The political and religious turmoil of the times fueled the appetite for political and military reporting among social groups that previously had little or no access to such information. The production and consumption of newsbooks and more extended reports of contemporary events meant that a profusion of fact-oriented reports circulated to new audiences. Chorographies and travel accounts similarly appealed both to the learned and to the unlearned but literate reader.

Histories and natural histories in the vernacular further broadened the production and consumption of the "discourses of fact," as did the *Philosophical Transactions*. Natural history was being produced in forms available to a broadening audience. Vernacular publication itself implied an audience broader than that of Latin publication. The social and educational composition of natural philosophy audiences expanded. In the area of religion the issues of the rationalizing theologians were of interest to substantial numbers of Englishmen worried about the inroads being made by Roman Catholicism and atheism. The novel, with its fictionalized "facts," was still another genre produced by and for an audience encompassing gentle and middling groups. The "discourses of fact" thus assumed the existence of a fairly wide range of individuals capable of both reporting "matters of fact" and comprehending and evaluating such reports. "Fact" combined the cultural powers of groups that crossed the gentle-nongentle divide.

While we have emphasized the similarity among the discourses of fact, not all of them followed the same path. Natural philosophy moved rapidly and decisively in the direction of hypothesis and to some extent to the search for factually derived laws of nature. Some natural historians attempted comparison and classification; civil historians and ethnographers did not. New or refined political classifications or explanations did not develop from political description. "Perfect" history continued to demand causal explanation, but historical discourse did not substantially expand the repertoire of historical explanation, which remained largely limited to explanation based on individual character or climate. The problems of partisanship and impartiality were voiced in all the discourses of fact but were most acute for those writing about political and religious topics of contemporary relevance.

Different epistemic communities followed divergent practices as they sought to establish "facts." Legal fact finders did their work in an adversarial context that natural philosophers and historians found distasteful, and legal systems could not tolerate the absence of finality that the English experimental community found so congenial. Nor could courts engage in experimental replication or utilize sense-enhancing instruments. The search for universal natural principles differed from the jurist's search for legal principles grounded in *English* legal experience. Historians often sought to derive moral precepts from historical facts; naturalists did not.

Once established, empirically grounded natural philosophy had less need to "borrow." If the direction of influence in the seventeenth century ran from law to natural history, it appears to have reversed in later centuries as writers on legal evidence began to draw on the authority of scientific fact finding. Over time the "facts" of the natural sciences would acquire a higher epistemological status than the "facts" of history or law.

This book has attempted to shed some light on questions relating to disciplinary development and permeability. If I have cast my study in a form that emphasizes disciplines and genres in order to investigate when and how "fact" became an important category for each, I have also drawn attention to the difficulty of placing certain kinds of intellectual productions in one category or another. Works thus might be considered "historical" either because they dealt with the past or because they dealt with particulars. Both natural history and civil history were "historical" in the latter sense. Chorography was "historical" because it dealt with particulars, both human and natural, and also because it sometimes treated "antiquities." The fact of a monster might be news, evidence of divine Providence, or the subject of a natural historian's descriptive account. The historian's preference for contemporary accounts sometimes made it difficult to distinguish between "news" and "history." Some topics so deeply intertwined religious and scientific communities that some historians now view them as part of the same intellectual enterprise, wishing to abolish the term "science" or "natural science" when dealing with the early modern period.

In emphasizing the legal origins of "fact," I have tried not to overestimate legal influences in the development of other disciplines. For instance, concepts of nonlegal provenance such as hypothesis and theory interacted with fact in natural philosophy, and history remained indebted to classical historiographical and rhetorical traditions. Proceeding largely discipline by discipline, while at the same time emphasizing the commonalities of the "discourses of fact," has, I hope, allowed me the best of both worlds, separate disciplines and general culture. The disciplines selectively absorbed concepts and methods from one another. As a result, they themselves were altered, as was the general culture. What emerged at the end of successive periods remains recognizable but had changed. By the end of the seventeenth century "fact," originally limited to historically and legally relevant human acts, extended to new forms of factual discourse, comprehended large portions of natural philosophy, and supported Christian belief. These intellectual dynamics tend to be lost when attention is devoted solely to developments over time in a single discipline or even when analysis is limited to the relation between "science" and religion. Though numerous studies have suggested important roles for Protestantism, Puritanism, and latitudinarianism in the development of natural philosophy and the permeability of natural philosophy and theology and metaphysics, few have explored possible links between legal thinking and the development of empiricist approaches to epistemology and natural philosophy.

Ideally, an even broader perspective would expose the extent to which changes were peculiarly English and to what extent the English pattern was shared by other European cultures. Subject to further research, it seems likely that the more formulaic method of legal fact determination characteristic of Continental courts and the exclusion of laymen from that process impeded the legal carryover into other fields that was so pronounced in England. The category "fact," however, was present in all countries touched by canon and Roman law, and "factum" and its cognates such as "fait" and "hecho" were used to designate human deeds and actions. One would, therefore, expect "fact" in the historical, newspaper, and travel literature that circulated throughout Europe.

As for Continental natural philosophy, it seems likely that "fact" would be less pervasively applied to natural phenomena in those locales where natural philosophy remained closer to the traditions of scholasticism than in England or where natural philosophy became more Cartesian and more wedded to the mathematical sciences. Our brief foray into French natural history at the Academy of Sciences suggests that the natural "fait" did make an appearance in France and that there were some parallel developments. The weaker foothold of skepticism in England, however, allowed for greater confidence in factual knowledge than in France.

Nowhere else did fact and hypothesis appear to have become knit together so closely as in England.

Although this book has focused on English cultural developments, we have noted commonalities shared by Continental and English legal systems, as well as those shared by the historiographical communities, both of which were shaped by classical exemplars and legal practice. But we have also drawn attention to the differences between the legal systems, pointing especially to the role of the jury and to the concern of English historians with contentious and often partisan accounts of the foundations of state and church. We have noted the Continental origins of the newspaper while emphasizing that the news media explosion during the English civil war and Interregnum brought this discourse of fact into the immediate and constant consciousness of the English public as military and political events were reported with breathless rapidity. English appetite for information, however much partisanly produced, was insatiable.

Although we cannot accurately speak about a purely English "science" or natural philosophy, given the interdependence of European naturalists, the English created a larger cluster of men devoted to empirical study than appeared elsewhere and created an institution that would trumpet the norms of a fact-oriented natural history. Bacon's fact-oriented natural history, his focus on experiment, and the call for an organized cooperative institution had its greatest impact in England. The peculiar combination of "fact" and hypothesis exemplified by Hooke and Boyle provided the characteristic stance of English natural philosophy.

Rational theology did not have its origins in England, but it blossomed there, particularly in the post-Restoration era as theologians embraced "fact" as a means of defending scriptural Christianity. And if several of the English literary trends had their French and Italian analogues, the development of the realistic, fact-oriented novel appears to be peculiarly English. Like other national European cultures, that of England was a unique amalgam of European and national developments. England was European to be sure, but it was also English.

Like most studies in intellectual and cultural history, this one raises the issue of "context." Few intellectual and cultural historians view cultural enterprises as having developed unaffected by the material, political, religious, and social environment. Some envision "context" in terms of broad socioeconomic environments, whereas for others, context suggests localized microenvironments. For still others, context implies viewing particular works in relation to commonly employed patterns of discourse. Those treating shared linguistic traditions as "context" have focused primarily on political discourse. Such approaches have not as yet had a substantial impact on religious or scientific topics.

This work has paid some attention to social and political context, particularly to social class and to the impact of the religio-political conflicts that were so central to the seventeenth century. There has also been some attention to the classical and medieval backgrounds of early modern English thought. Fundamentally, however, I have been concerned with how developments in each discipline provided contexts for the others and with the evolution of a general intellectual context that I have labeled the "culture of fact."

Studies concerned with development and change raise questions of causation. The jury appears to have played a central causal role in the development of a culture of fact. The institution of the jury, which operated not just in the metropolis but throughout the country and in venues open to a substantial public, not only disseminated the concept of fact broadly but implied a widely distributed competence for witnessing and fact determination that was easily assimilated in other fact-determining venues. The jury served as the focus for a general agreement that middling status coupled with impartiality and integrity was sufficient for the making of empirical judgments on the testimony of witnesses, who were on the whole treated as perceptually competent. The common law jury, then, provides a key to explaining the widespread English susceptibility to the kind of practical empiricism we have been describing.

Another factor that helps explain English familiarity and receptivity to "facts" is the enormously rapid expansion and broad dissemination of the news media in the revolutionary decades. The news media were to be found elsewhere in Europe, but the explosive growth fueled by the appetite for information about political and military events combined with the midcentury absence of press control was peculiar to England. A broadly based reading public was interested enough to purchase and deemed competent enough to understand the "facts" presented to it.

Something similar occurred with the "new philosophy" as new social and professional groups were recruited to participate in the practice of natural philosophy. Natural philosophy was no longer dominated by university-based academics but might be pursued by aristocrats, gentlemen, seamen, government officials, academic scholars, travelers, artisans, and the observant generally. Here again a fairly broad range of individuals and groups was viewed as sufficiently "perceptually competent" to participate in at least some stages of the "new philosophy." Much of the new philosophy, epitomized by literary productions associated with the Royal Society, was presented to the public in the vernacular, a development that made the terminology of "fact" more familiar. Popular interest in "wonders" and "marvels" fueled both the news media and scientific writing.

Widespread application of "fact" to religious issues in the latter portion of the seventeenth century further broadened the audience for "fact" as rational theologians used arguments from "fact" in their campaigns to buttress English Protestant Christianity. Religious writing and polemic thus provided still another arena in which facts were "consumed" by a broad spectrum of the population. Belief in scriptural "facts" was a matter of particular importance to the English in the latter decades of the seventeenth century. Then, at the end of the century, Locke provided fact with a newly enhanced philosophical status. It is no accident that "novels" appropriating the language of fact came to be produced for an audience familiar with and receptive to the language.

It is thus not wholly inappropriate to speak of the democratization of participation in the process of determining facts in England. Many, if not all, factual accounts could be produced by rather ordinary individuals and could be absorbed and understood by a similar audience. The factual discourses did not require an elite constituency, as did scholastic philosophy or mathematically oriented physics or epic poetry. A popular taste for facts was part and parcel of a broadening taste for the productions of print culture.

Of course, English culture had not become exclusively empirical nor was the culture of fact exclusively English. Tracing the English evolution, adoption, and dissemination of fact, however, does reveal the extent to which English culture had become a culture of fact and the special debt that this cultural evolution owed to the law's specific concerns for and techniques of fact finding. The adoption of fact by the experimental community was a central development in the history of natural philosophy. Over time "fact," as human deeds and actions, had been transformed into the best knowledge available to fallible human beings of a very broad spectrum of human and natural phenomena. This book has attempted to provide a better understanding of how fact was fashioned in law, adopted by historians, naturalists, theologians, and even novelists, and came to gain such intellectual currency. I have tried to show that a critical element in what has been called British empiricism was shaped out of legal materials and how "fact" grounded in human testimony became a central feature of the Anglo-American philosophical tradition and cultural practice.

Notes

Introduction

1. See Barbara Shapiro, *Probability and Certainty in Seventeenth-Century England: The Relationships between Religion, Natural Science, Law, History, and Literature* (Princeton, 1983). See also Donald Kelley, "The Problem of Knowledge and the Concept of Discipline," in *History and the Disciplines: The Reclassification of Knowledge in Early Modern Europe*, ed. Donald Kelley (Rochester, N.Y., 1997), pp. 13–28.

2. Sociologist Niklas Luhmann treats law as an autonomous intellectual and professional tradition that is nevertheless responsive to and capable of absorbing extralegal developments. *Autopoietic Law: A New Approach to Law and Society*, ed. Gunther Teubner (Berlin, 1988).

Chapter 1: "Fact" and the Law

1. R. C. Van Caenegem, "The History of European Civil Procedure," *Encyclopedia of Comparative Law* (Tubingen, 1972), 16:13. But see Robert Barett, *Trial by Fire and Water: The Medieval Judicial Ordeal* (Oxford, 1986), pp. 34–41. Barett suggests that the ordeal was not abandoned because it became irrational but became irrational because it had been abandoned (p. 86).

2. See Barbara Shapiro, *"Beyond Reasonable Doubt" and "Probable Cause": Historical Studies of the Anglo-American Law of Evidence* (Berkeley, 1991).

3. *Da Mihi facto dabo tibi ius*. The distinction appears in most canon and civil law procedurals but was not part of the law of the early Romans. See *Le fait et le droit: Etudes de logique juridique* (Centre Nationale de Recherches de Logique, Brussels, 1961), p. 25. The distinction appears in Quintilian, *Institutes of the Orator*, Loeb ed. (Cambridge, Mass., 1969), III, v, 4, 7.

4. In Latin "matter of fact" was sometimes rendered "res facta," The French used "fait" and "droit," the Spanish "questions de hecho" and "questions de derecho."

5. More is known about the practice of eighteenth-century courts.

6. Pleading by legal professionals in the central courts brought a case to an issue. When the issue had been reached, local juries determined the facts relating to that issue.

7. *Trial of Lawrence Bradden* (London, 1684), p. 61.

8. Sir Edward Coke, *The Third Part of the Institutes of the Laws of England* (London, 1819), p. 29; *A True Narrative of the Proceedings at the Hertford Assizes* (London, 1676), p. 76; *The Trial of John Giles* (London, 1681), p. 3; *The Trial of Lord Mohun* (London, 1699), p. 55.

9. William Lambarde, *Eirenarcha* (London, 1614), pp. 218, 219. See also Cicero, *De inventione*, I.34–43, 48; *Rhetorica ad herennium*, Loeb Classical Library, vol. 2 (Cambridge, Mass., 1954), 1.8.

10. See Van Caenegem, "History of European Civil Procedure," p. 29; Morris S. Arnold, "Law and Fact in the Medieval Jury Trial: Out of Sight, Out of Mind," *American Journal of Legal History* 18 (1974), 268–280; F. F. C. Milson, "Law and Fact in Legal Development," *University of Toronto Law Review* 17 (1969), 1–19; James Bradley Thayer, *Preliminary Treatise on Evidence at the Common Law* (1898; reprint New York, 1969), pp. 183–261; Jerome Lee, "The Law-Fact Distinction: From Trial by Ordeal to Trial by Jury," *AIPLA Quarterly Journal* 12 (1984), 288–294.

11. Thayer, *Preliminary Treatise on Evidence*, pp. 182–185. See also pp. 185–200. Thayer believed that Coke's formula came into existence in the sixteenth century. "Law and Fact in Jury Trials," *Harvard Law Review* (1890), 147–175. See also Alessandro Giuliani, "The Influence of Rhetoric on the Law of Evidence and Pleading," *Juridical Review* 62 (1969), 217.

"Choses en fait" does not appear in dictionaries of law French or the earliest English law dictionaries. See F. O., *Law French Dictionary*, 2d ed. (London, 1718). "Fait" appears as "deed," and meant deed in both senses of sealed documents and action. "Fait de dieu" was an act of God. J. H. Baker, *Manual of Law French*, 2d ed. (Aldershot, 1990). The term does not appear in John Rastell, *Expositions of the Terms of the Lawes of England* (1567) or in John Cowell, *The Interpreter or Book Containing the Significations of Words* (1607). Cowell and most subsequent writers distinguished "matter in deed" from "matter of record." "Matter in deed seemeth to be nothing else but a truth to be proved, . . . though not by any record." Giles Duncombe used "Choses en fait." *Tryals per Pais or the Law of England Concerning Juries by Nisi Prius* (London, 1682), p. 4.

12. See John Guy, ed., *The Debellacyon of Salem and Bizance*, in the *Complete Works of St. Thomas More* (New Haven, 1987), X, 1–232.

13. Francis Bacon, *Baconiana . . . Remains of Sir Francis Bacon*, 2d ed. (London, 1684), pp. 22–23, 30, 36.

14. Thomas Blount, *Law Dictionary* (London, 1670); Duncombe, *Tryals per Pais*, pp. 1–2. See also Edward Leigh, *A Philological Commentary* (London, 1658), p. 135; Anchitell Grey, *Debates of the House of Commons from the Year 1667 to the Year 1694*, 10 vols. (London, 1769), I, 448.

15. See Thomas A. Green, *Verdict According to Conscience: Perspectives on the English Criminal Trial Jury, 1200–1800* (Chicago, 1985), pp. 153–199. In special verdicts the judges dealt with both law and fact. Jurors sometimes engaged in "nullification," giving the verdict they wished regardless of the evidence. See ibid., pp. 255–257, 259.

16. See *Twelve Good Men and True: The Criminal Trial Jury in England, 1200–1800*, ed. J. S. Cockburn and Thomas A. Green (Princeton, 1988). Sir John Fortescue's fifteenth-century *De Laudibus Legum Angliae* already distinguishes witnesses from jurors (ed. S. B. Chrimes [Cambridge, 1942], chap. 26); J. H. Baker, *The Reports of Sir John Spelman*, 2 vols. (London, 1977–78), II, 106, citing *Deballacyon of Salem and Bizance* (1533).

17. See John Langbein, *Prosecuting Crime in the Renaissance* (Cambridge, Mass., 1974). For cross-examination, see Sir Thomas Smith, *De Republica Anglorum*, ed. Mary Dewar, 2 vols. (Cambridge, 1982), II, 15; Sir Geoffrey Gilbert, *The Law of Evidence* (London, 1805), pp. 61, 62, 132.

18. Coke, *Third Part of the Institutes* (1644), p. 163; Francis Bacon, *The Works of Francis Bacon*, ed. James Spedding, Robert Leslie Ellis, and Douglas Denon Heath, 15 vols. (London, 1857–72), I, 513.

19. Juries could reach verdicts in the absence of evidence presented in court.

20. See Matthew Hale, *Historia placitorum coronae or History of the Pleas of the Crown*, 2 vols.

(London, 1736), II, 241; Gilbert, *Law of Evidence*, p. 65. There were, however, concerns about forgery.

21. Gilbert, *Law of Evidence*, pp. 3, 148.

22. Ibid., pp. 139–140, 144.

23. Exclusion of interested testimony meant that not all the available evidence could be heard.

24. *The Tryal of . . . London Apprentices* (London, 1668), p. 44. See also *The Trial and Condemnation of . . . Charnock* (London, 1696), pp. 67–68; *The Tryal of Sir Tho. Gasgoyne for High Treason* (London, 1680), p. 444; Gilbert, *Law of Evidence*, p. 149.

25. M. Macnair, "'A Fragment on Proof,' by Francis North, Lord Guildford," *Seventeenth Century* 8 (1993), 143. Pardoned felons could serve as witnesses but not as jurors. Hale, *History of the Pleas of the Crown*, pp. 277–280.

26. Bacon, *Works*, I, 513; Hale, *History of the Pleas of the Crown*, 1736, I, 635; Sir Matthew Hale, *History of the Common Law of England*, ed. Charles M. Gray (Chicago, 1971), p. 164.

27. More, *Debellacyon*, p. 157; Gilbert, *Law of Evidence*, p. 147.

28. Hale, *History of the Common Law*, pp. 154, 165.

29. See Langbein, *Prosecuting Crime*; Shapiro, *Beyond Reasonable Doubt*, pp. 148–164.

30. Dalton, *The Country Justice* (London, 1635), p. 297. Several items on Dalton's list appear in Cicero and Quintilian. See Shapiro, *Beyond Reasonable Doubt*, p. 117.

Tancred's thirteenth-century treatise already noted that faced with conflicting testimony judges were to "follow those who are most trustworthy—the freeborn rather than the freedman, the older rather than the younger, the many of honorable estate rather than the inferior, the noble rather than the ignoble, the man rather than the woman. Further, the truthteller is to be believed rather than the liar, the man of pure life rather than the man who lives in vice, the rich man rather than the poor, anyone rather than he who is a great friend of the person for whom he testifies or an enemy of him against whom he testifies. If the witnesses are all of the same dignity and status, then the judge should stand with the side that has the greatest number of witnesses. If they are of the same number and dignity, then absolve the defendant." Charles Donahue, Jr., "Proof by Witnesses in the Church Courts of Medieval England: An Imperfect Reception of the Learned Law," in *On the Laws and Customs of England*, ed. Morriss Arnold (Chapel Hill, N.C., 1981), p. 131.

31. Cicero suggests inference might be drawn from the person of the accused from such personal attributes as age, ancestors, temperament, physical condition, way of life, fortune, and interest. *De inventione*, II, x, 34–36. See also II, xiii, 43.

32. See Shapiro, *Beyond Reasonable Doubt*, pp. 114–243.

33. Gilbert, *Law of Evidence*, p. 149.

34. John Langbein, "Historical Foundations of the Law of Evidence: A View from the Ryder Sources," *Columbia Law Review* 96 (1996), 1186–1190. But see John H. Wigmore, "History of the Hearsay Rule," *Harvard Law Review* 17 (1904), 436–458; R. W. Baker, *The Hearsay Rule* (London, 1950); Edward M. Morgan, *Some Problems of Proof under the Anglo-American System of Litigation* (New York, 1956).

35. Hale, *Primitive Origination*, p. 128; *Trial of Charnock*, p. 67; John Locke, *An Essay Concerning Human Understanding*, ed. A. Frasier, 3 vols. (New York, 1959), chap. 14, sec. 10.

36. Wigmore, "Hearsay Rule," pp. 443–447; Gilbert, *Law of Evidence*, p. 153, citing Francis Buller, *Introduction to . . . Trials at nisi prius*, pp. 294–295. See also James Oldham, "Truth-Telling in the Eighteenth-Century English Courtroom," *Law and History Review* 12 (1994), 104.

37. Courts, however, heard those under twelve without oath "which possibly being fortified with concurrent evidence may be of some weight, as in case of rape, buggery, witchcraft, and such crimes, which are practiced upon children." Hale, *History of the Pleas of the Crown*, 1736, II, 235–237; Gilbert, *Law of Evidence*, p. 143.

38. Macnair, "Fragment on Proof," p. 143. "Light and inconsiderable witnesses" were less credible. Hale, *Primitive Origination*, p. 128. Justicing manuals refer to upbringing, education,

whether suspects and witnesses were of idle or honest occupation, riotousness in diet or apparel, whether brawling, quarrelsome, or light-fingered, and whether they were gamesters or haunters of alehouses. Lambarde, *Eirenarcha* (1614), p. 218; Richard Crompton, *L'office et auctoritie de justice de peace* (London, 1606), p. 100r.

39. Quoted in Hubertus Schulte Herbruggen, "The Process against Sir Thomas More," *Law Quarterly Review* 99 (1983), 113–136. See also Shapiro, *Beyond Reasonable Doubt*, pp. 212–213. The defendant in the Trial of Throckmorton discussed the credibility of witnesses. T. B. Howell, *Complete Collection of State Trials*, 34 vols. (London, 1809–1826), I, 878–881. See also I, 1019, 1071.

40. Cynthia Herrup, *The Common Peace: Participation and the Criminal Law in Seventeenth-Century England* (Cambridge, 1987); *Historical Collections* (London, 1681), pp. 97, 102, 103, 106, 108. Hobbes, *Leviathan* (London, 1975), p. 57.

41. Hale, *History of the Pleas of the Crown*, 1736, II, 279.

42. Gilbert, *Law of Evidence*, p. 155.

43. For efforts to remove Roman Catholic justices of the peace, see J. S. Cockburn, *A History of the English Assizes, 1558–1714* (Cambridge, 1972), pp. 191, 200–219.

44. *The Trial of Sir Thomas Gascoyne* (London, 1680), pp. 64, 67. In a 1696 treason trial the defendant objected to the testimony of Roman Catholics witnesses because they might be absolved by pope or priest if they swore falsely. King's Counsel countered that "it was never allowed, or indeed objected, that I know of, before, that Roman Catholics were not good Witnesses. A Roman Catholick may be an honest man, not withstanding his religion." If they were competent to testify, their credibility was for the jury to weigh. *The Arraignment . . . of Sir John Friend* (London, 1696), pp. 36, 38. According to Gilbert, papist recusants could not be witnesses; neither could infidels, because they were not under the obligations of "our religion." The "binding force" of oaths ceased when the "reason and grounds of belief" were "absolutely dissolved." Jews might testify on the Old Testament because "their oaths do induce a belief of the fact, which they attest." Gilbert, *Law of Evidence*, p. 143.

45. Hale, *History of the Pleas of the Crown*, II, 276, 277; Hale, *History of the Common Law*, p. 163.

46. William Best's later work summarized the position of the seventeenth century. Best, *The Principles of the Law of Evidence*, 6th ed. (London, 1875), pp. 18–22. See also p. 24.

47. Gilbert, *Law of Evidence*, p. 155.

48. Physicians might be asked whether the "fact" was attributable to natural causes. See Shapiro, *Probability and Certainty in Seventeenth-Century England: The Relationships between Religion, Natural Science, Law, History, and Literature* (Princeton, 1983), pp. 204, 208; Robert Kargon, "Expert Testimony in Historical Perspective," *Law and Human Behavior* 10 (1986), 15–20; Catherine Crawford, "Legalizing Medicine: Early Modern Legal Systems and the Growth of Medico-Legal knowledge," in *Legal Medicine in History*, ed. Michael Clark and Catherine Crawford (Cambridge, 1994), pp. 89–116; Stephan Landsman, "One Hundred Years of Rectitude: Medical Witnesses at the Old Bailey, 1717–1817," *Law and History Review* 16 (1988), 445–495.

49. Hale, *History of the Common Law*, p. 164; Hale, *Primitive Origination*, p. 128; Locke, *Essay Concerning Human Understanding*, bk. 4, chap. 4, sec. 6. Keith Thomas, *Religion and the Decline of Magic* (New York, 1979), p. 473.

50. George Fisher, "The Jury's Rise as Lie Detector," *Yale Law Journal* 107 (1997), 575–714. Fisher emphasizes the necessity of believing either prosecution or defense witnesses, ignoring the possibility that the testimony of prosecution witnesses might vary and that only some might be believed. The jury is viewed as "lie detector" rather than as determiner of "reasonable belief." Isaac Watts, however, insisted on consideration of whether those who oppose testimony are "equally skillful and equally faithful as those who assert it." *Logick, or the Right Use of Reason in the Inquiry after Truth* [1724] (London, 1775), pp. 181–182. See also pp. 266–271.

51. Hale, *History of the Common Law*, p. 164.

52. Hale, *Primitive Origination*, p. 130; Gilbert, *Law of Evidence*, pp. 104, 147–148, 151. If wit-

nesses agreed in minute circumstances, it might be "a story laid and concerted beforehand." Ibid., p. 151.

53. State trials suggest that the need for two witnesses is sometimes agreed on by both prosecution and defense and at other times only the defendant insists on it. See *The Tryal of Henry Baron Delamere* (London, 1686); *The Trial and Conviction of John Hamden* (London, 1684). See also Samuel Reznick, "The Trial of Treason in Tudor England," in *Essays in History and Political Theory in Honor of Charles Howard McIlwain*, ed. Carl Wittke (Cambridge, Mass., 1936), pp. 258–288; L. M. Hill, "The Two-Witness Rule in English Treason Trials: Some Comments on the Emergence of Procedural Law," *American Journal of Legal History* 12 (1968), 95–111. *The Draught of a Bill, now in Parliament* (n.p., n.d.) discussed recent practice.

54. Macnair, "Fragment on Proof," p. 143.

55. Gilbert, *Law of Evidence*, p. 147.

56. Ibid.; More, *Works*, X, 157.

57. Crompton, *L'office*, p. 110v. The rule is also found in canon and civil law. *A True Relation of the Unjust Accusation of Certain French Gentlemen* (London, 1671), p. 19; Hale, *History of the Common Law*, p. 164; Gilbert, *Law of Evidence*, p. 147.

58. Hale, *History of the Common Law*, pp. 163, 164.

59. *The Book of Oaths* (London, 1649), p. 207. Oaths administered for civil and criminal trials contain the same language. The latter included a statement about the avoidance of malice, hatred, evil will, greed, favor, or affection. Ibid., pp. 205–207. See also *The Book of Oaths* (London, 1689), pp. 112–115. During the Anglo-Saxon era they swore, "In the name of Almighty God, . . . in true witness stand, unbidden and unbought, so I with my eyes over-saw and with my ears over-heard" that which I say. Benjamin Thorpe, ed., *Ancient Laws and Institutes of England*, 2 vols. (London, 1890), I, 181. See Helen Silving, "The Oath, I," *Yale Law Journal* 68 (1959), 1329–1390.

60. More, *Debellacyon*, p. 160.

61. Coke suggests perjury laws, which dated from the Conquest, were not enforced because the penalties were so harsh. *Third Part of the Institutes*, pp. 163, 165. See Michael Gordon, "The Invention of a Common Law Crime: Perjury and the Elizabethan Courts," *American Journal of Legal History* 24 (1980), 145–170.

62. Publications relating to oaths focused on their lawfulness, questioned by Quakers; oaths of loyalty and allegiance; and the common practice of "loose swearing." Discussion was indebted to scholastic treatments of assertory and promissory oaths. John Gauden's *Discourse Concerning Public Oaths* (London, 1662) indicated that the oath of the "common swearer" could not be given much credit (p. 17). For Hobbes, oaths were purposeless "without fear" on the part of those swearing. *The Elements of the Law*, ed. Ferdinand Tonnies (Cambridge, 1928), chap. 16, sec. 16. For perjury, witnesses, and oaths, see More, *Debellacyon*, pp. 155–162. For the importance of oaths in trials, see *A Guide to English Juries* (London, 1682), pp. 49–50; *Perjury the National Sin* (London, 1690), p. 4; John Cheney, *A Vindication of Oaths and Swearing* (London, 1677), pp. 6, 10, 14. Although oaths had "lost their ancient force," they were "the highest and strongest assurance that can be given of the truth in Cases of Testimony, depending upon the credit and veracity of him that swears." Cheney, *Vindication of Oaths*, pp. 23, 36. Thomas Comber's *Nature and usefulness of Solemn Judicial Swearing* (London, 1682) also noted the "slight and irreverent giving of Oaths (too common in our Courts of Justice)" (pp. 22, 25). John Allen, *Of Perjury* (London, 1682), similarly observed, "The times are notoriously pester'd disturb'd and endanger'd by the variety and frequency of Perjury" but nevertheless thought oaths remained "the best means to find out the truth of Matter of Fact, to determine of Right and Wrong . . . to clear the Innocent, and discover the Guilty" (pp. 1, 3, 15). John Tombes too assumed that perjury in judicial proceedings was common. One "should not swear a thing to be so or not unless he know it to be so or not; He must not relie on Conjectures, Rumours, or probabilities." *Sephersheba: or the Oath Book* (London, 1662), pp. 72 ff., 114, 133. Many believed perjuries to be "very little sins, or rather none at all." *Perjury the National Sin* (London, 1690), p. 4. See also pp. 10, 14–15. Isaac Barrow noted

the frequency of "rash and vain swearing" and its ill effect on legal proceedings. Barrow, *Works*, 3 vols. (London, 1700), I, 194, 195, 198. John Tillotson emphasized both the "growing evil and mischief" of breaking oaths and the oaths as "the surest ground of Judicial proceedings." Though oaths did not ensure "a certain and infallible decision of things according to truth and right," they provided "the utmost credit that we can give to any things, and the last resort of truth and confidence among men; . . . if the Religion of an Oath will not oblige men to speak truth, nothing will." An assertory oath is defined as one in which someone "affirms or denies upon oath a matter of fact, past or present; when he swears that a thing was, or is so, or not so." "And where mens estates or lives, are concerned, no evidence but what is assured by an Oath will be thought sufficient to decide the matters." *The Lawfulness and Obligation of Oaths; A Sermon Preached at the Assizes* (London, 1681), preface, pp. 3, 4, 6, 7, 10, 24, 26, 28, 29.

William Wake, noting that the frequency of swearing had "taken off from their Reverence . . . and disposed . . . [persons] to Swear more carelessly, and with lesser consideration than they ought to do," desired the perjury statutes to be solemnly declared at every assize and recommended "strict exaction of penalties." *A Practical Discourse Concerning Swearing* (London, 1696), preface, pp. 7, 15, 16, 34, 125, 138–139. Oaths, which were often "not to be trusted," left even the wisest men "not know[ing] which way to turn themselves in giving judgment." One must therefore "use all diligence, not only by examining witnesses, but observing circumstances, comparing testimonies, casting in Quaeries . . . to search out the matter." Thomas Bradley, *A Sermon Preached . . . at the Assizes* (York, 1663), pp. 34, 35. Both respect for and disregard of oaths in legal proceedings were obviously common. But see Fisher, "Jury's Rise as Lie Detector."

63. Because the presumption did not hold for those convicted of falsehood or crimes against the common principles of "honesty and humanity," their testimony was "of no weight." The same was true of notorious and public criminals. Such persons were excluded from testifying. Gilbert, *Law of Evidence*, pp. 140–141.

64. See Fisher, "Jury's Rise as Law Detector."

65. Hale, *History of the Pleas of the Crown*, 1736, II, 279; I, 635; Macnair, "Fragment on Proof," p. 143; Gilbert, *Law of Evidence*, p. 139, citing Coke Lit 6, b. 1561 and 1581. See also p. 140.

66. Macnair views the trials of this era as a turning point in the law of evidence. "Fragment on Proof," pp. 143–148.

67. Hale, *History of the Pleas of the Crown*, 1736, I, 635.

68. *The Petty Papers*, ed. Marquis of Lansdowne, 2 vols. (London, 1927), II, 204–206.

69. *Book of Oaths*, p. 203.

70. Coke, *The First Part of the Institutes of the Laws of England* (London, 1817), sec. l.6b. See also Shapiro, *Beyond Reasonable Doubt*, pp. 209–243.

71. *Trial of Charnock*, p. 68; *Arraignment . . . of Sir John Friend*, p. 43. *Arraignment . . . of Sir William Parkins* (London, 1696). p. 38. In another case the Solicitor General argued "that there may be Circumstances so strong and cogent, so violent" as to "fortify a positive Testimony, that will in Law amount to make a second Witness such as the Law requires." *The Tryal of Henry Baron Delamere* (London, 1686), pp. 78–79. The Lord Steward insisted "substantial Circumstances joyned to one Positive Testimony" was enough, according to the opinion of all the judges of England (p. 85). But one must distinguish between "bare Circumstances and bare Suspicions" that were "no Proof against any Man" and the "violent and necessary" circumstances that might substitute for a second witness (p. 82). See also *The Trial of John Hamden* (London, 1684), p. 39.

72. Violent presumption existed "when circumstances are proved that do necessarily attend the fact." Gilbert, *Law of Evidence*, pp. 147, 157, 158.

73. *Trial of Peter Cook* (London, 1696), p. 55.

74. Shapiro, *Beyond Reasonable Doubt*, pp. 1–41; Barbara Shapiro, "'To a Moral Certainty': Theories of Knowledge and Anglo-American Juries, 1600–1750," *Hastings Law Journal* 38 (1986), 153–193. We know very little about how the standard for civil cases evolved.

75. Baker, *Reports of Spelman*, II, 112, citing a 1465 case; More, *Debellacyon*, p. 160; Hale, *History of the Pleas of the Crown*, 1736, II, 314.

76. J. H. Baker, "Criminal Courts and Procedure at Common Law," in *Crime in England, 1550–1800*, ed. J. S. Cockburn (Princeton, 1977), pp. 37, 38.

77. Edward Waterhouse, *Fortescue Illustratus* (London, 1663), pp. 129, 259.

78. Hale, *History of the Common Law*, pp. 165, 167.

79. Macnair, "Fragment on Proof," p. 143.

80. Judge Vaughan in *State Trials*, VI, 1006.

81. *State Trials*, XXVI, 437, 457.

82. Cowell, *Interpreter*, s.v. "Jury."

83. Cockburn and Green, *Twelve Good Men and True*, pp. 377, 384, 385, 395, 397. See also pp. 129–130. London juries of the late seventeenth century were of higher status than provincial jurors. Ibid., p. 385.

84. Jurors were "such Persons as for Estate and Quality are fit to serve upon that Employment" and "of sufficient Freeholds, according to several Provisions of Acts of Parliament." Hale, *History of the Common Law*, pp. 160, 161.

85. William Walwyn, *Juries Justified* (London, 1650), pp. 4–5; Green, *Verdict According to Conscience*, p. 188. Some Interregnum reformers were hostile to juries. Donald Veall, *The Popular Movement for Law Reform* (Oxford, 1970), p. 117. The Hale Commission advocated literate jurors "of honest lives and conversations" and "good understanding."

86. See Cockburn, *History of the English Assizes*, pp. 118–120, 223, 331–332. See Waterhouse, *Fortescue*, p. 343; *Enchiridium Legum* (London, 1673), pp. 112, 114. *Commons Journals*, VIII, 610, 611, 613. Prosperous copyholders avoided jury duty by taking two-thousand-year leases. Anchitell Grey, *Debates of the House of Commons from 1667 to 1694* (London, 1763), I, 226.

87. Howell, *State Trials*, I, 52; *An Exact Account of the Trials . . . in the Old-Bailey . . . December 11, 1678* (London, 1678), p.31; Richard Bernard, *Guide to Grand Jury Men in Cases of Witchcraft* (London, 1627), p. 25.

88. Steven Shapin, *A Social History of Truth: Civility and Science in Seventeenth-Century England* (Chicago, 1994).

89. Cockburn, *History of the English Assizes*, pp. 104–105.

90. Quoted in Shapin, *Social History of Truth*, pp. 69, 69n, from William Segar, *Honor Military and Civil*, p. 229.

91. Those of profligate or "wicked temper or disposition" had diminished credit. And only if it was thought that a man's "bias is so strong upon him, as would incline a man of his disposition, figure, and rank in the world to falsify, you are to disbelieve him." Witness credibility was related one's "state and dignity in the world, for men of easy circumstances are supposed" less likely to commit perjury. At the same time, the testimony of "every plain and honest man affirming the truth" under oath is entitled to faith and credit. Gilbert, *Law of Evidence*, pp. 149, 155. St. Germain in the early sixteenth century also insisted witnesses were assumed to be "honest, good and indifferent, till the contrary was shown." Quoted in More, *Works*, X, 157.

92. See Lorraine Daston, "Baconian Facts, Academic Civility, and the Prehistory of Objectivity," *Annals of Scholarship* 8(1991), 338, 339; Shapin, *Social History of Truth*. But see Barbara Shapiro, "Science and Religion in Seventeenth-Century England," *Past and Present* 40 (1968), 16–41; Barbara Shapiro, "Early Modern Intellectual Life: Humanism, Religion, and Science in Seventeenth-Century England," *History of Science* 29 (1991), 45–71.

93. Hale, *History of the Common Law*, pp. 161, 162–163; Howell, *State Trials*, I, 897.

94. Howell, *State Trials*, I, 887. See also Richard Helmholz, "Canonists and Standards of Impartiality for Papal Judges Delegate," *Traditio* 25 (1969), 386–404.

95. Wilfred Prest, "William Lambarde, Elizabethan Law Reform, and Early Stuart Politics," *Journal of British Studies* 34 (1995), 465–466; Coke, *Third Part of the Institutes*, p. 29. See also Michael Dalton, *The Country Justice* (London, 1618), pp. 4–5.

96. *An Exact Account of The Trial between Sir William Pritchard . . . and Thomas Papillon* (Lon-

don, 1682), p. 25. See also T. S., *A Sermon Preached at the Assizes* (London, 1689), pp. 15, 19, 22, 24.

97. Hale, *History of the Common Law*, p. 163.

98. Coke, *Third Part of the Institutes*, p. 29.

99. Maija Jansson, "Matthew Hale on Judges and Judging," *Journal of Legal History* 9 (1989), 204, 206, 207. See also Gilbert Burnet, *Life of Hale* (London, 1833), p. 101.

100. Isaac Barrow, *Works*, 3 vols. (London, 1687), II, 28.

101. Hale, *History of the Common Law*, p. 165. Judge North wrote "in matters of Fact" a judge might aid jurors "by weighing the Evidence before them" and showing "his Opinion." Macnair, "Fragment on Proof," p. 144. Thomas Fuller, not a lawyer, insisted that although juries might need guidance in matters of law, they "need not be led by the nose in matter of fact." Quoted in Cockburn and Green, *Twelve Good Men and True*, p. 146.

102. See John H. Langbein, "The Criminal Trial before the Lawyers," *University of Chicago Law Review* 45 (1978), 263–306; John H. Langbein, "Shaping the Eighteenth-Century Criminal Trial; A View from the Ryder Sources," *University of Chicago Law Review* 50 (1983), 1–136; Cockburn, *History of the English Assizes*, pp. 109, 110, 122–123; Macnair, "Fragment on Proof," pp. 143–148.

103. Hale, *History of the Common Law*, p. 165; Hale, *History of the Pleas of the Crown*, 2 vols. (London, 1800), II, 312–314. See also S. E., *Tryals per Pais* (London, 1685), p. 75.

104. Hale, *History of the Pleas of the Crown*, 1800, II, 314. If judges, agents of the central authority, were deemed better fact evaluators, local lay juries would become unnecessary.

105. Quoted in Jansson, "Hale," pp. 206–207.

106. See D. A. Rubini, "The Precarious Independence of the Judiciary, 1688–1701," *Law Quarterly Review* 83 (1967), 343–355.

107. Hale, *Primitive Origination*, p. 128.

108. Gilbert, *Law of Evidence*, pp. 122, 155.

109. See Oldham, "Truth Telling," pp. 110–111. The prohibition of interested parties resulted in elaborate documentation that included as much circumstantial material as possible as a hedge against future legal problems.

110. Howell, *State Trials*, I, 872.

111. William Prest, "Elizabethan Law Reform and Early Stuart Politics," *Journal of British Studies* 34 (1995), 468–469. See also Hobbes, *Leviathan*, p. 209; Gilbert Burnet, *Lives, Characters, and an address to Posterity* (London, 1833), p. 127; Barrow, *Works*, II, 28.

112. Sir John Hawles, *The Englishman's Right* (London, 1680), pp. 120, 127; [Sir George Berkeley], *Historical Applications* (London, 1690), pp. 61–62. For praise of elegant speeches, see S. E., *Tryals per Pais*, preface.

113. Although we have sometimes spoken as if jury trials took place in "courtrooms," such structures did not exist. Jury trials took place in a wide variety of physical settings.

114. Gilbert, *Law of Evidence*, pp. 2, 4.

Chapter 2: "Fact" and History

1. See *Henry IV*, IV.i.48; *Timon of Athens*, III.v.25; *The Rape of Lucrece*, 346. I owe these references to Michael Witmore. See also Ben Jonson, *Volpone*, V.vii.155.

2. See Arnaldo Momigliano, *Classical Foundations of Modern Historiography* (Berkeley, 1990); Donald Kelley, "The Theory of History," in *Cambridge History of Renaissance Philosophy*, ed. Charles Schmitt and Quentin Skinner (Cambridge, 1988), pp. 746–762.

3. Sidney, Bacon, and Hobbes associated history with sense and memory and poetry with the imagination. See William Nelson, *Fact or Fiction: The Dilemma of the Renaissance Storyteller* (Cambridge, Mass., 1973).

4. Cicero, *De oratore*, II, 62–64; IX, 36.

5. Cicero, *Brutus*, X, 42. See also Quintilian, *Institutio oratoria*, III, viii, 66; X, i, 31.

6. Beatrice Reynolds, "Shifting Currents in Historical Criticism," in *Renaissance Essays*, ed. P. O. Kristeller and P. P. Wiener (New York, 1968), pp. 115–136; George Nadel, "The Phi-

losophy of History before Historicism," *History and Theory* 3 (1963), 298–99, 302; Arno Seifert, *Cognitio Historica: Die Geschichte als Namengeberin der frühneuzeitlichen Empire* (Berlin, 1976).

7. See Timothy Hampton, *Writing from History: The Rhetoric of Exemplarity* (Ithaca, 1990).

8. Donald Kelley, *Foundations of Modern Historical Scholarship: Language, Law, and History in the French Renaissance* (New York, 1970), pp. 120, 121, 132; Julian Franklin, *Jean Bodin and the Sixteenth-Century Revolution in the Methodology of Law and History* (New York, 1963), pp. 129–129; George Huppert, *The Idea of Perfect History: Historical Erudition and Historical Philosophy in Renaissance France* (Urbana, Ill., 1970). See also Seifert, *Cognitio Historica*.

9. Huppert, *Perfect History*, pp. 24, 31, 34, 50, 62–63.

10. Franklin, *Bodin*, pp. 128, 129, 137, 139n, 140–146, 150. Jean Bodin, *Method for the Easy Comprehension of History*, trans. Beatrice Reynolds (New York, 1945), pp. 13, 50.

11. Thomas Blundeville, *The True Order and Method of Writing and Reading Hystories*, ed. H. G. Dick, *Huntington Library Quarterly* 3 (1939–40), 157.

12. Wilfred Prest, *The Rise of the Barristers: A Social History of the English Bar, 1590–1640* (Oxford, 1986), p. 200.

13. Linda Van Norden, "The Elizabethan College of Antiquaries" (Ph.D. dissertation, University of California, Los Angeles, 1946), pp. 334, 333, 349, 391, 393, 403. See also Joan Evans, *A History of the Society of Antiquaries* (Oxford, 1956). Sir Edward Coke, however, advised men to be beware when laws were "delivered by historians," and Roger Twysden thought law delivered by historians is "much differing from that [which] comes from a lawyer, as declaring not only the fact, but the policy, reason, and matter of state in it, where the other resolved onely how it stood with the law." Twysden, *Certain Considerations upon the Government of England* (London, 1849), p. 23.

14. David Berkowitz, *John Selden's Formative Years* (Washington, D.C., 1988), p. 43; H. D. Hazeltine, "Selden as a Legal Historian," *Harvard Law Review* 47 (1932), 12–20. See also F. Frank Fussner, *The Historical Revolution: English Historical Writing and Thought, 1580–1640* (London, 1962), p. 286; D. R. Woolf, *The Idea of History in Early Stuart England* (Toronto, 1990), pp. 200–242.

15. See Barbara J. Shapiro, *Probability and Certainty in Seventeenth-Century England: The Relationships between Religion, Natural Science, Law, History, and Literature* (Princeton, 1983), pp. 119–193.

16. Thomas Hobbes, *Leviathan* (New York, 1975), p. 40.

17. See L. F. Dean, "Sir Francis Bacon's Theory of Civil History Writing," *ELH* 8 (1941), 161–165; G. H. Nadel, "History as Psychology in Francis Bacon's Theory of History," in *Essential Articles for the Study of Bacon*, ed. Brian Vickers (Hamden, Conn., 1968), pp. 236–252; Arthur B. Ferguson, "The Non-political Past in Bacon's Theory of History," *Journal of British Studies* 14 (1974), 4–20; Fussner, *Historical Revolution*, pp. 159–190.

18. Lord Bolingbroke, *Historical Writings*, ed. Isaac Kramnick (Chicago, 1972), pp. 4, 5, 8, 9, 10, 69.

19. White Kennett, *General History*, preface; Edmund Calamy, *A Letter to . . . Echard* (London, 1718), p. 6.

20. Gilbert Burnet, *Memoires of . . . James and William, Dukes of Hamilton* (London, 1677), preface.

21. Ludlow's were "based on personal experience" and what he learned from "persons well informed and of unsuspected fidelity." Edmund Ludlow, *Memoirs*, ed. C. H. Firth, 2 vols. (Oxford, 1891), I, 7. Denzil Holles, *Memoirs* (London, 1699), Preface to the Reader. Clarendon's "History" was sometimes considered a memoir. *Mr. Le Clerc's Account of the Earl of Clarendon's History of the Civil Wars* (London, 1710), p. 7.

22. William Dugdale, *Memorials of the English Affairs* (London, 1682), Publisher to the Reader.

23. Bulstrode Whitelocke, *Memorials of the English Affairs or an Historical Account* (London, 1682), Publisher to the Reader.

24. William Camden, *Britannia*, 1695 ed., s.v. "Life of Camden." See also David Lloyd, *Memorials* (London, 1668), preface; Holles, *Memoirs*, Publisher to the Reader, ix.

25. Whitelocke, *Memorials*, Publisher to the Reader.

26. Arthur Ponsonby, *John Evelyn* (London, 1933), pp. 176–178. See also Judith H. Anderson, *Biographical Truth: The Representation of Historical Persons in Tudor-Stuart Writing* (New Haven, 1984); Thomas F. Mayer and D. R. Woolf, eds., *The Rhetorics of Life-Writing in Early Modern England* (Ann Arbor, 1995), pp. 1–37.

27. *The Posthumous Works of Robert Hooke* (London, 1705), pp. i–x. This work, begun in 1697, was not the same as his diary.

28. Ibid.

29. Bacon, *De augmentis, Works*, VIII, 423–425. See Joseph Levine, "The Antiquarian Enterprise, 1500–1800," in *Origins of Modern English Historiography* (Ithaca, 1987), pp. 73–106.

30. For socioeconomic materials, see William Camden, *History of . . . Princess Elizabeth*, ed. Wallace MacCaffrey (Chicago, 1970), preface (this work is hereafter cited as *Annals*); Richard Brathwaite, *The Schollers Medley: or, an Intermixt Discourse upon Historicall and Poeticall Relations* (London, 1614), pp. 1, 3, 9. For lesser "worthies," see Thomas Fuller, *The History of the Worthies of England* (London, 1662); David Lloyd, *State Worthies*, 2d ed. (London, 1670). Samuel Clark, *Lives of Sundry Eminent Persons* (London, 1683), p. 2. Anthony Wood's *Athenae oxoniensis* was subtitled an "Exact History" (2 vols., London, 1691–92). John Aubrey, who assisted in Wood's "living and lasting History," wrote his *Brief Lives* to provide "the truth, and, as near as I can . . . nothing but the truth" about his contemporaries. Collective biographies increasingly included scholars and literary figures.

31. Dugdale's *Monasticon* was described as a "plentiful addition to English History." Quoted in Graham Parry, *The Trophies of Time: English Antiquarians of the Seventeenth Century* (Oxford, 1995), p. 116. See also pp. 226, 229, 230; D. C. Douglas, *English Scholars* (London, 1951).

32. For Selden, history included not only narrative political history but also "narrow particulars, and sometimes under other names." His own *Titles of Honor* (London, 1614) was also to be "reckoned for historie."

33. Edmund Bolton noted, "Many great volumes carry among us the titles of histories, but learned men . . . deny that any of ours discharge that office which the titles promise." *Hypercritica*, in *Critical Essays of the Seventeenth Century*, 3 vols., ed. Joel Spingarn (London, 1908–9), I, 83.

    For coins as historical evidence, see Henry Peacham, *The Complete Gentleman* (London, 1634), pp. 123–124. Coins and medals for John Evelyn provided "clear and perspicuous Testimony," better evidence for "fact" than documents. A series could furnish "an Historical Discourse with a Chain of Remarkable Instances, and Matters of Fact, without Fiction or Hyperbole." *Numismata; A Discourse of Medals, Ancient and Modern* (London, 1671), pp. 71, 150, 157, 160, 164, 260–291. See also Obadiah Walker, *The Greek and Roman History Illustrated by Coins and Medals* (London, 1697).

    Some were hostile or ambivalent to such antiquarian studies. John Locke criticized such pursuits as useless yet offered financial assistance for publication of John Aubrey's *Monumenta Britannica*. Locke, *Some Thoughts on Education*, in *The Educational Writings of John Locke*, ed. J. L. Axtell (Cambridge, 1968), pp. 268, 292–293, 307; "Letter to the Countess of Peterborough," in ibid., p. 89; "Of Study," in ibid., p. 410; *The Correspondence of John Locke and Edward Clarke*, ed. Benjamin Rand (London, 1927), pp. 214–220. See also Joseph Addison, *Dialogues Upon the Usefulness of Ancient Medals* [1726] (London, 1976), pp. 10–12, 154. See also Joseph Levine, *Battle of the Books: History and Literature in the Augustan Age* (Ithaca, 1991), pp. 285–287.

34. Brathwaite, *Schollers Medley*, pp. 25, 57.

35. John Selden, *Historie of Tithes* (London, 1618), p. xii. See also Camden, *Annals*, The Author to the Reader.

36. But see Robert Mayer, *History and the Early English Novel: Matters of Fact from Bacon to Defoe* (Cambridge, 1997).

37. Arthur B. Ferguson, *Utter Antiquity: Precepts of Prehistory in Renaissance England* (Durham, N.C., 1993), pp. 119–121, 122, 124; Joseph M. Levine, "Thomas More and the English Renaissance: History and Fiction in 'Utopia,'" in *The Historical Imagination in Early Modern En-*

gland, ed. Donald R. Kelley and David Harris Sacks (Cambridge, 1997), pp. 69–92; Bacon, *Works*, VIII, 439–444; Raleigh, *History of the World* (London, 1614), p. 536.

38. Quoted in Levine, *Battle of the Books*, p. 295. Daniel permitted himself the invented speech.

39. Blundeville, *True Order and Method*, p. 164; Camden, *Annals*, p. 6; Margaret Cavendish, *Life of Newcastle* (London, 1667), preface; Burnet, *Memoires of . . . Dukes of Hamilton*, preface; White Kennett, *A Register and Chronicle ecclesiastical and civil containing matters of fact* (London, 1728), preface. Hume employed invented speeches of a kind. See Philip Hicks, *Neoclassical History and English Culture* (New York, 1996), pp. 180–181.

40. For Camden, see Degory Wheare, *Method and Order of Reading Both Civil and Ecclesiastical Histories* (London, 1685), p. 133. Selden quoted in Berkowitz, *Selden's Formative Years*, pp. 41–42, 103. King Arthur might be acceptable as romance but not history. Selden, *Historie of Tithes*, pp. xii.

41. Bacon, *Works*, VIII, 423–425.

42. Richard Blome, *Britannia* (London, 1673), p. 2; Sir William Temple, *An Introduction to the History of England* (London, 1695), p. 31; Kennett, *General History*, preface; Daniel Defoe, *The Storm* (London, 1704), preface; David Hume, *History of England* (Boston, 1853), pp. 1, 2, 14, 22.

43. John Nalson, *An Impartial Collection of the Great Affairs of State*, 2 vols. (London, 1682–83), I, 1; Robert Brady, *A Complete History of England* (London, 1685), preface; George Scot, ed., *Memoirs of James Melvil* (London, 1683), preface. Thomas Sprat, *History of the Royal Society* (London, 1667), p. 215. See also Cavendish, *Life of Newcastle*, preface; *The History and Transactions of the English Nation* (London, 1689), p. 6; Gilbert Burnet, *Reflections on Mr. Varilla's History* (London, 1689), p. 10; Hamon L'Estrange, *The Reign of King Charles* (London, 1655), preface.

44. John Rushworth, *Historical Collections*, 8 vols. (London, 1682), I, preface.

45. Hazeltine, "Selden," p. 110; Rushworth, *Collections*, preface; William Howel, *The Elements of History* [1670] (London, 1700), preface; *Ravillac Redivivus* (London, 1678), p. 4; D. Jones, *The Secret History of White-Hall* (London, 1692), preface; Thomas Gumble, *The Life of General Monck, Duke of Albemarle* (London, 1671), preface; Edward Hyde, Lord Clarendon, *History of the Rebellion*, in *Versions of History from Antiquity to the Enlightenment*, ed. Donald Kelley (New Haven, 1991), p. 345. Brady contrasts "matter of Fact" with "fond Imaginations" and "mere conjectures." *A Historical Treatise of Cities and Burghs* (London, 1711), preface. Another wrote that the historian was "confined to the Facts and Occurrences he relates." *Supplement to Dr. Harris's Dictionary of Arts and Sciences* (London, 1744), unpaged.

46. *The Educational Writings of John Locke*, ed. J. L. Axtell (Cambridge, 1968), p. 292. See also pp. 393–395, 422. [Thomas Burnet], *Remarks upon . . . Lansdowne's Letter* (London, 1732), p. 20; Hume, *History of England*, II, 1; *The Royal Martyr* (London, 1660), p. 2. Joseph Addison complained that England had historians "able to compile Matters of Fact" but few to produce narratives comparable to those of classical historians. *The Freeholder*, no. 35, p. 194.

47. Roger L'Estrange, *A Brief History, Part III* (London, 1688), preface. Thomas Sprat, *True Account . . . of the Rye House Plot* (London, 1685), preface; Robert Brady, *A Complete History of England* (London, 1685), Dedicatory Letter; Thomas Hearne, *Remarks and Collections*, 11 vols. (Oxford, 1885–1921), II, 227, 228; Baxter, *Reliquiae Baxteriana* (London, 1696), preface by Matthew Sylvester. See also Hicks, *Neoclassical History and English Culture*, pp. 82–93.

48. *A General History of the Pyrates*, 2 vols. (London, 1713), I, preface.

49. Gumble, *Life of Monck*, preface. He admitted the historian could not really be acquainted with "the whole truth" though "very little did escape"; Thomas Fuller, *The Appeal of Injured Innocence* (London, 1650), p. 16.

50. Quoted in Michael Hunter, *John Aubrey and the Realm of Learning* (New York, 1975), p. 183; Van Norden, "Elizabethan College of Antiquaries," pp. 403–404; Sprat, *History of the Royal Society*, p. 44; Edward Stillingfleet, *Origines Brittanicae* (London, 1685), III, preface, iii–iv; Peter Whalley, *Essay on the Manner of Writing History* (London, 1736), pp. 16, 17.

51. Bacon, *Works*, III, 339. See also Robert Brady, *An Introduction to the Old English History* (London, 1684), An Epistle to the Reader.

52. Roger L'Estrange, *A Brief History of The Times* (London, 1687), p. 5; John Lewis, *A Specimen of the Gross Errors* (London, 1724), p. v; Langlet de Fresnoy, *A New Method of Studying History*, trans. (London, 1728), p. 289.

53. L'Estrange, *A Brief History of the Times: Part III*, n.p.

54. Jean Le Clerc, *Parrhasiana; Or Thoughts upon Several Subjects* (London, 1700), p. 136.

55. Whitelocke, *Memorials*, introduction by James Welwood, p. iv. See also Zachery Grey, *A Defense of our Antient and Modern Historians* (London, 1725), p. 2.

56. John Wallis, *A Defense of the Royal Society and the Philosophical Transactions* (London, 1678), p. 7. See also John Oldmixon, *The History of England During the Reigns of the Royal House of Stuart* (London, 1730), pp. iv, viii, ix.

57. Nalson, *Impartial Collection*, I, xxv; I, i, vii. See also Grey, *Antient and Modern Historians*, p. 212.

58. [Robert Brady], *A Full and Clear Answer to a Book* (London, 1681), p. 2. The controversy between Petyt and Brady was "concerning matter of Fact only." [Robert Brady], *Jani Anglorum facies Antiqua* (London, 1681), p. 1. Burnet, *Memoires of . . . Dukes of Hamilton*, preface. He also wrote that "Matters of Fact are falsely represented." Ibid. Matthew Smith wrote that some matters of fact might not "carry Conviction with them." *Memoirs of Secret Service* (London, 1699), p. vii. See also p. xv.

59. Bolingbroke, *Historical Writings*, p. 76.

60. Anthony Harmer [Henry Wharton], *A Specimen of Some Errors and Defects in the History of the Reformation of the Church of England* (London, 1693), p. 32; *Historical Collections Concerning Church Affairs* (London, 1696), preface.

61. Le Clerc, *Parrhasiana*, p. 101.

62. Roger North, *Examen: or, An Enquiry into the Credit and Veracity of a Pretended Complete History* (London, 1740), Dedicatory Preface, pp. 16–17, 110, 119.

63. Quoted in Bolingbroke, *Historical Writings*, p. xxxviii, from "Substance of Some Letters to Mr. De Pouilly" (1720), *Works of Lord Bolingbroke*, II, 490.

64. Langlet de Fresnoy, *A New Method of Studying History*, trans. (London, 1728), pp. 260, 289, 290, 294–295. The translator also referred to "historical facts." Ibid., pp. xi, 44, 45.

65. See Richard Popkin, *The History of Skepticism from Erasmus to Spinoza*, 2d ed. (Berkeley, 1979).

66. Selden, *Historie of Tithes*, p. xiii. See also Bolingbroke, *Historical Writings*, pp. 51, 55, 57.

67. Seth Ward, *A Philosophical Essay*, 4th ed. (London, 1667), pp. 84–88, 98–106.

68. Thomas Hobbes, *Elements of Law Natural and Politic*, ed. Ferdinand Tonnies (Cambridge, 1928), pt. I, chap. 6, sec. 9.

69. Thomas Gale, *Court of the Gentiles* (Oxford, 1668), p. 3. For moral certainty, see Shapiro, *Probability and Certainty*; Barbara Shapiro, *"Beyond Reasonable Doubt" and "Probable Cause": Historical Studies of the Anglo-American Law of Evidence* (Berkeley, 1991).

70. Bacon, *Works*, IV, 305.

71. James Howell, *Lustra Ludovici or, The Life of Lewis XIII* (London, 1646), Epistle Dedicatory; William Sanderson, *A Complete History of the Life and Raigne of Charles* (London, 1656), preface.

72. Hamon L'Estrange, *Reign of King Charles*, preface.

73. Quoted in William Lamont, "Arminianism: The Controversy That Never Was," in *Political Discourse in Early Modern Britain*, ed. Nicholas Phillipson and Quentin Skinner (Cambridge, 1993), p. 56.

74. Rushworth, *Collections*, I, preface.

75. Ibid. See also Peter Heylyn, *History of Episcopacy* (London, 1657), preface. Monk's biographer wrote that his history was derived from the duke's "own Relation" and testimony from the duke's "Associates and Companions." For some periods, the author was an eye and ear witness. For the battle with the Dutch, he used the journal of a principal flag officer. Gumble, *Life of General Monck*, preface.

76. Charles Firth, "Clarendon's History of the Rebellion," EHR 19 (1904), 454–456; Clarendon, *History of the Rebellion*, in *Versions of History*, ed. Kelley, p. 345. See also Hicks, *Neoclassical History and English Culture*, pp. 55–61.

77. Gilbert Burnet, *The History of My Own Times*, 2 vols., ed. Osmund Airy (Oxford, 1897–1900), I, xxxi.

78. But see D. R. Woolf, "A Feminine Past? Gender, Genre, and Historical Knowledge in England, 1500–1800," *American Historical Review* 102 (1997), 645–679.

79. William Dugdale, *A Short View of the Late Troubles in England* (London, 1681), preface.

80. Ludlow, *Memoirs*, p. viii.

81. A "more perfect history" was more likely if one waited until "party heat has cooled down." Such historians required "fresh" memorials and could use "acts, instruments, and negotiations of state." Bacon, *Works*, IV, 305. See also Gilbert Burnet, *Memoires of . . . Dukes of Hamilton*, preface; John Cockburn, *History of the General Assembly* (London, 1691), pp. 1–2. Cockburn used diaries, public accounts, and official correspondence. White Kennett thought "no prudent writer" would apply the "Name of history" to the "story of his own times." *Complete History of England* (London, 1706), I, preface, p. 169.

82. John Wilkins, *Essay on a Real Character and Philosophical Language* (London, 1668), p. 49; L'Estrange, *Brief History of The Times*, p. 1, included in *Observator*, vol. III.

83. Edward Stillingfleet, *Origines Sacrae* (London, 1662), preface, p. iii.

84. John Selden, *A Discoverie of Errors* (London, 1622), preface; Selden, *History of Tithes*, p. xii.

85. Quoted in Woolf, *Idea of History*, p. 205.

86. Brathwaite, *Schollers Medley*, pp. 6–7.

87. *The Acts and Monuments of John Foxe*, ed. G. Townsend and S. R. Cattley (London, 1837–41). See also F. J. Levy, *Tudor Historical Thought* (San Marino, Calif., 1967), pp. 103–104; Patrick Collinson, "Truth, Lies, and Faction in Sixteenth-Century Historiography," in *The Historical Imagination in Early Modern England*, ed. Donald R. Kelley and David Harris Sacks (Cambridge, 1997), pp. 37–68.

88. *History of the Most Renowned and Victorious Princess: Selected Chapters*, ed. Wallace T. MacCaffrey (Chicago, 1970), p. 3.

89. William Camden, *Britannia* [1586], trans. Philemon Holland (London, 1610), preface.

90. Selden, *Historie of Tithes*, p. xi; see also Berkowitz, *Selden*, p. 42. William Lambarde, *Archion* (London, 1635), p. 136; see also *A Peramubulation of Kent* [1576] (London, 1970), Dedicatory Letter, p. 67. William Dugdale, *The Antiquities of Warwickshire*, 2d ed., 2 vols. (London, 1730), preface.

91. Rushworth, *Collections*, preface.

92. *Historical Collections Concerning Church Affairs*, preface; Thomas Sheridan, *A Discourse of the Rise and Power of Parliament* (London, 1677), p. 72.

93. Burnet, *Memoires of . . . Dukes of Hamilton*, preface.

94. Gilbert Burnet, *History of the Reformation of the Church of England*, 3 vols. (London, 1679–1714), preface.

95. See James Welwood, *Memoirs of the Most Material Transactions in England* (London, 1700). Public records were the "most important and authentic of all." Thomas Madox, *History and Antiquities of the Exchequer* (London, 1711), pp. v, ix. John Oldmixon suggested that "the greatest Difficulty an Historian has in writing of our own Times" was deciding what documents to include. *The History of England during the Reigns of King William and Mary* (London, 1735), p. vii.

96. Nalson, *Impartial Collection*, I, ii, lxxviii, 2. For Clarendon's use of documents, see Hicks, *Neoclassical History and English Culture*, pp. 59–60.

97. Madox, *Exchequer*, p. 5. Defoe quoted in Paula Backscheider, *Daniel Defoe: A Life* (Baltimore, 1989), p. 410; Kennett, *Register and Chronicle*, preface. One early-eighteenth-century historian criticized "History Writers" who content themselves with "Copies of common Records, Gazetts, News-papers, and Pamphlets, stuffing their pieces with long Speeches in Parliament, Votes of the House of Commons, and even Proclamations." Another criticized the former for his failure to examine manuscripts. Grey, *Antient and Modern Historians*, pp. 99, 101.

98. Oldmixon, *History of England during the Reigns of the Royal House of Stuart*, p. xv. "Only a vain imagination" thought "that only Statesmen should relate Affairs of State." See also Old-

mixon, *History of England During the Reigns of King William and Mary,* p. vii; William Nicolson, *The Scottish Historical Library* (London, 1702), preface. For complaints about documentary excess, see *Supplement to Harris's Dictionary,* s.v. "History"; Laird Okie, *Augustan Historical Writing: Histories of England in the English Enlightenment* (New York, 1991); Hicks, *Neoclassical History and English Culture.* Historians were also criticized for "jumbling" records together, for providing partial citations, and for printing "only Ends and Shreds of Records." [Brady], *Full and Clear Answer,* Advertisement to the Impartial and Judicious Reader.

99. Parry, *Trophies of Time,* pp. 217, 249, 364; Hunter, *Aubrey,* p. 166.

100. See Arnaldo Momigliano, "Ancient History and the Antiquarian," *Journal of the Warburg and Courtauld Institutes* 13 (1950), 285–318; Momigliano, *Classical Foundations of Modern Historiography.*

101. Brathwaite, *Schollers Medley,* p. 80.

102. Inigo Jones, *The most notable Antiquity of Great Britain vulgarly called Stone-Heng* (London, 1655), p. 108. See also Walter Charleton, *Chorea Gigantum, or Stone-Heng Restored to the Danes* (London, 1663).

103. Hunter, *Aubrey,* pp. 180, 183; Kennett, *Register and Chronicle,* preface.

104. London, 1720. The translation in the subtitle was not that of Dugdale.

105. London, 1682.

106. In the Savoy, 1671, 2d ed.

107. See also William Dugdale, *The History of St. Paul's Cathedral* (London, 1657); Dugdale, *Antiquities of Warwickshire.* His *Short View of the Late Troubles in England* contained what had been within his "own cognisance" and quotations from mercuries and other publicly licensed narratives. Preface.

108. Kennett, *Register and Chronicle,* preface; White Kennett, *Parochial Antiquities* (Oxford, 1695), preface.

109. Kennett, *Parochial Antiquities,* Dedicatory Epistle.

110. Aubrey and Casaubon quoted in Hunter, *Aubrey,* pp. 171, 173.

111. Evelyn, *Numismata,* pp. 1, 3, 48–9, 50–51, 71, 156, 160, 163, 168. There should be medals of explorers, famous admirals, even buccaneers. Medals should memorialize events such as the Great Fire and honor inventors of machines, the penny post, and urban lighting as well as scholars, philosophers, and improvers of the practical arts. From medals and inscriptions we "discover'd the Religion, Rites and Superstitions of the Antients, . . . Events which have escap'd the Teeth of Time, and surviv'd all its Revolutions." Ibid., pp. 160, 163–168. See also Walker, *Greek and Roman History.*

112. Addison, *Usefulness of Ancient Medals,* pp. 14, 15, 17, 26, 148, 154; Arthur MacGregor, *Sir Hans Sloane* (London, 1994), p. 35. Nicolson's *Scottish Historical Library* included a section on medals and coins.

113. Selden was of two minds about antiquarian pursuits. He criticized overly "studious affection of bare and sterile antiquities" and at the same time condemned neglect of the "fruitful and precious part" that gave "necessarie light to the present in matter of state, law, history." *Historie of Tithes,* preface.

114. Blundeville, *True Order and Method,* p. 160; Brathwaite, *Schollers Medley,* p. 67. See also p. 69; Nalson, *Impartial Collection,* I, ii; Whitelocke, *Memorials,* Introduction by Welwood, p. ii. Bolingbroke, *Historical Writings,* p. 69.

115. Hobbes, *Leviathan,* p. 45.

116. Whalley, *Manner of Writing History,* p. 11; Gumble, *Life of General Monck,* p. 312.

117. See Rushworth, *Historical Collections; Second Part,* preface; Sir Edward Walker, "Observations upon the Annals Published by Hamon L'Estrange," in *Historical Discourses* (London, 1709), pp. 2, 5, 323, 327–328.

118. Raleigh, *History of the World,* bk. 2, chap. 5, sec. 10, p. 310. Cromwell quoted in C. H. Firth, "Sir Walter Raleigh's *History of the World*," in *Essays Historical and Literary* (Oxford, 1938), pp. 53–54.

119. Bolton, *Hypercritica,* I, 91.

120. See G. H. Nadel, "History as Psychology in Francis Bacon's Theory of History," *History and Theory* 5 (1966), 275–278.

121. Edward Hyde, Lord Clarendon, *History of the Rebellion*, 6 vols. (Oxford, 1888), III, 232. See also IV, 2; *Ravillac Redivivus*, p. 4.

122. Hobbes, *Leviathan*, p. 45.

123. Quoted in J. H. Hale, *Evolution of British Historiography* (Cleveland, 1964), p. 26.

124. See Dugdale, *Short View*, p. 600. See also Royce MacGillivray, *Restoration Historians and the English Civil War* (The Hague, 1974).

125. Sir William Temple, *Observations on the Netherlands* (London, 1674), preface, p. 247; Sir William Temple, *Memoirs*, 3d ed. (London, 1673), preface.

126. Rushworth, *Historical Collections: The Second Part*, preface; Burnet, *Memoires of . . . Dukes of Hamilton*, preface.

127. Raleigh, *History of the World*, pp. 534, 535–539, 573–574; Camden, *Britannia*, preface; Francis Bacon, *The Advancement of Learning*, ed. G. W. Kitchen (London, 1973), p. 74; Lambarde, *Perambulation of Kent*, p. 476.

128. Gale, *Court of the Gentiles*, preface, p. 3.

129. Berkowitz, *Selden*, p. 36; Gumble, *Life of General Monck*, preface; Brathwaite, *Schollers Medley*, p. 6; Brady, *Complete History of England*, To the Reader; Crouch, *History of Cromwell*; Edmund Bohun, *Continuation of the History of the Reformation* (London, 1680), preface; Rushworth, *Historical Collections: The Second Part*, title page, preface; Rushworth, *Historical Collections*, To the Reader.

130. Bacon, *Works*, IV, 302; Peter Heylyn, *Examen Historicum* (London, 1659), preface; Burnet, *Memoires of . . . Dukes of Hamilton*, Dedication to Charles II.

131. Scot, *Memoirs of James Melvil*, preface.

132. Kennett, *General History*, preface; L'Estrange, *Brief History of The Times*, p. 5.

133. *Ravillac Redivivus*, p. 4; Sprat, *True Account*, preface.

134. Kennett, *Parochial Antiquities*, preface.

135. Typically, fidelity was treated as a characteristic of the person producing the account, but it was sometimes treated as a characteristic of the account itself, which might described as a "faithful Representation" or a "faithful account."

136. Bolton, *Hypercritica*, I, 91. See also pp. 91–93.

137. Peter Heylyn, *The History of the Sabbath* (London, 1636), preface.

138. Laurence Echard, *The History of England*, 3 vols. (1707) I, preface; North, *Examen*, p. xiii; Gilbert Burnet, *A Letter to Mr. Thevenot* (London, 1690), p. 2. See also Stillingfleet, *Origines Sacrae*, xviii. Critics often labeled their opponents' histories "libels." See North, *Examen*, p. 659.

139. James Howell, *Familiar Letters* (London, 1655), I, 602; Clarendon, *History of the Rebellion*, in *Versions of History*, ed. Kelley, p. 345. For Clarendon's *History* as Tory propaganda, see Hicks, *Neoclassical History and English Culture*, pp. 62–81. Crouch, *History of Cromwell*, preface; Burnet, *History of My Own Times*, I, xxxiii.

140. See Thomas May, *History of Parliament* (London, 1647), preface; Echard, *History of England*, I, preface; Dugdale, *Memorials*, Publisher to the Reader; Rushworth, *Historical Collections*, preface; *The Life of Oliver Cromwell* (London, n.d.), preface; *Ephemeris Parliamentaria* (London, 1654), preface.

141. Nalson, *Impartial Collection*, pp. vi, xxv; Brady, *Complete History of England*, Dedicatory Letter; William Somner, *A Treatise of Gavelkind* (London, 1660), p. 97. Brady criticized others for "partial Citations, Falsity in leaving out and adding . . . wilful Wresting and abusing of Records." *Introduction to the Old English History*, Epistle to the Reader.

142. Burnet, *Memoires of . . . Dukes of Hamilton*, preface. See Isaac Kramnick, "Augustan Politics and English Historiography: The Debate on the English Past, 1730–1735," *History and Theory* 6 (1967), 33–55; MacGillivray, *Restoration Historians*.

143. Bolingbroke, *Historical Writings*, p. 55.

144. Whalley, *Manner of Writing History*, p. 3–4.

145. Andrew Marvell, *An Account of the Growth of Popery and Arbitrary Government* (London, 1677); Walter Charleton, *Two Discourses* (London, 1669), p. 25; Hunter, *Aubrey*, p. 69; James Welwood, *Memoirs of the Most Material Transactions in England* (London, 1700), preface; North, *Examen*, p. 672; Burnet, *Memoires of . . . Dukes of Hamilton*, preface. Burnet admitted

that readers might "find an Apology for the Reformation, interwoven with its History." Gilbert Burnet, *The Abridgement of the History of the Reformation of the Church of England* (London, 1682), part I, preface. Sprat admitted there was something of an apology in his *History of the Royal Society*, p. 322.

146. The historian would judge of the individual's "goodnesse or naughtinesse." Blundeville, *True Order and Method*, pp. 158, 160–161.

147. Brathwaite, *Schollers Medley*, pp. 5, 6; Peter Heylyn, *Examen Historicum* (London, 1659), part II, preface; Whalley recommended using "all the Powers and Artilleries of Rhetoric." *Manner of Writing History*, pp. 20–21, 22–24.

148. Nalson, *Impartial Collections*, I, 2; Whitelocke, *Memorials*, Publisher to the Reader; Lambert Wood, *The Life and Raigne of King Charles* (London, 1659), To the Reader; John Corbet, *A Historical Relation of the Military Government* (London, 1645), p. 4; Aubrey, *Brief Lives*, p. cv; Kennett, *Register and Chronicle*, preface; Marvell, *Growth of Popery*.

149. Whitelocke, *Memorials*, Publisher to Reader.

150. Brathwaite, *Schollers Medley*, pp. 21, 13–14; Bolton, "Hypercritica," in *Critical Essays*, I, 83; Whitelocke, *Memorials*, Publisher to the Reader; May, *History of the Parliament of England*, preface; Rushworth, *Historical Collections*, preface to the Reader; Charleton, *Two Discourses*, p. 26; Cavendish, *Life of William Cavendish*, preface; Camden, "Life of Camden"; A. W., *Medulla Historiae Scoticae* (London, 1685), To the Reader; Aylett Sammes, *Britannie Antigua Illustrata* (London, 1676), Preface to the Reader; Burnet, *Memoires of . . . Dukes of Hamilton*, preface; Harmer, *Specimen of Some Errors*, p. 40.

151. Kennett, *General History*, preface. Yet Kennett admired Camden because he chose the "plain form" of Annals. Camden preferred "to be Exact [rather] than Ornamental" and avoided "all superfluous Finery." *Complete History of England* (London, 1706), I, preface. An early-eighteenth-century work criticized Clarendon for using "florid expressions" though he favored natural and eloquent ornaments. *Clarendon and Whitlock Compar'd* (London, 1727), pp. ix, x, xi. See also pp. xii–xviii. See also *Supplement to Dr. Harris's Dictionary of Arts and Sciences* (London, 1744).

152. See Samuel Johnson, *A Dictionary of the English Language*, 2 vols., 2d ed. (London, 1755); D. Fenning, *The Royal Dictionary* (London, 1761).

153. Hume wrote of history as a "collection of facts" multiplying "without end." *History of England*, II, 1. See also III, 77.

154. Bolingbroke complained of the "inferior detail of history" and the difficulty of finding historians more interested in "ideas of the spirit, than in facts of the memory." *Historical Writings*, pp. xxvi–xxvii. See Joseph M. Levine, *Humanism and History: Origins of Modern English Historiography* (Ithaca, 1987).

Chapter 3: Discourses of Fact

1. Henry Oldenburg to Sir George Oxenden, President of English India Company, April 6, 1677, Royal Society, Original Letters.

2. See John Stoye, *English Travellers Abroad, 1604–1667* (New York, 1968); Charles Batten, *Pleasurable Instruction: Form and Convention in Eighteenth-Century Travel Literature* (Berkeley, 1978).

3. Cosmography mixed natural and civil history. *The Works of Francis Bacon*, ed. James Spedding, Robert Leslie Ellis, and Douglas Denon Heath, 14 vols. (London, 1857–74), IV, 311.

4. See Justin Stagl, "The Methodizing of Travel in the Sixteenth Century," *History and Anthropology* 4 (1990), 303–338. Stagl suggests that travel reporting was methodized similarly from c. 1570 to 1800. *A History of Curiosity: The Theory of Travel, 1550–1800* (Chur, Switzerland, 1995), p. 57. Robert Plot's *Natural History of Oxfordshire* (London, 1677) focused on the natural and artificial to supplement the existent "Civil and Geographical." Thomas Fuller's *History of the Worthies of England* (London, 1662) combined chorographical description with biographies of England's "worthies." Leslie Cormack distinguishes descriptive geography from chorography. *Charting an Empire: Geography at the English Universities, 1580–1620* (Chicago, 1997), p. 39.

5. Bacon's traveler was to observe princely courts, courts of justice, churches, fortifications, antiquities, libraries, colleges, great houses and gardens, armories, exchanges, and military training as well as cabinets and rarities. He was to meet the secretaries of ambassadors and other knowledgeable and eminent persons. "Of Travel," in *The Essays*, ed. John Pitcher (London, 1985), pp. 113–114. See also Philip Jones, *Certain Brief, and Special Instruction* (London, 1598); Robert Dallington, *A Method for Travel* (London, 1605). Twenty-eight descriptive geographical accounts were translated into English between 1580 and 1620. Cormack, *Charting an Empire*, p. 140. See also Esther Moir, *The Discovery of Britain: English Tourists, 1640–1840* (London, 1964).

6. See Barbara Shapiro, "History and Natural History in Sixteenth- and Seventeenth-Century England: An Essay on the Relationship between Humanism and Science," in *English Scientific Virtuosi in the Sixteenth and Seventeenth Centuries* Los Angeles, 1979), pp. 12–28; Stan Mendyk, *"Speculum Britanniae": Regional Study, Antiquarianism, and Science in Britain to 1700* (Toronto, 1989); Richard Helgerson, *Forms of Nationhood: The Elizabethan Writing of England* (Chicago, 1992), pp. 105–148; Lesley Cormack, "'Good Fences Make Good Neighbors': Geography as Self-Definition in Early Modern England," *Isis* 82 (1991), 639–661.

7. William Camden, *Britannia* (London, 1695), preface. The "description of a kingdom is a less intricate task than its history, because materials are more at hand, and impartiality less vitiated." Ibid. Thomas Sprat praised Camden for traveling every part of the country. *The History of the Royal Society*, ed. Jackson Cope and H. W. Jones (St. Louis, 1958), p. 20.

8. Lawyer-historian Lambarde hoped for "One whole and perfect bodie and booke of our English topography." *Perambulation of Kent* [1570] (London, 1970), p. 424. Aubrey's license from the Royal Cosmographer required justices of the peace, mayors, and sheriffs to provide "free Access" to public registers and books, to promote "the Geographical and Historical Description of Majesty's . . . Kingdom." *The Natural History and Antiquities of the County of Surrey*, 5 vols. (London, 1719), preface.

9. William Burton, *The Description of Leicestershire* (London, 1622), preface.

10. Daniel Defoe, *Tour thro' the Whole Island of Great Britain*, 2 vols. (London, 1727).

11. James Howell, *Londonopolis* (London, 1657), Advertisement to the Reader.

12. Thomas De-Laune, *The Present State of London* (London, 1681).

13. Sir Thomas Browne noted the need for an updated edition. *Hydriotaphia* (London, 1658), preface. See Richard Blome, *Britannia; Or, A Geographical Description of England, Scotland, and Ireland* (1673). Edmund Gibson's 1695 revision was a cooperative effort. See David Douglas, *English Scholars* (London, 1939); Graham Parry, *The Trophies of Time: English Antiquarians of the Seventeenth Century* (Oxford, 1995).

14. Defoe, *A Tour thro' the Whole Island of Great Britain*, I, 4. See also John Chamberlayne, *Magnae Britanniae Notitia; Or, The Present State of Great Britain* (London, 1718).

15. See *A Perfect Description of the Virginia* (London, 1649); *The Description of the Province of West-Jersey in America* (London, 1676); R. F., *The Present State of Carolina* (London, 1672); Richard Blome, *A Description of Jamaica* (London, 1678); Richard Blome, *The Present State of his Majesties Isles and Territories in America* (London, 1687).

16. *Perfect Description*, p. 1.

17. R. F., *Present State of Carolina*, p. 27.

18. Gerard Boate, *Ireland's Naturall History* (London, 1652); William Petty, *Political Anatomy of Ireland* (London, 1691); Laurence Echard, *Exact Description of Ireland* (London, 1691). See also William Petty, *The Present State of Ireland together with some Remarques upon the Antient State* (London, 1673).

19. Richard Hakluyt, *Principal Navigations* (New York, 1972). Hakluyt called his work "history." He occasionally relied on "some strangers as witnesses of the things done," but only "such as either faithfully remember or sufficiently confirm the travels of our own people." Preface to 1589 ed., pp. 33–34. Samuel Purchas, *Purchas his Pilgrimage* (London, 1613). Purchas emphasized the role of "Sense by Induction." 20 vols. (Glasgow, 1905), I, xl. See also Fynes Moryson, *Itinerary* (London, 1617); William Lithgow, *Rare Adventures and Painful Peregrinations* (London, 1632); George Sandys, *Relation of a Journey* (London, 1615); Henry Blount, *Voyages into the Levant* (London, 1636); Thomas Hariot, *A Brief and True Report of the*

new found land of Virginia (London, 1588); Capt. John Smith, *The General History of Virginia* (London, 1627); Richard Knolles, *General History of the Turks* (London, 1603).

20. For predecessors, see Mary B. Campbell, *The Witness and the Other World: Exotic European Travel Writing, 400–1600* (Ithaca, 1988).

21. Samuel Purchas, *Hakluytus posthumous, or Purchas His Pilgrimes* (London, 1625), I, To the Reader.

22. Percy Adams, *Travelers and Travel Liars, 1660–1800* (New York, 1980).

23. Ibid., pp. 93–94. See also Stagl, *History of Curiosity,* pp. 171–207.

24. Awnsham Churchill and John Churchill, *A Collection of Voyages and Travels,* 4 vols. (London, 1704), I, xcix.

25. Lithgow, *Rare Adventures and Painful Peregrinations,* To the Reader. Richard Brathwaite in 1616 complained that travelers sometimes invented "strange things." *The Schollers Medley: or, an Intermixt Discourse upon Historicall and Poeticall Relations* (London, 1614). John Fryer's *New Account of East-India and Persia* (London, 1698) contrasted his treatment with "Poetical Fictions." Preface.

26. Joshua Childrey, *Britannia Baconia* (London, 1661), Preface to the Reader.

27. Edmund Halley, *Correspondence and Papers,* ed. Eugene MacPike (Oxford, 1932), p. 82.

28. Edward Chamberlayne, *Anglia notitia: or, The Present State of England* (London, 1669), Preface to the Reader. See also Stagl, *History of Curiosity,* p. 51.

29. See Barbara Shapiro, "Early Modern Intellectual Life: Humanism, Religion, and Science in Seventeenth-Century England," *History of Science* 29 (1991), 46–71; K. M. Reeds, "Renaissance Humanism and Botany," *Annals of Science* 33 (1976), 519–542. See also Frank Lestringant, *Mapping the Renaissance World: The Geographical Imagination in the Age of Discovery* (Berkeley, 1994); Ann Blair, "Humanist Methods in Natural Philosophy: The Commonplace Book," *Journal of the History of Ideas* 53 (1992), 541–551.

30. Bacon, *Works,* I, 191. See also Nathaniel Carpenter, *Geography Delineated* (Oxford, 1625). Descriptive geography, often combined with history, was a common study for university undergraduates. Cormack, *Charting an Empire,* p. 161.

31. David N. Livingstone, *The Geographical Tradition: Episodes in the History of a Contested Enterprise* (Oxford, 1992), p. 60.

32. Henry Oldenburg, *Correspondence,* ed. and trans. A. Rupert Hall and Marie Boas Hall, 13 vols. (Madison, Wis., 1965–86), I, 79; II, 65; III, 168. Charles II expressed an interest in surveying the empire even before the Royal Society was incorporated. James Jacob, *Boyle and the English Revolution* (New York, 1977), p. 155, citing B. M. Egerton MSS 2395, fol. 296r. In 1661 a committee was formed to consider "questions to be inquired of in the remotest part of the world." See Daniel Carey, "Compiling Nature's History: Travellers and Travel Narratives in the Early Royal Society," *Annals of Science* 54 (1997), 274.

33. Robert Knox, *A Historical Relation of the Island of Ceylon* [1681] (Glasgow, 1961), preface by Robert Hooke, p. lxiv; Oldenburg, *Correspondence,* III, 34. Hooke's 1697 lectures emphasized the importance of travel books in collecting natural history information.

34. London, 1692. Boyle complained about the scarcity of travel books and indicated their importance for eyewitness accounts. See Carey, "Compiling Nature's History," p. 281.

35. London, 1696, pp. 1, 9.

36. *Collection of Voyages and Travels,* I, lxxvi. The traveler was to collect information on climate, government, places of strength, religion, language, trade and manufacturing, public buildings, arts and artists, customs, laws, "strange Adventures," "surprizing Accidents," and "rarities." He should observe princely courts and "converse with the most celebrated men in all the arts and sciences." Ibid.

37. Quoted in John Heilbron, *Physics at the Royal Society during Newton's Presidency* (Los Angeles, 1983), p. 25.

38. Oldenburg, *Correspondence,* III, 87, 200, 603–607; IV, 451; VII, 347, 417; IX, 311. See also *Philosophical Transactions* I (1665–66), 415, 424, 467, 471–472.

39. Edmund Halley, "An Historical Account of the Trade-Winds," in *Miscellanea Curiosa,* 3d ed., 3 vols. (London, 1726), I, 61, 75.

40. They were requested to keep "an exact Diary," one copy to be sent to the Lord High Admiral and another to Trinity House for the use of the Society. *Philosophical Transactions* I (1665–66), 141–143.

41. Oldenburg, *Correspondence*, II, 161; IV, 279, 337.

42. Knox, *Island of Ceylon*, preface by Hooke, p. xlvii. The East India Company testified, "We esteem Captain Knox a Man of Truth and Integrity, and that his Relations and Accounts of Ceylon . . . are worthy of Credit." Ibid., p. xxx.

43. *Memoirs for a Natural History of Animals*, trans. Alexander Pitfield (London, 1688), preface; Charles Webster, *The Great Instauration: Science, Medicine, and Reform, 1626–1660* (London, 1675), pp. 437–438, 445; *Philosophical Transactions*, I (1665–66), 11.

44. John Ray, *A Collection of Curious Travels and Voyages* (London, 1693). Ray, *Observations Topographical and Physiological: Made in a Journey* (London, 1673), preface.

45. Francis Willughby, *The Ornithology* (London, 1678), preface by John Ray.

46. *Miscellanea Curiosa*, 3d ed., III, 160–168.

47. Martin Lister, *A Journey to Paris in the Year 1698* (London, 1699). See also *The Present State of France and Description of Paris*, p. 2. Although Lister's observations inclined toward "nature," he reported on buildings, monuments, ancient statuary, book collections, food, wine, opera, the theater, and paintings. See also Edward Browne, *Brief Account of Some Travels in Hungary, Serbia* (London, 1673); Browne, *Account of Several Travels through a Great Part of Germany* (London, 1677); *Memoirs and Travels of Sir John Reresby* (London, 1904); John Fryer, *A New Account of East-India and Persia* (London, 1698).

48. 2 vols. (London, 1707), preface.

49. Steven Shapin, *The Social History of Truth: Civility and Science in Seventeenth-Century England* (Chicago, 1994).

50. London, 1670, preface. Edward Tyson and Nehemiah Grew used travel accounts. Carey, "Compiling Nature's History," p. 284. Hooke's library contained an extensive collection of travel and chorographic literature. Leona Rostenberg, *The Library of Robert Hooke: The Scientific Book Trade of Restoration England* (Santa Monica, Calif., 1989), pp. 134–139.

51. William Dampier, *A New Voyage Round the World* (1699–1705); Dampier, *A Collection of Voyages* (London, 1724). See also Philip Edwards, *The Story of the Voyage: Sea Narratives in Eighteenth-Century England* (Cambridge, 1994).

52. See Charles Smith, *The Ancient and Present State of the County of Kerry* (Dublin, 1766), p. xviii; Livingstone, *Geographical Tradition*, p. 126.

53. Oldenburg continued to press Winthrop about "the Composure of a good History of New England, from the beginning of ye English arrival there, . . . containying ye Geography, Natural Productions and Civill Administration thereof, together with the Notable progresses of yr Plantation, and the remarkable occurrences." *Correspondence*, III, 525; VII, 142.

54. London, 1676. See also John Josselyn, *New England's Rarities Discovered* (London, 1672); Joseph and Nesta Ewant, *John Bannister and His Natural History of Virginia, 1678–1692* (Urbana, 1970); Raymond Stearns, *Science in the British Colonies of America* (Urbana, 1970), pp. 218, 223, 225, 227.

55. For exceptions, see W. H. Greenleaf, *Order and Empiricism: Two Traditions of English Political Thought, 1500–1700* (London, 1964); Stagl, *History of Curiosity*, p. 57.

56. *The Petty Papers*, ed. Marquis of Lansdowne, 2 vols. (London, 1927), I, 175–178. See also "Observations on England," ibid., I, 208 ff. As early as 1574 Thomas Blundeville suggested that trade, the public revenue, military forces, and manner of government should be included in histories of cities and countries.

57. Newton wished attention be given to the policies and state of affairs of nations, taxation, trades, and commodities, "laws and customs," and "how far they differ from ours," as well as fortifications and the "power and respect belonging to the degrees of nobility or magistrates." Stephen Rigaud, *Correspondence of Scientific Men of the Seventeenth Century*, 2 vols. (Oxford, 1841), Newton to Aston, May 18, 1668, II, 293.

58. 2d ed. (In the Savoy, 1669).

59. *The Present State of Ireland* (London, 1673). Thomas Sprat in 1665 claimed, "The English

have describ'd, and illustrated, all parts of the Earth." *A Letter Containing Some Observations on Monsieur de Sorbier's Voyage into England* (London, 1665), p. 60. Although the *Philosophical Transactions* in 1676 complained that the natural history of most countries was lacking, a correction noted, "Now I see very much done in that kind; and I hear of much more." *Philosophical Transactions* XI (1676), 552; XII (1677), 816.

60. Sir William Temple, *Observations upon the United Provinces* (London, 1673), preface. See also Sir William Temple, "Essay on Government," in *Miscellany* (London, 1672); Owen Feltham, *Batavia* (London, 1677); A. W., *The Present State of the United Provinces* (London, 1669), written by a member of the Royal Society; Richard Peers, "Description of the Seventeen Provinces," in Moses Pitt, *The English Atlas: or, a Compleat Chorography of England and Wales* (Oxford, 1680–83), IV.

61. See Sir George Carew, *A Relation of the State of France*, ed. Thomas Birch [1609] (London, 1749); Peter Heylyn's hostile *Survey of the Estate of France* (London, 1656) provided little information; John Evelyn, *The Present State of France* (London, 1652). Evelyn advised reporters to inform themselves about the "mysteries of Government and Polity." Preface. *The Present State of France* (London, 1687) was a translation. Sir Anthony Weldon's *Perfect Description of the People and Country of Scotland.* (London, 1649) was an attack on the Scots in the form of chorographical description.

62. Jean J. Gailhard, *The Present State of . . . Italy* (London, 1668), Preface to the Reader.

63. *The Present State of Denmark* (London, 1683), Dedicatory Letter.

64. *An Account of Denmark as It was in the Year 1692*, 3d ed. (London, 1694), preface. Observation of the "more polish'd and delicious Countries of France, Spain, or Italy" dazzled travelers and "cast a disguise upon the Slavery of those Parts." Ibid., preface. His impartial account of Denmark "might save the Curious the labour and expence of the Voyage." Preface.

65. J. Crull, *Denmark Vindicated* (London, 1694), Prefatory Letter, pp. 89, 166–167. John Robinson, *An Account of Sweden: Together with an Extract of the History of that Kingdom* (London, 1694) promised, "You will find here a Relation of Matter of Fact only." The Publisher to the Reader.

66. London, 1695, pp. iv, viii, 2–3, 109. *The Present State of Germany* emphasized political concerns and policy issues. Though Europeans might be "languid" about the empire of China and "treat their Story and Description with little more attention than we do a well-drawn Romance," this attitude was inappropriate for the politically important German empire. Its author, Samuel Pufendorf, described its political condition as well as its strength, "disease," and "interest" (London 1690). Publisher to Reader. He included nothing "but what I had received upon the Credit of those that had been Eye-Witnesses of their own Relations." Ibid., To the Reader.

67. London, 1670, preface, pp. 1–8, 11.

68. Ibid., p. 11. Moses Pitt's *English Atlas* included material on the "Governments, Civil and Military, . . . Magistrates, Laws, Assemblies, Courts" as well as historical accounts of the "actions and successes of each Nation, or their Princes, remarkable actions." Preface.

69. Sir Henry Blount, *A Voyage into the Levant*, 8th ed. (London, 1671), pp. 3, 4, 6, 7, 80. See also George Sandys, *A Relation of a Journey . . . Containing a description of the Turkish Empire* (1615), in Churchill and Churchill, *Collection*; Henry Marsh, *A New Survey of the Turkish Empire and Government* (London, 1665); Karl. H. Dannenfeldt, *Leonhard Rauwolf: Sixteenth-Century Physician, Botanist, and Traveler* (Cambridge, Mass., 1968).

70. London, 1668, Dedicatory Letter, Preface to the Reader. Every government had its "maxims and rules" that were its "foundations and pillars: . . . not subject to the alteration of time." Ibid., p. 3. William Eton, *A Survey of the Turkish Empire* (London, 1799). Eton would "reason only from facts" and draw "conclusions from facts recorded in their own history." Preface, p. 3.

71. But see Sir William Temple, *A Survey of the Constitutions and Interests*, in *Miscellanea I* (London, 1681); [Sir Peter Paxton], *Civil Polity, a Treatise Concerning the Nature of Government, Wherein the Reasons of that Diversity to be observed in the Customs, Manners, and Usage of Natives are Historically Explained* (London, 1703); William Batz, "The Historical Anthropology of John

Locke," in *Philosophy, Religion, and Science in the Seventeenth and Eighteenth Centuries*, ed. John Yolton (Rochester, N.Y., 1990), pp. 385–395.

72. Graunt "deduc'd many true conclusions, concerning the gravest, and most weighty Parts of civil Government" from the bills of mortality. Sprat, *History of the Royal Society*, p. 243. Discussion of national "interest" is often found in books labeled "The Present State of X."

73. William Letwin, *The Origins of Scientific Economics* (New York, 1964), p. 139. See also William Petty, *Political Arithmetick* (London, 1671); Sprat, *History of the Royal Society*, p. 243; Mary Poovey, *A History of the Modern Fact: Problems of Knowledge in the Sciences of Wealth and Society* (Chicago, 1998), pp. 120–137.

74. London, 1604, preface by translator E. G.

75. See Anthony Pagden, "Ius et Factum: Text and Experience in the Writings of Bartolomé de las Casas," in *New World Encounters*, ed. Stephen Greenblatt (Berkeley, 1991), pp. 91, 94; Anthony Pagden, *European Encounters with the New World: From Renaissance to Romanticism* (New Haven, 1993), pp. 74–80. See also Lestringant, *Mapping the Renaissance World*, pp. 13, 138.

76. The term "moral history," however, was used by Awnsham and John Churchill, *Collection*, I, lxxii, and by Sir John Narborough, *An Account of Several Late Voyages and Discoveries* (London, 1694), p. v. See also John Fryer, *A New Account of East-India and Persia* (London, 1698), title page.

77. See Margaret Hodgen, *Early Anthropology in the Sixteenth and Seventeenth Centuries* (Philadelphia, 1964); J. L. Myers, "The Influence of Anthropology on the Course of Political Science," *University of California Publications in History* 11 (1916), 22–33; John Howland Rowe, "The Renaissance Foundations of Anthropology," *American Anthropologist* 67 (1965), 1–20; Greenblatt, *New World Encounters*; Lestringant, *Mapping the Renaissance*; Denise Albanese, *New Science, New World* (Durham, N.C., 1996); Pagden, *European Encounters with the New World*; Clarence J. Glacken, *Traces on the Rhodian Shore: Nature and Culture in Western Thought from Ancient Times to the End of the Eighteenth Century* (Berkeley, 1967); Anthony Grafton, *New Worlds, Ancient Texts* (Cambridge, Mass., 1991).

78. John Woodward, *Brief Instructions for making Observations in all parts of the World* (London, 1696), pp. 1, 9.

Chapter 4: "News," "Marvels," "Wonders," and the Periodical Press

1. See Carolyn Nelson and Matthew Seccombe, *British Newspapers and Periodicals, 1641–1700* (New York, 1987); M. A. Shaaber, *Some Forerunners of the Newspapers in England* (Philadelphia, 1929); Stanley Morison, "The Origins of the Newspaper," inaugural lecture, University of London, Oct. 5, 1954; Joseph Frank, *The Beginnings of the English Newspaper, 1620–1660* (Cambridge, 1961); Joad Raymond, *The Invention of the Newspaper: English Newsbooks, 1641–1649* (Oxford, 1996); James Sutherland, *The Restoration Newspaper and Its Development* (Cambridge, 1986); C. John Sommerville, *The News Revolution in England: Cultural Dynamics of Daily Information* (Oxford, 1996); R. B. Walker, "The Newspaper Press in the Reign of William III," *Historical Journal* 17 (1974), 691–709; Michael Harris, *London Newspapers in the Age of Walpole* (London, 1987); Jeremy Black, *The English Press in the Eighteenth Century* (Beckenham, Kent, 1987); Jeremy D. Popkin, "Periodical Publication and the Nature of Knowledge in Eighteenth-Century France," in *The Shapes of Knowledge from the Renaissance to the Enlightenment*, ed. Donald R. Kelley and Richard H. Popkin (Dordrecht, 1991), pp. 203–214; Elizabeth Eisenstein, *The Printing Press as an Agent of Change: Communication and Cultural Transformation in Early-Modern Europe*, 2 vols. (Cambridge, 1979). See also M. D. Saiz, *Historia del periodismo en España*, 2 vols. (Madrid, 1983), I; Folke Dahl, *Les débuts de la presse française* (Goteborg, 1951); Eugene Hatin, *L'histoire du journal en France* (Paris, 1846); R. Levois, *Histoire de la presse française* (Lausanne, 1965).

2. Robert Burton, *The Anatomy of Melancholy* [1621], 2 vols. (New York, 1977), I, 118. See also Richard Cust, "News and Politics in Early Seventeenth-Century England," *Past and Present* 112 (1986), 60–90.

3. See Joy Kenseth, "The Age of the Marvelous: An Introduction," in *The Age of the Marvelous*,

ed. Joy Kenseth (Hanover, N.H., 1991), pp. 27, 29, 31, 40, 51; Jean Céard, *La nature et les prodiges: L'insolite au XVI-siècle* (Geneva, 1977); Katherine Park and Lorraine Daston, "Unnatural Conceptions: The Study of Monsters in Sixteenth- and Seventeenth-Century France and England," *Past and Present* 92 (1981), 20–54; Daston, "Marvelous Facts and Miraculous Evidence in Early Modern Europe," in *Rethinking Objectivity*, ed. Allan Megill (Durham, N.C., 1994); Daston and Park, *Wonders and the Order of Nature, 1150–1750* (New York, 1998); Jerome Friedman, *The Battle of the Frogs and Fairford's Flies: Miracles and the Pulp Press during the English Revolution* (New York, 1993).

4. Levois, *Histoire de la presse française*, pp. 124–125, 142–143, 148; Howard Solomon, *Public Welfare, Science, and Propaganda in Seventeenth-Century France: The Innovations of Theophraste Renaudot* (Princeton, 1972), pp. 100–162; Michael Frearson, "London Corantos in the 1620s," in *Studies in Newspaper and Periodical History 1993 Annual* (Westport, Conn., 1994), pp. 3–18; Goran Leth, "A Protestant Public Sphere: The Early European Newspaper Press," in ibid., pp. 67–92.

5. *The Wonderful discoverie of witches in Lancaster* (1613) provided "nothing but . . . matter of fact, . . . carefully set forth and truly reported." Quoted in J. Osborn, *Lives of the most Remarkable Criminals*, 2 vols. (London, 1735), II, 255. See also Peter Lake, "Deeds against Nature: Cheap Print, Protestantism, and Murder in Early-Seventeenth-Century England," in *Culture and Politics in Early Stuart England*, ed. Kevin Sharpe and Peter Lake (Stanford, 1993), pp. 257–283.

6. Shaaber, *Forerunners of the Newspaper*, pp. 144–156.

7. John Wilkins, *An Essay Towards a Real Character and a Philosophical Language* (London, 1668), p. 49.

8. Sommerville, *News Revolution*, pp. 35, 75–84. See also Joad Raymond, *Making the News: An Anthology of Newsbooks of Revolutionary England* (Moreton on the Marsh, 1993).

9. Nigel Smith, *Literature and Revolution in England, 1640–1660* (New Haven, 1994), pp. 54–69.

10. The *Faithfull Scout* and the *London Courant* quoted in Frank, *Beginnings of the English Newspaper*, pp. 214, 265.

11. Quoted in ibid., p. 84.

12. Quoted in ibid., p. 122.

13. Ibid., pp. 54–55.

14. The *Kingdom's Weekly Intelligencer*, quoted in Frank, *Beginnings of the English Newspaper*, pp. 187–188; the *Moderate Intelligencer*, p. 124, quoted in ibid., pp. 228–229. The earliest American colonial newspaper (1690) promised "faithful relations." Its editor requested that "Diligent Observers" provide information and added that he would print only "what we have reason to believe is true, repairing to the best fountains for our informations." Sidney Kobre, *The Development of the Colonial Newspaper* (Pittsburgh, 1944), p. 14.

15. Frank, *Beginnings of the English Newspaper*, p. 68, from *A Continuation of Certain Speciall and Remarkable Passages* (1644). See also ibid., pp. 97, 228–229; Lois Schwoerer, "Press and Parliament in the Revolution of 1689," *Historical Journal* 20 (1977), 558–559.

16. John Wilkins, *Essay*, p. 49. Bracton, many centuries earlier, had distinguished rumor from common fame.

17. Frank, *Beginnings of the English Newspaper*, p. 97.

18. Burton, *Anatomy of Melancholy*, II, 199.

19. *News from Fleetstreet* (London, 1675), p. 1.

20. Quoted in Sommerville, *News Revolution*, p. 89.

21. *Protestant Oxford Intelligencer*, no. 1 (1681); *Oxford Gazette*, Nov. 20, Nov. 23, 1665; *Mercurius Aulicus* (Oxford, 1642–44), pp. 93, 100. See also p. 151; *The Intelligencer*, July 10, 1665, p. 553; Frank, *Beginnings of the English Newspaper*, p. 300. See also *Mercurius Britanicus* (pp. 35–36). It was not uncommon for foreign sources to be translated and printed without verification.

22. *Mercurius Aulicus*, pp. 93, 151; *Perfect Diurnal*, in Frank, *Beginnings of the English Newspaper*, p. 43; *Mercurius Britanicus*, pp. 35–36.

23. *Mercurius Politicus*, pp. 137–138. See also p. 139.

24. Frank, *Beginnings of the English Newspaper*, p. 84.

25. Ibid., p. 122.

26. Ibid., p. 187.

27. See Sommerville, *News Revolution*, pp. 64–65.

28. For example, the *Complete Intelligencer*, the *Impartial Intelligencer*, the *Moderate Intelligencer*. Restoration examples include the *Protestant Oxford Intelligencer*, the *London Intelligence*, the *Domestick Intelligence*, and the *Currant Intelligence*.

29. Sir Bulstrode Whitelocke, *A Journal of the Swedish Ambassy*, 2 vols. (London, 1772).

30. Oldenburg also sent political "intelligence" to Joseph Williamson. Oldenburg, *Correspondence*, 13 vols., ed. M. B. Hall and R. Hall (Madison, Wis., 1965–77).

31. Thomas Hobbes, *Behemoth: or an Epitome of the Civil Wars in England* (London, 1679), p. 155; Harcourt Brown, *Scientific Organizations in Seventeenth-Century France* (Baltimore, 1934), p. 188. Letter, Meric Bigot to N. Heinsius. Oldenburg wrote, "If . . . printing Journals spread overall, we have a good general Intelligence of all ye Learned Trade and its Progress." Oldenburg, *Correspondence*, IV, 275. There was interest in a briefer and less costly "philosophical gazette" in the 1680s. Michael Hunter and Paul Wood, "Towards Solomon's House: Rival Strategies for Reforming the Royal Society," *History of Science* 24 (1986), 59–61. See also David Kronick, *A History of Science and Technical Periodicals: The Origins and Development of the Scientific and Technological Press, 1665–1790* (New York, 1962); David Knight, "The Growth of European Scientific Journals Published before 1850," in *Scientific Publishing in Europe*, ed. A. L. Meadows (Amsterdam, 1980), pp. 8–10; Adrian Johns, "History, Science, and the History of the Book: The Making of Natural Philosophy in Early Modern England," in *Publishing History* 30 (1991), 6–30; Adrian Johns, *The Nature of the Book* (Chicago, 1988); Dwight Atkinson, *Scientific Discourse in Sociohistorical Context: The Philosophical Transactions of the Royal Society of London, 1675–1975* (Mahwah, N.J., 1999), pp. 20–21.

32. The *St. James Post* would have regard "to time, place, and fact, as may together make a useful history." The *British Observator* in 1733 chose "news rather than conjectures," "facts rather than speculations." Cited in Black, *English Press*, pp. 28, 32. Daniel Defoe's *Daily Post* provided "just Accounts of Facts in plain Words." Quoted in Paula R. Backscheider, *Daniel Defoe: His Life* (Baltimore, 1989), p. 459. The *Reading Mercury* (1742) wished "to insert nothing but Facts . . . what they know to be true." R. M. Wiles, *Freshest Advices: Early Provincial Newspapers in England* (Columbus, 1965), p. 193.

33. Frank, *Beginnings of the English Newspaper*, pp. 84, 155; Raymond, *Invention of the Newspaper*, pp. 129–130. *Mercurius Civicus*, Jan. 8, 1645. The plain or "low style" was also favored by the French *Gazette*.

34. When the paper changed editors in 1653, it reverted to more straightforward reporting. For the relationship between newsbooks and pamphlets, see Raymond, *Invention of the Newspaper*, pp. 184–231.

35. *Currant Intelligence*, April 26, 1681. *Daily Current*, in Sommerville, *News Revolution*, p. 14.

36. *A Continuation of Certain Speciall and Remarkable Passages*, quoted in Frank, *Beginnings of the English Newspaper*, p. 68; *Kingdom's Weekly Intelligencer*, quoted in ibid., p. 187. Another wrote that although newsletters were filled "with their own Inventions instead of truth," he would write nothing "But Matters of Fact." *Ravillac Redivivus* (London, 1682), p. 1. See also Joad Raymond, *The Crisis of Eloquence: Reading and Writing English Newsbooks, 1649–69* (Ph.D. dissertation, 1994), p. 102.

37. Quoted in Frank, *Beginnings of the English Newspaper*, p. 70.

38. Ibid.

39. See, for example, *Mercurius Dogmaticus*, *Mercurius Insanus Insanismus*, *Mercurius Phanaticus*, *Mercurius Phreneticus*, and *Phanatick Intelligencer*.

40. John Cleveland, *A Character of a London Diurnal* (London, 1644), p. 1.

41. *The Works of Mr. John Cleveland* (London, 1687), pp. 1, 3. His *Character of a Moderate Intelligencer* maligned the journal for harsh and unpleasant prose, "gross hyperbole, and for telling Lies by the Gross." To call a newsman "an Historian is to knight a Mandrake: 'Tis to . . .

give the Reputation of an Engineer to a Maker of Mouse-traps." "When those weekly Fragments shall pass for History, let the poor man's Box be entitled the Exchequer." "[It] is the Embryo of a History slink'd before Maturity." Ibid., pp. 79–80. See also Cleveland, *Character of a London Diurnal*, pp. 3, 4, 6.

42. See Sutherland, *Restoration Newspaper*; Sommerville, *News Revolution*, pp. 75–97; Peter Fraser, *The Intelligence of the Secretaries of State and Their Monopoly of Licensed News, 1660–1688* (Cambridge, 1956).

43. *Loyal Impartial Mercury*, Sept. 5, 1682.

44. See, for example, *True Domestick Intelligence*, 1679, no. 16, 18, 22, 29, 32, 71; Sutherland, *Restoration Newspaper*, pp. 76–78, 81.

45. See *A True and Perfect Narrative of the late Terrible and Bloody Murther of Sir. Edmondberry Godfrey; Who was found Murthered on Thursday the 17th of this Instant October, in a Field near Primrose Hall, with a full Accompt of the manner of his being Murthered, and in what manner he was Found* (London, 1678), p. 3. See also *A Succinct Narrative of the Bloody Murther of Sir Edmondbury Godfrey* (London, 1683), self-described as "faithfully collected out of the several respective Depositions." For a typical crime report, see *The True and Perfect Account of a Young Man was found dead in a Pond in Wood's Close Fields on Sunday the 7th Instant, in the Parish of . . . supposed to be murdered by some Bloody Villains* or *Bloody News from Clarken-well, being a True Relation of a horrid Murther* (London, 1661); *The Strange and Wonderful Discovery of Mr . . . found Murthered and cast up by the Tyde* (London, 1684); *A Full and True Relation of a most Barbarous and Dreadful Murder: committed on the Body of Mrs. Kirk* (London, 1684); *Murther upon Murther; Being A full and True Relation of a Horrid and Bloody Murther* (London, 1691); *Barbarous and Bloody News . . . being a True Account of two Horrid Murders* (London, 1690). Sensational events such as the killing of Mary Jenkinson, the keeper of the lions in the Tower, by a lion was the kind of news that might appear in broadside, pamphlet, or brief serial form.

46. See *Intelligencer*, Jan. 18, 1663, and Jan. 8, 1664; *Loyal Protestant and True Domestic Intelligencer*, no. 16, 18, 20. See Sutherland, *Restoration Newspaper*, pp. 44–45, 50–59; Sommerville, *News Revolution*, p. 132. Reporting on some political trials was quite full.

47. *The Late Famous Tryal of Mr. Hickeringill* (London, 1681). See also *A Perfect Narrative of the Robbery and Murder . . . of Mr. John Talbot* (London, 1669), p. 38. See also *News From Newgate or An Exact and true Account of the most remarkable Tryals of Several Notorious Malefactors; . . . in the Old Baily* (London, 1674); *The Truest News from the Sessions* (London, 1674); *A True Narrative of the Proceedings at the Sessions House* (London, 1677), p. 2.

48. Roger L'Estrange, *A Brief History of the Times, in a Preface to the Third Volume of Observators* (London, 1687), p. 4.

49. *Loyal Protestant*, March 9, 1680.

50. *A True Account of the Behavior, Last Dying Words and Execution of John Hutchins; Domestick Intelligence*, Nov. 11, 1679; *The Intelligencer*, Jan. 8, 1663, p. 35, and June 20, 1664, p. 393.

51. London, 1684, preface. See also John Temple, *The Irish Rebellion: or an History* (London, 1646), reporting the "latest news from Ireland."

52. London, 1677.

53. *The Military Scribe* (1644), in Frank, *Beginnings of the English Newspaper*, p. 70.

54. Samuel Pepys, *The Portugal History* (London, 1677), p. 2. The press supplied modern historians with "more Store of Matter for a Month than . . . [ancient historians'] Registers and Fasti could do for years." John Oldmixon, *History of England* (London, 1735), p. vii.

55. Laurence Eachard, *The History of the Revolution and the Establishment of England in the Year 1688* (London, 1725), preface.

56. Ibid.

57. Sommerville, *News Revolution*, pp. 66–67.

58. London, 1661.

59. London, 1679. See also *Five Strange Wonders concerning the flying in the Air of a Black Coffin* (London, 1659); *Strange and wonderful News from Chipping Norton . . . of certain dreadful Apparitions* (London, 1679); *Strange News from Lemster . . . being a True Narrative Given Under sev-*

eral *Persons Hands there, of a most Strange and Prodigious Opening of the Earth, . . . Attested by several persons of Worth and Reputation* (London, 1679). This news was "Attested on Oath."

60. London, 1672.

61. London, 1681. The *Protestant Oxford Intelligence* reported a huge cloud shaped like a chariot drawn by four horses and a man holding a spear. No. 4, 1681.

62. London, 1674. See also *The Full and True Relation of a Dreadfull Storm . . . Accompanied with . . . Hail-stones, some of them being above Two Pounds in weight* (London, 1680); *A True Account of the great Damages done by the Late Storm* (London, 1689). *Modest Observations of the Present extraordinary Frost* (1684) promised to be "studious in matter of fact, past," but "sparing as to Sequels."

63. *True Protestant Mercury,* no. 3. See also *Moderate Intelligencer,* no. 24, Aug. 1682; *Royal Protestant, and True Domestick Intelligencer,* no. 8, April 12, 1681. A list of credible witnesses was appended to *A Full and True Relation of the Death and Slaughter of a Man and his Son . . . slain by the Thunder and Lightening* (London, 1680).

64. Robert Hooke's *Philosophical Collections* included "A Relation of a strange Apparition in the Air." V, Feb. 1681–82.

65. Defoe, *The Storm,* preface, p. 58. See also Nathaniel Crouch, *Admirable Curiosities, Rarities and Wonders* (London, 1684).

66. Robert Hooke, "A Discourse of Earthquakes," *Posthumous Works,* ed. Richard Waller (London, 1705), pp. 417, 426. For earthquakes, see *True Protestant Mercury,* no. 3; *Athenian Gazette,* April 25, 1691. See also *A True and Exact Relation of the Late Prodigious Earthquake and Eruption of Mount Aetna* (London, 1669).

67. Nathaniel Crouch, *The General History of Earthquakes* (London, 1684), pp. 127, 128, 150; John Aubrey, *The Natural History of Wiltshire* (Devon, 1969), To the Reader; Oldenburg, *Correspondence,* III, 54, 57. Joseph Williamson, who as secretary of state was responsible for the *Gazette,* was a member of the Royal Society and served as its president from 1677 to 1680.

68. Bacon, "The Advancement of Lerning," *Works,* III, 330; Bacon, "Preparation for a Natural and Experimental History," ibid., XIV, 223; *The Works of Sir William Petty,* ed. Marquis of Lansdowne, 2 vols. (London, 1927), I, 175–178. See also I, 208 ff. Evelyn's plan for the Royal Society library included the category "monsters." Carey, "Compiling Nature's History," pp. 287–288. Thomas Sprat, however, reported that the Royal Society "promise no Wonders, nor endeavor after them." *The History of the Royal Society,* ed. Jackson Cope and H. W. Jones (St. Louis, 1958), p. 318. For a "preternatural philosophy" based on marvels, see Daston and Park, *Wonders and the Order of Nature.*

69. *Strange News from Lemster,* pp. 3, 6, 7.

70. *Mercurius Politicus,* Dec. 3, 1657; Oldenburg, *Correspondence,* II, 277, 280.

71. Rose-Mary Sargent, *The Diffident Naturalist: Robert Boyle and the Philosophy of Experiment* (Chicago, 1995), p. 143; Robert Boyle, *Some Considerations about the Reconcileableness of Reason and Religion* (London, 1675), pp. 54–55. See also Oldenburg, *Correspondence,* II, 177; III, 164, 362. Boyle wrote, "For my part, though I be very backward to believe any strange thing in particular, though but purely natural, unless the testimonies that recommend it be proportionable to the extraordinariness of the thing." *Works,* I, lxxvi. Locke reported a "monstrous" growth to Boyle, noting his interest in such things "even when they seem extravagant." John Locke, *The Correspondence,* 8 vols., ed. E. S. de Beer (Oxford, 1976–89), II, 40. Hooke, however, sometimes had reservations about "Surprisingness," favoring investigation of more obvious but neglected things. Ellen Tan Drake, *Restless Genius: Robert Hooke and His Earthly Thoughts* (New York, 1966), p. 160.

72. *The Intelligencer,* July 13, 1665; Nicholas H. Steneck, "Greatrakes the Stroker: The Interpretations of Historians," *Isis* 73 (1982), 161–177; Eamon Duffy, "Valentine Greatrakes, the Irish Stroker: Miracle, Science, and Orthodoxy in Restoration England," in *Religion and Humanism,* ed. Keith Robbins (Oxford, 1981), pp. 251–273.

73. Experiments could not "suddenly conclude all extraordinary events to be the immediate Finger of God," and many "effects" that once frightened the ignorant were now recog-

nized as having been "brought forth by the common Instruments of Nature." Members were reluctant to assent about "future contingencies" because they were "rigid, in examining all particular matters of Fact." Sprat, *History of the Royal Society*, pp. 359–360.

74. See, for example, *Wonders from the Deep or a true and exact Account and Description of the Monstrous Whale* (London, 1677).

75. *The Marine Mercury, or, A True Relation . . . of a Man-Fish* (London, 1642); James Grant, *The Newspaper Press*, 2 vols. (London, 1871), I, 35–36.

76. John Edwards, *Cometomantia* (London, 1684). See Sara Gentuh, *Comets, Popular Culture, and the Birth of Modern Cosmology* (Princeton, 1997).

77. *Royal Impartial Mercury*, June 9, 1682; Sommerville, *News Revolution*, p. 62. The *Domestick Intelligence* occasionally reported on the activities of the Royal Society and its members. Sept. 19, 1679, and Oct. 31, 1679.

78. Hunter and Wood, "Towards Solomon's House," pp. 59–60.

79. *Athenian Gazette*, May 12, May 19, 1691; preface to vol. VI, Dec. 1, 1691–Jan. 30, 1692.

80. Ibid., vol. 4, Nov. 17, 1691. See Atkinson, *Scientific Discourse*.

81. *True Protestant Mercury*, June 10, 1681.

82. Obadiah Walker, *Of Education, Especially of Young Gentlemen* (Oxford, 1673), pp. 248–249.

Chapter 5: The Facts of Nature I

1. But see R. S. Westfall, *Force in Newton's Physics* (New York, 1971); Norma Emerton, *The Scientific Reinterpretation of Form* (New York, 1984); Jan Wojcik, *Robert Boyle and the Limits of Reason* (Cambridge, 1996); Barbara Shapiro, *Probability and Certainty in Seventeenth-Century England: The Relationships between Religion, Natural Science, Law, History, and Literature* (Princeton, 1983); Lorraine Daston, *Classical Probability in the Enlightenment* (Princeton, 1988); Ian Hacking, *The Emergence of Probability* (New York, 1975); Margaret Osler, "From Immanent Nature to Nature as Artifice: The Interpretation of Final Causes in Seventeenth-Century Natural Philosophy," *The Monist* 79 (1996), 388–407.

2. Steven Shapin and Simon Schaffer, *Leviathan and the Air Pump: Hobbes, Boyle, and the Experimental Life* (Princeton, 1985); Shapin, *The Social History of Truth: Civility and Science in Seventeenth-Century England* (Chicago, 1994); Peter Dear, "Miracles, Experiments, and the Ordinary Course of Nature," *Isis* 81 (1990), 663–683; Dear, *Discipline and Experience: The Mathematical Way in the Scientific Revolution* (Chicago, 1995); Lorraine Daston and Katherine Park, *Wonders and the Order of Nature, 1650–1750* (Cambridge, Mass., 1997). See also Daniel Garber, "Experiment, Community, and the Constitution of Nature in the Seventeenth Century," *Perspectives in Science* 3 (1995), 173–205.

3. See Arno Seifert, *Cognitio Historica* (Berlin, 1976); Paolo Rossi, "Hermeticism, Rationality, and the Scientific Revolution," in *Reason, Experiment, and Mysticism in the Scientific Revolution*, ed. M. L. Bonelli and William R. Shea (New York, 1995), pp. 255–274; Antonio Perez-Ramos, *Francis Bacon's Idea of Science and the Maker's Knowledge Tradition* (Oxford, 1988); Hans Blumenberg, *The Genesis of the Copernican World*, trans. R. M. Wallace (Cambridge, Mass., 1987). See also Brian Vicars, "Francis Bacon and the Progress of Knowledge," *Journal of the History of Ideas* 53 (1992), 495–517. Interest in "fact" as a philosophical topic developed with Mill, Peirce, Bertrand Russell, F. H. Bradley, and Wittgenstein. See Kenneth Russell Olson, *An Essay on Facts* (Stanford, 1987).

4. It was one of the common ways Bodin and others distinguished civil and natural history.

5. See Dear, *Discipline and Experience*. See also Margaret Cook, "Divine Artificer, Corpuscular Mechanism, and Chemical Experiment: Robert Boyle's Experimental Philosophy of Nature" (paper delivered Nov. 11, 1997, at History of Science Society meeting, San Diego). Bacon's experimentally based natural philosophy also rejected the distinction between artificial and inartificial proofs.

6. See Paul Kocher, "Francis Bacon on the Science of Jurisprudence," *Journal of the History of Ideas* 18 (1957), 3–26; Harvey Wheeler, "The Invention of Modern Empiricism: Juridical Foundations of Francis Bacon's Philosophy of Science," *Law Library Journal* 76 (1983), 78–

120; Harvey Wheeler, "Science out of Law: Francis Bacon's Invention of Scientific Empiricism," *Toward a Humanistic Science of Politics: Essays in Honor of F. D. Wormuth,* ed. F. D. Nelson and R. L. Sklar (London, 1983), pp. 101–143; Kenneth Cardwell, "Inquisitio Rerum Ipsarum: Francis Bacon and the Interrogation of Nature" (Ph.D. dissertation, University of California, 1986); Kenneth Cardwell, "Francis Bacon, Inquisitor," in *Francis Bacon's Legacy of Texts,* ed. William A. Sessions (New York, 1990), pp. 269–289; Rose-Mary Sargent, "Scientific Experiment and Legal Expertise: The Way of Experience in the Seventeenth Century," *Studies in the History and Philosophy of Science* 20 (1989), 19–45; Mark Neustadt, "The Making of the Instauration: Science, Politics, and Law in the Career of Francis Bacon" (Ph.D. dissertation, Johns Hopkins University, 1987); Julian Martin, *Francis Bacon, the State, and the Reform of Natural Philosophy* (Cambridge, 1992); Daniel Coquillette, *Francis Bacon* (Stanford, 1992).

7. Francis Bacon, "De augmentis," in *The Works of Francis Bacon,* ed. James Spedding, Robert Leslie Ellis, and Douglas Denon Heath, 14 vols. (London, 1857–74), IV, 193, 292.

8. Bacon, "Novum Organon," book I, aphorism xcviii, *Works,* IV, 94.

9. Bacon, "Great Instauration," *Works,* IV, 19.

10. William Ashworth, "Natural History and the Emblematic World View," *Reappraisals of the Scientific Revolution,* ed. David Lindberg and Robert Westman (Cambridge, 1990), pp. 303–332. See also Michel Foucault, *The Order of Things: An Archeology of the Human Sciences* [1966] (New York, 1973).

11. See Joseph Levine, "Natural History and the History of the Scientific Revolution," *Clio* 13 (1983), 57–73; Alice Stroup, *A Company of Scientists* (Berkeley, 1990); Harold Cook, "The Cutting Edge of a Revolution? Medicine and Natural History near the Shores of the North Sea," in *Renaissance and Revolution: Humanists, Scholars, Craftsmen, and Natural Philosophers in Early Modern Europe,* ed. J. V. Field and Frank James (Cambridge, 1993), pp. 45–61; Nicholas Jardine, J. A. Secord, and E. C. Spary, *Cultures of Natural History* (Cambridge, 1996).

12. Bacon, "Preparative," aphorism ix, *Works,* IV, 261; "Parasceve" (Latin), *Works,* I, 402. See also "Parasceve," *Works,* IV, 252, 254; Paula Findlen, "Francis Bacon and the Reform of Natural History in the Seventeenth Century," in *History and the Disciplines: The Reclassification of Knowledge in Early Modern Europe,* ed. Donald R. Kelley (Rochester, N.Y., 1997), pp. 239–260.

13. Bacon, "Great Instauration," *Works,* IV, 26. Nature was to be interrogated. Bacon, "Preparative towards a Natural and Experimental History," *Works,* IV, 263.

14. Bacon, "Great Instauration," *Works,* IV, 32. See also "Novum Organon," *Works,* IV, 26, 30. Bacon, however, does not use "fact" consistently. "For questions are at our command, though facts are not." *Works,* V, 135. This translation is Cardwell's: "Bacon, Inquisitor," p. 280.

15. See Michael Witmore, "Culture of Accidents: Unexpected Knowledges in Early Modern England" (Ph.D. dissertation, University of California, Berkeley, 1997); Katherine Park and Lorraine Daston, "Unnatural Conceptions: The Study of Monsters in Sixteenth- and Seventeenth-Century France and England," *Past and Present* 92 (1981), 20–54.

16. Bacon, "Parasceve," aphorism viii, *Works,* IV, 260. Traditional natural history was "very different from that kind of history which I have in view." "Advancement of Learning," *Works,* IV, 299. See also "Parasceve," *Works,* IV, 252, 254.

17. See "Great Instauration," *Works,* IV, 12, 19, 32; "Novum Organon," book I, aphorism cxii, *Works,* IV, 102; aphorism cxxiv, *Works,* IV, 110. See also I, 203, 218; IV, 123. In the latter he used *de facto naturae.* See *Works,* I, 210. He also referred to the "inquisition of the fact itself" [*inquisitio facti ipsius*], *Works,* IV, 123; I, 232. See also "Preparative," aphorism ix, *Works,* IV, 261. In new and particularly subtle experiments it was necessary to show how the experiment was conducted so as to allow others to determine "whether the information obtained . . . be trustworthy or fallacious." *Works,* IV, 161.

18. "Great Instauration," *Works,* IV, 291. See also "Parasceve," *Works,* IV, 252.

19. Nature was to be interrogated, vexed, coerced, and manipulated in various ways to yield information. For Bacon's use of "inquisitio," see Cardwell, "Bacon, Inquisitor."

20. For "transmutation histories" providing narratives of matter of fact replete with witnesses and designation of exact times and places, see Laurence Principe, *The Aspiring Adept: Robert Boyle and the Alchemical Quest* (Princeton, 1998).

21. Thomas Hobbes, *Leviathan*, ed. M. Oakeshott (New York, 1962), p. 69.

22. Ibid., p. 45. "And whereas sense and memory are but knowledge of fact, which a thing past and irrevocable; Science is the knowledge of consequences, and dependence of one fact upon another" (p. 45). "Regular effects" might be a storehouse for prudence, which was "nothing but to conjecture from experience." Thomas Hobbes, *The Elements of Law*, in *English Works*, 11 vols., ed. William Molesworth (1839–45; reprint Aalen, Germany, 1962), IV, 16, 18.

23. Robert Hooke suggested that hypotheses might be "confirm'd by Fact or Effect." Hooke, *Posthumous Works*, ed. Richard Waller (London, 1705), p. 536.

24. William Harvey, *Disputations Touching the Generation of Animals* (Oxford, 1981), trans. Gweneth Whitteridge. Harvey's methods, however, were not those of the natural historian.

25. John Henry, "The Scientific Revolution in England," in *The Scientific Revolution in National Context*, ed. Roy Porter and Mikulas Teich (Cambridge, 1992), pp. 202–203; J. A. Bennett, "The Magnetical Philosophy," *Journal of the History of Astronomy* 12 (1981), 165–177.

26. John Aubrey, *Brief Lives*, ed. O. L. Dick (1949; reprint Ann Arbor, Mich., 1957), p. 320. *Philosophical Transactions* IV (1669), Dedicatory Letter to Seth Ward. Daniel Garber contrasts Baconian and Restoration Royal Society "facts," suggesting that the former were individual and the latter social. Garber, "Experiment." For the Hartlib circle, see Charles Webster, *The Great Instauration* (London, 1975). For Oxford, see Barbara J. Shapiro, *John Wilkins: An Intellectual Biography* (Berkeley, 1968), pp. 118–147; Shapiro, "Science and the Universities in Seventeenth-Century England," *Journal of British Studies* 10 (1971), 47–82; Margaret Purver, *The Royal Society: Concept and Creation* (Cambridge, Mass., 1967); Robert G. Frank, *Harvey and the Oxford Physiologists* (Berkeley, 1980).

27. Thomas Sprat, *The History of the Royal Society*, ed. Jackson Cope and H. W. Jones (St. Louis, 1958), pp. 70, 83, 99, 100. By the 1670s there were serious attendance problems. If members might take issue with some of Sprat's statements, there is no indication that he misrepresented Society views on the centrality of "matters of fact."

28. See Peter Dear, "Totius in Verba: Rhetoric and Authority in the Early Royal Society," *Isis* 76 (1985), 145–161.

29. Joseph Glanvill, *A Prefatory Answer to Mr. Henry Stubbe* (London, 1671), pp. 143–144; Glanvill, *Scepsis Scientifica* (London, 1665), p. 118; Glanvill, *Essays on Several Important Subjects in Philosophy and Religion* (London, 1676), essay II, pp. 46, 49–50.

30. Glanvill, *Essays*, essay VI, pp. 48–49, 56; essay I, p. 15. See also Glanvill, *Scepsis Scientifica*, Address to the Royal Society.

31. Henry Oldenburg, *Correspondence*, ed. and trans. A. R. Hall and M. B. Hall, 13 vols. (Madison, Wis., 1965–86), VIII, 538; VII, 260; III, 525. See also II, 14; XIII, 397; *Philosophical Transactions* I (1665–66), 65. See also pp. 130, 150.

32. Oldenburg, *Correspondence*, II, 401. See also III, 8–9, 384; M. B. Hall, "Science in the Early Royal Society," in *The Emergence of Science in Western Europe*, ed. Maurice Crosland (New York, 1976), pp. 57–78; John Henry, "The Origins of Modern Science: Henry Oldenburg's Contribution," *British Journal of the History of Science* 21 (1988), 103–110.

33. See Henry, "Scientific Revolution in England," pp. 178–209; K. Theodore Hoppen, "The Nature of the Early Royal Society," part 2, *British Journal for the History of Science* 9 (1976), 243–273; Michael Hunter, *Establishing the New Science* (Woodbridge, Suffolk, 1989), pp. 45–71; Oldenburg, *Correspondence*, V, 263.

34. Robert Hooke, *Lectures and Collections* (London, 1678), pp. 22–24. See also Ewen A. Whitaker, "Selenography in the Seventeenth Century," *History of Astronomy* 2, 119–143.

35. Quoted in David R. Oldroyd, "Some Writings of Robert Hooke on Procedures for the Prosecution of Scientific Inquiry, Including His 'Lectures of Things Requisite to a Natral History,'" *Notes and Records of the Royal Society* 41 (1987), 146–47, 152, 157.

36. Quoted in Ibid., pp. 152, 157.

37. R. T. Gunther, *Early Science in Oxford*, 15 vols. (Oxford, 1920–45), VI, 112.

38. Oldenburg, *Correspondence*, II, 383.

39. Humphrey Ridley, *Anatomy of the Brain* (London, 1695), preface; Peter Wyche, trans., *A*

Short Relation of the River Nile (London, 1669), preface; Robert Hooke, "Cometa," in *Lectiones Cutlerianae* (London, 1678), p. 34; *An Attempt to Prove the Motion of the Earth from Observation* (London, 1674), preface; *Philosophical Transactions* I (1665–66), 65; Oldenburg, *Correspondence*, II, 383, 384; John Ray, *The Wisdom of God* (London, 1692), preface. See also pp. 49, 126; Francis Willughby, *The Ornithology* (London, 1678), preface; John Evelyn, *Sylva* (London, 1664). For Lister, see Oldenburg, *Correspondence*, VII, 342. See also VII, 437, 462, 492; VIII, 318. For Wallis, see ibid., IX, 307. For Newton, see Stephen Rigaud, *Correspondence of Scientific Men of the Seventeenth Century*, 2 vols. (Oxford, 1841), II, 386.

40. John Woodward, *An Essay toward a Natural History of the Earth* (London, 1695); Hans Sloane, *A Voyage to the Islands Madera, Barbadoes, . . . with the Natural History*, 2 vols. (London, 1701), I, preface. Sloane used "phenomenon" synonymously with "Matter of Fact." Arthur MacGregor, *Sir Hans Sloane* (London, 1994), p. 14.

41. Oldenburg, *Correspondence*, III, 162. Sprat, in emphasizing the Royal Society's "submissive way of Registring nothing, but Histories, and Relations," also noted that "they have left room for others, . . . to change, to augment, to approve, to contradict them." *History of the Royal Society*, p. 116.

42. Shapin and Schaffer, *Leviathan and the Air Pump*; Marie Boas Hall, *Robert Boyle and Seventeenth-Century Chemistry* (Cambridge, 1958); James Jacob, *Robert Boyle and the English Revolution* (New York, 1977); Frederick O. Toole, "Robert Boyle's Concept of Science and Nature" (unpublished paper); Rose-Mary Sargent, *The Diffident Naturalist: Robert Boyle and the Philosophy of Experiment* (Chicago, 1995); Jan W. Wojcik, *Robert Boyle and the Limits of Reason* (Cambridge, 1997); Michael Hunter, ed., *Robert Boyle Revisited* (Cambridge, 1994); Margaret Osler, "The Intellectual Sources of Robert Boyle's Philosophy of Nature: Gassendi's Volunteerism and Boyle's Physico-Theological Project," in *Philosophy, Science, and Religion in England, 1640–1700*, ed. Richard Kroll, Richard Ashcraft, and Perez Zagorin, (Cambridge, 1992); Lawrence Principe, *Aspiring Adept: Robert Boyle and the Alchemical Quest* (Princeton, 1998).

43. But see Garber, "Experiment."

44. Robert Boyle, *General Heads for the Natural History of a Country, Great or Small Drawn Out for the Use of Travellers and Navigators* (London, 1692), p. 1.

45. Robert Boyle, *New Experiments Touching the Spring of Air* (London, 1662), preface; Robert Boyle, *The Christian Virtuoso* (London, 1690), p. 52; Robert Boyle, *The Works of the Honourable Robert Boyle*, ed. Thomas Birch, 6 vols. (London, 1772), II, 742, 744; I, 34. See Robert Kargon, "The Testimony of Nature: Boyle, Hooke, and Experimental Philosophy," *Albion* 3 (1971), 72–81.

46. Boyle, *Works*, VI, 524, 525; Boyle, *Christian Virtuoso*, pp. 57–58.

47. See Shapin, *Social History of Truth*. For a critique, see Sargent, "Scientific Experiment and Legal Expertise."

48. Boyle, "Experimental and Observationes Physicae," *Works*, V, 569; Boyle, "Certain Physiological Essays," *Works*, I, 313–314. See also Oldenburg, *Correspondence*, II, 177.

49. Robert Plot, *The Natural History of Oxfordshire*, 2d ed. (Oxford, 1705), To the Reader; Royal Society, Original Letters, I, fol. 177; Oldenburg, *Correspondence*, VII, 23–28; William Derham, *Philosophical Letters* (London, 1718), p. 175.

50. Thomas Birch, *The History of the Royal Society*, 4 vols. (London, 1760), I, 32, 33; Robert Hooke, *Micrographia* (London, 1665). [Matthew Hale], *Observations Touching the Principles of Natural Motions* (London, 1677), Preface to the Reader. Hale thought Bacon and his followers distinguished their approach too sharply from that of Aristotle. *Observations*, p. 105.

51. Sprat, *History of the Royal Society*, p. 215. Many reports, however, were incapable of experimental proof.

52. Henry Power, *Experimental Philosophy . . . With some Deductions, and Probable Hypotheses raised from them* (London, 1664), p. 58.

53. Richard Lower, *Justification of the Discourse on Fevers by Thomas Willis* [1665] (Oxford, 1983), p. 215. See also p. 218; *A Brief Account of Mr. Valentine Greatrakes and Divers of the Strange Cures* (London, 1666), pp. 37, 40.

54. Oldenburg approached diplomats Sir John Finch, Sir Paul Rycaut, and Sir Robert South-well to contribute to their "philosophical correspondence." The Society wished "all sorts of Intelligent and Publick minded men in all parts of the world to contribute." Diplomat members of the Royal Society, often viewed as inactive because rarely present, thus contributed substantially to the Society's endeavors. Sir Joseph Williamson, secretary of state, a member since 1663, served as president from 1677 to 1680. See Oldenburg, *Correspondence*, III, 525; VII, 8–9; IX, 338; X, 483; Royal Society Letterbook I, Original Letters, fols. 299, 303, 336.

55. Oldenburg, *Correspondence*, III, 525; VII, 8–9; Margaret Deacon, *Scientists and the Sea, 1650–1900* (New York, 1971), p. 84; Hooke quoted in David R. Oldroyd, "Geological Controversy in the Seventeenth Century: 'Hooke vs Wallis' and Its Aftermath," in *Robert Hooke: New Studies*, ed. Michael Hunter and Simon Schaffer (Woodbridge, Suffolk, 1989), pp. 223–224; Edmund Halley, *An Historical Account of the Trade-Winds and Monsoon, observable in the Tropics*, in William Derham, *Miscellanea Curiosa*, 2 vols., 3d ed. (London, 1726), I, 61.

56. Sprat, *History of the Royal Society*, p. 200; Henry Stubbe, *Legends No Histories* (London, 1670), pp. 21, 120. For emphasis on the positive role of merchants, see Mary Poovey, *A History of the Modern Fact: Problems of Knowledge in the Sciences of Wealth and Society* (Chicago, 1998).

57. Boyle's interest in projects connected with the sea led him to rely on seamen of varying status. Deacon, *Scientists and the Sea*, pp. 119, 112, 124, 126, 127, 134.

58. Sprat, *History of the Royal Society*, pp. 432, 72. Sprat overestimated the contributions that merchants and husbandmen would make. He admitted many reports lacked "sufficient confirmation to raise Theories, or Histories on them." Ibid., p. 195.

59. Ibid., p. 257; Oldroyd, "Some Writings of Robert Hooke," pp. 157–158; Royal Society, Original Letters, II, fol. 281. See also W. E. Houghton, "The History of Trades: Its Relation to Seventeenth-Century Scientific Thought," in *Roots of Scientific Thought: A Cultural Perspective*, ed. P. P. Wiener and A. Holand (New York, 1957), pp. 354–381; K. H. Ochs, "The Royal Society of London's History of Trade Programme," *Notes and Records of the Royal Society* 39 (1985), 129–158.

60. Oldenburg, *Correspondence*, IV, 337; Oldroyd, "Some Writings of Robert Hooke," pp. 165–167; John Aubrey, *The Natural History and Antiquities of the County of Surrey* (London, 1718–19), p. 410.

61. Shapin and Schaffer, *Leviathan and the Air Pump*; Shapin, *Social History of Truth*; Sargent, *Diffident Naturalist*.

62. Oldenburg, *Correspondence*, X, 198. He favored using "Register-books of Merchants, English and Dutch, to observe" natural rarities. Ibid.

63. Shapin, *Social History of Truth*, p. 293, quoting from Boyle, *Certain Physiological Essays*.

64. Boyle, "Experimenta et observationes physicae," *Works*, V, 608. See also *Works*, V, 605, 607.

65. Boyle, *Works*, III, 396, 442–445. For earlier connections between craftsmen and gentleman investigators, see Leslie Cormack, *Charting an Empire: Geography at the English Universities, 1580–1620* (Chicago, 1997), p. 51.

66. Boyle, "Certain Physiological Essays," *Works*, I, 306, 314. Observation required "either skill or curiosity, or both in the Observer." Boyle, "The Usefulness of Experimental Philosophy," *Works*, III, 472.

67. R. S. Westfall, "Unpublished Boyle Papers Relating to Scientific Method," *Annals of Science* 12 (1956), 71, 73. See also Boyle, *Some Considerations about the Reconcileableness of Reason and Religion* (London, 1675), p. 61.

68. Boyle, *Christian Virtuoso*, p. 72.

69. Quoted in Oldroyd, "Some Writings of Robert Hooke," p. 152. Shapin, *Social History of Truth*, pp. 363, 365, 376, 383, 392; Shapin, "Who Was Robert Hooke?" in *Robert Hooke: New Studies*, ed. Michael Hunter and Simon Schaffer (Woodbridge, Suffolk, 1989), pp. 253–286. But see Ellen Tan Drake, *Restless Genius: Robert Hooke and His Earthly Thoughts* (New York, 1966); *The Diary of Robert Hooke, 1672–1680*, ed. Henry Robinson and Walter Adams (London, 1935).

70. For Boyle, "faithfulness in truly delivering what he knows" was one of two essential qual-

ities of a witness. Oldenburg, *Correspondence*, I, 434; VII, 8–9; VIII, 538; Boyle, *Works*, I, 314; Boyle, *Christian Virtuoso*, pp. 52–72.

71. Boyle, however, questioned More's competence and implied that More was subject to "hallucinations." Shapin, *Social History of Truth*, pp. 297–298. See also "A Calculation of the Certainty of Humane Testimony," *Philosophical Transactions* XXXI (Oct. 1699), 359–360.

72. Royal Society, Original Letters, III, fol. 14.

73. See *The Four Footed Beast* (London, 1668), Dedicatory Letter; Derham, *Miscellanea Curiosa*, I, 61. Oldenburg, in connection with a strange case of triplets, wrote that though the report came from "an excellent Oculist," the Society wished the "double attestation" of the two physicians present. *Correspondence*, I, 277, 280.

74. Robert Hooke, *Micrographia* (London, 1665), preface; *Philosophical Experiments and Observations*, ed. William Derham (London, 1726), pp. 27, 28; Oldroyd, "Some Writings of Robert Hooke," p. 158. Leeuwenhoek in 1677 sent testimonials from eight witnesses to support his observations. Edward G. Ruestow, *The Microscope in the Dutch Republic: The Shaping of Discovery* (Cambridge, 1996), pp. 154–155.

75. Robert Boyle, "Some Considerations about the Reconcileableness of Reason and Religion," *Works*, IV, 182.

76. Sir Matthew Hale, *The Primitive Origination of Mankind* (London, 1678), p. 128. An anonymous article in the *Philosophical Transactions* attempted to calculate how increasing numbers of concurrent reports might approximate moral certainty. A single witness might be certain to half a full certainty; the second with the first yielded three-fourths; the third, seven-eighths. By the tenth it would reach 1023/1024 of certainty, and the twentieth, over two million to one. "Calculation of the Certainty of Humane Testimony." XXXI (1669), 359–360.

77. Michael Hunter and Paul B. Wood, "Towards Solomon's House: Rival Strategies for Reforming the Early Royal Society," *History of Science* 24 (1986), 79.

78. Harvey Wheeler and Rose-Mary Sargent suggest that scientific principles and legal principles were developed by similar procedures. See Wheeler, "Science out of Law"; Sargent, "Scientific Experiment and Legal Expertise"; Sargent, *Diffident Naturalist*, pp. 42–61. It is difficult to see how Coke's distinction between ordinary reason and the reason of the law, accessible only to judges and lawyers of long experience, can be equated to Boyle's use of the term "reason," which rejects arcane learning. Jurists distinguished between the unchanging laws of nature and the mutable laws of man, recognizing that different nations operated according to different legal principles. Common and civil laws thus might treat the same set of facts differently. English judges would not, as Sargent suggests, have recognized their activity as "interpreting facts." Nor would naturalists have thought that principles regulating natural phenomena would vary from place to place and time to time.

79. Oldenburg, *Correspondence*, III, 163.

80. Christopher Merret, *Self-Conviction: Or an Enumeration of the Absurdities, . . . [and] Falsities in Matters of Fact* (London, 1670).

81. Differences of opinion with respect to hypotheses would be far less difficult to deal with because they were, by definition, uncertain. See Chapter 6.

82. Hevelius, a wealthy magistrate, was "Europe's premier telescopic observer." Albert Van Helden, "Telescopes and Authority from Galileo to Cassini," *Osiris*, 2d ser., 9 (1994), 19. Both Hevelius and Auzout were members.

83. Oldenburg, *Correspondence*, II, 653.

84. *Philosophical Transactions* IX (Feb. 1666), 150–151.

85. Oldenburg, *Correspondence*, III, 6.

86. Oldenburg, *Correspondence*, III, 6, 24, 30, 170–171, 219. Gilles De Launay also referred to the Royal Society as a "tribunal." Ibid., IV, 218.

87. Oldenburg, *Correspondence*, III, 219, 324; Royal Society, Original Letters, II, fol. 376. *Philosophical Transactions* I (1665–66), 151; Oldenburg, *Correspondence*, II, 653. For a somewhat different interpretation, see Shapin, *Social History of Truth*, pp. 286–289. Disputes over astronomical "facts" were not unusual. Eugene Fairfield MacPike, *Hevelius, Flamsteed, and*

Halley: Three Contemporary Astronomers and Their Mutual Relations (London, 1937), pp. 81–102; Van Helden, "Telescopes and Authority," pp. 9–29.

88. Oldenburg, *Correspondence*, VII, 284. See also VII, 286.

89. Extreme cold seemed incredible to those living in the Congo. East Indian travelers were disbelieved when they claimed that a "fluid body of water" could, in a few hours, become a solid and compact body, such as ice. Quoted in Shapin, *Social History of Truth*; Boyle, "New Experiments and Observations touching Cold," *Works*, II, 477, 573.

90. Galileo contrasts the "eyes of an idiot" with those of a "careful and practiced anatomist or philosopher." "Letter to the Grand Duchess Christina," in *Discoveries and Opinions of Galileo*, trans. Stillman Drake (New York, 1957), p. 196. For Descartes, inventions that increased the power of the senses were "undoubtedly among the most useful there can be." *The Philosophical Writings of Descartes*, trans. and ed. J. Cottingham et al. (Cambridge, 1985), p. 152. See also Albert Van Helden, "The Birth of the Modern Scientific Instrument, 1550–1700," in *The Uses of Science in the Age of Newton*, ed. John J. Burke (Berkeley, 1983), pp. 49–84; J. A. Bennett, "The Mechanics' Philosophy and the Mechanical Philosophy," *History of Science* 24 (1986), 1–28.

91. Experimentalists without sense-enhancing instruments were no more than "empty conjecturalists." Power, *Experimental Philosophy*, preface. See also Oldroyd, "Some Writings of Robert Hooke," pp. 145–167; Sprat, *History of the Royal Society*, pp. 94, 246–252, 384–385; William Gibson, "The Medical Interests of Christopher Wren," in *Some Aspects of Seventeenth-Century Medicine and Science* (Los Angeles, 1969), p. 8.

92. Hooke, *Micrographia*, preface. Instruments immensely extended Hooke's "empirical horizon." See Catherine Wilson, *The Invisible World: Early Modern Philosophy and the Invention of the Microscope* (Princeton, 1995). Nehemiah Grew also spoke of revealing "a new world." *Anatomy of Plants* (London, 1682), preface. Boyle wrote, "If we were sharp-sighted enough, or had such perfect microscopes, . . . our promoted senses might discern" the minute differences that explain colors we see in visible objects. Boyle, *Works*, V, 680. Microscopes would provide sight of what the "Atomical and Corpuscularian Philosophers durst but imagine." Power, *Experimental Philosophy*, preface. See also Sprat, *History of the Royal Society*, pp. 384–385; Joseph Glanvill, *Plus Ultra* (London, 1668), p. 57; Ruestow, *Microscope in the Dutch Republic*, pp. 15, 17–18, 24.

93. Wilson, *Invisible World*, pp. 57, 68, 100. See also ibid., pp. 140–175.

94. It was recognized, however, that instruments had their problems. Leeuwenhoek's observations were doubted in part because his critics were unable to obtain similar instruments and because Royal Society members did not see what Leeuwenhoek claimed to have seen, even though witnesses vouched for him. Microscopists were aware of the difficulties in interpreting what had been observed. Enthusiasm abated after 1690. See Wilson, *Invisible World*, pp. 100–101, 215–256; Oldenburg, *Correspondence*, II, 653. Astronomical disputes sometimes turned on the issue of instrument quality. See Robert Hooke, *Animadversions on the First Part of the Machina Coelestis of . . . Johannes Hevelius* (London, 1674).

95. Hale, *Primitive Origination of Mankind*, p. 130.

96. Sprat, *History of the Royal Society*, pp. 214–215, 243–245.

97. *Philosophical Transactions* I (1665–66), 193; Boyle, *Works*, III, 614–615, 624–628.

98. John Woodward, *The Natural History of the Earth* (London, 1726), p. 158.

99. Quoted in Michael Hunter, *Science and the Shape of Orthodoxy* (Woodbridge, Suffolk, 1995), p. 182.

100. Robert Hooke, "A Discourse of Earthquakes," in *The Posthumous Works of Robert Hooke*, ed. Richard Waller (London, 1705), p. 335. See also p. 321. Hooke wrote, "I conceive it Lawful and Philosophical to Jurare in Verba, when Nature speakes or dictates." Quoted in Drake, *Restless Genius*, p. 324.

101. Boyle, "An Hydrostatical Discourse," *Works*, III, 626.

102. William Derham, *Philosophical Letters* (London, 1718), p. 62.

103. *Martin Lister's English Spiders* (1678), trans. M. Davies and B. Harley (Colchester, 1992), p. 48.

104. Moses Pitt's *English Atlas* exhibited "a true Representation of the Universe . . . there being nothing more conducive to the assistance of the understanding and memory than a plain
simple, clear and uncompounded representation of the Object of the Sense." Preface. He
suggested "pictures of . . . Observables" could show what might "not otherwise be so fully and
sensibly expressed by Verbal Description." Robert Hooke, *Of the True Method of Building a Solid
Philosophy, or of a Philosophical Algebra*, in *Posthumous Works*, p. 64. See also John T. Harwood,
"Rhetoric and Graphics in *Micrographia*," in *Robert Hooke: New Studies*, ed. Michael Hunter
and Simon Schaffer (Woodbridge, Suffolk, 1989), pp. 119–147; Michael Aaron Dennis,
"Graphic Understanding: Instruments and Interpretation in Robert Hooke's *Micrographia*,"
Science in Context 3 (1989), 309–364. Hooke's microscopic illustrations were composites of
repeated observations, not records of particular observations. *Micrographia*, Preface. See also
Wilson, *Invisible World*, pp. 86–88. For Hooke's illustrative sketches, see Oldroyd, "Some
Writings of Robert Hooke," pp. 147, 155–156. Hooke had been apprenticed to a portrait
painter and considered a career as a painter. Drake, *Restless Genius*, p. 11.

Evelyn provided engravings of natural objects he had seen himself or for which he had
"unquestionable testimony." *Sylva* (London, 1664), preface. For Evelyn, a collection of prints
was "a kind of Encyclopedia of all intelligibles, and memorable things that either are, or have
been *in rerum Natura*." Richard Nicolas, *The Diaries of Robert Hooke, the Leonardo of London,
1635–1703* (Lewes, Sussex, 1994), p. 141. See also Willughby, *Ornithology*; Nehemiah Grew,
Musaeum Regalis Societatis (London, 1681); Eleazar Albin, *A Natural History of English Insects*
(London, 1724). John Ray noted that many "looked upon a history of plants without figures
as a book of geography without maps." Ray, *Correspondence*, 1848, p. 155, quoted in Gill Saun-
ders, *Picturing Plants* (Berkeley, 1995), p. 7. See also Robert W. Unwin, "A Provincial Man of
Science at Work: Martin Lister, F.R.S., and His Illustrators, 1670–1683," *Notes and Records of
the Royal Society* 49 (1995), 202–230.

For Dutch painters and natural history, see Ruestow, *Microscope in the Dutch Republic*,
pp. 48–56, 68–77, 134–136. See also Mary G. Winkler and Albert Van Helden, "Represent-
ing the Heavens: Galileo and Visual Astronomy," *Isis* 83 (1991), 195–217; Winkler and Van
Helden, "Johannes Hevelius and the Visual Language of Astronomy," in *Renaissance and
Revolution: Humanists, Scholars, Craftsmen, and Natural Philosophers in Early Modern Europe*, ed.
J. V. Fields and Frank James (Cambridge, 1993), pp. 97–116.

105. Steven Shapin, "Pump and Circumstance: Robert Boyle's Literary Technology," *Social
Studies of Science* 20 (1982), 481–520. Peter Dear suggests that circumstantial detail was provided to enhance the sense of actuality. Dear, "Narratives, Anecdotes, and Experiments:
Turning Experience into Science in the Seventeenth Century," in *The Literary Structure of Scientific Argument*, ed. Dear (Philadelphia, 1991), pp. 135–163.

106. Hooke, *Posthumous Works*, p. 63. See also Hooke, *Philosophical Experiments and Observations*, pp. 26–28; Boyle, "Certain Physiological Essays," *Works*, I, 314.

107. Sprat, *History of the Royal Society*, p. 73.

108. Ibid. See also p. 7. Evelyn referred to the Society as "acute and learned Judges." John
Evelyn, *A Philosophical Discourse of Earth* (London, 1676), p. 8.

109. Wilkins related judgment to evidence. *Essay Towards a Real Character and a Philosophical
Language* (London, 1668), p. 202.

110. See Oldenburg, *Correspondence*, IX, 658; II, 27; Hooke, *Micrographia*, preface. For Newton, see Rigaud, *Correspondence of Scientific Men*, II, 317. See also Peter Dear, "From Truth to
Disinterestedness in the Seventeenth Century," *Social Studies of Science* 22 (1992), 619–632.

111. Royal Society, Boyle Letters, I, 108r, 131r; Boyle, "New Experiments," *Works*, II, 626;
Oldenburg, *Correspondence*, III, 342; Woodward, *Natural History of the Earth*, preface.

112. Locke's views and role are discussed in Chapter 8.

113. See W. B. Brockliss, "The Scientific Revolution in France," in *The Scientific Revolution in
National Context*, ed. Roy Porter and Mikulas Teich (Cambridge, 1992), pp. 55–89; Roger
Hahn, *The Anatomy of a Scientific Institution: The Paris Academy of Sciences, 1666–1803* (Berkeley, 1971); Robin Briggs, "The Académie Royale des Sciences and the Pursuit of Utility," *Past
and Present* 131 (1991), 38–87; Dear, *Discipline and Experience*.

114. Rabelais, however, used the expression "des faictz de nature." Cited in Edwin M. Duval, *The Design of Rabelais's Pantagruel* (New Haven, 1991), p. 49. "Faict" was sometimes used in the medieval era in referring to monsters (I owe this information to Michael Witmore). See also Stroup, *Company of Scientists*; Lorraine Daston, "Strange Facts, Plain Facts, and the Texture of Scientific Experience in the Enlightenment," in *Proof and Persuasion: Essays on Authority, Objectivity, and Evidence*, ed. S. Marchand and E. Lunbeck (Brepols, Belgium, 1996), pp. 42–59; Christian Licoppe, *Le formation de la pratique scientifique: Le discours de l'expérience en France et en Angleterre (1630–1820)* (Paris, 1996).

115. Christian Huygens felt the Académie des Sciences should concentrate on a "natural history . . . according to the plan of Verulamus." R. Hooykaas, "The Rise of Modern Science: When and Why?" *British Journal of the History of Science* 20 (1987), 453–473. Auzout in 1666 used "fait" in connection with his observations of comets. Oldenburg, *Correspondence*, III, 294; Stroup, *Company of Scientists*, pp. 66–67, 69, 71, 73. See also D. Dodart, *Mémoires pour servir à l'histoire des plantes* (1676); Rio C. Howard, "Guy de la Brosse and the Jardin des plantes in Paris," in *The Analytic Spirit*, ed. Harry Woolf (Ithaca, 1981), pp. 195–224; Harold J. Cook, "Physicians and Natural History," in *Cultures of Natural History*, ed. Nicolas Jardine, J. A. Secord, and E. C. Spary (Cambridge, 1996), p. 102.

116. *Mémoires pour servir à l'histoire naturelle des animaux* (Paris, 1671), preface. A translation was ordered by the Royal Society in 1688. I quote from the translation unless otherwise indicated. Perrault's "Projet pour les expériences et observations anatomiques" employs two categories, fact (*de fait*) and law. The latter seems to refer to explanation. "Fait" covered witnesses of sight and touch, law, reasoning, and interpretation. Experiment involved both. Preface.

117. Perrault, *Mémoires*, preface. See also Kevin John Muhall, *Claude Perrault, 1613–1688, ou, la curiosité d'un classique* (Paris, 1988), pp. 44–45. For fact and hypothesis, see ibid.

118. Perrault, *Mémoires*, preface.

119. Ibid. For the rhetoric of proof in the Academy, see Licoppe, *La formation de la pratique scientifique*, pp. 52–87.

120. Sprat, *History of the Royal Society*, pp. 125–126, 253; Oldenburg, *Correspondence*, III, 140; IV, 153, 192. For Huygens's adoption of the first-person narrative for experiments, see Licoppe, *La formation de la pratique scientifique*, p. 61.

121. Bernard de Fontenelle, *Memoirs of the Royal Academy of Science*, preface, cited in Derham, *Miscellanea Curiosa*. See also Hahn, *Anatomy of a Scientific Institution*, pp. 26, 28, 32, 33. The collective review of facts and experiments was typical of the period 1667–92. It was replaced by collective adjudication of individual projects. Ibid., p. 28. Fontenelle's *Elogium of Sir Isaac Newton* (London, 1708) referred to Newton's experiments as "matters of fact" (p. 17).

The adoption of "fact" by French naturalists was not recognized in seventeenth-century dictionaries. See *Le dictionnaire de l'Académie Française*, 2 vols. (1694). By the mid-eighteenth century "fait" had become part of the vocabulary of both English and French natural investigators. The *Encyclopédie, ou Dictionnaire Raisonné des Sciences, des Arts, et des Métiers* (1761) noted its uses in law, history, and natural philosophy (VI, 383). The entry discussed witnessing and precautions against passion and prejudice. Buffon wrote that both civil and natural history were founded "sur des faits." Quoted in Seifert, *Cognitio Historica*, p. 181n.

In France, too, the "discourse of fact" appears to have been associated with a relatively plain style. In 1699 the Académie des Sciences "declared that nature would appear there quite unadorned, not having thought fit to borrow from the gentlemen of the *Académie française* any of the finery and bedizenments they have in stock." Quoted in Paul Hazard, *The European Mind, 1680–1715*, trans. J. Lewis May (Cleveland, 1963), p. 310. See also Christian Licoppe, "The Crystallization of a New Narrative Form in Experimental Reports (1660–1690)," *Science in Context* 7 (1994), 205–244.

122. Daston, "Strange Facts, Plain Facts," pp. 42–59.

123. See David Goodman, "The Scientific Revolution in Spain and Portugal," in *The Scientific Revolution in National Context*, ed. Roy Porter and Mikulas Teich (Cambridge, 1992), pp. 178–210; David Goodman, "Iberian Science: Navigation, Empire, and Counter-Reformation," in *The Rise of Scientific Europe*, ed. David Goodman and Colin Russell (Kent, 1991), p. 125;

R. Hooykaas, *Humanists and the Voyages of Discovery in Sixteenth-Century Portuguese and Letters* (Amsterdam, 1979), pp. 14–15; Antonello Gerbi, *Nature in the New World*, trans. J. Moyle (Pittsburgh, 1985); Anthony Pagden, "Ius et Factum: Text and Experience in the Writings of Bartolomé de las Casas," in *New World Encounters*, ed. Stephen Greenblatt (Berkeley, 1991), pp. 91, 94; Paula Findlen, "Courting Nature," in *Cultures of Natural History*, ed. Nicolas Jardine, J. A. Secord, and E. C. Spary (Cambridge, 1996), pp. 57–74. See also Margaret Hodgen, *Early Anthropology in the Sixteenth and Seventeenth Centuries* (Philadelphia, 1964); Howard F. Cline, "The Relaciones Geográficas of the Spanish Indies, 1577–1586," *Hispanic American Historical Review* 44 (1964), 341–374; Anthony Pagden, *European Encounters with the New World* (New Haven, 1993), pp. 55, 57, 58, 60–61, 74–75, 82–83; José de Acosta, *The Naturall and Morall History of the Indies* (London, 1604); Daniel Banes, "The Portuguese Voyages and the Discovery and the Emergence of Modern Science," *Journal of the Washington Academy of Sciences* 28 (1988), 47–88. Like most European legal systems, that of Spain distinguished between fact (*hecho*) and law (*derecho*).

124. I wish to thank Justin Suran and Harold Cook for assistance with Dutch materials. The closest equivalents to "matter of fact" and "matter of law" appear to be "een feitelijke kwestie" and "een rechskwestie." Cook suggests that the term "werkelijk" was closer to Dutch use in natural history and medicine than "feit."

125. See Harold J. Cook, "The New Philosophy in the Low Countries," in *The Scientific Revolution in National Context*, ed. Roy Porter and Mikulas Teich (Cambridge, 1992), pp. 115–149; Cook, "Cutting Edge of a Revolution?" pp. 45–61; L. C. Palm, "Leeuwenhoek and Other Dutch Correspondents of the Royal Society," *Notes and Records of the Royal Society* 43 (1989), 191–207; Svetlana Alpers, *The Art of Describing: Dutch Art in the Seventeenth Century* (Chicago, 1983).

126. Oldenburg, *Correspondence*, III, 162; IX, 968, 658. See also Derham, *Miscellanea Curiosa*, I, 200.

127. Oldenburg, *Correspondence*, III, 162.

128. Peter Dear, however, suggests that all matters of fact were of moral certainty and that the phrase "probable matter of fact" was an oxymoron. "From Truth to Disinterestedness

Chapter 6: The Facts of Nature II

1. Steven Shapin and Simon Schaffer, *Leviathan and the Air Pump: Hobbes, Boyle, and the Experimental Life* (Princeton, 1985); Steven Shapin, *The Social History of Truth: Civility and Science in Seventeenth-Century England* (Chicago, 1994). Mario Biagoli similarly suggests, "A claim would become a matter of fact only through the gentlemen acting like gentlemen around it." "Tacit Knowledge, Courtliness, and the Scientist's Body," in *Choreographing History*, ed. S. L. Foster (Bloomington, Ind., 1995), p. 75.

2. See Steven Shapin, "Who Was Robert Hooke?" in *Robert Hooke: New Studies*, ed. Michael Hunter and Simon Schaffer (Woodbridge, Suffolk, 1990), pp. 253–286; Stephen Pumphrey, "Ideas above His Station: A Social Study of Hooke's Curatorship of Experiments," *History of Science* 29 (1991), 1–37. For review symposia and Shapin's response, see *MetaScience* 6 (1994), 1–23. For the epistemological importance of merchants, see Mary Poovey, *A History of the Modern Fact: Problems of Knowledge in the Sciences of Wealth and Society* (Chicago, 1998).

3. It is thus unclear whether John Wilkins, one of founders of the Royal Society and the son of an Oxford goldsmith, would have been considered a gentlemen or, if so, whether he attained that status when he became a doctor of divinity, warden of Wadham College, or bishop of Chester. Could John Ray, the most praised natural historian of his generation but a dependent of gentleman Sir Francis Willughby, have been outside the range of credible witnessing? For the view that Boyle's conception of virtue rejected the traditional emphasis on noble and gentle status, see James R. Jacob, *Robert Boyle and the English Revolution: A Study in Social and Intellectual Change* (New York, 1977), p. 71.

4. See Shapin, "Who Was Robert Hooke?" But see also Ellen Tan Drake, *Restless Genius: Robert Hooke and His Earthly Thoughts* (New York, 1996).

5. Thomas Sprat, *History of the Royal Society*, ed. Jackson Cope and H. W. Jones (St. Louis,

1958), p. 67. Hooke occasionally met with the king. Robert Hooke, *The Diary of Robert Hooke, 1672–1680,* ed. Henry Robinson and Walter Adams (London, 1935), passim. Few members were tradesmen or artisans. Michael Hunter, *The Royal Society and Its Fellows, 1660–1700: The Morphology of an Early Scientific Institution* (Chalfont St. Giles, England, 1982).

6. See Barbara Shapiro, "The Universities and Science in Seventeenth-Century England," *Journal of British Studies* 10 (1971), 47–82. See also Mordecai Feingold, "What Facts Matter," *Isis* 87 (1996), 131–139.

7. Steven Shapin, "Pump and Circumstance: Robert Boyle's Literary Technology," *Social Studies of Science* 14 (1984), 481–521; Jan Golinski, "Robert Boyle: Skepticism and Authority in Seventeenth-Century Chemical Discourse," in *The Figural and the Literal: Problems of Language in the History of Science and Philosophy, 1630–1800,* ed. A. E. Benjamin, G. N. Cantor, and John R. R. Christie (Manchester, 1987), pp. 58–82.

8. Nigel Smith, *Literature and Revolution in England, 1640–1660* (New Haven, 1993), p. 57.

9. See also Steven Shapin, "The House of Experiment in Seventeenth-Century England," *Isis* 79 (1986), 373–404. Though many experiments were performed before the assembled Royal Society, others took place in smaller, even private, yet legitimate venues such as Boyle's laboratory or the Interregnum lodgings of Petty and Wilkins. English legal experience exhibits some analogs. Although common law suits were tried publicly, trials often took place in a variety of semipublic, semiprivate venues when judges toured their circuits. The "courthouse" of modern times existed no more than the modern "laboratory." The judicial activities of quarter and especially petty sessions often were conducted in private locations. Felony suspects were frequently examined in justices' homes.

10. Sprat holds up Christopher Wren as the embodiment of the ideal naturalist.

11. See Michael Walzer, "Good Aristocrats/Bad Aristocrats: Thomas Hobbes and Early Modern Political Culture," in *The Presence of the Past,* ed. R. Bienvenue and M. Feingold (Amsterdam, 1991), pp. 41–51; Frank Whigham, *Ambition and Privilege: The Social Tropes of Elizabethan Courtesy Literature* (New York, 1984).

12. Humanist intellectuals self-consciously confronted the disparity between knowledge and power.

13. See Michael Hunter and Paul Wood, "Towards Solomon's House: Rival Strategies for Reforming the Early Royal Society," *History of Science* 24 (1996), 49–108.

14. Sprat, *History of the Royal Society,* p. 36.

15. John Wilkins, *The Principles and Duties of Natural Religion* (London, 1675), pp. 26–27.

16. See Ralph M. Blake, "Theories of Hypothesis among Renaissance Astronomers," in *Theories of Scientific Method: The Renaissance through the Nineteenth Centuries,* ed. Edward Madden (Seattle, 1960); Edward Grant, "Hypotheses in Late Medieval and Early Modern Science," *Daedalus* 91 (1962), 599–616; Larry Lauden, *Science and Hypothesis* (Dordrecht, 1981); Margaret Morrison, "Hypotheses and Certainty in Cartesian Science," in *An Intimate Relation: Studies in History and Philosophy of Science Presented to Robert E. Butts,* ed. J. R. Brown and J. Mittelstrass (Dordrecht, 1989); Desmond Clarke, *Descartes' Philosophy of Science* (University Park, Pa., 1982); Daniel Garber, *Descartes' Metaphysical Physics* (Chicago, 1992). Gassendi believed that all empirical knowledge is conjectural.

17. But see Peter Urback, *Francis Bacon's Philosophy of Science: An Account and a Reappraisal* (La Salle, Ill., 1987), pp. 34, 38 ff.; L. Jonathan Cohen, *The Probable and the Provable* (Oxford, 1977).

18. See Barbara J. Shapiro, *Probability and Certainty in Seventeenth-Century England: The Relationships between Religion, Natural Science, Law, History, and Literature* (Princeton, 1983), pp. 44–61; Blake, "Theories of Hypothesis." "Doctrine" too was sometimes used interchangeably with "theory." Dictionary definitions of "conjecture" and "hypothesis" did not conform to virtuosi usage. "Hypothesis" was treated as a supposition or something conditional. "Theory" was characterized as the speculative part of any science and distinguished from practice. Occasionally, it was treated the same as "hypothesis." "Theorem" was also associated with mathematics. "Conjecture" was sometimes defined as "guess." See H. D., *The English Dictionary* (London, 1626); Edward Philips, *The New World of English Words* (London, 1658). (The 1671

and 1696 editions had assistance from leading antiquaries and virtuosi, e.g., Boyle, Wallis, Hooke, Ray, Flamsteed, Glisson, Sydenham, and Evelyn). See also Elisha Coles, *A Dictionary* (London, 1671); T. Blount, *Glossographia* (London, 1681); N. Bailey, *A Universal Etymological English Dictionary* (London, 1721); John Kersey, *Dictionarium Anglo-Britannicum* (London, 1708).

19. Sprat, *History of the Royal Society*. There is scholarly disagreement over the *History*'s aims and representativeness. Michael Hunter finds it more Baconian than most members would have accepted and suggests that Sprat's statements on hypothesis were unrepresentative. "The Early Royal Society and the Shape of Knowledge," in *The Shape of Knowledge from the Renaissance to the Enlightenment*, ed. D. R. Kelley and R. H. Popkin (Dordrecht, 1991), pp. 189–202. See also Michael Hunter, "Latitudinarianism and the 'Ideology' of the Early Royal Society: Thomas Sprat's *History of the Royal Society* (1667) Reconsidered," in *Establishing the New Science* (Woodbridge, Suffolk, 1989), pp. 199–216. P. B. Wood recognizes Wilkins's control of the shape and content of the *History* but views it as a "subtle misrepresentation and selective exposition." "Methodology and Apologetic: Thomas Sprat's *History of the Royal Society*," *British Journal for the History of Science* 13 (1980), 1–26. Margaret Purver views the *History* as an authoritative statement of the Society's Baconianism. See also Peter Dear, "Totius in verba: Rhetoric and Authority in the Early Royal Society," *Isis* 76 (1985), 145–161; H. Fisch and H. W. Jones, "Bacon's Influence on Sprat's History of the Royal Society," *Modern Language Quarterly* 12 (1951), 399–406. Some have inferred Society dissatisfaction from failure to reprint the *History* immediately. It seems more likely that the *History* served its immediate apologetic purpose and that its latitudinarianism no longer was politic after defeat of the 1667–68 comprehension proposals. Hooke referred to Sprat's "excellent History." *Lectiones Cutlerianae*, ed. R. T. Gunther (Oxford, 1931), p. 150.

20. Sprat, *History of the Royal Society*, pp. 255–257, 311–318.

21. Henry Oldenburg, *Correspondence*, ed. and trans. A. R. Hall and M. B. Hall, 13 vols. (Madison, Wis., 1965–86), VII, 260.

22. Sprat, *History of the Royal Society*, pp. 18, 28, 30, 32, 38–39.

23. Ibid., pp. 311–318. Wren had added to "the Theory of Dioptrics," contributed to the "Theory of Refraction, which exactly anser'd every Experiment," made observations on Saturn and "a Theory of that Planet, truly ansering all Observations," and produced a "theory of the Moon's Libration, as far as his Observations could carry him." Ibid., p. 315.

24. Sprat, *History of the Royal Society*, p. 311; J. A. Bennett, "Hooke and Wren and the System of the World: Some Points toward an Historical Account," *British Journal for the History of Science* 8 (1975), 55. Sprat's characterization of some members' efforts as "theory" and others as "hypothesis" did not clarify the distinction between the two. His usage is rather odd given Wilkins's supervisory role. Wilkins's *Essay on a Real Character* placed "theorem" under the category "Rule" along with maxim, axiom, principle, and canon; "hypothesis" was placed in the category "supposition." John Wilkins, *Essay towards a Real Character and a Philosophical Language* (London, 1668), pp. 48, 49.

25. *Philosophical Transactions* XVI (1686), 001–2.

26. *Philosophical Transactions* II (1667), 105; Royal Society, Original letters, II, fols. 300, 314. Oldenburg highlighted the "faithfull history" of nature and art derived from careful observation and experiment, which eventually would raise a "body of natural philosophy, that may give a rational account of ye effects of nature, and enable men to inferr from confirmed cause and, effects, such deductions may conduce" to man's benefit. *Correspondence*, VII, 260.

27. Oldenburg, *Correspondence*, IX, 16–17, X, 109. William Derham refers to Newton's theory of the moon. *Miscellanea Curiosa*, 3d ed., 3 vols. (London, 1726), I, 279.

28. C. H. Weld, *A History of the Royal Society*, 2 vols. [1848] (New York, 1975), II, 526–527; M. B. Hall, "Science in the Early Royal Society," in *The Emergence of Science in Western Europe*, ed. Maurice Crosland (New York, 1976), pp. 57–78.

29. Joseph Glanvill, *Scepsis Scientifica* (London, 1665), Address to the Royal Society.

30. *Letters and Poems in Honour of the Incomparable Princess, Margaret, Duchess of Newcastle* (London, 1676), p. 124.

31. Joseph Glanvill, *The Vanity of Dogmatizing* (London, 1661), p. 189; Glanvill, "Against Confidence in Philosophy and Matters of Speculation," *Essays on Several Important Subjects in Philosophy and Religion* (London, 1676), p. 15; Glanvill, "Modern Improvements of Useful Knowledge," *Essays*, pp. 48–49; Glanvill, *Plus Ultra* (London, 1668), pp. 81, 89; Glanvill, "Against Confidence," *Essays*, p. 15. See Henry Van Leeuwen, *The Problem of Certainty in English Thought, 1630–1680* (The Hague, 1963), pp. 71–89; Jackson I. Cope, *Joseph Glanvill, Anglican Apologist* (St. Louis, 1956).

32. See Pierre Duhem, *To Save the Phenomena: An Essay on the Idea of Physical Theory from Plato to Galileo* (Chicago, 1969); Grant, "Hypotheses"; Blake, "Theories of Hypothesis"; Robert Westman, "Kepler's Theory of Hypothesis and the Realist Dilemma," *Studies in the History and Philosophy of Science* 3 (1972), 233–264. Hypotheses themselves were not novel in the seventeenth century, and astronomers frequently employed mathematical suppositions about the heavens. Because it was not considered necessary to assert that such hypotheses conformed to physical phenomena, they coexisted with Aristotelian physics.

33. Henry Power, *Experimental Philosophy . . . With some Deductions, and Probable Hypotheses raised from them* (London, 1664), preface. See also pp. 72, 192, 193. See also Power to William Croone, Royal Society Letter Book I, fol. 35; Thomas Birch, *The History of the Royal Society of London*, 4 vols. (London, 1756), I, 81, 165; George Garden, "A Discourse concerning the Modern Theory of Generation," in *Miscellanea Curiosa*, I, 142–152; "A Short Discourse concerning Concoction," ibid., pp. 153, 169.

34. Ralph Bohun, *A Discourse Concerning the Origine and Properties of Wind* (Oxford, 1671), preface; Robert Plot, *The Natural History of Oxfordshire* (London, 1675), 1704 ed., pp. 28, 43, 169; Oldenburg, *Correspondence*, VIII, 120. "A Theory might be established in the philosophical world, which might agree as much as possible with Observations and Experiments, which should be often repeated with due Care and Fidelity." *Philosophical Transactions*, 3 vols., 5th ed. (London, 1749), I, 461.

35. Samuel Parker, *A Free and Impartial Censure of the Platonicke Philosophie* (Oxford, 1666), pp. 44–45, 46–47; Sprat, *History of the Royal Society*, p. 233.

36. John Evelyn, *Sylva* (London, 1664), Preface to the Reader; Walter Charleton, *Immortality of the Human Soul* (London, 1657), p. 116

37. Walter Charleton, *Natural History of the Passions* (London, 1674), p. 4.

38. Nehemiah Grew, *The Anatomy of Plants* [1682] (New York, 1965), pp. 7, 221. "Conjecture" was aided by analogy. Nehemiah Grew, *The Idea of a Phytological History Propounded* (London, 1673), p. 40.

39. Oldenburg, *Correspondence*, X, 209. See also VII, 346.

40. See E. Zilzel, "The Genesis of the Concept of Physical Law," *Philosophical Review* 51 (1942), 245–279; Francis Oakley, "Christian Theology and Newtonian Science: The Rise of the Concept of the Laws of Nature," *Church History* 30 (1961), 433–457; Jane Ruby, "The Origins of Scientific '''Law,''' *Journal of the History of Ideas* 47 (1986), 341–359; John Milton, "The Origin and Development of the Concept of the 'Laws of Nature,'" *Archives Européennes de Sociologie* 22 (1981), 173–195. Boyle occasionally used the expression "laws of nature," and several members of the Royal Society spoke of the "laws of motion." Milton suggests that Hooke was the first to describe an empirically determined regularity of their own discovery as "a law or rule of nature." Nature was treated as being governed by laws long before there were attempts to state any laws, and theological voluntarism played a significant role. For Hooke, philosophical inquiry was a means of "finding out the ways and Means Nature use, and the Laws by which she is restrain'd in producing divers Effects." See Robert Hooke, *Micrographia* (London, 1665), preface; Hooke, *Posthumous Works*, ed. Richard Waller (London, 1705), p. 26. Margaret Osler suggests that the language of the laws of nature goes back at least to Lucretius and was often used by medieval philosophers. She suggests that what was new in the seventeenth century was the identification of particular propositions as laws of nature (personal communication). See also Benjamin Milner, "Francis Bacon: The Theological Foundations of the Valerius Terminus," *Journal of the History of Ideas* 58 (1997), 255–256; *Laws of Nature: Essays on the Philosophical and Historical Dimensions*, ed. Friedel Weinert (Berlin, 1995).

41. Royal Society, Letter Book, I, fol. 37, 63. See also fol. 42–46; Stephen Rigaud, *Correspondence of Scientific Men of the Seventeenth Century*, 2 vols. (Oxford, 1841), I, 94; Christian Huygens, *The Celestial Worlds Discovered* (London, 1968), p. 10; Aant Elzinga, "Huygens' Theory of Research and Descartes' Theory of Knowledge," *Zeitschrift fur Allegemeine Wissenschaft* 3 (1972), 17, 19. See also pp. 16–22; part I (1971), 174–194.

42. Neile manuscript quoted in Hunter and Wood, "Towards Solomon's House," pp. 79, 80. Experiments alone were "but a dry entertainment without the indagation of causes." Ibid., p. 53. Neile criticized Christopher Wren for his reluctance to "explain his principles" and find "a reason for his experiments" on motion.

43. Quoted in Hunter and Wood, "Toward Solomon's House," p. 59; William Petty, *Political Arithmetic* (London, 1690), preface. See also John Henry, "The Scientific Revolution in England," in *The Scientific Revolution in National Context*, ed. Roy Porter and Mikulas Teich (Cambridge, 1992), pp. 178–209.

44. If Moray suggested that "promiscuous" experiments be replaced by a "continued series," another member felt no observations or experiments "if truly made" should be "slighted." Quoted in Hunter, "Early Royal Society," pp. 197, 193. Still another suggested that the society examine all "Systems, Theories, Principles, Hypotheses, . . . and experiments," ancient and modern, in order to compile "A Complete System of Solide Philosophy, for explicating all phenomenon" and "rendring a rationall account of the causes of things." Until that time the Society was not to "own any hypothesis, system or doctrine in principles of Natural Philosophy, nor the explication of any phaenomenon. . . . Nor dogmatically define, nor fixe Axiomes of Scientificall things . . . adhering to none, till by mature debate & clear arguments, chiefly such as are deduced from legitimate experiments, the truth of such positions be demonstrated invincibly. . . . And till then be a sufficient collection made, of Experiments, Histories & observations, there are no debates to be held . . . concerning any Hypothesis or principle of philosophy, nor any discourse made for explicating any phenomena, except by special appointment of the Society, or allowance of the president." Although this statement has been traditionally attributed to Hooke, Hunter and Wood suggest that Moray is its author. "Towards Solomon's House," p. 81.

45. Hooke to Brouncker, quoted in F. F. Centore, *Robert Hooke's Contribution to Mechanics: A Study in Seventeenth-Century Natural Philosophy* (The Hague, 1970), p. 8.

46. Oldroyd, "Some Writings of Robert Hooke," pp. 157–158.

47. Hooke, *Posthumous Works*, pp. 393, 417; Birch, *History of the Royal Society*, I, 128–130, 175.

48. Hooke, *Posthumous Works*, p. 280.

49. Hooke, Royal Society Classified Papers, fols. 92–94, quoted in Hunter and Wood, "Towards Solomon's House," p. 90.

50. Hooke, *Micrographia*, preface. For Hooke's methodology, see Hunter and Schaffer, *Robert Hooke: New Studies*; D. R. Oldroyd, "Robert Hooke's Methodology of Science as Exemplified in His Discourse of Earthquakes," *British Journal for the History of Science*, 6 (1972), 110–130; Margaret 'Espinasse, *Robert Hooke* (Berkeley, 1962), pp. 28–33.

51. Quoted in Hunter and Wood, "Towards Solomon's House," p. 79.

52. Hooke, *Micrographia*, preface. About 1668 Hooke wrote that though the Royal Society "have hitherto seem'd to avoid and prohibit preconceived Theories and Deductions from particular, and seemingly accidental Experiments; yet I humbly conceive, that such, if knowingly and judiciously made, are Matters of the greatest Importance, as giving a Characteristick of the Aim, Use, and Significancy thereof, and without which man, and possibly the most considerable Particulars, are passed over without Regard and Observation." Quoted in Drake, *Restless Genius*, p. 160. The Royal Society, prior to the publication of *Micrographia*, emphasized that though they had licensed his work, "yet they own no theory, nor will they be thought to do so; and that several hypotheses and theories laid down by him therein, are not delivered as certainties, but as conjectures." They were not to be presented "to the world as the opinion of the Society." Nov. 23, 1664, Birch, *History*, I, 491.

53. Quoted in Robert Gunther, *Early Science in Oxford*, 15 vols. (Oxford, 1930), VI, 112.

54. An example was his own hypothesis on "animal Motion," which "no Man ever did or will

be able to explicate either this or other Phenomenon in Nature's true way and Method." *Philosophical Collections* (London, 1682), no. 2, 25.

55. Hooke, "Cometa," in *Lectiones Cutlerianae* (London, 1679), pp. 24–25, 53, 34.

56. Quoted in Bennett, "Hooke and Wren," p. 43. See also pp. 35–37. "Probable arguments" were appropriate to the Copernican and Tychonic hypotheses because there could never be determination of the controversies "without some positive observations from determining whether there were a Parallax or no of the Orbs of the Earth." Robert Hooke, *An Attempt to Prove the Motion of the Earth from Observations* (London, 1674), p. 4.

57. For Hooke's natural philosophy, see Oldroyd, "Hooke's Methodology of Science," pp. 109–130; D. R. Oldroyd, "Some Writings of Robert Hooke on Procedures for the Prosecution of Scientific Enquiry, including his 'Lectures of Things Requisite to a Natural History,'" *Notes and Records of the Royal Society of London* 41 (1987), 145–167; J. A. Bennett, "Robert Hooke as Mechanic and Natural Philosopher," *Notes and Records of the Royal Society of London* 35 (1980), 33–47. See also Lotte Mulligan, "Robert Hooke and Certain Knowledge," *Seventeenth Century* 7 (1992), 151–169; Hunter and Schaffer, *Robert Hooke: New Studies*.

58. Hooke, *Posthumous Works*, p. 3.

59. Robert Boyle, "Excellency of Theology," *The Works of the Honourable Robert Boyle*, ed. Thomas Birch, 6 vols. (London, 1772), IV, 59. "Things discovered in after times" might "overthrow doctrine" based on current observations.

60. Robert Boyle, "Certain Physiological Essays," *Works*, I, 303, 311.

61. Ibid., pp. 302, 303. See also Robert Boyle, *Hydrostatical Paradoxes* (London, 1666), preface; Boyle, "The Experimental History of Colors" (1664), *Works*, I, 662; Boyle, *A Defense of the Doctrine Touching the Spring of Air* (London, 1662), preface. See Richard Westfall, "Unpublished Boyle Papers Related to Scientific Method," *Annals of Science* 12 (1956), 63–73; Frederick J. O. Toole, "Robert Boyle's Concept of Science and Nature" (unpublished paper). M. B. Hall suggests that Boyle may have changed his views of hypothesis, initially feeling that his experiments "illustrated" the corpuscular philosophy and later claiming that they could prove it. Hall, "Science in the Early Royal Society," in *The Emergence of Science in Western Europe*, ed. Maurice Crosland (New York, 1976), p. 73. For Sargent, Boyle's "facts" occasionally involved statements about regularly occurring events and causes rather than particular events. The spring of air, which Boyle initially treated as hypothetical, therefore became "factual." Rose-Mary Sargent, *The Diffident Naturalist: Robert Boyle and the Philosophy of Experiment* (Chicago, 1995), pp. 132, 134, 136. See also Jan Wojcik, *Robert Boyle and the Limits of Reason* (Cambridge, 1997), pp. 161–180.

62. Robert Boyle, *An Essay about the Origen and Nature of Gems* (London, 1672), preface, p. 123.

63. See *Philosophical Transactions* I (1665–66), 192.

64. Boyle, "Origine of Particular Qualities," *Works*, IV, 347.

65. Boyle, "Some Considerations touching the Usefulness of Experimental Natural Philosophy," *Works*, II, 45. The same effect might be produced by different causes. Ibid. Boyle also wrote "Of the Excellency and Grounds of the Mechanical Hypothesis."

66. Westfall, "Unpublished Boyle Papers," pp. 63–73. See also Boyle, "Of the Excellency and Grounds of the Corpuscular Hypothesis," *Works*, IV, 68–78; *Works*, I, 30; Marie Boas Hall, *Robert Boyle on Natural Philosophy* (Bloomington, Ind., 1965), pp. 134–135; Marie Boas, "Boyle as a Theoretical Scientist," *Isis* 46 (1950), 261–268.

67. Boyle, "Certain Physiological Essays," *Works*, I, 302. See also Boyle, *Works*, III, 739–740.

68. Boyle, *Hydrostatical Paradoxes*, preface.

69. Boyle, *Works*, IV, 182.

70. Robert Boyle, "The Christian Virtuoso," *Works*, V, 339–340.

71. Boyle, *Hydrostatical Paradoxes*, preface. See also Oldenburg, *Correspondence*, III, 100–101; Boyle, *Works*, II, 125. "Doctrine" and "theory" were occasionally used interchangeably. See "An Introductory Essay to the Doctrine of Sounds" (1683), in Derham, *Miscellanea Curiosa*, I, 121.

72. Boyle, "Certain Physiological Essays," *Works*, I, 303. In connection with his "theorie and

conjectures concerning the mechanical production of qualities," Boyle insisted he did not "debar himself of the liberty either of altering them or substituting others" if "progress in the history of qualities shall suggest better hypotheses or explications." *Works*, IV, 236. See also "Experiments and Considerations Touching Colours," *Works*, I, 688, 695.

73. Boyle, *Works*, IV, 462.

74. See Margaret J. Olser, "The Intellectual Sources of Robert Boyle's Philosophy of Nature: Gassendi's Volunteerism and Boyle's Physico-Theological Project," in *Philosophy, Science, and Religion in England, 1640–1700*, ed. Richard Kroll, Richard Ashcraft, and Perez Zagorin (Cambridge, 1992), pp. 178–198; Shapiro, *Probability and Certainty*; Van Leeuwen, *Problem of Certainty*; J. J. MacIntosh, "Robert Boyle's Epistemology: The Interaction between Science and Religious Knowledge," *International Studies in the Philosophy of Science* 6 (1992), 91–122. Sargent rejects the probabilistic assessment and the characterization of Boyle as an empiricist. *Diffident Naturalist*, pp. 104, 210, 211.

75. Oldenburg, *Correspondence*, II, 170; IX, 20, 307.

76. *Philosophical Transactions* I (1665–66), 192, 193, 263, 264, 265, 266, 271, 281–282, 288; III (1668), 652; Oldenburg, *Correspondence*, III, 136, 148, 154, 159, 277, 346. Oldenburg also referred to the "hypothesis" of the tides. Ibid., III, 8.

77. Oldenburg, *Correspondence*, VII, 103, 563–564. See also VIII, 26, 72–74, 79. Oldenburg replied to Leibniz that matters lying outside the rigor of mathematics typically resulted in a variety of opinions. Ibid., VII, 103.

78. See William A. Wallace, "Galileo and Reasoning ex suppositione," in Wallace, *Prelude to Galileo* (Dordrecht, 1981); Margaret Morrison, "Hypothesis and Certainty in Cartesian Science," in *An Intimate Relation . . . Studies Presented to Robert E. Butts*, ed. James R. Brown and Jurgen Mittelstrass (Dordrecht, 1989).

79. See Dear, *Discipline and Experience*.

80. Oldenburg, *Correspondence*, IX, 27–28, 149.

81. *Isaac Newton's Papers and Letters on Natural Philosophy*, ed. I. B. Cohen (Cambridge, Mass., 1958), pp. 2, 106. Peter Dear suggests that Newton's work on colors was typical of the geometrical optics, which sought universal propositions, and although Newton used reasoning and experience to support these truths, they were not part of the proof itself. Newton was not attempting to use "facts" to support a still hypothetical generalization but aimed at universal statements derived from mathematical natural philosophy and experiment. *Discipline and Experience*, p. 232. See also Zev Bechler, "Newton's Optical Controversies: A Study in the Grammar of Scientific Dissent," in *The Interaction between Science and Philosophy*, ed. Y. Elkana (Jerusalem, 1974), pp. 118–119, 122–124, 129–134; Richard S. Westfall, "The Foundation of Newton's Theory of Colours," *Isis* 53 (1962), 339–358.

82. Oldenburg, *Correspondence*, IX, 119, 249; "un hypotheses fort vraisemblable." Ibid., IX, 247. See also ibid., IX, 383, 555.

83. Oldenburg, *Correspondence*, IX, 16–17; IX, 109. Flamsteed referred to it as a theory. Pardies denied he had called Newton's theory a hypothesis out of contempt. Ibid., IX, 63, 119.

84. Rigaud, *Correspondence of Scientific Men*, II, 390. Gregory to Collins, April 1672. See also Hall, "Science in the Early Royal Society," pp. 69–71.

85. Some translators render this, "I frame no hypotheses"; others, "I feign no hypotheses."

86. Isaac Newton, *Mathematical Principles of Natural Philosophy*, ed. F. Cajori (Berkeley, 1934), pp. 546, 547. I. B. Cohen traces the evolution of Newton's views on hypothesis in succeeding editions of *Principia*. "Hypotheses in Newton's Philosophy," in *Seventeenth-Century Natural Scientists*, ed. Vere Chappell, 12 vols. (New York, 1992), VII, 206–236; François Duchesneau, "The 'More Geometrico' Pattern in Hypotheses from Descartes to Leibniz," in *Nature Mathematized*, ed. William R. Shea (Dordrecht, 1983), pp. 197–214; Anita M. Pampusch, "'Experimental,' 'Metaphysical,' and 'Hypothetical' Philosophy in Newtonian Methodology," *Centaurus* 18 (1974), 289–300.

87. Ephraim Chambers, *Cyclopaedia or An Universal Dictionary of the Arts and Sciences*, 4 vols. (London, 1727). Science included "things as men may discover by the use of sense and reasoning," such as the laws of nature. I, ix. In the "Experimental Philosophy" the "laws of na-

ture and the Properties and Powers of Bodies" were deduced from "sensible experiments and observations." I, 281.

88. John Locke, *On Education*, ed. Peter Gay (New York, 1964), p. 160. See also G. A. J. Rogers, "Locke's *Essay* and Newton's *Principia*," *Journal of the History of Ideas* 39 (1978), 217–232.

89. John Keill, *An Examination of Dr. Burnet's Theory of the Earth* (Oxford, 1698), p. 22. See also Halley's review of the *Principia* in Cohen, *Newton's Papers and Letters*, pp. 405–424.

90. Richard Sorrenson, "Towards a History of the Royal Society in the Eighteenth Century," *Notes and Records of the Royal Society* 50 (1996), 29–46. Sorrenson rejects the view of Society decline. Hans Sloane, *A Voyage to the Islands . . . with the Natural History* (1701), quoted in Harold Cook, "The Cutting Edge of a Revolution? Medicine and Natural History near the Shores of the North Sea," in *Renaissance and Revolution: Humanists, Scholars, Craftsmen, and Natural Philosophers in Early Modern Europe*, ed. J. V. Field and Frank James (Cambridge, 1993), p. 49. See also Charles Leigh, *Natural History of Lancashire* (Oxford, 1700), pp. 35, 48, 100–101, 106.

91. Cook, "Cutting Edge," p. 46, quoting *Philosophical Transactions* L (1757), 461.

92. Sorrenson, "Towards a History of the Royal Society," pp. 39–41.

93. Woodward, *Natural History of the Earth*, pp. 73–74.

94. Ibid., pp. xii, xiii. He was not yet ready to offer "a complete Theory" (p. xii). No conjecture would "abide the Test; because they have not due warrant from Observation" and are "repugnant thereunto." Ibid., p. 40.

95. Woodward, *An Attempt Towards a Natural History of Fossils*, 2 vols. (London, 1726), I, xiv. His *Fossils of all Kinds, digested into a Method* (London, 1728), addressed to Newton, claimed that his "Method," if not Newton's own, "is wholly owing to you; it being begun, carried on, and finished at your Request" (pp. 1–2).

96. For Matthew Hale, "the Laws of Nature are stable, and sealed and regular, and not like the Laws of Men," which are changeable. *Difficiles Nugae: Or, Observations Touching the Torricellian Experiment* (London, 1674), pp. 6–7.

97. Chambers, *Cyclopaedia*, I, 281.

98. Oliver Goldsmith, *A Survey of Experimental Philosophy*, 2 vols. (London, 1776), Advertisement to the Reader, I, 4, 6. Cartesian natural philosophy is characterized as a "romance." Ibid., I, 13.

99. "Fact" for Chambers was something actually done or "done indeed." *The Royal English Dictionary*, ed. D. Fenning (London, 1761), in addition to defining fact a "thing done," refers to it as "A Reality, opposed to meer supposition or speculation." The purpose of experiments is to "discover their effects, their laws, and relations, or to be able to arrive at the true cause of phaenomenon occasioned thereby." Samuel Johnson's *Dictionary of the English Language*, 4 vols., 2d ed. (London, 1755), also defined "fact" as "Reality; not supposition; not speculation." John Kersey, *Dictionarium Anglo-Britannicum* (London, 1708), retains traditional legal usage. Fact "is a Truth that may be prov'd tho not by Record, and Matter of Record is that which is prov'd by some Record." See also N. Bailey, *A Universal Etymological English Dictionary* (London, 1721).

100. Harvey Wheeler, "Science out of Law: Francis Bacon's Invention of Scientific Empiricism," in *Towards a Humanistic Science of Politics*, ed. F. D. Nelson and R. L. Sklar (London, 1983), pp. 101–143; Rose-Mary Sargent, "Scientific Experiment and Legal Expertise: The Way of Experience in Seventeenth-Century England," *Studies in the History and Philosophy of Science* 20 (1989), 19–45. Sargent argues that Boyle's natural philosophy followed legal methods for deriving legal principles. *Diffident Naturalist*, pp. 42–50. Legal emphasis on moral certainty, however, was centered on the individual "facts" rather than the "law" or legal principles.

101. Hale, *Difficiles Nugae*, p. 6.

102. Literary scholars first explored the role of English science in modifying English prose style in the direction of greater "plainness." R. F. Jones argued that the "new philosophy" played a substantial role in the seventeenth-century critique of highly ornamented and rhe-

torically sophisticated prose and poetry. R. F. Jones, *The Seventeenth Century: Studies in the History of English Thought and Literature from Bacon to Pope* (Stanford, 1951). But see Brian Vickers and Nancy Streuver, *Rhetoric and the Pursuit of Truth: Language Change in the Seventeenth and Eighteenth Centuries* (Los Angeles, 1985); Richard Kroll, *The Material Word* (Baltimore, 1991); Robert E. Stillman, "Assessing the Revolution: Ideology, Language, and Rhetoric in the New Philosophy of Early Modern England," *Eighteenth Century* 35 (1994), 99–118. The contributions of latitudinarianism, humanist academies, and the ideology of courtly and gentlemanly behavior have also been invoked in connection with the linguistic norms of the virtuosi. The "polite," however, often ridiculed the virtuosi. See Lawrence Klein, *Shaftesbury and the Culture of Politeness: Moral Discourse and Cultural Politics in Early-Eighteenth-Century England* (Cambridge, 1994).

103. See also Sir Philip Sidney, *An Apology for Poetry* [1595], ed. Forrest G. Robinson (New York, 1970). Richard Blome separated style from logic. *The Gentleman's Recreations . . . being the Enclycopedy of the Arts and Sciences* (London, 1686). But Chambers's *Cyclopaedia* defined rhetoric as the means of persuasion and included invention, amplification, argument, narration, and style.

104. Sprat, *History of the Royal Society*, p. 112. Bacon insisted that the study of nature required the rejection of "pugnatious disputations" and "probable oratory." *The Works of Francis Bacon*, ed. James Spedding, Robert Leslie Ellis, and Douglas Denon Heath, 14 vols. (London, 1857–74), III, 636.

105. Sprat, *History of the Royal Society*, pp. 62, 111, 113. "Who can behold, without indignation, how many mists and uncertainties, these specious Tropes and Figures have brought on our Knowledge. How many rewards . . . have been . . . snatch'd away by the vanity of fine speaking." Ibid., p. 112. Sprat, who was hired by the Royal Society for his rhetorical skill, also promoted an "impartial Court of Eloquence" akin to the French Academy.

106. Weld, *History of the Royal Society*, II, 527.

107. Hooke, *Posthumous Works*, p. 63.

108. See Shapiro, *Probability and Certainty*, pp. 227–256. Natural history was to be recorded without embellishment and would set "forth a simple narrative of the facts . . . to be described with perspicuity." Bacon, *Works*, V, 510–511. See also Hooke, *Micrographia*, preface; John Ray, *The Ornithology of Francis Willughby* (London, 1678), preface. Stylistic pronouncements did not always result in a plain style. Boyle's prose was complex and convoluted.

109. See Dear, "Totius in verba," pp. 145–161. The unembellished first-person account was preferred but not always practiced. Dear shows that compilers sometimes compressed firsthand reports into summaries and that portions of reports dealing with the setting up of experiments were often written in the passive voice.

110. *The Royal English Dictionary* (London, 1761) defined narrative as "giving an account of fact or a series of facts as they happened."

111. *Philosophical Transactions* V (1670), 1152–1153; P. B. Wood, "Methodology and Apologetic: Thomas Sprat's History of the Royal Society," *British Journal for the History of Science* 13 (1980), 1–24.

112. Hooke, *Micrographia*, preface; Oldenburg, *Correspondence*, VIII, 51, 74, 324. Samuel Sorbière associated the Society's moderate mode of discourse with hypothesis. *A Voyage to England* (London, 1709), p. 38.

113. Oldenburg condemned "Arguing and disputing." *Philosophical Transactions* II (1667), 503–504. Boyle thought the natural philosophy of the schools "litigious" and "barren." *Some Considerations Touching the Usefulnesse of Experimentall Naturall Philosophy* (Oxford, 1663), pp. 2–3. Locke attacked the competitiveness and wrangling of the disputation, where "victory" was "adjudged not to him who had Truth . . . but the last word in the Dispute." John Locke, *Essay Concerning Human Understanding* (London, 1690), III, x, 7. See also IV, vii, 11; Peter Walmsley, "Dispute and Conversation: Probability and the Rhetoric of Natural Philosophy in Locke's *Essay*," *Journal of the History of Ideas* 54 (1993), 381–394.

Members of the Royal Society whose professional lives shifted back and forth between London and the universities—e.g., Wilkins, Wallis, Goddard, Barrow, Wren, Willis, and Newton—should be characterized as both Society members and university-oriented intellectuals. Humanist scholars often used the dialogue, a genre that could be employed either contentiously or politely. The legal advocate's necessarily partisan mode of argumentation and the winner-loser model of the courts were also rejected. But see Shapin and Schaffer, *Leviathan and the Air Pump*; Shapin, *Social History of Truth*; Lorraine Daston, "Baconian Facts, Academic Civility, and the Prehistory of Objectivity," *Annals of Scholarship* 9 (1991), 337–363; Mario Biagoli, "Etiquette, Interdependence, and Sociability in Seventeenth-Century Science," *Critical Inquiry* 22 (1996), 193–238.

114. See Paula Findlen, *Possessing Nature: Museums, Collecting, and Scientific Culture in Early Modern Italy* (Berkeley, 1995); Mario Biagoli, *Galileo Courtier: The Practice of Science in the Culture of Absolutism* (Chicago, 1993). No precedence was permitted in the Royal Society except for the president, secretary, and distinguished visitors.

115. Baldasar Castiglioni, *The Book of the Courtier*, trans. Charles S. Singleton (Garden City, N.Y., 1959), p. 294.

116. See Daniel Javitch, *Poetry and Courtliness in Renaissance England* (Princeton, 1978); Royal Society, Original Letters, fol. 214, Sept. 21, 1664.

117. See Anne Goldgar, *Impolite Learning: Conduct and Community in the Republic of Letters, 1680–1750* (Cambridge, Mass., 1995); *Commercium Litterarium: Forms of Communication in the Republic of Letters, 1600–1650*, ed. H. Bot and F. Waquet (Amsterdam, 1994); Lorraine Daston, "The Ideal and Reality of the Republic of Letters in the Enlightenment," *Science in Context* 4 (1991), 367–386; H. Bot and F. Waquet, *La republique des lettres* (Paris, 1997).

118. Exclusion did not mean that participants were uninterested or uninvolved with religious issues or that philosophical topics did not have important religious implications.

119. Barbara Shapiro, "Latitudinarianism and Science in Seventeenth-Century England," *Past and Present* 48 (1968), rpt. in *The Intellectual Revolution of the Seventeenth Century*, ed. Charles Webster (Oxford, 1974), pp. 286–316.

120. See ibid.; Shapiro, *Probability and Certainty*.

121. Glanvill, *Plus Ultra*, p. 149. The virtuoso possessed "a sense of his own fallibility . . . and never concludes but upon resolution to alter his mind upon contrary evidence. Thus he conceives warily and he speaks with . . . caution . . . and with great deference to opposite persuasion, candour to dissenters, and calmness in contradictions, . . . he gives his reasons without passion . . . discourses without wrangling, and differs without dividing. . . . He suspends his judgment when he does not clearly understand." Ibid., p. 147. An "open inquiry in the great Field of Nature" led men to "more indifferency toward those petty Notions, in which they were before apt to place a great deal of Religion; and to reckon that [it] lies, in the few, certain, operative Principles of the Gospel, . . . and not . . . upon Questions that engender strife." Joseph Glanvill, *Essays on Several Important Subjects* (London, 1676), essay IV, p. 27. The natural philosopher must "proceed with wariness and circumspection without too much forwardness in establishing maxims and positive doctrines; to propose their opinions as hypotheses that may probably be the true account; without peremptory affirming that they are." The "principal rule" was "to be wary and diffident, not to be hasty in our conclusions, or overconfident of opinions; but to be sparing of our assent and not to afford it but to things clearly and distinctly perceived." Ibid., p. 51.

122. Sprat, *History of the Royal Society*, p. 53; John Wilkins, *Sermons Preached on Several Occasions* (London, 1682), p. 414.

123. Oldenburg emphasized the "great difference between a regulated, unprejudiced mind, and those who speak about everything with a decisive air, and wish to have their ideas pass for . . . demonstrations." *Correspondence*, X, 22. The Royal Society laid "aside all set Speeches and Eloquent Harangues as fit to be banisht out of all Civil Assemblies, as a thing found by woeful experience, especially in England, fatal to Peace and good Manners." Edward Chamberlayne, *Anglia notitia: or, The Present State of England* (London, 1673), p. 345.

124. Sprat, *History of the Royal Society*, pp. 32–34. See also p. 341.

125. Klein questions the notion of "polite science." *Shaftesbury and the Culture of Politeness*;

Lawrence Klein, "Enlightenment as Conversation" (unpublished paper). Addison as well as Shaftesbury dismissed natural science as irrelevant to the culture of politeness.

Chapter 7: Facts of Religion

1. See Barbara J. Shapiro, *Probability and Certainty in Seventeenth-Century England: The Relationships between Religion, Natural Science, Law, History, and Literature* (Princeton, 1983); Henry Van Leeuwen, *The Problem of Certainty in Seventeenth-Century England, 1630–1690* (The Hague, 1963); Gerard Reedy, *The Bible and Reason: Anglicans and Scripture in Late-Seventeenth-Century England* (Philadelphia, 1985).

2. Hugo Grotius, *The Truth of the Christian Religion*, ed. Simon Patrick (London, 1680), p. 21. The Resurrection and Christ's miracles, questions of "Matter of Fact," were confirmed "by unexceptionable Testimonies." Ibid.

3. William Chillingworth, *The Religion of Protestants: a Safe way to Salvation*, 2d ed. (London, 1638), pp. 57, 88, 115. See also Robert Orr, *Reason and Authority: The Thought of William Chillingworth* (Oxford, 1967); Van Leeuwen, *Problem of Certainty*.

4. Seth Ward, *A Philosophical Essay Toward the Eviction . . . of God* [1654], 4th ed. (London, 1677), pp. 84–88.

5. Ibid., pp. 99–101, 102, 107 ff., 117.

6. London, 1662, preface, pp. 120–136. See also Edward Stillingfleet, *A Rational Account of the Grounds of Protestant Religion* (London, 1664); Robert Carroll, *The Common Sense Philosophy of Religion of Bishop Edward Stillingfleet, 1635–1699* (The Hague, 1975). The word "martyr" has its origin in the Greek root meaning "witness."

7. Edward Stillingfleet, *Origines Sacrae* (London, 1662), p. 285. See also Thomas Sprat, *History of the Royal Society*, ed. Jackson Cope and H. W. Jones (St. Louis, 1958), pp. 362–363.

8. Stillingfleet, *Origines Sacrae*, p. 286.

9. Ibid., pp. 260, 287–288.

10. Ibid., p. 297.

11. Stillingfleet condemned "pedantic flourishes, flattering insinuations," and "affected cadences." Ibid., pp. 199, 293, 295.

12. John Tillotson, *The Rule of Faith* (London, 1666), pp. 85, 102, 118. "Matters of Fact" were proved by "credible Testimony." One can have "an undoubted assurance of them, when . . . prov'd by the best Arguments that the nature and quality of the thing will bear." Tillotson, *The Works* (London, 1696), preface. For Locke, see John Marshall, *Resistance, Religion, and Responsibility* (Cambridge, 1994), p. 128. See also Thomas Smith, *Sermon of the Credibility of the Mysteries of the Christian Religion* (London, 1675), p. 25; Jan Wojcik, *Robert Boyle and the Limits of Reason* (Cambridge, 1997).

13. John Wilkins, *The Principles and Duties of Natural Religion* (London, 1675), pp. 9–10. See also Charles Wolseley, *The Reasonableness of Scripture Belief* (London, 1672); John Evelyn, *The History of Religion* (London, 1850), p. 393. See also p. 392.

14. Robert Boyle, *Some Considerations about the Reconcileableness of Reason and Religion* (London, 1675), pp. 93, 95, 96.

15. Boyle, "Reconcileableness of Reason and Religion," *The Works of the Honourable Robert Boyle*, ed. Thomas Birch, 6 vols. (London, 1772), IV, 182. See also "A Discourse of Things Above Reason," *Works*, IV, 449.

16. Robert Boyle, "The Christian Virtuoso," *Works*, VI, 525.

17. "Since we scruple not to be believe such Prodigies, as Celestial Comets, Vanishing and Reappearing Stars . . . and like amazing Anomalies of Nature, upon the credit of Human Histories; I see not that Vicarious Experience should not be more trusted, which has divers peculiarly current Circumstances to Confirm it." *The Christian Virtuoso* (London, 1690), p. 81. See also R. M. Burns, *The Great Debate on Miracles from Joseph Glanvill to David Hume* (London, 1981), pp. 51–54.

18. Robert Boyle, *Reasons Why a Protestant should not turn Papist* (London, 1687), p. 17.

19. Gilbert Burnet, *A Rational Method for proving the Truth of the Christian Religion* (London, 1675), preface, pp. 27–28.

20. Ibid., p. 28. See also Sir Matthew Hale, *Contemplations Moral and Divine* (London, 1676), p. 162; Nehemiah Grew, *Theologica Sacra* (London, 1701), pp. 292, 298, 299, 305, 310.

21. Richard Allestree, *The Divine Authority and Usefulness of Holy Scripture* (Oxford, 1673), p. 16.

22. Ibid., pp. 16–17.

23. See Samuel Parker, *A Demonstration of the Divine Authority of . . . the Christian Religion* (London, 1681); Thomas Tenison, *A Discourse Concerning a Guide in Matters of Faith* (London, 1681).

24. John Edwards, *A Complete History of Religion*, 2 vols. (London, 1696). "Without sense evidence All the Passages . . . concerning Christ's Birth, Life, Miracles, death, Resurrection, and Ascension are of no Credit; For those are to be proved as other Matters of fact are, by the Testimony of Witnesses who heard or saw those things." II, 436–437. The Apostles were not "mad or senseless," "had a share of Understanding as well as others, and their Ears and Eyes were as good as others Mens." They were "competent Judges," having the "Means and Opportunities" of informing themselves about the things they related. The "Matters of Fact were so frequent, and so often repeated." The acts were "done publically." Conspiracy or combination "in a Lie" was impossible because of the "Thousands alive who knew the Facts." The Apostles were "Honest, Plain and True-Hearted men," not "idle and loose Persons." II, 436–437, 440–441, 443–445, 446, 447, 449–450. *Athenian Mercury*, no. 29. See also Burns, *Great Debate on Miracles*.

25. *Philosophical Transactions* XXI (Oct. 1699), 359–360. The article was reprinted in William Derham, *Miscellanea Curiosa*, 3 vols. (London, 1726), II, i, 6–8. See also Ephraim Chambers, *Cyclopaedia or An Universal Dictionary of the Arts and Sciences*, 4 vols. (London, 1727), II, 334.

26. Scholastic theology used arguments from design and natural theology but did not focus on particular facts.

27. The connections between English religion and natural philosophy has long attracted the attention of scholars. The relationship between Puritanism and natural philosophy and then latitudinarianism has been explored. The integration of religion and natural philosophy is currently under investigation. For the role of Puritanism, see Robert K. Merton, *Science, Technology, and Society in Seventeenth-Century England* (New York, 1970); Christopher Hill, *Intellectual Origins of the English Revolution* (London, 1965); Charles Webster, *The Great Instauration: Science, Medicine, and Reform, 1626–1650* (London, 1976). For latitudinarianism, see Barbara Shapiro, "Latitudinarianism and Science in Seventeenth-Century England," *Past and Present* 48 (1968), 16–40; James R. Jacob and Margaret C. Jacob, "The Anglican Origins of Modern Science," *Isis* 71 (1980), 25–67. For integration, see Amos Funkenstein, *Theology and the Scientific Imagination from the Middle Ages to the Seventeenth Century* (Princeton, 1986); Margaret J. Osler, *Divine Will and the Mechanical Philosophy* (Cambridge, 1994); Margaret J. Osler, "Mixing Metaphors: Science and Religion or Natural Philosophy and Theology in Early Modern Europe," *History of Science* (forthcoming); Betty Jo Dobbs, *The Janus Face of Newton: The Role of Alchemy in Newton's Thought* (New York, 1991); Andrew Cunningham and Perry Williams, "Decentring the 'big picture': The Origins of Modern Science and the Modern Origins of Science," *British Journal for the History of Science* (1993), 407–432; Andrew Cunningham, "Getting the Game Right: Some Plain Words on the Identity and Invention of Science," *Studies in History and Philosophy of Science* 19 (1988), 365–389.

28. John Ray, *The Wisdom of God Manifested in the Works of Creation* (London, 1692), preface. See also John Ray, *Three Physico Theological Discourses* (London, 1693).

29. See Wilkins, *Natural Religion*; Stillingfleet, *Origines Sacrae*, pp. 379, 401–420; Nathaniel Grew, *The Phytological History Propounded* (London, 1673), pp. 98–101; William Derham, *Christo-Theology, or, A Demonstration of the Divine Authority of the Christian Religion* (London, 1730); William Derham, *Astro-Theology, or a Demonstration of the Being and Attributes of God from a Survey of the Heavens* (London, 1715); William Derham, *Physico-Theology: or, A Demonstration*

of the Being of God from his Works of Creation (London, 1724). Neal C. Gillespie describes two varieties of physico-theology, one derived from natural history, the other from Newtonian cosmology. "Natural History, Natural Theology, and Social Order: John Ray and the 'Newtonian Ideology,'" *Journal of the History of Biology* 20 (1987), 1–49.

30. John Evelyn, *Acetaria: A Discourse of Sallets* (London, 1699), preface; Nehemiah Grew, *The Anatomy of Plants* [1682] (New York, 1965), p. 8; Boyle, "Christian Virtuoso," *Works*, VI, 516. See also Robert Boyle, *The Usefulness of Experimental Philosophy* (London, 1663); Joseph Glanvill, *Essays on Several Important Subjects* (London, 1676), pp. 5–6; Nehemiah Grew, *Cosmologia Sacra* (London, 1701).

31. Robert Hooke, *Micrographia*, in R. W. T. Gunther, *Early Science in Oxford*, 14 vols. (London and Oxford, 1920–45), XIII, 80, 135–137, 165–167, 210; Hooke, *Posthumous Works*, ed. R. Waller (London, 1705), p. 121.

32. See Margaret Cooke, "Divine Artifice, Corpuscular Mechanism, and Chemical Experiment: Robert Boyle's Experimental Philosophy of Nature" (unpublished paper).

33. John Gascoigne, *Cambridge in the Age of the Enlightenment: Science, Religion, and Politics from the Restoration to the French Revolution* (Cambridge, 1989), p. 117.

34. Matthew Hale, *The Primitive Origination of Mankind* (London, 1677), To the Reader, p. 129.

35. Ibid., pp. 128–129, 130, 131–132, 139, 151, 162–163, 164, 166, 192, 240, 339.

36. See Cecil Schneer, "The Rise of Historical Geology in the Seventeenth Century," *History of Science* 11 (1954), 256–268; Roy Porter, *The Making of Geology: Earth Science in Britain, 1660–1815* (Cambridge, 1977); Paolo Rossi, *The Dark Abyss of Time* (Chicago, 1984); Roger Ariew, "A New Science of Geology in the Seventeenth Century?" *Studies in Philosophy and the History of Philosophy* 24 (1991), 81–94; Roy Porter, "Creation and Credence: The Career of Theories of the Earth in Britain, 1660–1820," in *The Natural Order: Historical Studies of Scientific Culture*, ed. Barry Barnes and Steven Shapin (Beverly Hills, Calif., 1979), pp. 97–123; Rachel Laudan, *From Mineralogy to Geology: The Foundation of a Science, 1650–1830* (Chicago, 1987).

37. See Robert Hooke, "A Discourse of Earthquakes," *Posthumous Works*; David R. Oldroyd, "Geological Controversy in the Seventeenth Century: 'Hooke vs Wallis' and Its Aftermath," in *Robert Hooke: New Studies*, ed. Michael Hunter and Simon Schaffer (Woodbridge, Suffolk, 1989), pp. 207–234; Ellen Tan Drake, *Restless Genius: Robert Hooke and His Earthly Thoughts* (Oxford, 1996). Yushi Ito, "Hooke's Cyclic Theory of the Earth in the Context of Seventeenth-Century England," *British Journal for the History of Science* 21 (1988), 295–314; Edward Lhwyd preferred natural history to the "romantick theories" of Burnet and Woodward. Gunther, *Early Science in Oxford*, XIV, 269.

38. Thomas Burnet, *The Sacred Theory of the Earth*, 2 vols. (London, 1684–90), I, 96; John Ray, *Three Physico-Theological Discourses*, 3d ed. (London, 1713), p. 5.

39. John Woodward, *The Natural History of the Earth* (London, 1726). Woodward insisted on "the exact Agreement betwixt Nature and Holy Writ from Observations, and Facts at this time demonstrable in the whole terraquous Globe." He would steer his "Course entirely on Observation of Fact" (pp. 29, 128). See also Woodward, *Essay Towards a Natural History of the Earth* (London, 1695); Woodward, *An Attempt Toward a Natural History of the Fossils of England*, 2 vols. (London, 1726), I, iv, xii; II, 3, 5; Nicholas Steno, *The Prodromus to a Dissertation Concerning Solids* (London, 1671), trans. Henry Oldenburg; Erasmus Warren, *Geologia: or, A Discourse concerning the Earth before the Deluge* (London, 1690); John Keill, *An Examination of Dr. Burnet's Theory of the Earth* (Oxford, 1698); Joseph M. Levine, *Dr Woodward's Shield: History, Science, and Satire in Augustine England* (Berkeley, 1977).

40. Woodward, *Fossils of England*, I, iv, xii. See also II, 3, 5.

41. Most of those engaged in geological discussion were Anglican clerics. Porter, *Making of Geology*, p. 23.

42. See Shapiro, *Probability and Certainty*, pp. 194–226; Barbara Shapiro, *"Beyond Reasonable Doubt" and "Probable Cause": Historical Perspectives on the Anglo-American Law of Evidence* (Berkeley, 1991), pp. 51–54, 164–168, 209–212, 320–321.

43. John Cotta, *The Triall of Witchcraft* (London, 1616), pp. 80–81; Richard Bernard, *Guide to Grand Jurymen in Cases of Witchcraft* (London, 1627).

44. Reginald Scot, *The Discoverie of Witchcraft* [1594] (London, 1964), pp. 42, 43.

45. Meric Casaubon, *Of Credulity and Incredulity in Things Natural, Civil and Divine* (London, 1668), pp. 159, 312. See also Casaubon, *A Treatise Proving Spirits, Witches, and Supernatural Operations* (London, 1672).

46. Casaubon, *Of Credulity and Incredulity*, pp. 164, 165.

47. Bacon, "The Advancement of Learning," *Works*, IV, 296.

48. Joseph Glanvill, *Saducismus Triumphatus* (London, 1681), pt. II, pp. 4, 10–11; Glanvill, *A Blow at Modern Sadducism* (London, 1668), pp. 5–6.

49. Glanvill, *Saducismus Triumphatus*, II, 10–12; Glanvill, *Blow at Modern Sadducism*, pp. 115–118. "The Credit of matters of Fact depends much upon the Relatours, who if they cannot be deceived themselves nor supposed any ways interested to impose upon others, ought to be credited.... matter of Fact is not capable of any proof besides, but that of immediate sensible evidence." *Saducismus Triumphatus*, pp. 4, 111.

50. Glanvill, *Blow at Modern Sadducism*, pp. 116–117. See Shapiro, *Probability and Certainty*, pp. 214–216, 320. Boyle warned Glanvill to be "very careful to deliver none but well attested narratives." Boyle, *Works*, VI, 120.

51. Richard Baxter, *The Certainty of the World of Spirit* (London, 1691), pp. 1, 2, 17. See also George Sinclair, *Satan's Invisible World Discovered* (Edinburgh, 1685).

52. *Athenian Mercury*, March 31, 1690. "As for humane Testimony, this matter has all the Requisites of Credibility that any thing is capable of; 'tis affirmed by most Men, prudent Men, good Men, who had no Interest nor Temptation to impose on the World." Ibid.

53. John Webster, *The Displaying of Supposed Witchcraft* (London, 1677), pp. 55, 57, 60–62, 64. See also John Wagstaffe, *The Question of Witchcraft Debated* (London, 1671), pp. 112–113, 123–124, 146; Shapiro, *Probability and Certainty*, pp. 104–226; T. J. Jobe, "The Devil in Restoration Science: The Glanvill-Webster Debate," *Isis* (1981), 343–356.

54. *Spectator*, July 11, 1711, no. 117.

55. Shapiro, *Probability and Certainty*, pp. 204–211.

56. *A Brief Account of Mr Valentine Greatrake's ... Strange Cures in a Letter ... to Robert Boyle* (London, 1666), pp. 28, 33, 35, 37, 39–40, 61, 95. See also Eamon Duffy, "Valentine Greatrakes, the Irish Stroker: Miracle, Science, and Orthodoxy in Restoration England," in *Religion and Humanism: Papers Read at ... Ecclesiastical History Society*, ed. Keith Robbins (Oxford, 1981), pp. 251–273; Nicholas Steneck, "Greatrakes the Stroker: The Interpretations of Historians," *Isis* 73 (1982), 161–177; Barbara Kaplan, "Greatrakes the Stroker: The Interpretations of His Contemporaries," *Isis* 73 (1982), 178–185; James Jacob, *Henry Stubbe, Radical Protestantism, and the Early Enlightenment* (Cambridge, 1983), pp. 48–60, 164–174.

57. See William Burns, "'Our Lot is Fallen into an Age of Wonders': John Spencer and the Controversy over Prodigies in the Early Restoration," *Albion* 27 (1995), 239–252. John Edwards, a Calvinist divine, rejected comets as portents of "calamitous Events" but believed them to be warnings of God's wrath and displeasure. *Cometomantia* (London, 1684), pp. 1–2, 67. Plot was "very diffident" about connecting wars, plagues, and other "prodigious events" to natural phenomena. *The Natural History of Stafford-Shire* (Oxford, 1686), p. 49.

58. See David C. Douglas, *English Scholars* (London, 1939).

59. See Thomas Fuller, *The Church History of Britain* (London, 1655); Fuller, *The Appeal of Injured Innocence* (London, 1659); Peter Heylyn, *Examen Historicum* (London, 1659).

60. London, 1684.

61. Stillingfleet, *Origines Britannicae* (London, 1685), preface, p. lxxxii; Douglas, *English Scholars*, p. 255.

62. London, 1679–1714, 3 vols., I, preface; II, preface.

63. Burnet, *History of the Reformation*, II, preface. John Strype wrote that he was "only a historian, and related passages and events, and matters of fact, as I find them, without any design of favoring and exposing any side." "My relations of things are not hearsays, nor taken up at second hand, or compiled out of others men's public writings; but I have gone as near

the fountain head as possible; that is to archives, state papers, registers, records and original letters, or else to books of good credit, printed in those times; directing more surely to the knowledge of how affairs then stood." *Annals of the Reformation and the Establishment of Religion,* 2 vols. (Oxford, 1822), I, vii, xii.

64. Anthony Harmer [Henry Wharton], *A Specimen of Some Errors and Defects in the History of the Reformation of the Church of England* (London, 1693), pp. iv–v, 11, 17, 25, 32. See also *A Letter to Dr. Burnet Occasioned by his late Letter to Mr. Lowth* (London, 1685); *An Answer to a Letter to Dr. Burnet, occasioned by his Letter to Dr. Lowth* (London, 1685); Simon Lowth, *A Letter to Edward Stillingfleet* (London, 1687), p. 40. Lowth offered to put himself to open trial, which is by "God and my Country." Stillingfleet and Burnet were "excepted out of the Jury" because incapacitated by "manifest prejudice and interest." *A Letter Occasioned by the second to Dr. Burnet* (London, 1685), p. 40.

65. Quoted in J. A. I. Champion, *The Pillars of Priestcraft Shaken: The Church of England and Its Enemies, 1660–1730* (Cambridge, 1992), p. 49.

66. Anon., *Historical Collections Concerning Church Affairs* (London, 1696), preface.

67. Thomas Salmon, *An Impartial Examination of Bishop Burnet's History of his Own Time* (London, 1724), pp. vi, ix, 513.

68. Champion, *Pillars of Priestcraft Shaken,* pp. 11, 12, 20. But see Joseph Preston, "Ecclesiastical Historians and the Problem of Bias, 1559–1742," *Journal of the History of Ideas* 32 (1971), 203–220; Laird Okie, *Augustan Historical Writing* (London, 1991).

69. Gilbert Burnet, *The Abridgement of the History of the Reformation of the Church of England* (London, 1682), preface.

70. Douglas, *English Scholars,* p. 260. See also Preston, "English Ecclesiastical History," pp. 203–220.

71. See J. H. Hexter, "Historiography: The Rhetoric of History," *International Encyclopedia of the Social Sciences,* 19 vols. (New York, 1968), VI, 368–394; Hayden White, *Metahistory: The Historical Imagination in Nineteenth-Century Europe* (Baltimore, 1973); White, *The Content of the Form: Narrative Discourse and Historical Representation* (Baltimore, 1987).

Chapter 8: Cultural Elaboration of "Fact"

1. See John Marshall, *John Locke: Resistance, Religion, and Responsibility* (Cambridge, 1994).

2. *The Educational Writings of John Locke,* ed. J. A. Axtell (Cambridge, 1968), p. 292. See also *Elements of Natural Philosophy by John Locke,* ed. Mons. des Maiseaux (Whitehaven, 1764), pp. 66–68.

3. Locke was active in Oxford scientific circles during the 1660s. See Kenneth Dewhurst, "Locke's Contribution to Boyle's Researches on the Air and on Human Blood," *Notes and Records of the Royal Society of London* 47, 198–206; M. A. Stewart, "Locke's Professional Contacts with Robert Boyle," *Locke Newsletter* 12 (1982), 19–44. Locke was one of Boyle's literary executors. See also Awnsham Churchill and John Churchill, *A Collection of Voyages and Travels,* 4 vols. (London, 1704).

4. See Barbara Shapiro, *Probability and Certainty in Seventeenth-Century England: The Relationships between Religion, Natural Science, Law, History, and Literature* (Princeton, 1983).

5. John Locke, *Essay Concerning the Human Understanding,* 2 vols., ed. A. C. Fraser (New York, 1959), bk. IV, chap. XV, sec. 2.

6. Ibid., bk. IV, chap. XV, sec. 2.

7. Ibid., bk. IV, chap. XV, sec. 5, 6.

8. Ibid., bk. IV, chap. XV, sec. 6; bk. IV, chap. XVI, sec. 1, 6.

9. Ibid., bk. IV, chap. XVI, sec. 6.

10. Ibid., bk. IV, chap. XVI, sec. 9.

11. Ibid., bk. IV, chap. XVI, sec. 10.

12. Ibid., bk. IV, chap. XVI, sec. 10.

13. Ibid., bk. II, chap. I, sec. 10. Locke's views on hypothesis were similar to those of Hooke and Boyle. See Laurens Laudan, "The Nature and Source of Locke's Views of Hypothesis,"

Journal of the History of Ideas 28 (1967), 211–233; Margaret C. Osler, "John Locke and the Changing Ideas of Scientific Knowledge," *Journal of the History of Ideas* 31 (1970), 1–16; G. A. J. Rogers, "Boyle, Locke, and Reason," in *Philosophy, Religion, and Science in the Seventeenth and Eighteenth Centuries*, ed. John Yolton (Rochester, N.Y., 1990), pp. 339–350; James Farr, "The Way of Hypothesis: Locke on Method," *Journal of the History of Ideas* 48 (1987), 51–72.

14. Letter to Molyneux, quoted in John W. Yolton, *The Locke Reader* (Cambridge, 1977), pp. 100–102. See also p. 310.

15. Ibid., p. 310, citing *Familiar Letters*, pp. 223–224.

16. Locke, *Essay Concerning the Human Understanding*, bk. II, chap. I, sec. 10; bk. IV, chap. XII, sec. 10.

17. Yolton, *Locke Reader*, p. 102; *Essay Concerning the Human Understanding*, bk. II, chap. VIII, sec. 1–2, 7–23; bk. IV, chap. III, sec. 16. See also G. A. J. Rogers, "Locke's *Essay* and Newton's *Principia*," *Journal of the History of Ideas* 39 (1978), 217–237.

18. Locke, *Some Thoughts on Education*, in *Educational Writings*, ed. Axtell, pp. 230, 231, 232.

19. Locke, *Conduct of the Understanding* (London, 1706), sec. 13. Locke was critical both of those who refuse to use matters of fact to build knowledge and of those who draw "general conclusions and raise axioms from every particular they meet with." Ibid., sec. 13.

20. Ibid.

21. By the mid-eighteenth century Locke's *Essay* had become the logic text at Oxford. G. A. J. Rogers, "John Locke, Conservative Radical," in *The Margins of Orthodoxy, Heterodox Writing, and Cultural Response, 1660–1750*, ed. Roger Lund (Cambridge, 1995), p. 105.

22. Sir Geoffrey Gilbert, *The Law of Evidence* (Dublin, 1754).

23. See Barbara Shapiro, *"Beyond Reasonable Doubt" and "Probable Cause": Historical Perspectives on the Anglo-American Law of Evidence* (Berkeley, 1991), pp. 25–61.

24. Isaac Watts, *Logick, or the Right use of Reason in the Inquiry after Truth* [1724] (London, 1775), pp. 181–182, 266–271, 457, 458, 469. Watts treated the Resurrection as a matter of fact. Ibid., p. 471.

25. Watts, *Logick*, in *The Works*, 9 vols. (Leeds, 1812), VII, 314, 474.

26. *Observations on Man*, 2 vols. (London, 1749), I, 6. See also George Campbell, *The Philosophy of Rhetoric*, ed. L. Bitzer (Carbondale, Ill., 1963).

27. Thomas Reid, *Essays on the Intellectual Powers of Man* (Cambridge, 1850), pp. 270, 271, 273, 499, 559, 671, 692.

28. See Shapiro, *Beyond Reasonable Doubt*.

29. Thomas Reid, *An Inquiry into the Human Mind on the Principles of Common Sense* (Edinburgh, 1764), p. 3. See also p. 46. Bacon "delineated the only solid foundation on which natural philosophy can be built." Newton "reduced the principles laid down by Bacon into three or four axioms." Reid, *Essays on the Intellectual Powers of Man* (Edinburgh, 1785), p. 652. Hume was very critical of Reid.

30. Reid, *Intellectual Powers of Man*, p. 51.

31. Reid, *Human Mind*, p. 15.

32. Reid, *Intellectual Powers of Man*, p. 114.

33. Ibid., pp. 696–697. "The great part, and the most interesting part of our knowledge" was therefore "probable." Ibid.

34. Reid, *Human Mind*, p. 4. Theories such as those dealing with the formation of the earth and the generation of animals "so far as they go beyond a just induction from facts are vanity and folly." Ibid., p. 5. The historian "builds upon testimony, and rarely indulges conjecture. The antiquarian mixes conjectures with testimony. . . . The Mathematician . . . deduces everything, by demonstrative reasoning, from his definitions and axioms. Indeed whatever is built upon conjecture, is improperly called science." Conjectures in philosophical matters "have commonly got the name of hypotheses, or theories." Hypotheses were in their nature uncertain and should be assented to in proportion to the evidence. *Intellectual Powers of Man*, pp. 46, 48–49.

35. Reid, *Intellectual Powers of Man*, p. 88.

36. See Shapiro, *Beyond Reasonable Doubt*; Alexander Welsh, *Strong Representations: Narrative and Circumstantial Evidence in England* (Baltimore, 1992); Barbara Shapiro, "Circumstantial Evidence: Of Law, Literature, and Culture," *Yale Journal of Law and the Humanities* 5 (1993), 219–241.

37. D. Fenning, *The Royal English Dictionary* (London, 1761); Samuel Johnson, *A Dictionary of the English Language*, 2d ed. (London, 1755).

38. See William Nelson, *Fact or Fiction: The Dilemma of the Renaissance Storyteller* (Cambridge, 1973); Ian Watt, *The Rise of the Novel* (Berkeley, 1957); Lennard J. Davis, *Factual Fictions: The Origins of the English Novel* (New York, 1983); Michael McKeon, *The Origins of the English Novel, 1600–1740* (Baltimore, 1987); J. Paul Hunter, *Before Novels: The Cultural Contexts of Eighteenth-Century Fiction* (New York, 1990); Jack D. Durant, "Books about the Early English Novel: A Survey and a List," in *The First English Novelists: Essays in Understanding*, ed. J. K. Armistead (Knoxville, Tenn., 1985), pp. 269–284; Robert Newsom, *A Likely Story: Probability and Play in Fiction* (New Brunswick, N.J., 1988).

39. See Russell Fraser, *The War against Poetry* (Princeton, 1970); K. G. Hamilton, *The Two Harmonies: Prose and Poetry in the Seventeenth Century* (Oxford, 1963); Nelson, *Fact or Fiction*, p. 56.

40. Cicero, *De legibus*, I.i.4.

41. Sir Philip Sidney, *An Apology for Poetry* [1590], ed. Forrest Robinson (Indianapolis, 1970), pp. 18, 21, 24, 26. The historian's "mouse-eaten records" are associated with something less than truth since the historian authorized "himself (for the most part) upon others histories, whose greatest authorities are built upon the notable foundation of hearsay" (p. 33). For Jonson, the poet was "a Maker or fainer; . . . the Fable and Fiction is (as it were) the form and Soul of any Poeticall worke." "Discoveries," in *Ben Jonson*, 11 vols., ed. C. H. Herford and Percy Simpson (Oxford, 1925–63), VIII, 635. For Bacon on poetry as "feigned" history, see *The Advancement of Learning*, ed. G. W. Kitchen (London, 1981), bk. II, pt. IV, sec. 1–5.

42. See Arthur B. Ferguson, *Utter Antiquity: Perceptions of Prehistory in Renaissance England* (Durham, N.C., 1993), pp. 102–131.

43. See A. C. Howell, "*Res* and *Verba*: Words and Things," in *Seventeenth-Century Prose*, ed. Stanley Fish (London, 1971), pp. 187–199; James Bono, *The Word of God and the Languages of Man: Interpreting Nature in Early Modern Science and Medicine* (Madison, Wis., 1995).

44. Richard Helgerson, *Self-Crowned Laureates: Spenser, Jonson, Milton, and the Literary System* (Berkeley, 1983), pp. 212–213, 225–227; Robert Hinman, *Abraham Cowley's World of Order* (Cambridge, Mass., 1960); Thomas Sprat, *History of the Royal Society*, ed. Jackson Cope and H. W. Jones (St. Louis, 1958), pp. 414, 417.

45. Quoted in Boris Ford, *From Dryden to Johnson* (London, 1966), p. 54.

46. Neither naturalists nor travel writers consistently adhered to the plain style.

47. Percy G. Adams, *Travelers and Travel Liars, 1660–1800* (Berkeley, 1962), pp. 1, 91–92, 94. See also Percy G. Adams, *Travel Literature and the Evolution of the Novel* (Lexington, Ky., 1983).

48. Raleigh also reported that Don Pedro de Sarmiento told him that an island in the Straits of Magellan ought to be called the Painter's Wives Island, "saying that whilst the Fellow drew that Map, his Wife . . . desired him to put in one Country for her; that she, in imagination, might have an Island of her own." Sir Walter Raleigh, *History of the World* (London, 1687), pt. I, bk. 2, chap. xxiii, sec. 4. Peter Heylyn's *Cosmographie* (London, 1652) mentions fictional locales, including Utopia, New Atlantis, Faerie land, the Painter's Wives Island, and those of *Don Quixote* (pp. 195, 196).

49. Cited in Adams, *Travelers*, p. 102.

50. *Athenian Gazette*, July 21, 1691.

51. Thomas More, *The Complete Works* (New Haven, 1963–90), IV, 39. He also insisted on the need to record distances with exactitude. See Joseph M. Levine, "Thomas More and the English Renaissance: History and Fiction in Utopia," in *The Historical Imagination in Early Modern England*, ed. Donald R. Kelley and David Harris Sacks (Cambridge, 1997), pp. 69–92. A

similarly playful mixture of "facts" and fantastic fictions informed portions of Rabelais's *Pantagruel*, which borrowed material from Jacques Cartier and other travel accounts. Adams, *Travelers*, p. 113.

52. *The Present State of Betty-Land* (London, 1684), p. 12. *The Present State of Fairy-Land* (London, 1713).

53. London, 1717.

54. Jonathan Swift, *Gulliver's Travels* (New York, 1960), pp. 313–314. His traveler calls for legislation requiring travel writers take an oath before the Lord High Chancellor swearing that everything reported was true to the best of his knowledge. Ibid. For Dampier's influence, see Willard Bonner, *Captain William Dampier, Buccaneer-Author: Some Account of a Modest Buccaneer and of English Travel Literature in the Early Eighteenth Century* (Stanford, 1934).

55. [William King], *The Transactioneer* (London, 1700), preface, pp. 19, 20, 43, 66–67, 69.

56. Quoted in Davis, *Fact or Fiction*, pp. 108, 110.

57. Aphra Behn, "The Fair Jilt," in *The Histories and Novels of Mrs. Behn* (London, 1696), preface. See also pp. 19, 24, 35, 161.

58. Aphra Behn, *Oroonoko or, The Royal Slave, A True History* [1688] (New York, 1973), p. 1. It was the "Hero himself, who gave us the whole Transactions of his Youth." Ibid. "I have often seen and conversed with this Great Man, and been a Witness to many of his mighty Actions." Ibid., p. 7. See also McKeon, *Origins of the English Novel*, pp. 111–114.

59. Adams, *Travelers*, p. 111. See also Charles Batten, *Pleasurable Instruction: Form and Convention in Eighteenth-Century Travel Literature* (Berkeley, 1978); Philip Gove, *The Imaginary Journey in Prose Fiction* (London, 1961). Gove located 215 eighteenth-century imaginary journeys. Criminal biographies, which also blended into the novel, often assured readers, "Here is no Fiction, as is commonly used in Pamphlets of this Nature." Quoted in Lincoln B. Faller, *Turned to Account: The Forms and Functions of Criminal Biography in Late-Seventeenth- and Early-Eighteenth-Century England* (Cambridge, 1987), p. 198.

60. See Watt, *Rise of the Novel*; McKeon, *Origins of the English Novel*; Davis, *Factual Fictions*; Hunter, *Before Novels*; John Richetti, "The Legacy of Ian Watt's *The Rise of the Novel*," in *The Profession of Eighteenth-Century Literature*, ed. Leo Damrosch (Madison, Wis., 1992), pp. 95–112.

61. Daniel Defoe, *A Tour thro' the Whole Island of Great Britain* (London, 1722), p. vi. Despite his claims of personal observations, Defoe consulted Camden and Gibson's revisions of Camden. See Ilse Vickers, *Defoe and the New Sciences* (Cambridge, 1996), pp. 154–176.

62. Daniel Defoe, *Journal of the Plague Year* (London, 1722); Benjamin Moore, "Governing Discourse: Problems of Narrative Authority in *Journal of the Plague Year*," *Eighteenth Century* 33 (1992), 136–140.

63. [Daniel Defoe], *A General History of the Robberies and Murders of the Most notorious Pyrates, and also Their Policies, Disciplines and Government from the first Rise . . . to the present year*, 2 vols. (London, 1714), I, preface.

64. Ibid., I, 25. "If there are some Incidents and Turns in their Stories, which may have in them a little of the Air of a Novel, they are not invented or contrived." The account of the pirate Captain Avery, unlike the recent play about Avery, was a history, "not false report." Ibid., I, 25, 26.

65. I owe this information to Robert Ritchie. See also [Daniel Defoe], *Madagascar: or, Robert Drury's Journal, during Fifteen Years of Captivity on that Island* (London, 1729). The editor insisted "so far as every Body concern'd in the Publication knows, it is nothing else but a plain honest narrative of Matter of Fact." Preface. See also Arthur W. Secord, *Robert Drury's Journal and Other Studies* (Urbana, Ill., 1961).

66. [Daniel Defoe], *Madagascar*, Prefatory Letter, p. iii.

67. Ibid., pp. iv, v, vi, 1, 456.

68. *The Storm* (London, 1704), preface.

69. Ibid.

70. London, 1720.

71. Daniel Defoe, *Memoirs of a Cavalier* (1972), p. 4.

72. Daniel Defoe, *Roxanna* (London, 1724), preface.

73. Daniel Defoe, *Moll Flanders*, ed. Mark Schorer (New York, 1950), p. xix. The account ends in 1683 because "nobody can write their own life to the full end of it, unless they write it after they are dead" (p. xxiii).

74. *Robinson Crusoe*, preface, p. 1. The *Farther Adventures of Robinson Crusoe* (London, 1720) denies that it is a romance. Preface.

75. Quoted in Adams, *Travel Literature*, p. 90.

76. See Welsh, *Strong Representations*. For the emphasis on "history" in the new novel, see Henry Fielding, *The History of Tom Jones, A Foundling* (London, 1749); Samuel Richardson, *Clarissa: or the History of a Young Lady* (London, 1747); Leo Braudy, *Narrative Form in History and Fiction: Hume, Fielding, and Gibbon* (Princeton, 1970).

77. But see Robert Mayer, *History and the Early English Novel: Matter of Fact from Bacon to Defoe* (Cambridge, 1977). See also John F. Tinkler, "Humanist History and the English Novel in the Eighteenth Century," *Studies in Philology* 85 (1988), 510–537

78. But see Mary Poovey, *A History of The Modern Fact: Problems of Knowledge in the Sciences of Wealth and Society* (Chicago, 1988).

Conclusion

1. For exceptions, see the work of Donald Kelley and Harold Berman.

Index

circumstances (*continued*)
and natural philosophy, 131; in religion 171, 175
circumstantial evidence, 9, 21–22, 178–179, 206, 209
civility, 25, 142, 143. *See also* politeness
classification, 78, 81, 83–85, 157
Cockburn, J. S., 220, 222, 225, 226
coffeehouses, 90, 204
Cohen, I. B., 259
Cohen, Jonathan, 254
coins, 49, 51–53, 61, 228. *See also* antiquities
Coke, Sir Edward, 10, 11, 12, 21–23, 78, 220, 225, 226, 249; artificial reason of the law, 159; behavior, 28; and history, 227; impartiality, 27; perjury, 223
Collinson, Patrick, 231
comets, 54, 140, 183, 252, 263, 266; as news, 99–100, 103
conjecture, 5, 100, 101, 103–104, 151, 158, 160, 254; Boyle, 151; and experiment, 148; and fact, 166, 196; in France, 135; in history, 55–56, 60–61, 229; Locke, 191; in natural philosophy, 114, 144, 147–148, 160, 246; Reid, 195, 268
Conner, Bernard, 79–80
conscience: of juries, 12–14, 22–23; satisfied, 22–23, 209. *See also* juries; reasonable doubt, beyond; verdicts
context, 105, 216–217
Cook, Harold, 252, 253, 260
Cooke, Margaret, 244, 265
Copernican hypothesis, 164, 191. *See also* hypothesis
Coquillette, Daniel, 245
Cormack, Leslie, 234, 235, 236, 248
corpuscularianism, 147, 151, 258
cosmography, 136. *See also* chorography; geography
Cotton, Sir Robert, 37
courtiers, 25, 118–119, 141, 142. *See also* social status
courts, 141–142, 214, 226, 254. *See also* judges; juries; law
Cowell, John, 220, 225
Cowley, Abraham, 199–200
Crawford, Catherine, 222
Creation, 7, 168, 177, 178, 188
credibility (of witnesses), 4, 8, 166, 197, 207; calculations of, 123, 244; in chorography and travel writing, 112–113; in law, 8, 11–17, 23; in natural history and philosophy, 112–113; in news reporting, 86, 88–89, 92, 96, 98, 103; in religion, 177, 179; Locke, 190; Royal Society, 113, 117–118, 119–121. *See also* witnesses
crime, 86, 87, 89
Crompton, Richard, 222
Crouch, Nathaniel, 101, 243

Cudworth, Ralph, 182
Cunningham, Andrew, 264
Cust, Richard, 239

Dalton, Michael, 14, 16, 221
Daniel, Samuel, 41
Daston, Lorraine, 2, 135, 225, 252; and civility, 262; and marvels, 2, 106, 240, 243–245
Davenant, Sir William, 34–35, 199
Deacon, Margaret, 248
Dean, L. F., 227
Dear, Peter, 2, 106, 244, 251, 252, 255, 259; first-person accounts, 261
Defoe, Daniel, 50, 71, 203–207; on Camden, 270; chorography and travel, 68, 69, 203; and fact; 234; on lives, 42, 43, 229; and news, 241; and novel, 203; *Robinson Crusoe*, 71; *The Storm*, 100–101
de Fresnoy, Langlet, 45
deism, 174
deity, proofs of, 159, 175–177, 180, 188, 264
demonstration, 23, 172–174, 191
Derham, William, 255, 274–275
Descartes, René, 110, 127, 133, 146, 250
description, of places, 63–85; political, 73. *See also* chorography
Dewhurst, Kenneth, 267
diaries, 38, 39
dictionaries, 2, 69, 220
diplomats: reports by, 78, 94; and Royal Society, 248
disciplines, 2, 214, 215
"discourses of fact," 77, 83–85, 91, 103, 137, 165, 213, 252; audience for, 213, 218; divergence among, 213–214; ethnography, 82–83; expansion of, 97, 285; and fiction, 71, 206; first-person accounts, 161; and hearsay, 161; history, 140, 167, 206, 213; and impartiality norm, 4, 132, 212, 214; language of, 160–167, 172, 200; law, 140, 206, 213; natural history and natural philosophy, 106, 140, 160–167, 213–215; news, 84, 86, 90, 91, 94, 104, 206; and novel, 91, 166, 203–206, 213; overlap among, 59, 65–66, 59, 72, 81, 84, 94, 97–99, 109–110; popularity of, 199; rhetoric of, 29, 97; romance, 166; Royal Society, 206; social status of readers, 218; style, 54, 200, 212, 252; "virtual witnessing," 142; witnesses, 70–72, 84, 91, 98–100, 167, 212. *See also* impartiality; witnesses
disinterested witnesses, 17, 140, 177, 181, 190, 200; in natural history and philosophy, 110, 124, 126, 128, 129, 132, 137; in news, 98; in religion, 171, 180. *See also* impartiality; interest; witnesses
disputation, 140, 162, 164–165, 261

8, 31; treatises on evidence, 192–194; witnesses, 8, 11–31, 113. *See also* fact; judges; juries; law and science; moral certainty; reasonable doubt, beyond; verdicts; witnesses

law and science, 112, 118–119, 121, 126–128, 137–139, 156, 159–160, 208, 214, 260

laws of nature, 5, 105, 148, 157–160, 166, 196, 207, 249, 252; and Boyle, 151–152, 256; Hale, 159, 260; Hooke, 256; Newton, 155, 156, 166; post-Newtonian era, 194; Reid, 195

lawyers, 5, 61, 127, 131, 133, 159, 173, 192, 193; and history, 33–37; partiality of, 29–30; and rhetoric, 29–30, 176, 187

Leeuwenhoek, Antonie van, 141, 249, 250

Leibniz, 153, 259

L'Estrange, Roger, 48, 97

L'Estrange, Hamon, 232

Lestringant, Frank, 236, 239

Levine, Joseph, 228, 229, 234, 245, 265, 269

Levy, F. J., 231

Lhwyd, Edward, 265

Licoppe, Christian, 252

Lister, Martin, 116, 247; chorography and travel, 70, 75, 83, 227; natural history, 83, 130

Livingstone, David N., 236

Lloyd, William, 184

Locke, John, 133, 174, 194, 195, 251; assent, 101; axioms, 268; and Boyle, 156, 189, 190, 191, 243, 267; conjecture, 191; disputation, 261; experiment, 192; fact, 133, 156, 167, 189–192, 212, 218; generalization of fact, 5, 180–192; and Gilbert, 192; hearsay, 191; and history, 42, 190, 229; hypothesis, 156, 190, 191, 267; and latitudinarians, 189; legal language of, 190–91; and moral certainty, 190; and Newton, 156, 191–192, 260; observation, 190; probability, 190, 191, 267; Revelation, 189; and Royal Society, 190; testimony, 15; and travel, 76, 167, 172; witnesses, 172, 190

logic, 46, 267; and rhetoric, 160, 261, 267

Lower, Richard, 110

Lowth, Simon, 185, 267

Lucian, 35

Ludlow, Edmund, 38, 48, 227

Luhmann, Niklas, 219

MacGregor, Arthur, 232

Machiavelli, Niccolò, 53, 78, 82

MacIntosh, J. J., 259

Macnair, M. R. T., 220, 223, 224, 225, 226

Marshall, John, 262, 266

Martin, Julian, 245

Marvell, Andrew, 58

marvels and wonders, 2, 3, 70–71, 81, 104, 106, 175, 180, 182, 206, 240–245; Bacon, 101, 102, 109, 191, 242, 249; monstrous births, 101, 183, 240–245; as news, 4, 40, 49, 80, 86–88, 93, 97, 99, 180, 214, 242, 249. *See also* rarities

mathematical certainty, 151, 156

mathematics, 110, 111, 148, 154, 215

matter in deed, 220

matter of fact. *See* fact

matter of fact and matter of law, 9–11, 136, 197, 211

matter of record, 12

May, Thomas, 37

Mayer, Robert, 271

Mayer, Thomas, 228

McKeon, Michael, 269, 270

medals, 40, 52, 53, 61, 228, 232. *See also* antiquities; coins

medicine, 110, 111, 112, 136

Melanchthon, Phillip, 160

memoir, 38, 39, 50, 227; fictional, 205–206; in natural history, 134–135

memorials, 39, 61, 98. *See also* antiquities; history

memory, 13, 26, 30, 35, 39, 41, 46, 50, 99, 125, 137, 226; Bacon, 246, 251; Hobbes, 110, 246, 251; Reid, 195

Mendyk, Stan, 235

merchants, 161, 253; and travel reporting; 74, 134–135; as witnesses, 16–18, 26, 121, 248. *See also* chorography; social status; travel accounts

metaphor, 161, 200

microscope, 4, 127–128, 136, 140, 141, 176, 250; Boyle, 250; Hooke, 148–150, 176, 247, 265

Milner, Benjamin, 246

Milsom, F. F. C., 220

Milton, John, 256

miracles, 171, 173, 174, 263. *See also* Resurrection; Scripture

Molesworth, Robert, 79, 238

Momigliano, Arnaldo, 51, 226, 232

monsters. *See* marvels and wonders

Montesquieu, 78

Moore, Benjamin, 270

moral certainty, 129, 224, 230; and fact, 125, 134, 144, 166, 244; in history, 46, 230; in law, 23, 30, 31, 224, 230; Locke, 190; in natural history and natural philosophy, 113, 133, 135, 137, 138, 252; in religion, 169, 170, 173, 175, 177–178. *See also* conscience: satisfied; reasonable doubt, beyond

Moray, Sir Robert, 50, 135, 163; experiment, 159, 251, 258

More, Henry, 123, 180–182, 249

Hevelius, 126; hypothesis, 146, 259; intelligencer, 94, 101, 291; and Newton, 155; Royal Society, 112, 114, 120, 135, 246, 247; on rhetoric, 162; *Philosophical Transactions*, 94, 114, 126; seeks foreign information, 74, 64, 76, 234, 236, 248; theory, 146, 256; witnesses, 123
Oldham, James, 221, 226
Oldmixon, John, 51, 231, 242
Oldroyd, David R., 246, 248, 249, 250, 257, 258
optics, 146, 157, 195
Orr, Robert, 263
Orviedo, Gonsálo Fernández de, 136
Osler, Margaret, 244, 247, 256, 259, 264
O'Toole, Frederick, 247
Overbury, Sir Thomas, 11
Oxford, University of, 118; physiologists, 112

Pagden, Anthony, 239, 253
panegyric, 58, 59
Paracelsians, 106
Park, Katherine, 106, 240, 243, 244, 245
Parker, Samuel, 256
Parry, Graham, 228, 235
partiality, 25, 30, 130, 212; of lawyers, 29–30. *See also* impartiality
Pepys, Samuel, 99
Perez-Ramos, Antonio, 106, 244
perjury, 10, 12, 18–19, 31, 97, 223
Perrault, Claude, 134, 252
Petty, Sir William, 77–78, 101, 103, 140, 237, 243; experiment, 149, 257; on Ireland, 69, 75, 233; oaths, 21; political description, 77–78; style, 161; Wadham College, 111, 254
philology, 37, 49, 50
Philosophical Collections, 101, 103
Philosophical Transactions, 94, 114, 126, 241, 255; and fact, 213; ridiculed, 201–212. *See also* Oldenburg
physico-theology, 176, 178, 179, 285. *See also* rational theology
physics, 110, 150
Pitt, Moses, 237, 251
Plato, 198
Plot, Robert, 67, 119, 147, 234, 247, 256, 266
poetry, 40, 41, 58, 197–199, 218, 226; Bacon on, 226, 269; and history, 23, 40–41, 197–199; Hobbes on, 35, 226; Sprat on, 199–200
poesie-historical, 40–41, 60, 198–199
politeness, 142, 162, 164, 166, 262–263
political description, 77–82. *See also* chorography
Polybius, 15, 35
Poovey, Mary, 207, 239, 248, 253, 271
Pope, Walter, 119

Popkin, Jeremy, 239
Popkin, Richard, 230. *See also* skepticism
Porter, Roy, 265
Power, Henry, 147, 150, 256
Prest, Willam, 225, 226, 227
Preston, Joseph, 267
presumption, 21–22, 179, 209, 224. *See also* circumstantial evidence
Principe, Laurence, 245, 247
probability, 1, 31, 105, 211
prodigies, 181, 183, 266. *See also* marvels and wonders
proof. *See* documents; witnesses
Protestantism, 168, 170
Providence, 35, 53–43, 88–89, 176
prudence, 53, 246
Pumphrey, Stephen, 253
Purchase, Samuel, 70, 71, 235, 236
Purver, Margaret, 246, 255
Puttenham, George, 198
Pzalmanazar, George, 200–201

Quakers, 223–224
Quintilian, 15, 219, 221

Rabelais, François, 252
Raleigh, Sir Walter, 15, 40, 53–54, 55, 201, 220, 269
Ramus, Peter, 160
rape, 17, 21, 221
rarities, 68, 81, 121. *See also* marvels and wonders
Rastell, John, 220
rational theology, 116, 125, 169–172, 175–188, 216, 217; and natural history and natural philosophy, 5, 176, 217. *See also* latitudinarianism; physicotheology
Ray, John, 119, 247, 254; chorography and travel, 70, 75, 77, 78, 83, 130, 237; fact, 116; natural history, 83, 130; on plain style, 161; religion and fact, 176–177, 264; scientific illustration, 251; social status, 141
Raymond, Joad, 239, 240, 241
reason, 110, 125, 152, 212
reasonable doubt, beyond, 3, 125, 129, 133, 137–138, 158, 161–162, 167, 169, 170, 209, 211; in law, 23, 31; in natural history and natural philosophy, 133; in religion, 169, 172. *See also* moral certainty
Reeds, Karen, 235
Reformation, 183, 184, 186, 267. *See also* Protestantism
Reid, Thomas, 194–196, 268
religion, 5, 276, 217–218; and science, 118, 119, 215. *See also* Christianity; latitudinarianism; Protestantism; rational theology; Scripture
republic of letters, 165, 166, 262

Resurrection, 171, 173, 263, 264. *See also* Christianity; Scripture

Reynolds, Beatrice, 226

Reznick, Samuel, 223

rhetoric: and chorography and travel writing, 72; Cicero, 160; courtly, 165; critics, 160; and discourses of fact, 29, 97; and history, 3, 35, 41, 58–59, 62, 215, 234, 267; impartiality, 57, 97, 132; and law, 9, 14, 29–30, 137, 220; and lawyers, 29–30, 176, 187; and logic, 160, 261, 267; and natural philosophy, 5, 160–165; and news reporting, 95; Oldenburg, 162; and Royal Society, 160–165, 268; Sprat, 161

Rhetorica ad herrennium, 10

Richardson, Samuel, 206

Ritchie, Robert, 270

Rogers, G. A. J., 268

Roman Catholicism, 9, 123; and arguments of fact, 133, 169, 170, 172–175, 188, 264

romance, 91, 161, 166, 199, 204, 206, 207; and chorography, 71; and discourses of fact, 166; and history, 40–42, 45, 55–56, 58, 187, 205–206; hypothesis as, 45, 55–56, 114, 145, 205

Rossi, Paolo, 104, 244, 265

Royal Society, 3, 44, 99, 110, 113, 131, 136, 143, 146, 246, 261; articles of inquiry, 70–72; chorography, 66; conjecture, 257; and diplomats, 78, 94; discourse and language of, 140, 145, 160–165, 253, 261, 262; and discourses of fact, 137, 206; disinterdness, 113; in eighteenth century, 157; ethnography, 83, 110; and Evelyn, 251; experiment, 106, 113, 120, 124, 129, 254; and fact, 5, 89, 105–138, 142; and France, 134–135; Glanvill, apologist for, 112–114; hearsay, 113, 139; Hevelius-Auzout dispute, 126–127; *History of the Royal Society*, 145, 234, 255; and Hobbes, 110; hypothesis, 144–151, 257; judgments, 251; and latitudinarianism, 164–165; and Locke, 190; monstrous births, 101, 102; natural history, 114–117; natural philosophy, 114; news of, 99; and Oldenburg, 112, 113, 120, 135, 246–247; political description, 79; rarities, 121; origins, 111–112; register, 39; research program, 112–116, 137; and rhetoric, 160–168, 268; social status of members and correspondents, 139–140, 165, 253; style, 2–3, 5, 95, 96, 160–168; and travel reporting, 70, 72–80, 82–84, 116, 140; trust, 113. *See also* natural history; natural philosophy; *Philosophical Transactions*; Sprat

Rubini, D. A., 226

Ruby, Jane, 256

Ruestow, Edward, 249, 251

rumor, 64, 92, 100, 108, 119, 240. *See also* hearsay

Rushworth, John, 42, 47–48, 55, 98, 229

Rycaut, Paul, 80–81, 248

Sanderson, William, 47

Sargent, Rose-Mary, 122, 159, 243, 245, 247, 249, 258, 259

satire, 58, 201–202

Schaffer, Simon, 2, 4, 162–163; *Leviathan and the Air Pump*, 105–106, 116–117, 122, 139–143, 165, 244, 248, 253, 262. *See also* credibility; Shapin; social status; witnesses: credibility

scholasticism, 143, 218

Schwoerer, Lois, 240

science. *See* experiment; natural history; natural philosophy; Royal Society

science and law. *See* law and science

scientific revolution, 110, 114, 246

scientist, 5

Scot, Reginald, 180, 266

Scripture, 5; facts of, 168, 169–174; rational belief in, 172

seamen, 75, 120–121, 135. *See also* chorography; social status

Selden, John, 37, 39–42, 46, 49–51, 55, 58, 60, 78, 228, 229–232

senses, 109, 174, 180; best evidence, 172; Boyle, 173, 182; fallibility of, 46, 65, 127, 129, 154, 157; Hobbes, 171, 246; observations, 109; and reason, 125, 137; Reid, 195; visual, 119

Shaaber, M. A., 239

Shakespeare, William, 34, 40, 198–199

Shapin, Steven, 2, 4, 75–76, 162–163, 262; *Leviathan and the Air Pump*, 105–106, 116–117, 244, 253, 254; *Social History of Truth*, 225, 237, 244, 248; social status and matters of fact, 24–25, 118, 122–123, 139–143, 165, 248, 249; "virtual witnessing," 84, 131. *See also* credibility; gentlemen; social status; witnesses: observation

Shapiro, Barbara J.: *Beyond Reasonable Doubt*, 219, 221, 222, 224, 230, 268, 269; circumstantial evidence, 269; *John Wilkins*, 246; latitudinarianism and science, 262, 264; moral certainty, 224, 230; *Probability and Certainty in Seventeenth Century England*, 2, 219, 222, 227, 230, 244, 259, 261, 262, 263, 266; religion and science, 225, 236, 264; universities and science, 215, 217

Sidney, Sir Phillip, 34, 226, 261

Siefert, Arno, 227, 244

Silving, Helen, 223

skepticism, 31, 45–46, 72, 84, 170, 17, 179, 180–181, 214–215

Vicars, Ilse, 270
voyages. *See* travel

Wadham College, Oxford, 111–112, 140, 163, 253
Wagstaffe, John, 182, 266
Wake, William, 224
Walker, Obadiah, 103–104, 244
Wallis, John, 111, 116, 126–127, 132, 153–154, 261
Walmsley, Peter, 261, 225
Walwyn, William, 24, 225
Walzer, Michael, 254
Ward, Seth, 101–102, 111, 140, 244, 246; on historical faith, 46–47, 169–170, 230, 263, 230
Waterhouse, Edward, 23
Watt, Ian, 269, 270
Watts, Isaac, 193–196
Webster, Charles, 237, 246
Webster, John, 182, 266
Weldon, Sir Anthon, 238
Welsh, Alexander, 171, 205, 269, 271
Welwood, James, 53
Westfall, R. S., 244, 258, 259
Westman, Robert, 256
Whalley, Peter, 58, 234
Wharton, Henry, 185, 267
Wheeler, Harvey, 159, 239, 244, 245, 260
Whigham, Frank, 254
White, Hayden, 266
Whitelocke, Bulstrode, 37, 38, 94
Wigmore, John H., 221
Wiles, R. M., 241
Wilkins, John, 140, 189, 255; classification, 130; discourse and style, 161, 182; and fact, 158; and factual genres, 48, 89, 92, 240; hypothesis, 145–136, 255; and latitudinarianism, 164; social status, 253, 262; and Sprat's *History of the Royal Society*, 145, 255; Wadham College, 111–112, 254
Williams, Perry, 264
Williamson, Joseph, 241, 243, 248, 256, 259
Willis, Thomas, 111, 140, 247, 261
Willughby, Francis, 75, 76, 77, 83, 116; social status, 141, 253
Winkler, Mary, 251
Wilson, Catherine, 250
Wilson, Thomas, 14
Winthrop, John, 76, 120, 237
witchcraft, 17, 19, 21, 88, 188, 221; Boyle, 181, 182; and fact, 178–180; Glanvill, 180–182, 266; and juries, 179, 180; witnesses, 179
Witmore, Michael, 226, 245
witnessing. *See* witnesses: observation

witnesses, 11–13, 165, 166, 170–73, 179–82; ability, 172; accessories, 21; Bacon, 109; Boyle, 117, 119, 152; children, 16, 221; competence, in law, 13–14; concurrent, 48, 190; concurrent in law, 18, 113; consistency, 171; contradictory, 19, 190, 221; cross-examination of, 19; and culture of fact, 211; Defoe, 203–205; demeanor of, 17; and discourses of fact, 70–72, 84, 91, 99, 100, 212; exclusion of, 221; expertise, 14, 17–18, 121–123, 213, 222; experience in, 118, 121–123; 140; experiments and, 76, 119, 128, 130, 139; fallibility of, 125; faith, 8, 11–31, 113, 174; fictional, 205–206; fidelity in, 112, 118, 123–124, 172, 248–249; first hand, 5; Gilbert on, 222; Hale on, 124, 221, 249, 250; Hooke, 115, 124, 150, 253; interested, 17, 18, 25, 26, 132, 182; and juries, 24, 140; Locke, 172, 190, 192; merchants, 16, 17–18, 26, 121, 248; midwives, 16; moral character of, 173, 190; and news, 26, 88, 91, 92, 96, 98, 100, 103; oaths of, 13; partiality, 125; physicians, 17, 22; propertyholders, 16; prosecution, 20; qualifications, 165, 173, 177; reputation, 16; Royal Society, 102, 113, 117–118, 119–121, 179; Roman Catholic, 8–9, 221; and scientific instruments, 127, 129, 132, 137; Scriptural, 179; seamen, 120–121; servants, 16; skilled, 118, 121–123, 132, 137, 190; social status, 1, 25–26, 28, 118–122, 129, 139, 190, 213; two witnesses rule, 18, 223; "virtual witnessing," 84, 131, 142; yeoman, 17, 102; witchcraft, 179–180; women, 16, 221; wonders and marvels, 87, 102; women, 16, 221. *See also* credibility; disinterested witnesses; eye and ear witnesses; impartiality (of witnesses); multiple witnesses
Wojcik, Jan, 244, 247, 258, 263
wonders. *See* marvels and wonders
Wood, Paul, 241, 249, 254, 255, 261
Woolf, D. R., 227, 228, 231
Woodward, John, 73, 83, 116, 239, 247, 250, 251; on Deluge, 178–179, 265; and fact, 158; and Newton, 260
Wren, Sir Christopher, 76, 111, 140, 146, 251, 254, 255; and hypothesis, 146, 148, 255
Wren, Matthew, 111

yeomen, 17, 24
Yolton, John, 268

Zilzel, E., 256

CPSIA information can be obtained at www.ICGtesting.com
Printed in the USA
BVOW02s0347200616

452576BV00001B/21/P